STAGE MAKEUP

By the same author:

FASHIONS IN HAIR

FASHIONS IN EYEGLASSES

RICHARD CORSON

STAGE MAKEUP

Fourth Edition

Prentice-Hall, Inc., Englewood Cliffs, New Jersey

PRENTICE-HALL INTERNATIONAL, INC., *London*
PRENTICE-HALL OF AUSTRALIA, PTY. LTD., *Sydney*
PRENTICE-HALL OF CANADA, LTD., *Toronto*
PRENTICE-HALL OF INDIA PRIVATE LIMITED, *New Delhi*
PRENTICE-HALL OF JAPAN, INC., *Tokyo*

FOREWORD

The actor's dream is to play a wide range of characters, to explore many facets of life in roles that encompass all humanity. To fulfill this dream he requires not only talent and training but an unstinting devotion to his art.

In many areas of this endeavor the actor is assisted and supported by the artistry and technical skills of brilliant craftsmen. From the original script to the set, lighting, and costume, every effort is made to achieve perfection. Curiously, in the field of makeup the actor is left quite to his own devices. Except for the rare production which is so exotic or stylized that a specialist is necessary, the actor must design and execute his own makeup.

It is therefore of considerable concern that many young professionals in the theater are unfamiliar with even so elementary a problem as projection of the actor's features, essential to the fullest communication of the character's inner life. Even on the rare occasions when a professional makeup artist is available, it is still the actor who is more aware than anyone else of the special problems posed by his own features and by the character he is playing. Thus, it is the responsibility of each actor to learn the craft of makeup, that final dressing of the character which will enable him to perform his role as fully and effectively as possible.

In addition to such fundamentals as the assimilation and projection of the character in terms of age, environment, and health, there is an area of psychological support which makeup can give the actor comparable only to the assistance of a perfect costume. Just as robes or rags can give the actor the "feel" of a character, so also can makeup. The visual image reflected in his dressing room mirror can be as important to the actor as it will later become to the audience.

The authority of the arch of a brow or the sweep of a profile can be as compelling as Lear's crown and scepter. The psychological effect of shadows and pallor or glowing health can be as conducive to mood and manner on stage as in life, while an impudent tilt to a nose or the simple graying of the hair will inevitably make more specific the delineation of character. The most detailed and subtle characterization can be performed only with full freedom and authority when the actor knows that the visual image supports and defines his work.

The actor untrained in makeup is deprived of an invaluable aid to his art—and little is done to remedy the situation. Large universities give courses in makeup intermittently or not at all. Drama schools often merely glance at the problem or train in outmoded techniques. And the actor must shift for himself or hope for the casual assistance and hand-me-down techniques of fellow artists.

It is therefore most exciting and encouraging to all actors when a book such as this comes to our rescue. Richard Corson's approach to makeup is meticulous and eminently practical. Perhaps even more important is his stress on the creative aspects of makeup and the avoidance of stereotypes and formulae. The insistence on supporting technical skill and imagination and individuality reflects a positive and rewarding approach. With fullest exploitation of the mind and senses, an unsuspected range of roles exists for each of us. It is through the assistance of the art and craft of makeup presented in this book that we can hope for a more complete realization of our goals in acting.

UTA HAGEN

PREFACE

Makeup is often regarded as a necessary but unfortunate adjunct to dramatic productions. The majority of actors and directors both on and off Broadway not only fail to realize its vast possibilities in contributing to the effectiveness of a production, but they regard it as a series of formulas to be followed blindly and mechanically. Assuredly makeup is not, or should not be, formulary or routine. Yet makeup as it is usually learned is frequently just that. There is a formula for middle age, one for old age, another for Irishmen, yet another for butlers. Such makeup is stultifying to the actor and an affront to the audience.

It is the purpose of this book to acquaint the student with the basic principles of the art and technique of makeup so that he may use them creatively in the design and execution of makeups which, beyond being technically commendable, will materially assist the actor in the development and projection of his character.

The book is intended for both the actor and the makeup artist, professional and nonprofessional. It is designed to be used as a text and subsequently as a reference book.

The fourth edition includes nearly two hundred new illustrations, some of them of student makeups, which should provide a certain amount of encouragement for the beginner. In addition, all of the hair style plates have been redone and greatly expanded, and the color chart and the appendix on makeup materials have been brought up to date.

The chapter on three-dimensional makeup now includes many new techniques for skin-texture effects, there is a new section on makeup for actors of various races, a new chapter on fashions in makeup, and an outline for a condensed course in makeup for students with limited time. Perhaps one of the most useful additions, for both study and reference, is the picture collection in Appendix F—portraits taken from works of art and collages of photographs of eyes, noses, mouths, chins, foreheads, and hands.

It is important in using this book as a text to understand each chapter thoroughly and to master the material before proceeding to the next. It is always a temptation to skip to the practical work in makeup and especially

the advanced character work. This temptation should be scrupulously re-
sisted. The approach in this text is based upon understanding principles,
not upon learning rules. An understanding of these principles is basic to
imaginative and skillful makeup.

The value of recordings of students' voices in a speech class has long
been recognized. In a makeup class, photographs of the students' work serve
the same purpose. They not only provide a record of a student's progress,
but they point up dramatically the faults in his makeup and they serve
as a spur to greater progress. They also demonstrate how the student can
strive for greater perfection in detail. Two photofloods and a camera are
the only equipment needed. The immediate benefits of the photographs are
increased if a Polaroid camera is available. This makes it possible for the
student to compare the original makeup with the photograph and make
any changes which seem desirable. The photographs of students' makeups
in this book were taken as routine classroom procedure. A few odds and
ends of props and costumes should be available to students. Improvised
costumes which give the general effect are sufficient. It is both interesting
and useful to have the better photographs displayed on a board in the classroom. In order to show development in skill as well as contrast in makeups,
the work of each student can be organized into a group.

But no matter how limited or extensive the available equipment,
success in makeup is in large part the result of approaching it with a completely professional attitude. This implies an enthusiasm for learning and a
refusal to settle for less than one's best. Only when the study of makeup
is undertaken with such an attitude will its tremendous potentialities for
helping the actor be fully realized.

ACKNOWLEDGMENTS

Since the first edition of this book was in preparation, many people,
including Dr. C. L. Shaver, Dr. C. M. Wise, and Mrs. Lester Hale, have
given generously of their time and experience and made important con-
tributions. For the current edition I am most grateful for the cooperation
of Mr. Peter Owen, Mr. James Hart Stearns, Miss Shirley Jac Wagner, Mr.
Bill Smith, Mr. Mike Carrington, Mr. Bert Roth, Dr. Harold K. Stevens,
Mr. John W. Parker, Mr. Alvin Cohen, Mehron's, Leichner of London,
and the M. Stein Cosmetic Company.

For a number of years Mr. Dick Smith, one of the most imaginative and dedicated television makeup artists in the country, has been more than generous in sharing the results of his own experimentation. I am again indebted to him for permitting me to use his own photographs of his remarkable television makeup for Hal Holbrook's Mark Twain.

I particularly wish to express my appreciation to Mr. Mitchell Erickson, who has once again spent long hours reading the manuscript and suggesting improvements.

R. C.

CONTENTS

ILLUSTRATIONS

STAGE MAKEUP

1

AN APPROACH TO
MAKEUP

Theatrical makeup can conceal or distort one of the actor's most essential means of communication, and it can mislead or distract the audience. On the other hand, it can, as an integral part of the characterization, illuminate the character for the actor as well as for the audience and provide the actor with an extraordinarily effective means of projecting a subtle and striking character portrait.

Makeup does not create character; it only helps to reveal it. No makeup is complete without an actor underneath. And a makeup which is conceived as a work of art in itself, unrelated to a specific performance, no matter how brilliant the execution may be, is worse than useless—it can destroy the actor's characterization.

A makeup which is too heavy or masklike will immobilize facial expression. And one which veers off in a direction not intended by the actor and is thus unrelated to what he is trying to project will only sabotage his work and confuse the audience. A makeup which by its very ineptitude calls attention to itself is an even greater tragedy. Therefore, since makeup has as great a potential for harm as for good, it must not be approached casually. Nor can it be avoided. Aside from its essential role as an integral part of visual character projection, it is equally essential in counteracting the often devastating effects of stage lighting and stage distance, which may reduce the actor without makeup to an ashen blob.

Since makeup is essential, it is important that it be approached posi-

1

tively with full knowledge of its power to help the actor. A young actor playing King Lear (Figures 127, 128) must rely heavily on makeup for visual effectiveness. Also, in such a play as *Separate Tables,* in which one actress is required to play two strikingly different characters, the makeup is an essential part of the performance. There are other roles in which the contribution of makeup is less obvious but no less important. In some of these the makeup can be neglected with perhaps a minimum of damage to the actor's work, but the pity of it is that the actor will never know how much an intelligently conceived and skillfully executed makeup might have helped him psychologically as well as visually to develop the characterization. Often precisely the right sort of makeup can provide a steppingstone to the characterization and can enable the actor to see himself more clearly in the role, thus providing a powerful psychological springboard.

But this does not mean that the makeup may be used as a crutch. Quite the contrary. It is the final step in the actor's efforts to bring the character to life and provides him with valuable and often necessary help after he has done all that he can without it.

In the case of the really skillful actor it is astonishing how much he can accomplish physically without any aid from makeup at all. If you are familiar with the work of those two great artists in the solo drama field, Angna Enters and the late Ruth Draper, you know the unbelievably wide range of characters they portray with no change in makeup. Miss Draper, of course, depended on suggestion throughout her performance, and consequently the imagination of the audience automatically played an important part. But Miss Enters uses complete costumes and numerous properties and still manages with only some changes in hair style and none at all in her strikingly pale, almost stylized facial makeup to suggest, to a remarkable degree, any character of any age.

The photographs in Figures 1–6 will serve to illustrate the point. They are from a series of character sketches in which changes are made solely by means of spectacles, hat (the same hat in every case), cigar, and necktie. There is no time for any makeup change. These photographs were taken with no makeup other than a Pan-Stik base.

The photographs are not intended as examples of characters completely realized visually. Most of them could be improved with skillfully applied makeup. On the other hand, all of them could easily be ruined by makeup not so skillfully applied. They are included here only as examples of how much can and should be achieved by the actor before he even begins to think about adding makeup. Then when he sits down at his makeup table, he must be careful only to accentuate and to extend, never to de-

FIGURES 1–6. Character portrayal without makeup. All photographs are of the young actor in Figure 7 as characters in a series of monologs which are presented as shown, with no makeup other than a Pan-Stik base. These studies show how much the actor can and should do before makeup is added.

stroy, what he has already accomplished. It is of the greatest importance that during the makeup process he maintain psychologically and, to some extent, physically the character he has developed and never for a moment allow himself to become merely an artist's model.

An understanding of the relationship of makeup to the character, though basic to the art, is only the beginning. An infinite amount of understanding will do little to stay the havoc which can be wrought by an untrained eye and an unskillful hand. In acting, the will to act and an understanding of the character are insufficient to insure even an acceptable performance. Skill in translating the will and the understanding into physical and vocal terms on a stage is essential. It is so with makeup. And, as with acting, this skill involves more than a mere learning of specific techniques.

First of all, it is essential to learn to observe people closely and analytically, mentally cataloguing details of skin coloring and texture, bone structure, hair growth, conformation of wrinkles and sagging flesh, and so on, always matching these with the type of person on which they are found. Then, we must understand the principles involved in re-creating these effects on an actor—simple principles of light and shade and of color which have been used by artists for centuries. And lastly, we must learn to apply our understanding and our observation to the use of specific tools and techniques of makeup in order that it may become a help, not a hindrance, in the projection of a character.

As stated in the preface, this book is intended for both the actor and the makeup artist. In the theater it is essential that the actor be skilled in makeup, though he may need at times to rely on the professional makeup artist when particularly difficult or unusual technical problems are presented. Like speech and body movement, makeup is part of an actor's craft, and the actor who neglects his makeup risks failure to project visually the precise and carefully drawn character-concept he has in his mind. His body is his sole means of visual communication with his audience, and neglect of a single visual aid will certainly lessen the possible impact of his performance and may spell the difference between success and failure.

Although the makeup artist, through his great technical knowledge and skill, can be of invaluable service to the actor in many ways, he should not be relied upon to do work the actor ought more logically to do himself. After all, no other person can understand the character he is trying to project quite so well as the actor himself; nor can any other person know quite so specifically the probable effect of various kinds of makeup on his particular face. Furthermore, in the theater the makeup artist can rarely devote as much time to the exccution of any one makeup, night after night, as can the individual actor. Therefore, the actor who must rely on the skill of the makeup artist is an artistic cripple. He may have the use of all of his faculties but one, but without that one he can never really stand on his own.

The makeup artist, on the other hand, can go beyond the actor in developing skills which the actor simply has no time or no real need to learn. It is the makcup artist and not the actor who needs to be able to ventilate beards on net, for example, to make plaster casts and rubber prosthetic pieces, and with his critical and objective eye to appraise the completed makeup from the house under stage lights.

But whether the skill is the actor's or the makeup artist's or a blending of the two, the basis for all makeup lies in the character which is being brought to life. A makeup which functions positively in helping the actor to project his character is performing a service to the actor, to the playwright, and to the audience.

2

CHARACTER
ANALYSIS

The source of our information about a character is the play. Directly through the stage directions and indirectly through the dialogue we come to know the character. We become acquainted not only with his physical appearance but with his background, environment, personality, age, and relationships with other characters in the play. Although this probing into the character is basically an acting problem, it is also essential preparation for the makeup, and it is important that we be able to translate the information into visual terms.

Take, for example, Cyrano's nose. This would appear at first glance to be the basis for Cyrano's makeup. But is it sufficient to put on a big nose and let it go at that? Without it there is no Cyrano, but there is a good deal more that we must know in order to bring the man to life.

To what extent, we may ask, is the nose comic and to what extent tragic? What elements of nobility and courage and kindness should appear in the visual impression aside from the one monstrous feature? And from a purely practical point of view we must ask what effect any given shape of nose will have on a particular actor's face. A nose which is exactly right for Cyrano on one face may on another appear so outrageously grotesque that the visual characterization is destroyed.

Such questions as these must be asked not only about Cyrano but about any character you are trying to develop. And, in answering each question, there is a choice to be made. You may not always make the right choice, but you must make a positive one. In makeup, as in acting, you must not be content just to let things happen. A fine makeup, like a fine painting or a fine performance, is a product of thorough preparation, intelligent selection, and meticulous execution.

This holds equally true when you are trying to reflect in specific physical terms in an actor's face his state of health, his disposition, or even his occupation. All of these may be specified in the script, and it is essential not to deny them in the makeup. If a character walks on stage with a deep suntan and announces that he is a coal miner from Wales, the audience will immediately assume that he is lying or, perhaps, if they are a bit more cynical, that the actor doesn't know much about makeup. If the character *is* lying, fine. But if he is not, the makeup has come very close to ruining the performance on the first entrance. If Marguerite Gautier plays her death scene with rosy cheeks and a bloom of health, the credulity of the audience is going to be severely strained. Therefore, it is essential at the very least to provide the minimum requirements of the physical appearance so as to correlate what the audience sees and what it hears. But beyond this you have an obligation to use the resources of makeup creatively to solve more subtle problems.

It is, for example, not only possible but commonplace to find members of the same family who have similar backgrounds and similar environments as well as a family resemblance but who are still very different people. The two sisters, Stella and Blanche, in *A Streetcar Named Desire* may quite logically resemble each other, but there is a vast difference between them, and this difference must be projected visually. The makeup must help the actress playing Blanche convey to the audience the realization that things are not as they seem—or as she would have them seem. Without the assistance of the makeup it would be very difficult indeed to make the audience accept the facts of Blanche's recent experiences and her present mental state. Obviously, a makeup which will do this for Blanche would be disastrous for Stella. And yet it is quite conceivable that the same actress might at different times play both parts. Were she to do so, she would most certainly depend partly on the makeup in order to express as fully as possible the individuality of each of the characters. And her choices in planning each of the makeups would depend upon a searching analysis of the character.

Such an analysis can be simplified by classifying the determinants of physical appearance into six groups—*heredity, race, environment, temperament, health,* and *age.* These are not, of course, mutually exclusive. Race, for example, is merely a subdivision of heredity, but it presents such a special problem that it requires individual and specific attention. Nor are the six groups usually of equal importance in analyzing a character. Race, for example, may be a basic consideration in such a play as *Raisin in the Sun* and of no significance at all in a play like *Waiting for Godot*, which was, in fact, performed on Broadway with both white and Negro casts. Temperament is obviously a more important consideration than environment in studying such a character as Lady Macbeth, whereas with Blanche in *A Streetcar Named Desire* both environment and temperament are basic to an understanding of the character and the play. In any character analysis, therefore, it is well to concentrate one's attention on those groups which are of most significance to the character. It is not important to know precisely in which group any specific feature or character trait belongs. The divisions are laid out merely as a practical aid in organizing one's research.

HEREDITY

Without going into problems of genetics, we can say that generally speaking this group includes those characteristics, physical and mental, with which a person is born. The red hair of all the boys in *Life With Father* is obviously hereditary. Since it is required by the play, there is no choice to be made. But in most instances we must decide for ourselves such questions as the color of the hair, the shape of the nose, and the line of the eyebrow, and we must base our decision on a knowledge of the relationship between physical features and character and personality. We must beware of the attitude that one kind of feature will do as well as another In the character analysis it is our problem to choose exactly the kind of feature which will tell the audience most about the character and which will best support the character portrait the actor is trying to present. Since this is the subject of the next chapter, we need not elaborate here but can merely specify it as one of the items to be noted and used in the analysis.

RACE

Racial differences bring up special makeup problems which require a solution somewhat less obvious than it might seem at first glance. In makeup in general there has always been an unfortunate tendency to rely upon types rather than individuals. This is particularly pernicious in dealing with different races and nationalities. If we are Caucasians, we tend to think of Orientals, Negroes, and Indians as each belonging to a clearly defined group with an invariable set of specific characteristics involving color of skin, type of hair, form of features, and other physical traits. This is untenable simply because it is untrue. It is true that pink skins are not characteristic of Negroes, Orientals, or Indians; but within the general color limits of the race there is wide variety, particularly in view of widespread intermingling of the races. Similarly, there are very definite trends in shape of features and kind of hair, and the trends are sufficiently clear-cut to make each race identifiable. But that still leaves wide latitude for individual characterization. If we have a Japanese character in an American play, for example, how often is the Japanese character analyzed in terms of his environment? To most people a Japanese makeup is a Japanese makeup. Yet if we do a Japanese play (*Rashomon*, for example), are we to make up all the characters alike? Let us hope not. Non-Caucasian characters in a Caucasian play should be revealed as no less individual than the rest of the characters.

That leaves us with our usual makeup problem plus one additional one—that of race. In other words, race is significant and must be dealt with, but it must not overshadow everything else—unless, of course, the play is a symbolic one concerned with races of mankind. Furthermore, it is necessary always to decide how important to make the racial element. The usual solution to the problem is to suggest the race sufficiently to answer the requirements of the playwright (and, of course, the audience) and beyond that to concentrate on other elements in the character analysis.

As the racial question becomes more subtle (in dealing with various strains of the Caucasian race, for example), it usually decreases in importance. It is true that a Norwegian must be clearly distinguished from an Italian, but the distinction can usually be made quite satisfactorily in coloring, which is hardly a major problem. To distinguish between an Englishman and an Irishman is of considerably less importance (to the makeup artist, that is—not, perhaps, to the Englishman or the Irishman).

It is, of course, not only the scientifically accepted differences among the races which are important, but also the differences which exist in the minds of the audience. Although we must not accept and perpetuate clichés in makeup, the way of the pioneer is often a thorny one. And all of the scientific backing in the world can be of no avail if the audience fails to see what it thinks it should. The immediate function of makeup is to help the actor, and if strong racial characteristics are important in projecting the character, at least in terms of audience acceptance, the makeup must provide them.

Appendix E includes a chart and a plate of drawings (Figure 196) which indicate specifically the characteristics of the various races and racial strains. These are of no particular importance now and can be referred to when needed. But the information there, brief though it is, must be used with the discussion on these pages in mind. It must not be looked upon as definitive but as a practical guide.

ENVIRONMENT

In addition to race and other hereditary factors, environment is of considerable importance in determining the color and texture of the skin. A farmer, a bookkeeper, and an athlete will all have different colors of skin, and a color which is right for one would be completely incongruous on another. A man who has lived all of his life in Finland is not likely to look the same as his twin brother who has lived most of his life in Brazil.

One must take into consideration not only the general climatic conditions of the part of the world in which the character lives but also the physical conditions under which he works and spends his leisure time. Offices, mines, fields, foundries, night clubs, slums, and penthouses all have different effects upon the people who work or live in them. But remember that a character may have had a variety of environments. Monsieur Madeleine in Hugo's *Les Miserables* may be a wealthy and highly respected mayor, but his physical appearance will still bear the marks of his years of imprisonment as the convict Jean Valjean.

If environment is to be construed as referring to all external forces and situations affecting the individual, then custom or fashion may logically be considered a part of the environmental influences and a very important one. These influences arising from social customs and attitudes have throughout the centuries brought about superficial and self-imposed changes in appearance.

During the first half of the twentieth century it was assumed that men's hair would be short and that women's hair would be longer. A man might be capable of growing long hair and might even prefer long hair, but ordinarily social pressures were at work to prevent his letting his hair grow. During other periods in history, however, customs were different, and men wore their hair long and in certain periods wore wigs. The drawings in Appendix G indicate the great variety in hair styles through the centuries, and, of course, those styles must be taken into consideration in analyzing a character and planning his makeup.

The matter of makeup off stage must also be considered. Now we assume that women customarily wear makeup and men do not. Yet during certain periods men did wear makeup, and during certain others well-bred women did not. If an eighteenth-century fop appears to be wearing makeup, no harm is done because he might very well be, but if any of the men in *Mr. Roberts* are obviously made up, they immediately become less believable.

Until the present century it has been fashionable for women (and occasionally for men) to make their skins as pale and as delicate as possible. It is necessary, therefore, to bear in mind that a healthy, fashionable woman of a period other than the present one will be considerably paler than a comparable woman of today. Dark skin on a Caucasian woman in most past centuries would be a mark of a lower social class.

Furthermore, styles in street makeup vary. The plucked eyebrows, brilliant rouge, and bizarre lips which were commonplace in the late twenties would seem completely anachronistic in any other period. Even "nice" girls in that period wore too much makeup. Similar eccentricities can be found for other periods in history. The heavy, stylized eye makeup of the ancient Egyptians is perhaps the most obvious example, and the decorative patches of the eighteenth century also come to mind.

Remember, then, that makeup should look like makeup on the stage only when the character would normally be wearing it. That means that your character must be analyzed in the light of social customs to determine not only possible hair styles but also the accepted usage in regard to makeup.

For every character that you make up, always analyze the skin color, hair style, and street makeup in terms of environmental influences.

TEMPERAMENT

An individual's temperament, which may be interpreted as including personality, disposition, and personal habits, affects his physical appearance in many ways.

The adventurer and the scholar, the Bohemian artist and the shrewd business man, the prizefighter and the philosopher—all are widely different in temperament, and these differences are to a greater or lesser degree apparent in the physical appearance. The convivial Sir Toby Belch and the melancholy Sir Andrew Aguecheek, for example, are, aside from all other differences, widely contrasting in temperament and could not conceivably look alike.

The March sisters in *Little Women* are products of the same environment and the same heredity; yet temperamental differences make them strongly individual, and their individuality must be reflected in the makeup.

In addition to these intrinsic differences, there are others which involve conscious choices by the character himself. This is related to the matter of makeup and hair discussed under "Environment." It may be, for example, that bizarre makeup was the custom in the twenties, but every girl did not use it. Perhaps well-bred girls in 1900 did not wear obvious makeup, but there were not-so-well-bred girls who did.

A shy, mousy librarian in, say, 1953 would certainly not be ostracized if she wore false eyelashes, but she would never dream of doing so. Or, perhaps, she might dream of it, but she would still not do it. Or if she did do so, it would be so significant as to require an explanation. And the idea of her wearing green eyeshadow is preposterous. Yet green eyeshadow might be quite right for a dissolute, aging actress, such as Tennessee Williams' leading character in *Sweet Bird of Youth*. For that matter, it would be quite acceptable in the same period for any fashionable young woman, but not all fashionable young women would choose to wear it. In the mid-sixties colored eyeshadow became nearly as commonplace as lipstick had been previously and was therefore less useful in suggesting temperament and personality.

Similarly, the hair is an even more striking and obvious reflection of personality. Granted, it depends first of all on fashion, but to what extent the fashion is followed depends on personality. One would expect the mature and socially correct Mrs. Higgins in *Pygmalion* (or *My Fair Lady*, if you will) to have her hair beautifully done, not a hair out of place, perhaps not in the latest fashion but in one considered proper for a woman of her years and of her elevated social station. The Cockney flower girl, Eliza Doolittle, on the other hand, might be expected to give her hair no attention at all, except, perhaps, to push it out of her eyes. When she is transformed into a "lady," her hair, as well as everything else about her, must reflect the change. In fact, it is an integral part of it.

There are fewer opportunities for men to express their personality in this way, but the ones which exist must not be slighted. When a beard or a mustache is to be worn, there is often a splendid opportunity to reflect personality. First of all comes the choice of whether to wear facial hair at all. And the choice is always related to fashion. In other words, it would take as much courage not to wear a mustache or a beard in 1870 as it would to wear one in, say, 1940. In 1960 it would take less courage than in 1940, but the mere fact of wearing a beard would still be significant and a clear reflection of personality.

Secondly, once the decision to wear the beard has been made, there is the equally important decision as to what kind of beard to wear. Again, this depends on fashion. We must know first of all what kind of beards were being worn in the period. If fashions were very limiting, there is less freedom of choice; if the character departs from the fashion, and there are always those who do, it is doubly significant. But there are several periods in history, especially at the end of the nineteenth century, for example, when facial hair was the rule and the style was limited only by the imagination, taste, and hair-growing capability of the individual. In such a period there is an extraordinary opportunity to express personality through conscious choice of style in facial hair.

The same principles apply to hair on the head as well. There are the usual limitations of style, but even during periods when convention is very limiting, as in the middle of the twentieth century, there are still possible variations in length, in wave or absence of it, in the manner of combing, and in color. The latter in most periods has seldom been a conscious choice with men but has often been an important one for women.

An interesting case of temperamental differences resulting in both conscious and unconscious physical changes is found in the *Madwoman of Chaillot*. There are, in fact, four madwomen, each completely different from the other temperamentally, each showing that difference in her face. Countess Aurelia, the Madwoman of Chaillot, is calm, compassionate, clever, rather tragic, and completely charming. Mme. Constance, the Madwoman of Passy, is garrulous, argumentative, bad tempered, flighty, and quick to take offense. Mlle. Gabrielle, the Madwoman of St. Sulpice, is shy, retiring, and easily hurt. And Mme. Joséphine, the Madwoman of La Concorde, is forthright, practical, and very businesslike. A makeup which would be appropriate for one of the madwomen would be completely wrong for any of the others.

These are not problems which must be faced only with certain striking characters like the madwomen or Sir Toby or on special occasions when circumstances demand it. They must be considered and solved for every character.

An actress of 25 who is playing a contemporary character of 25 must not assume that her own hair style or her own way of making up her eyebrows or her lips will necessarily be suitable for the character. Although she might be able to get by with it in some instances, getting by should hardly be an actor's objective. The problem becomes particularly acute in stock when an actor is playing a different role every week, sometimes with very little variation in age. It is then more important than ever that every legitimate means possible of distinguishing among the characters be found. This means not making changes just to be different but finding the precise way in which the character would express himself. And so long as the personality is fully and accurately expressed in visual terms, the characterization will have taken a long step toward individuality.

HEALTH

In most cases a character's state of health is such that it results in no noticeable physical changes. But sometimes, as with Mimi or Camille, such changes are very noticeable and very specific and are important in validating characterization or plot. At other times, as with Elizabeth Barrett or with Laura in *The Glass Menagerie,* there is no specific illness, just a state of delicate health which is, nonetheless, important in understanding the character and often essential to the plot. Then there are many characters, frequently among refugees, for example, who are undernourished and must give physical evidence of this. By contrast there are those who are overnourished and suffer from gout. And there are others who are bursting with health and must show it in their faces as well as in their physical movements. Again, this is not a problem to be considered for only occasional characters but is significant for all.

In most cases normal good health will be assumed, and that can be considered in making up. Even when the health is not normal, it is rare that a specific illness is indicated. It is seldom necessary, therefore, to try to reproduce medically accurate physical symptoms. Any physical suggestion of the illness can usually be confined to changes in the skin color, the eyes, and, occasionally, especially when mental illness is involved, in the eyebrows and the hair. As always, it is better to do too little than too much. Above all, avoid attributing to certain illnesses specific physical symptoms which are inaccurate and which will immediately be spotted by doctors and nurses in the audience. In certain areas of makeup it is best to curb the imagination and rely strictly on factual information.

AGE

Since age invariably affects all people in physical terms, it is an essential consideration in every makeup. But it must not be allowed to overshadow other determining factors in the physical appearance. There are actors (or so-called makeup artists) who ask the age of a character, then proceed confidently with the makeup with no further questions. Aside from the flagrant lack of understanding of either acting or makeup which this betrays, it also indicates failure to observe the relationship of chronological age to physical appearance.

In makeup, we are interested primarily in the apparent, not the actual, age. If a woman is supposed to look 50, that is what we should try to make her look, whatever her chronological age may be. But that is still only the beginning. All women who look 50 do not look 50 in the same way. A hard-working charwoman of 40 will look 50 in quite a different way from a society woman of 60 who takes excellent care of herself and looks 50. In one, we are aware of a disintegration, a breaking down, a letting go, a loss of youthful vigor with no effort to maintain it. In the other, the normal disintegration may have taken place, but it is to some extent concealed and mitigated by a way of life, a state of mind, and an active attempt to counteract it in every possible way. The results, in terms of makeup, are vastly different. It is true, of course, that in determining exactly how to express the apparent age of 50 in each case we must also deal with questions of heredity, environment, temperament, and health, and it is for that reason that the question of age has been left until last. Its effects can never be determined without reference to the total character, past and present.

In discussing specific effects of age, we can only generalize and indicate the kind of changes which usually take place. The extent to which such changes occur must always be determined in relation to the individual. The conventional divisions of youth, middle age, and old age are serviceable for this discussion.

Youth. There is an unfortunate custom in the theater of referring to any youthful makeup as a *straight* makeup. This is a pernicious term which means simply that you do nothing but heighten the color and project the features. Designating a makeup as "straight" is a trap which leads to neglect of essential work. Conceivably, the term has a certain validity in the fortuitous event that a specific role is so ideally cast that the actor's features are precisely right with not a hair to be changed. But he must be perfect. If there is one single thing about him which is not exactly right, then he requires a makeup which will change him to fit the character he is playing, and this we call a *character* makeup.

Now, there are instances when there is no clearly defined character or perhaps none at all. In photographic portraiture, in some platform appearances, sometimes in choruses it is expected that the actor shall appear as himself. But it is rare to find an actor who cannot profit by some improvement in his face, and a straight makeup does not improve—it merely projects. When we wish to improve the actor's face without relating

FIGURE 7. Corrective makeup for youth. For character makeups of the same actor see Figures 33, 48, 49, 88, 117, 139, 140, 157, 158, 164, and 166.

it to a specific character, we use a *corrective* makeup. This is not, however, a term which is used to refer exclusively to youthful makeups.

Makeup for youth, then, except when an actor is appearing as himself, requires as complete an analysis as for age. The makeup will no doubt be simpler, but the character must be studied no less thoroughly. The physical results of the youthfulness are usually a smooth skin, a good deal of color in the face, a delicately curved mouth (Figures 7, 34, 38, 53), smooth brows following the shape of the eye (Figures 7, 14-F, 25, 51-A, 53, 65-A), an abundance of hair, and so on. Those are average results, of course. Heredity, environment, temperament, and health may counteract the normal effects of youth, as in the case of Richard III. Despite the fact that Richard is a young man at the time of the play, he is hardly an average, normal one. Although there may be little in the face to suggest age, it will probably not seem particularly youthful. Temperament and environment will have had strong influences on his physical appearance.

Ophelia is a young girl, but any young actress who plays her throughout in a conventional youthful makeup is in trouble. Her profound unhappiness and her confusion which finally result in a complete mental breakdown and eventual suicide must certainly, along with other elements in the personality, be reflected in some way in the makeup. This need not and should not be obvious, but it must be there, despite her youthfulness.

Middle age. This is an indefinite period somewhere in the middle of life. It reaches its climax perhaps in the 50's, depending on the individual. For purpose of discussion it may be considered as including all ages between 40 and 65. As we have already pointed out, however, it is the apparent age rather than the actual age which is important in makeup.

Provided nature is allowed to take its course, the color of the skin and the hair will change; muscles will sag (Figures 63, 82); wrinkles will form; youthful curves in lips, eyebrows, and cheeks will become more angular (Figures 65-E-F-H-J, 71-D, 80-E); and hair will fall out. The exact nature of the changes will depend upon factors other than mere age. A good working basis can be achieved by analyzing your character in terms of the results of his age on skin, muscle tonus, teeth, and hair (including eyebrows). Some middle-aged women of 50 look more nearly 30. Others look over 60. So it is important in every case to determine how seriously age has affected the appearance. And remember that the effects of age are modified radically by health, environment, and temperament.

Characters falling into this middle-age group are shown in Figures 39, 45, 48, 49, 63, 88, 140, 151, 153, 175, and 178.

Old age. As a person advances beyond middle life, the skull structure usually becomes more prominent (Figures 8, 71-D, 204), especially if he is thin. If he is fat, then there will be a greater tendency toward flabbiness with pouches and puffs and double chins (Figures 8-H, 201). Along with a general sagging of the flesh, the tip of the nose may droop, hair may fall out, eyebrows may become bushy or scraggly (Figures 8, 197, 198, 209, 210), lips invariably become thinner (Figures 8, 201-A-C-E, 204, 206), teeth fall out, skin and hair color change, neck becomes scrawny (Figures 8-G, 204) and hands bony (Figure 202-B), and the face may be a mass of wrinkles (Figure 8-G-H). It is up to you to decide which of these effects apply to your character. Again, changes will be affected by health, environment, and temperament.

The foregoing analysis is one which should be applied to every charac-

FIGURE 8. Studies of elderly faces showing contrast in effects of age.

ter for which you create a makeup. It will obviously involve some time in studying the play and discussing the character with the actor and the director. If you are an actor doing your own makeup, then your problem will be greatly simplified. Following such a plan of character analysis means, of course, that all consideration of makeup cannot be left until the night of dress rehearsal. It is something which must be planned as carefully as the set and the costumes.

There was a time when there were standard stage sets for drawing room, palace, cottage, and forest, and they were in no way related to the individual play. Sets were not designed—they were put up. But we have now passed that stage in our theatrical development. Makeups should not just be "put on"—they should be designed with as much care as the set. Since the focus of the play is the actor, the makeup, though less obvious (let us hope) and less expensive than nearly any other aspect of the production, is more closely related to the development of the actor's characterization.

The creative aspect of makeup lies in the mind of the artist and stems directly from his understanding of the character. If before you sit down at your dressing table you have intelligently planned in specific terms the physical changes you wish to make for the character, you will have mastered the creative part of your problem and will have left only the technical one of the execution of your ideas.

PROBLEMS

1. Turn to Appendix F and see what impressions you get from the following numbered drawings, paintings, and photographs and try to put these into a few words or sentences: 197-A-B-E-F-H, 198-C-G-I, 199-B-C-E-F, 200-H-J-L, 201-A-B-C-H-I-J, 203, 204, 205, 206, 209, 213, 216.

2. What impression do you get of each of the characters represented by the stylized masks in Figures 223–228?

3

PHYSIOGNOMY

While many people assume that there is no relationship between physical appearance and personality, at the same time they continually form impressions of others, consciously or unconsciously, on the basis of what they look like. Sometimes the impressions prove to be reliable, sometimes not. But most people like to think that they are good judges of character, and their judgment is based largely on their visual impressions.

Thus, there has grown up over the centuries a body of beliefs concerning the relationship of the human face to the character of the individual. The professional physiognomist has refined and organized these beliefs into very complex principles which he believes enable him to read character accurately.

It is interesting to speculate on the validity of his claims, but it is hardly profitable for the makeup artist since the principles, valid or not, are far too complex to be useful. Were one to try to follow the principles of physiognomy in detail, the only solution to the makeup problem would be a mask since all of the actor's features would have to be altered. Therefore, our use of the term *physiognomy* is a more general one and refers to any equating of character with physical appearance.

In these terms almost every person in a theater audience is an amateur physiognomist. Whether we approve or disapprove of this is beside the point. It is a fact which an actor must face. This does not mean, however, that we must accept and cater to clichés and superstitions, but we can use the prejudices of the audience constructively in helping the actor project his characterization in visual terms.

Many of our commonplace attitudes about the features as related to

20

character are simplifications and generalizations of basic truths. Facial structure, it must be remembered, depends not only on the bones of the skull, which change relatively little after maturity, but upon musculature, which changes a great deal. Muscles which are used develop, and those which are not used atrophy. As age advances, there is a relaxation of certain muscles. But the changes which take place are not the result of a whim of nature. They may not be affected very much by massage or by creams, but they are affected greatly by attitudes of mind and by behavior patterns which bring about habitual expressions. These expressions eventually cause permanent creases and hollows and bumps which distinguish the man from the boy. This is one of the reasons some faces become more interesting and attractive with age whereas others wither and decay, reflecting an inactive mind and body. Still others betray misuse of the mind and the body or pain and suffering and maladjustment to one's environment.

People who do not frown, for example, do not develop deep vertical wrinkles at the root of the nose. But there are various reasons for frowning. It may come from a nagging, fretful, dissatisfied disposition, or it may be the result of deep concentration and serious thought. Both cause vertical creases, but the creases are not the same. Thus the face changes, even from year to year, and reflects the mind.

The changes which most clearly reflect the individual occur primarily around the eyes and the mouth, and it is in those areas that we can concentrate our makeup efforts. And though we should take full advantage of these physical changes in order to assist the actor in the visual projection of his characterization, we must once again avoid oversimplification resulting in stereotypes.

Let us take, for example, the frequently held belief that small eyes, close together, are a sign of dishonesty. Since most of the audience will be familiar with this idea and many of them, at least subconsciously, will believe it, it can be useful to the actor and is worth considering from both a positive and a negative point of view. If an open-faced actor is to play a dishonest character, it may be to his advantage to make his eyes smaller and closer together. Or if an actor with small eyes, close together, wishes to play an honest, open, perhaps ingenuous character, he may—and, in most cases, will—wish to enlarge his eyes and make them appear farther apart.

But this is not to say that honesty must invariably be equated with the size and the placement of the eyes. This would be an oversimplification resulting in a reliance on conventional character types. The desirability of using this particular negative physical characteristic, or any other one, must be carefully weighed in the case of each character for whom you propose to use it.

Suppose, for example, that the character to be portrayed is dishonest but that it is important to the plot that other characters be completely taken in by his apparent trustworthiness. Then do we want small, close-set eyes? On the other hand, we may wish to give the audience something to distrust—so that they can feel superior to the characters in the play when the truth comes out.

Carrying the matter still further, there are, perhaps, though the character is dishonest, other more important qualities, often conflicting ones, to be expressed. In *Black Chiffon*, for instance, the leading character, brilliantly played by Flora Robson in London and New York, is a kleptomaniac. This is the thread which holds the plot together, and it is the tragic flaw in an otherwise warm, compassionate, and thoroughly admirable and respectable woman with a devoted family. Surely we would not choose to give the woman small, close-set eyes.

And thus the searching and the questioning should go for every character. It is obvious that we must make very careful decisions as to exactly what we should like to express in the makeup before we even consider how to do it. Rarely will we be able to do everything we should like to; but fortunately we are not painting a portrait, we are merely adding to the one the actor has already begun.

It is hoped that the suggestions in this chapter will be used intelligently not as firmly established rules but only as a guide in making decisions. In making up the eyes and the eyebrows particularly, such decisions must continually be made. When one has had considerable experience in both life and makeup and has developed his powers of observation, he will not need such a guide, but at the beginning one may very well become lost and confused. A decision based only on a whim of the moment or a desire merely to try something different is not likely to be very helpful.

Too often, changes—any kind of changes—are made simply to disguise the actor with no knowledge or thought of their suitability to the character. The purpose of this chapter is merely to give guidance when such changes are to be made so as not only to support the actor's characterization but also to avoid making changes which may, in the mind of the audience, tend to deny what the actor is trying to express.

Usually in a study of makeup there is a great gap between the analysis of a character and the actual makeup process. We are told to decide what the character looks like, but we are given no help in making our decisions.

In this chapter we shall try to bridge that gap by providing a slender thread of guidance. The slenderness is deliberate since the stronger the thread the greater will be the tendency to misuse it and to rely upon it instead of on one's own considered judgment.

In using the following information, remember that it includes only a relatively small number of details which may be of practical use to the makeup artist and is not a scientific study to be used as a basis for analyzing one's friends.

EYES

Perhaps no other feature betrays the inner man so clearly as his eyes. Fortunately, the area surrounding the eye is easily changed with makeup.

In general, prominent eyes (Figures 197-F, 198-A, 199-D) are thought to be found on dreamers and aesthetes and those who live largely through their senses whereas deep-set eyes (Figures 197-G, 198-C, 199-H, 200-B-K) appear in many cases to be an indication of an observant, analytical mind. We might say that one is the eye of a Romeo, the other of a Cassius. Contrast, for example, the deep-set eyes of Abraham Lincoln with the prominent ones of Henry VIII or the deep-set ones of Plato, Aristotle, and Socrates with the prominent ones of Garrick, Macready, and Sarah Siddons. Many eyes will be neither strongly one nor the other, and thus the individuality might be expected to include characteristics of both types.

Dark, narrow, deep-set eyes, too close together (normal eyes are the width of an eye apart) may be found in association with sullenness and suspicion and sometimes, if corroborated by other indications, deceit. If the eyes are oblique and pointed as well as small and too close, and particularly if the eyebrows also follow the oblique line, the indications of deceitfulness are thought to be stronger (G—Plate 5s). (Plates 1–21 appear in Appendix G.)

Small eyes, close together, with a well-developed brow and without negative indications are usually taken as an indication of shrewdness.

It is a matter of common observation that prominent eyes, too far apart, with an arching brow at a considerable distance above the eye (Figure 65-D) are often an indication of credulity and a not-overly-active mind. This kind of eye would, for example, be quite appropriate for Bottom.

The eyes and the mouth often change markedly during one's lifetime. We usually associate the changes with the aging process, but the kind of changes which take place will depend upon the kind of life one leads. As a very obvious example, we can cite the wrinkles which develop at the corner of the eye (Figure 8-E-H). Since these are developed through frequent laughter, it is clear that they may logically be used as an indication of a pleasant, happy, kindly disposition. One could hardly find a better example than Albert Einstein (Figure 8-C).

EYEBROWS

Here we have one of the most expressive and most easily changed features of all. Even a slight change in the eyebrow can affect the whole face. The expressiveness of the eyebrows can be demonstrated by a simple experiment. Draw two circles (representing eyes) on a piece of paper and draw eyebrows over them. Then draw two more with a different kind of eyebrows. Do at least a half a dozen or so. Or, if you prefer, use the same set of circles and keep changing the eyebrows in which to observe the rather striking change in the impression which is conveyed.

Eyebrows vary in placement, line, thickness, color, length, and direction of the hairs. Heavy eyebrows (Figures 8-G, 65-K-L, 197-A-F, 200-L-N, 203, 217) are usually associated with energy, physical or mental, whereas faintly developed brows (Figures 65-J-P, 197-B-E, 199-D) suggest less energy, sometimes even weakness and vacillation—provided other indications support this. Suppose we consider Beethoven and Mendelssohn. Judging from the music, we can assume that Beethoven was probably the more energetic of the two, and we find that his eyebrows were much the heavier. In studying pictures of military men it is very difficult indeed to find eyebrows which are not well developed. Julius Caesar (Plate 2k), Hannibal, Richard Coeur de Lion, Wellington, Cromwell, Charles XII— all had heavy brows. And we find equally heavy ones on Plato, Galileo, and Cicero. In fact, it is seldom that we find men who have achieved prominence through their own efforts with faintly developed eyebrows. Once again, Abraham Lincoln and Henry VIII show a striking contrast. Try, for example, to visualize a rugged military leader with faint, delicately arched eyebrows. Whether or not such a person could exist is beside the point. The picture he presents to our mind verges on the ludicrous.

We have already mentioned that high, arched brows (Figure 65-D) are associated with credulity and lack of concentration. An active mind and body are seldom found with delicate, raised eyebrows. Bushy eyebrows with smooth hair (Figures 8-G, 197-A-F-G, 200-H-L, 203, 205) suggest a vigorous personality. If the hairs of the brow are erratic, they are likely to give the impression of an erratic mind.

It is interesting to note and easy to verify that the concrete thinker tends to knit his brows deeply, developing deep vertical wrinkles between the brows (Figures 197-G, 199-H, 200-B-H, 205, 213) whereas the abstract thinker tends to have brows which are more evenly compressed and often well built out at the outer corners (Figures 197-I, 198-G). A comparison of pictures of a group of inventors (Guttenberg, Morse, Daguerr, Watt, Whitney) with a group of religious leaders (Calvin, Edwards, Swedenborg) or even musicians (Mozart, Handel, Liszt, Gluck) will show this contrast.

More finely etched vertical creases associated with lighter, often partially raised brows slightly knit at the inner ends (Figures 39, 65-F) are often observed on a fretting, nagging type of person. This is simply a result of the way the muscles are habitually used.

If the inside corners are drawn downward and together but the outer corners seem to be lifted (Figure 198-F), the impression is created of an individual who is abrupt and egotistical.

Brows which angle upward in almost a straight line (Figure 197-E-I) are thought to be found on untrustworthy, sycophantic people. Brows which slant downward (Figures 65-B-F, 140, 198-A-H, 218) are frequently associated with egotism, pessimism, weakness, or, if knit at the inner corners, suffering. If you want to suggest treachery or cunning, you may find it helpful to put a curve or a wave in a brow which is angled upward (Figures 65-C, 158, 208). This would be an appropriate brow for Iago or Richard III and is, in fact, the brow of Henry VIII.

NOSE

The nose is the one bony feature which is relatively easy to remodel in three dimensions. As we all know, a very little added to or subtracted from the nose can, like a change in the eyebrows, alter the whole face. And since the change is so dramatic, it is important that the right kind of change be made.

Here, of course, we get away from the logical and verifiable changes which are the result of habitual expressions and into a more controversial area. Probably the most we should do is to suggest in a very general way the impression that various forms of the nose usually create for the average person.

For example, whether or not we accept any sort of relationship between the nose and the personality, we must admit that certain kinds of noses do nothing to further the impression of a particular kind of character. Not even the professional physiognomist would contend that a great military leader must always have a large, strongly developed nose. But at the same time if we try to portray such a character with a delicate little nose with a turned-up tip, the actor may find his characterization taking a different turn from the one he had anticipated. Whereas he intended to be strong and implacable, he may seem only blustering and comic. If he wishes to be comic, fine. If not, it behooves him to choose a nose which will seem suitable to the audience.

In general, it is important to remember that beautiful, delicate modeling in the nose, whatever its size, gives an impression of a similar delicacy or sensitivity in the personality. Crudeness in the personality may well be reflected in crudeness in the nose structure. This refers largely to inherent character traits, not to superimposed ones, since the nose changes relatively little (as compared to the eyes and the mouth) and is related primarily to qualities with which one is born. Cyrano may have had a nose which was outrageously prominent, but one would not expect it to be coarse or crudely formed since Cyrano was an extraordinarily sensitive, refined person. Falstaff, on the other hand, may have been lovable and a jolly companion, but one would hardly expect him to have a sensitively modeled nose.

Large noses, though not in our day considered to be a mark of beauty, are, when they are well modeled, often looked upon as a positive sign of character and of strength. As a matter of fact, an examination of history will reveal relatively few important men (successful through their own merit, that is) with small noses. However, if the nose is narrow and pinched (Figures 49, 57), one expects to find more reserve in the personality and sometimes a suspicious, secretive nature.

The Roman nose (Figures 199-B-F, 200-J-M, 205) always seems relatively energetic and determined. It is often found on military men—Caesar (Plate 2i), Hannibal, Wellington, Cromwell, Charles XII, and Simón Bolívar, for example, as well as on prominent men in all fields—including Dante, Schiller, Plato, John Locke, DeSoto, Archimedes. The concave type of nose (Figures 80-P, 86, 206, Plate 13h-i-o-q) corresponds to the concave face. There is likely to be a lack of energy and ambition. This may be overcome, as it was in the case of Socrates, but it is thought to be the natural tendency.

The Grecian nose (Figure 200-G) suggests refinement, taste, and sensitivity. A straight nose turned up at the end (Figures 80-M, 200-K) gives a feeling of optimism and enthusiasm and a general curiosity about life. This impression is modified considerably if the nose is coarsely formed (Figure 203). A turned-down tip (Figures 80-O, 124) may accompany coldness and deliberateness and sometimes melancholy. Shortness combined with broadness (Figure 199-H) seems to indicate vitality, and flatness is thought to betray secretiveness and suspicion, sometimes cunning.

The nose does change slightly throughout life, and it is a matter of common observation that with dissipation and overindulgence the change will be in the direction of coarseness (Plates 13q, 18l). It is also felt by some that fine concentration in thought and action and an active self-control will tend to refine and sharpen the lines.

The nose can be used to indicate the sort of temperament and capabilities the individual was given to start with, and the eyes and the mouth provide reflections of what has been done with them.

MOUTH

Whereas the eye is usually found to reveal the kind of mentality and the type of thought processes, the mouth seems much more likely to reveal the physical side of the nature. It is a matter not only of logic but of common observation that the greater the intensity of mental control, the harder will be the muscles of the mouth, resulting in thinner lips with sharper lines (Figures 8-B-G-K, 200-L, 201-H-J, 204). The greater the emotionalism, the more relaxed the mouth muscles will be and the fuller and more separated the lips (Figures 201-F, 207, 215, 216, Plate 13q). The full, sagging lower lip of certain mental defectives is an extreme example. It is interesting to note that among military men and explorers (including Caesar, Napoleon, Wellington, Pershing, Bolívar, Cromwell, Charles XII, Cabot, Columbus, DeSoto, Hudson) there is usually much greater firmness in the lips than, for example, among the poets (Milton, Shakespeare, Byron, Burns, Poe).

Thin, uneven lips with the corners turned down (Figures 45, 201-A, 208, 221) are usually taken as a warning of bad temper and fault-finding. If the lips are well-colored with turned-up ends (Figure 201-D-G-I), they are quite logically a token of optimism and good humor. To confirm this, however, observe the eyes. In the makeup in Figure 163, for example, the smiling mouth is obviously anything but good-humored or kindly.

Loose, swollen lips (Figure 207) may suggest dissipation, whereas compressed lips with strongly developed nasolabial folds (Figures 8-K, 57, 201-J, 204) are associated with strong, purposeful activity.

It has been observed that determination and tenacity are frequently found to accompany a large mouth with the upper lip drawn down and the under one rolled outward, especially if supported by a strong chin (Figures 88, 200-H-J, 201-J, 220). There is no better example than Abraham Lincoln.

It is also a matter of common observation that the greater the expansion in the mouth, the greater the expansion in the personality. Shy, introverted, or self-centered people tend to contract the mouth, whereas genial, outgoing people tend to expand it (Figures 199-B, 200-D-H-J). Any competent actor will do this automatically and will need a minimum of help from the makeup. Again, it is to the point to compare the sympathetic, outgoing Abraham Lincoln with the self-centered Henry VIII, the one with a large, expansive mouth, the other with a tiny, contracted one.

It cannot be repeated too often that suggestions in this chapter are to be used only as guides if you feel you need them. Under no circumstances should you adopt the attitude that, for example, small eyes mean cunning or a large nose means passion. Use these brief suggestions with discretion and try always to correlate the features and not rely on only one to suggest the character. You will never be able to make all of the changes you consider ideal, but the purpose in a character analysis is to try to discover the determining factors in the character's behavior, then to visualize as nearly as possible what he should look like. Later you will have to meet the practical problem of recreating this image on the face of a specific actor. But remember always that a single feature cannot define character.

And remember, too, that the more changeable features, such as the eyes and the mouth, may belie the indications of the hereditary bone structure. Socrates' head, for example, has many indications of strongly negative personality traits, all of which Socrates admitted to possessing at one time. But through persistence and determination he overcame them. This happens to some extent to most of us—sometimes, unfortunately, in reverse. It must be remembered that all of the features must be correlated if a useful analysis is to be made.

PROBLEMS

1. Repeat Problem 1 at the end of Chapter 2, using suggestions in this chapter in making your judgments. Compare the impressions you have now with your original ones. They may be exactly the same, or they may be quite different. In most cases they should be somewhat more specific.

2. Follow the same procedure with photographs of people. They must not be well-known people, however; the faces should be completely new to you. This time try to be more specific in your analysis, first studying the

face as a whole and the general impression you receive, then analyzing the features to see which ones support that impression and which ones may offer contradictions. If you are working in a class, results of both Problems 1 and 2 should be discussed. There will undoubtedly be arguments. It will, of course, not be possible to reach any definite conclusions about who is right and who is wrong, but it should prove enlightening to compare reactions, and it should also sharpen your awareness of faces.

3. Choose three characters from well-known plays and write brief descriptions of exactly how you think they should look, being specific about such features as mouths, noses, and eyes. Do not be misled by photographs of actors who may have played the parts, for there you are seeing the individual actor's interpretation, not the ideal one. Do not be concerned with practical problems of makeup.

4

FACIAL ANATOMY

Before beginning to remodel a house it is essential to understand how houses are constructed. Similarly, there is little hope of remodeling a human face successfully unless we know how faces are constructed. When we model a new nose for a character, for example, we must be able to make a nose that looks as if it has bone and cartilage in it. When we try to hollow a cheek, we must place the shadow in precisely the right spot in relation to the cheekbone so that our painted shadow will look like a depression in the face and not like a superimposed patch of dark paint. In other words, we must work from the inside out. Although the bones of the head are concealed from direct view, the whole shape of the head depends upon their exact conformation. And a makeup which ignores the basic bone structure can be no more be successful than a job of remodeling which is not related to the basic house.

BONES OF THE FACE

A thorough and highly technical knowledge of anatomy, though not to be scorned, is not really essential to the makeup artist. It is not even necessary to remember the technical names of bones and muscles so long as you know where they are. There is, for example, no particular virtue in referring to the *zygomatic arch* when the term *cheekbone* is simpler and more generally understood. In a few instances, however, when the precise location of shadows and highlights is to be discussed, it is certainly advantageous to be able to refer to the precise area. The term *forehead* is useful only if we really mean the entire forehead, which in makeup we seldom do. There are two separate and distinct eminences, the *frontal* and the *superciliary*, which must ordinarily be considered separately in highlighting. In this case, then, the technical terms become useful, though it is possible to refer simply to the upper and lower forehead.

A knowledge of the bones of the face becomes increasingly important with the advancing of the character's age for the simple reason that muscles lose their tonus and begin to sag, flesh is no longer firm, and the face begins to take on the effect of a skull draped with skin. This is an effect impossible to achieve unless you know exactly where the bones of the skull are located.

Figure 9 shows a three-dimensional drawing of a skull, stripped of all cartilage, muscle, and skin. This is the basic structure of all faces, though there are, naturally, variations in exact shapes of bones which provide the

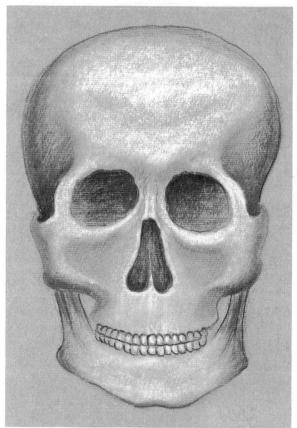

FIGURE 9. Charcoal and chalk drawing of a human skull to demonstrate principles of three-dimensional modeling.

first step in distinguishing one individual from another. Notice how the prominent bones catch the light while the hollows are in shadow.

Figure 10 is a diagrammatic representation of a skull indicating the names of the various bones and hollows (or fossae). The *maxilla* and the *mandible* are simply the upper and lower jaw, which you would hardly be able to miss. The *nasal bone* is equally obvious. But observe that only the upper section of the nose is part of the skull. The lower, more movable part is constructed of cartilage attached to the nasal bone.

We have already mentioned the importance of distinguishing between the two eminences of the forehead. In some individuals these are very clearly defined, especially when the source of light is from directly over-head, forming a slight shadow between the two. This can be seen in Figure

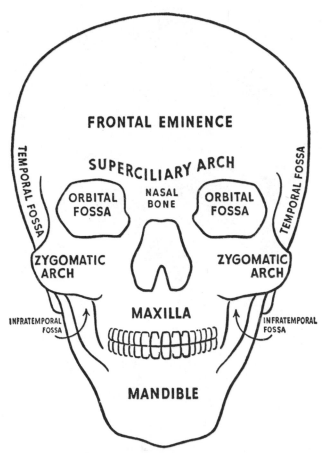

FIGURE 10. Diagram of human skull, locating important prominences and depressions.

205. In other individuals, the whole forehead may be smoothly rounded with no hint of depression between the two normally prominent parts of the skull. If your own forehead is of the latter type, study someone else's so that you will understand the conformation.

The *cheekbone* or *zygomatic arch* is one of the most important bones of the face for the makeup artist and the one which seems to give the most trouble. In many individuals the cheekbone is very prominent, making it quite easy to locate. But in others it is often necessary to prod the flesh with the fingers in order to find its precise location. In studying the bones of your own face, you should always locate them by feel as well as by sight since this will frequently be a part of normal makeup procedure, especially when makeup is being applied with the fingers. In the case of the cheekbone, prod the flesh along the entire length of it from the ear to the nose until you know its exact shape. It is especially important to find the top of the bone, then feel how it curves around underneath. Keep prodding until you can locate accurately a distinct top and bottom to the bone, for it is at this point that most cheek shadowing and highlighting goes wrong. Figure 71-A, which shows a side view of the cheekbone, may clarify in your mind the general shape.

Then there are the hollows in the skull. The *orbital* ones are clear-cut and easy to feel with your finger. The *temporal* hollows are what you normally refer to as the *temples*. These are not deep, but there is a slight depression which shows up increasingly with age (Figure 205). The *infratemporal* hollows, which are extremely important in makeup, you will have already found in the process of prodding the cheekbone. The lack of bony support here allows the flesh to sink in underneath the cheekbone, resulting in the familiar hollow-cheeked effect (Figures 8-D, 205). In extreme old age or starvation this sinking-in can be very great indeed.

Study the bone structure of your own face thoroughly. Then, if possible, study several different types of faces both visually and tactually.

The skull is, as you know, covered with various muscles which operate the mandible (the only movable part of the skull) and the mouth, eyelids, and eyebrows. In order that the study of these may be made more immediately applicable, they will be discussed in Chapter 12 in connection with the individual features which they affect.

CONSTRUCTION OF A HEAD

The next step, now that we have studied the basic framework of the head, is to cover it with flesh and skin to make it resemble a living being. The best way to arrive at a practical understanding of the structure of the head is actually to construct one. This should be done with artists' modeling clay (such as Plastolene) on a thin but sturdy board. A piece of Masonite about 12 x 16 inches is excellent. Only the front half of the head (from the ears forward) or perhaps the front third need be done. Figures 11, 12, and 13 show such a head being modeled.

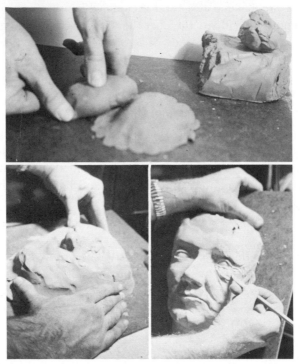

FIGURES 11, 12, 13. Modeling a head in clay. Shown at the top is the first step—pressing the clay against the board to make sure that it sticks. The second step shows the general form of the head, with the nose begun. The third step shows the completed head being aged with a modeling tool.

In addition to the primary advantage of learning by actual practice the basic construction of a human head, there are two additional advantages. One is the actual practice in modeling features (especially the nose), which is essential in making any prosthetic addition to the face, whether it be of nose putty or rubber. The second is that this same head can be remodeled indefinitely to study the actual three-dimensional form of sagging flesh, such as wrinkles or pouches, which you are trying to reproduce with paint, or to experiment with various shapes of noses, eyebrows, or chins in planning a makeup for a specific character. In other words, once the original model is made, it should be kept for subsequent use.*

For the benefit of those who are at a loss as to how to go about the modeling, here are some fairly specific instructions which should anticipate most of the usual pitfalls.

MODELING A HEAD IN CLAY

Five pounds of an oil-base clay will enable you to model a face of approximately life size. The area to be developed can be bounded by the hairline, a point just below the jaw, and a point halfway to the ear on either side (Figure 12). If you wish to carry the head back as far as the ear, another three or four pounds of clay should be sufficient. The clay may come in either five- or one-pound blocks. For easy working, it should be cut into half- or quarter-pound cubes. These cubes should be kneaded and worked with the hands until the mass is soft and pliable. As each piece is softened, it should be pressed to the board with the thumbs, as shown in Figure 11, and additional pieces mashed onto it in the same way. If this is done properly, the completed face can be carried about or hung perpendicularly on the wall with no danger of the clay's pulling away from the board.

As the pieces of clay are blended to the board, the general facial area to be developed should be kept in mind. A face about 7 to 9 inches long and about 5 or 6 inches wide is the most satisfactory. Making a larger face from five pounds of clay results in too flat a construction, while a smaller face does not take full advantage of the material.

The softened clay (except for about half a pound, which will be used later) should be molded into a mound which might very well resemble half an egg sliced lengthwise. It is by cutting away and building up the various areas in this mound that the face is developed.

Figure 14-A shows a stylized head construction, emphasizing its three-dimensional quality. In 14-B you can see how this is related to a real head. In many ways the head, especially the front half, is closer to a cube than to an egg. You will probably prefer to use the basic egg shape for your clay model, but it is frequently helpful to visualize the cube in order to be sure that your head is really three-dimensional. It is important to be aware that the forehead, for example, has a front plane and two side planes

---

* Such a project as this almost invariably brings forth cries of protest from students, who seem to feel that only experienced artists can model heads. Actually, it's much simpler than it looks, and I have yet to find a student who has not enjoyed doing it. The results may or may not be artistically commendable, but that is not important. The important thing is to learn through building up a head yourself how it is actually formed.

(the temples). The depression for the eyes actually forms a sort of bottom
to the forehead box, and of course the top of the head makes a rounded
top.

The nose forms a smaller, elongated box with definite front, sides, and
bottom. The front, sides, and bottom of the jaw are clear-cut. Notice particularly the horseshoe shape of the teeth. Don't let your lips follow the
flat plane of the forehead! Remember that there are teeth which the lips
must follow.

The normal face is divided into three equal parts horizontally, and
that division should be your first step. The forehead occupies the top third,
the eyes and nose the middle third, and the upper and lower jaws (including the mouth, of course) the lower third. It is probably well to model the

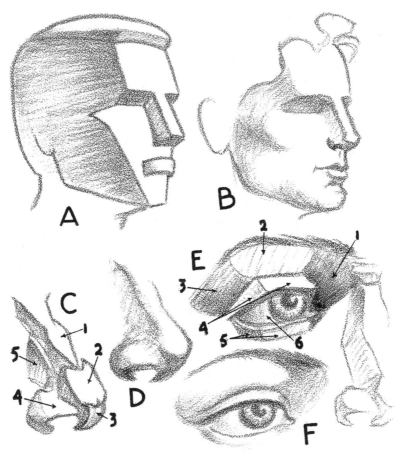

FIGURE 14. Third dimension in the head. A, C, and E show in
exaggerated form the planes of the head and the features.

larger areas and develop the general shape of the head, defining the fore-head, the jaw, and the eye sockets before starting on any detailed modeling.

Nose. This is usually the simplest single feature to model because its size and location can easily be changed without much damage to the rest of the modeling. This is where you will use that extra bit of clay that was left over. In adding the clay here or for any feature, it is always best to add more than seems necessary, for it is always easier to cut away excess clay than it is to add on to a feature which has been carefully modeled and found to be too small.

Figure 14-C shows a breakdown of the nose into its component parts. Plane 1 represents the slender nasal bone, 2 and 3 show the two planes of the cartilage which forms the tip. In 4 we see the roughly cylindrical flesh of the nostrils, and 5 represents the side planes. D shows the nose more realistically as it actually looks to the observer. But notice in both C and D the subleties of shape.

The front plane of the nose (1 and 2) is not of even width all the way down. It is narrow at the bridge, then widens and narrows again as it fits into the still wider cartilage of the tip (2). Examine a number of noses carefully to observe this construction. In some noses it will be quite obvious. In others the change will be so subtle that it will be difficult to distinguish it. On your clay head, model these planes carefully to give the feeling of bone and cartilage beneath the skin. Don't let it be a shapeless lump. Since you will use this particular bit of modeling frequently in your makeup work, it becomes especially important to become proficient at it now. And you will find the modeling in clay much easier than it will be later with nose putty.

Mouth. Modeling the mouth is a process of shaping and carving, working for the rounded fleshiness of the lips as opposed to a straight thin gash in the clay. As we have suggested above, start with a cylindrical shape, and model the mouth on that. Refer to Figure 14-A. It is usually helpful in laying out the mouth to establish the exact center of the mouth with the small indention or cleft which extends from the nose down to the cupid's bow of the upper lip.

Eyes. Before beginning on the eyes, be sure the superciliary arch and the cheekbones are carefully modeled since these, along with the nose, will form the eye socket. It is usually wise to make an actual eye socket before building up an eye. This can be done quite simply by pressing with both thumbs where the eyes are to be. This, as we have mentioned before, can be done during the preliminary laying out of the face. Bear in mind that eyes are normally the width of an eye apart (Figure 51-A).

As with the nose, the eyes are modeled with extra clay. A piece about the size of a walnut set into each socket should prove more than sufficient. This should give you a good start in laying out the correct planes.

Figure 14-E shows schematically the planes of the eye, while 14-F shows the normal eye for comparison. Planes 1, 2, and 3 represent the slope from the upper edge of the orbital fossa downward and inward to the eyeball, but this slope lies in three planes which blend gently and imperceptibly into each other. Plane 1 is the deepest part of the eye socket, formed by the meeting of the nasal bone and the superciliary arch. Plane 2 is the most prominent part of the upper socket, pushed forward by the bone of the superciliary arch. This is in essentially the same horizontal plane as the forehead. Plane 3 curves backward into the plane of the temple.

Plane 4 represents the upper lid, which comes forward over the eyeball and follows it around so that it is actually in three planes, only two of which are visible in this three-quarter view. Plane 5 represents the lower lid which, though much less extensive than the upper, follows the same general pattern. Plane 6 represents the eyeball itself.

On your clay head it would probably be well to model the eye as if closed, then with the modeling tool carefully cut down into the clay as if removing a section of the lid in order to form the eyeball itself and give the lid thickness. It is possible, if you prefer, to model the eyeball and lay on thin pieces of clay for the lids. The important thing is to have a three-dimensional eye, correctly placed in the face, well shaped, and set properly into the eye sockets. As with all other features, avoid flatness.

When all of the features are in place, smooth out rough edges, and carefully check all planes of the face and of each feature. If the result is too far from reality, analyze it to find your missteps, and redo those sections.

But the best way to avoid a catastrophe is first to lay out proportions with great care, measuring your own features if you like, then to make sure the basic head is three-dimensional, not flat. There is a tendency among beginners to make heads which are either excessively egg-shaped or very flat. Avoid this. Try to develop a feeling for both roundness and squareness in the head. Both qualities are there. Be sure your individual features are carefully constructed with all of their individual parts. Relate the size and placement of features to the head and to each other. A careful modeling of each feature should then result in a satisfactory head.

The important thing is to follow through each step logically and carefully, progressing from large areas to small ones, and not trying to finish a head at one sitting. The skill and understanding you will gain will repay a good deal of time and effort.

PROBLEMS

1. Locate on your own face the various prominences and depressions shown in the drawing in Figure 10.

2. In the photographs you used for Problem 2, Chapter 3, in others which you may have collected, or in Figures 197–201, point out the bones and hollows in the face.

3. Following the instructions in this chapter, model a head in clay. You may use yourself or someone else as a model. Use actual measurements of the real head if you find you can't trust your own eye. There is no need to try for a likeness, though you may occasionally achieve one unexpectedly. The two most important objectives are to get the general proportions of the face right and to model the head as a whole and the individual features so that there is a feeling of solidity—as if there were an actual bone structure giving the whole thing form. Keep this head for future use.

5

EQUIPMENT FOR
MAKEUP

Before beginning even to experiment with the application of makeup, it is necessary to have available materials with which to work—not just any materials, but carefully chosen ones. It is true that the final test of a good makeup lies in its effectiveness on the stage, and the makeup artist is responsible to a very large degree for the success or failure of the makeup, but the artist's equipment can help or hinder him to a great extent. Since the beginner has not yet learned the tricks of doing acceptable work with mediocre tools, it is greatly to his advantage to start out with the best he can obtain.

The artist's equipment consists not only of the paints, powders, and brushes used in makeup but also of the surroundings in which he works and the informational material he collects for reference.

The term *greasepaint*, through long association with anything theatrical, is well known even to the layman. But greasepaint is only one of a great many materials used by the makeup artist. A list of these materials is included in Appendix A. The average kit will, of course, include only a fraction of these. Since a study of the complete list at this time would only prove confusing, certain items have been starred (*). These are the ones with which you are likely to be immediately concerned, and they should be read through now. The others can be used for reference when you need them.

THE MAKEUP KIT

After you have become somewhat familiar with a few of the materials listed in Appendix A, you will want to select those best suited to your needs and organize them into a makeup kit. When you have selected your materials, you will need a container of some sort in which to carry them. The individual kit should always be portable. The group kit may be or not, depending upon where and how it is to be used.

The most convenient individual kit is probably a portable unfitted woman's makeup case, obtainable in most department and leather goods stores. Those with handles on the side are usually about 8" x 10" x 5". Those with handles on the top are likely to be deeper but not so wide. There is usually a built-in mirror. The case should have a tray with a few divisions. If it hasn't, then make your own tray out of plywood or other sturdy material. One of the purposes of the makeup case is to keep the materials in order, and for that reason a divided tray is necessary.

The selection of a kit is, of course, a personal matter, and many actors will prefer other types of kits. For professional actors on tour, if they are sending their kits with the company luggage, a sturdy metal box with a good lock may prove more satisfactory. Some actors may prefer cantilever trays to the kind that must be lifted out. It doesn't really matter what kind of makeup box you use so long as it holds the amount of makeup you need, keeps the makeup in order, is convenient to use, and is generally practical for you.

For small group kits (or well-stocked individual ones) a large fishing tackle box with cantilever trays (Figure 15) is practical and not unreasonable in price. These boxes come in many sizes with varying numbers of trays. Similar boxes designed primarily as sample cases are also splendid for makeup. Figure 16 shows a particularly good one. Many other models of various sizes are also available. Then there are several kits with trays and drawers designed specifically for makeup. Your needs and your budget will no doubt determine which one you choose.

If there is no occasion to carry the group makeup materials from place to place, then cabinets with small drawers or with shelves and pigeonholes are more easily accessible. The drawers or shelves can then be labeled and the paints and powders arranged according to color.

Professional makeup artists will undoubtedly prefer the professional makeup kit with trays and drawers or a sample kit such as the one illustrated (Figure 16). The sample kits are available in fiber, artificial leather, or top grain cowhide with from 1 to 20 trays and varying widely in price.

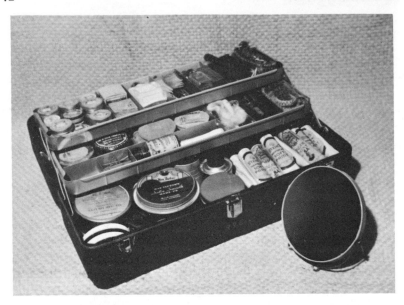

FIGURE 15. Makeup kit containing materials from several makeup companies. The kit is a metal fishing tackle box.

There are excellent kits available from Paramount and from the makeup companies. It would be well to investigate current styles and prices from several sources before choosing the kit best suited to your needs.

It is also possible to buy filled kits from the makeup companies, but it is far cheaper and far more practical to select your own makeup box and the materials to fill it, for only in that way will you be able to have the best of everything and those particular materials which you will need.

Since you will not know what you will need until you have had some experience, you may wish to refer to the sample kits listed in Appendix C. One of them can probably be adapted, with only slight changes, to your needs. The primary purpose in the student kits is to keep the price as low as possible. That means fewer colors to work with and more mixing to be done—not at all a bad thing. For purposes of more advanced work in the makeup class it might be arranged to supplement the simple student kits with materials from a large group kit.

For reasons of economy you may wish to use one of the inexpensive student kits containing small tubes and tins of makeup. These are not ideal, but they provide enough material for a satisfactory beginning, and they can always be supplemented with additional materials. Available kits are discussed in Appendix A under "Student Makeup Kits."

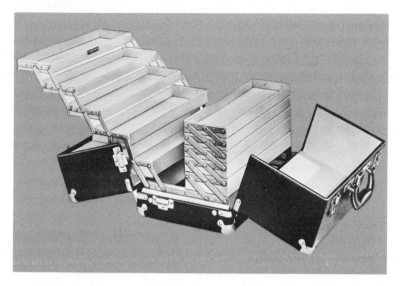

FIGURE 16. Ten tray case suitable for the professional makeup artist or for use as a group kit. Similar cases are available in various sizes from Fibre Products Mfg. Co. (See Appendix B for address.)

If all makeup materials for a class are furnished, the dispensing of makeup from the general kit is a problem but can usually be managed, in the case of greasepaint, by using glass slides approximately three by four inches. Each student should possess one of these slides, or the whole group of slides can be kept by the instructor. When the student needs a base from the large kit, he can squeeze a small amount onto his glass slide and leave the tube in the kit for others to use. When he needs one of the shading colors, he can remove a very small amount from the container with an artist's palette knife. Or it may be that the instructor will prefer either to designate an assistant to dispense the paint or to do it himself. But no matter how the paint is dispensed, the glass slide method, though not without its disadvantages, makes possible the use of an average-sized supplementary kit by the whole class and eliminates the hectic "tube grabbing," which always causes much confusion and waste.

When using cake makeup, you will need to have a sufficient number of cakes, large or small, so that any one cake will not have to be shared by more than two students. Every student must have his own sponge and at least one brush, preferably more.

All paints in both individual and group kits should be labeled in accordance with the color chart in Appendix H, as suggested in Chapter 6.

THE MAKEUP ROOM

Given the necessary materials, one can do a makeup in any surroundings. But one can work far more efficiently in a room designed to fill the requirements of the makeup artist.

The focus of such a room, whether it be an individual dressing room or a large room for group makeup, is the makeup table and mirror. The most one can expect in the average dressing room is a mirror surrounded by rows of naked bulbs. A more satisfactory arrangement would be to have the light source recessed and a slot provided for slipping in colored gelatines to approximate the stage lighting (see Figure 17). This will never give the same effect as the stage lights, but it will come considerably nearer than the usual dressing room lights, especially when very warm or very cool lights are being used on stage. If such an arrangement is not possible, and it usually is not, at least be sure the amount of illumination is adequate.

The dressing table should be about 30 inches high containing a drawer with lock for storing the makeup between performances and for keeping the actor's valuables or personal effects during performances. A dispenser for cleansing tissues either above or to one side of the mirror is a great convenience. Either a wastebasket or a special section built into the table

FIGURE 17. Dressing table designed to permit the use of gelatine slides over the mirror lights to approximate the stage lighting.

should be provided for disposing of tissues. If there is an additional space above or at the sides of the mirror, a row of small shelves or pigeonholes for makeup will help in avoiding some of the usual clutter on the table itself.

In the professional theater, actors customarily do their own makeup, but in the nonprofessional theater there is usually a makeup artist or even a makeup crew. This places an additional burden on dressing rooms which are usually overcrowded anyway, or it necessitates moving to a vacant room which has no adequate facilities for makeup. Either situation does not make for efficiency. It is wise in all nonprofessional theaters to provide a special makeup room large enough to accommodate quite a number of actors in addition to the makeup artists. A row or two of chairs for actors who are waiting to be made up is an excellent addition.

There should be long tables with a continuous row of large mirrors above them. A large mirror in one corner is also very helpful in keeping the actors who have already been made up away from the dressing tables, where they are likely to slow down the makeup work.

A lavatory or two is indispensable. So are clothes hooks on the wall and a large cabinet in which to keep the makeup and makeup smocks. A case of small drawers, as suggested in the section on the makeup kit, is preferable here to a portable makeup box. Dentists' cases with large but very shallow traylike drawers are excellent but very expensive. Metal filing cabinets with drawers about 9" x 12" x 3" are quite practical. A reclining barber's chair is enormously helpful to the makeup artist and should be standard equipment in any professional makeup room.

If possible, a general makeup room should be adjacent to the dressing rooms and as near the stage as possible. The latter consideration is really the more important one, for makeup often needs to be hurriedly touched up between acts or during an act. Good ventilation is so essential as hardly to need mention.

Remember that though a good makeup can be done in poor surroundings, a better one will probably result from more favorable conditions. Even the most capable makeup artist can hardly be expected to do his best if compelled to work for very long under handicaps imposed by poor physical conditions.

THE MAKEUP MORGUE

One of the first requisites of a good makeup artist is a keen sense of observation. Skill in makeup techniques can be learned through study and practice, but artistry comes from observing people closely and then using that skill in making a dramatic character as real as those people.

But no matter how closely you observe people, you cannot possibly retain every detail of observation. For this reason, a makeup *morgue* (a term frequently used to designate a file of clippings) is indispensable. Since our best source-book for information on makeup is life itself, the morgue should contain, first of all, unretouched photographs of men and women of all ages and all kinds. Magazines (particularly *Life* and *National Geographic*) are the best source. For fictional characters, both drawings and photographs of other makeups are helpful. Reproductions of great paintings are a good source for historical hair styles. There is also much valuable material to be found in secondhand bookstores. In addition, your morgue should contain makeup catalogs, price lists, and any information you can collect on makeup techniques. In fact, anything which has a direct bearing upon your present or future problems should be included.

A practical container is a letter-size expanding file made of stiff paper reinforced with cardboard on the front and back (Figure 18). There are usually about 21 divisions. Such files can be obtained at any stationery store.

A great deal of clutter is avoided if small clippings are pasted on sheets of 8½ x 11 inch paper before being filed. This has an additional advantage. For a particular show those sheets which are most likely to be useful can be removed from the file and put temporarily into a hard-cover spring binder,

FIGURE 18. A makeup morgue of pictures and information to be used for reference.

a loose-leaf notebook, or paper manuscript-covers. They are much more manageable and less likely to be lost.

Below is a suggested classification for your morgue. As your collection grows, you may want to make certain changes and add subdivisions. For a professional makeup artist one file is far from sufficient. A single item or two in the following list may be expanded into a whole file with numerous subdivisions. For the average actor, however the following arrangement of material for one file makes a good beginning:

AGE, Male	LIGHTING
AGE, Female	MULTIPLE MAKEUPS
BEARDS AND MUSTACHES	NOSES, EYES, MOUTHS, ETC.
COLOR	PHOTOGRAPHY
CORRECTIVE MAKEUP	PROSTHESIS
EQUIPMENT AND SUPPLIES	RACIAL AND NATIONAL
FICTIONAL, Male	STYLIZED MAKEUP
FICTIONAL, Female	TECHNIQUES
HISTORICAL, Male	WIGS AND HAIR, Male
HISTORICAL, Female	WIGS AND HAIR, Female
LIGHT AND SHADE	

As you work with your morgue, you will probably find other divisions which are more practical for you. And it is important that you do work with it continually. The makeup morgue is not something you work up overnight as a class project or that you gather together hurriedly on a free weekend. It is as important a part of your makeup equipment as greasepaint or nose putty. You cannot do successful makeup work without it. The source of your knowledge and your inspiration is people. Since you cannot keep people on file for easy reference, you must keep photographs of them. The visual impressions you store up in your memory are important, but they are not always extensive or dependable enough to help you solve every problem you will meet. The makeup morgue is your private, portable library. You should start now to collect material and keep adding more whenever you run across any. Your morgue will, of course, never be complete. You should continue to add to it as long as you do makeup.

We have in this chapter and in Appendix A covered all of the equipment you will need as a makeup artist. The problem now is to use that equipment as effectively as possible. A kit stocked with good materials, a well-lighted dressing table, and an extensive morgue will by no means insure good makeups; but they will, at least, provide no excuse for bad ones. And they will go a long way toward simplifying your makeup problems.

PROBLEMS

1. Start your own makeup morgue, using the photographs you have already gathered for the problems in Chapters 3 and 4. Work out whatever filing system you find most convenient, but be sure there is adequate room for expansion. Label all material you find according to the category in which you file it. This will simplify putting it back each time you have used it. Make a point of bringing as many pictures as possible to class each day.

6

COLOR IN PIGMENT

Before we can actually use the makeup paints discussed in the last chapter, it is essential that we be able to select and to mix colors intelligently. This necessitates a basic understanding of the principles of color, which can then be applied specifically to makeup paints.

Scientifically speaking, color can be approached from three different points of view—those of the chemist, the physicist, and the psychologist. The makeup artist, though primarily not a scientist, must at one time or another use each of these approaches. When he mixes paints, he is a chemist. When he estimates the effect of stage lights on his makeup, he is a physicist. And when he selects a certain color of makeup pigment for the effect it will have on the audience, he is a psychologist.

All color comes originally from the source of light, whether it be natural or artificial. White light is a mixture of light rays of all colors. Technically speaking, pigment has no color of its own but has, rather, the ability to absorb certain rays and reflect others. The rays it reflects are the ones which are responsible for the pigment's characteristic color. A "red" dress, for example, absorbs all light rays except the red ones, which it reflects, making the dress appear red.

But since we are artists first and scientists second, suppose we merely accept for the moment the existence of color in pigment and begin by examining the relationships characteristic of the various colors we see.

CHARACTERISTICS OF COLOR

In order to be able to talk intelligently about color and to approach the problem with a certain amount of organization in our thinking, it is

49

convenient to know three terms used to designate distinct color characteristics. Many of the best color psychologists deprecate the use of these terms
—nevertheless, they are practical for our purpose. They are usually known
as *hue, intensity,* and *value*.

Hue. The hue of a color is simply the name by which we know it—red
or green or blue or yellow. Pink and maroon are both variations of the
basic red hue; brown is a variation of orange; ivory is a variation of yellow.

If we take samples of all of the major hues with which we are familiar and drop them at random on a table, the result, of course, is chaos.
But as we place next to each other hues which are somewhat similar, we
begin to see a progression which by its very nature becomes circular—in
other words, a color wheel. That is the traditional form of hue arrangement and for our purposes the most practical one.

Since, however, the progression from one hue to another is a steady
one, that means that the circle might contain an unlimited number of
hues, depending only on the threshold of perception of the individual—
that point, in other words, at which two hues become so nearly alike as to
be indistinguishable to the naked eye and, consequently, for all practical
purposes identical. But though a tremendous number of hues results in an
aesthetically attractive wheel, it confuses the issue in actual practice. There-

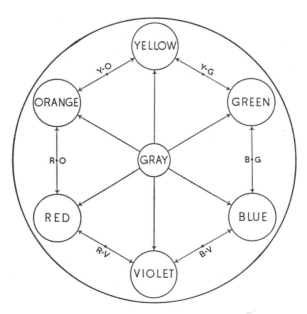

FIGURE 19. The Prang color wheel.

fore a certain number of hues must be selected at regular intervals on the circumference of the wheel. Every authority on color has his own pet arrangement of the color wheel. For purposes of this discussion, I have chosen the conventional Prang color wheel (Figure 19), not because of its technical accuracy, but simply because it is the one customarily used in schools and is consequently more familiar to the average student of makeup than some of the more recent arrangements.

The hue of a color, then, is the name by which we know it and is determined by its position on the periphery of the color wheel.

Intensity. Thus far we have been speaking only of very brilliant colors. But more often than not we shall be using colors of less than maximum brilliance. A gray-blue is still blue in hue, but it is far different from the blue on the color wheel. Although of the same hue, it is lower in *intensity*. This color would be shown as being nearer the center of the wheel—more gray, in other words. Colors on the periphery are brilliant. Colors nearer

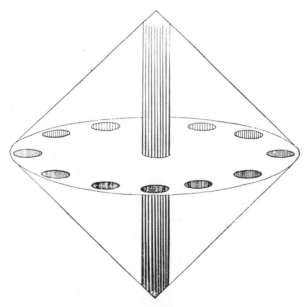

FIGURE 20. The double color cone, formed by placing the bases of two imaginary cones against either side of the color wheel. Brilliant hues are found on the periphery of the central wheel. Variations in value are indicated by a vertical movement in either direction within the cone, while variations in intensity are indicated by movement to and from the center of the cone.

the center are less brilliant or of lower intensity and are commonly referred to as *tones*.

Value. But in addition to being blue and low in intensity, a specific color may be light or dark—light gray-blue, medium gray-blue, dark gray-blue. Thus a third dimension enters our descriptive terminology. This darkness or lightness of a color is called its *value*. A light value is high; a dark value is low. Pink is a high value of red; ivory is a high value of yellow; midnight blue is a low value of blue.

Since the color wheel is only two-dimensional, it obviously cannot be used to show this third color dimension. A simple way of doing it is to

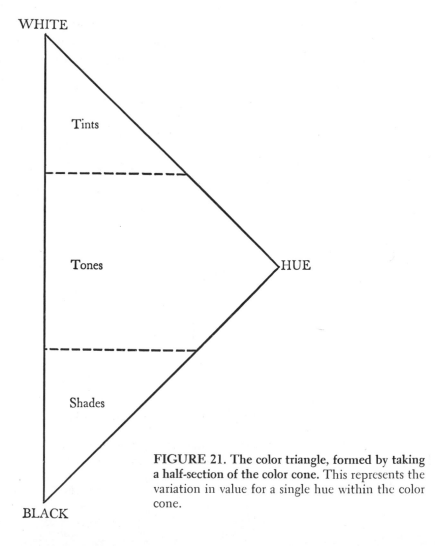

FIGURE 21. The color triangle, formed by taking a half-section of the color cone. This represents the variation in value for a single hue within the color cone.

visualize two solid cones placed base to base with the flat round color wheel between them, as in Figure 20. This gives us our third dimension.

From the color wheel we can go up or down within the cone. As we go up, we approach white; as we go down, we approach black. Colors in the upper part of the cone are called *tints*; those in the lower part are known as *shades*. (Figure 21.) Straight up the center from tip to tip you must imagine an even progression from black to white; around the periphery there will be an even progression from one brilliant hue to another; and from any point on the outside to the center will be a similar progression from a brilliant hue to gray.

Since a color can be at any point whatever in the color cone, you can easily imagine what a vast number of colors is possible. But every one can be located with reasonable accuracy in terms of *hue*, *intensity*, and *value*.

A SYSTEM OF COLOR CLASSIFICATION

If you have had any experience at all in makeup, you know how complex the problem of color selection is. There is every imaginable flesh color to choose from and numerous brilliant colors for rouge, eyeshadow, and other accents. Choosing the right one is as important as it is difficult. Manufacturers of makeup materials have been less than helpful. Their color numbering systems, each differing completely from every other, progress vaguely and erratically from light to dark, but that is the most one can say for them. The numbers must be memorized in combination with the colors to be of any practical use.

What color, for example, is Factor's 4½ and how does it differ from 4? One might expect it to be darker, but there is nothing to lead one to expect it to be in the red family, as it is, rather than in the yellow. Stein's 1 and 22 are somewhat similar, whereas 1 and 1½ are totally different. Stein's 12 is a fairly bright yellow, whereas 13 has a very grayed, purplish color in the tube and is much less purple on the skin. The color names applied to the various flesh colors are, on the whole, as unenlightening as the numbering systems and only contribute to the total picture of astonishingly complete inconsistency. Mehron's foundation 5 and Factor's greasepaint 2½ are for all practical purposes nearly identical in hue, value, and intensity. One is called "Olive" and the other "Flesh." Mehron's "Sunburn" is essentially the same as Factor's "Flesh Juvenile." No wonder the beginner is confused. The only logical and practical solution to the problem seems to be to ignore the manufacturers' numbers and color labels completely and to organize the colors in some consistent fashion.

The basic problem in such an organization is to determine exactly what color the paint in each tube or tin actually is and to label it appropriately so that all paints can be interrelated, using a system of numbering which will be not only logical but meaningful. The chart in Appendix H represents such an organization of colors. It is designed to simplify the makeup artist's problem by eliminating memorization of endless numbers, guessing at colors, and peeking into tubes. By becoming familiar with the system used in formulating the chart, you can decide exactly what shade you want and the number which logically indicates that shade without any time-consuming search or memorization.

All makeup colors are divided into two basic groups according to hue

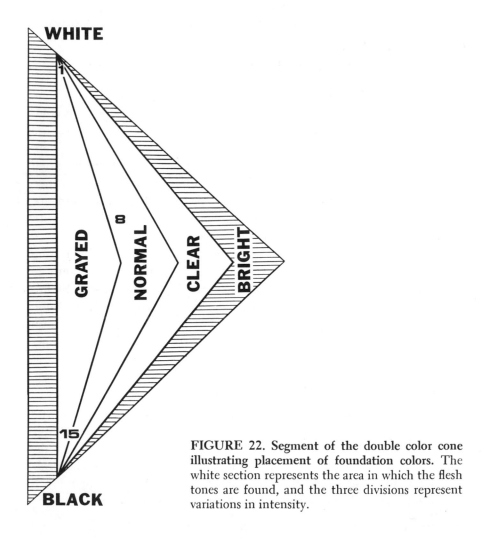

FIGURE 22. Segment of the double color cone illustrating placement of foundation colors. The white section represents the area in which the flesh tones are found, and the three divisions represent variations in intensity.

and intensity. Foundation or flesh colors (lower intensity and a limited number of hues) are in one group, while shading colors or liners (higher intensity and full range of hues) are in the other.

Foundation colors. All foundation colors, also called base colors, are to be found in a wedge-shaped segment of the color wheel formed by connecting "gray" with both "red" and "yellow" by straight lines. Since the colors are not brilliant, they lie somewhere in the central portion of the wedge rather than at the periphery of the circle. Most of them also lie above or below the circle—toward white or black, that is. (See Figure 20.) In other words, they vary in value, giving us tints and shades as well as tones. In fact, the variation in value is considerably greater than the variation in intensity.

The foundation colors fall logically into seven hue groups—*yellow, orange-yellow, yellow-orange, orange, red-orange, red,* and *purple-red,* which may be abbreviated as Y, OY, YO, O, RO, R, and P. Technically speaking, there are many more than seven variations in hue. There are, for example, colors which are just a little more red or orange than the standardized orange of the O group. There are others which are almost exactly halfway between orange and red-orange. This means that all colors put into the O group will not be of *exactly* the same hue, but for practical purposes (considering the changes in makeup which result from differences in skin color and the even greater ones made by stage lighting) the differences are not important. Now, then, we have separated makeup colors according to hue.

The second dimension of color is the value—the lightness or darkness. This is the simplest of all to indicate and can be done merely by a scale of numbers; 1–15 seems to provide an adequate number of steps. 1 is the lightest value of any hue, and 15 is the darkest. Thus, O1 would be a very pale orange (actually a light cream), whereas O15 would be an extremely dark orange (actually a dark brown). O8 would represent a medium value, fairly bright orange flesh tone, which would still not be so bright as an orange rouge, which is not included in this division of the color chart.

Perhaps a glance at Figure 22 will clarify the value scale in relationship to the double color cone. This is a segment of the cone representing all the possible variations of one specific hue. The white section represents the area of the segment in which the makeup foundation colors may be found. The shape of this area is simplified somewhat for the diagram. As you will see, 8 is located somewhat above the middle. Although it is approximately the center of the flesh tone value scale and represents the "normal" flesh tone for men, 10 would be more nearly on a value level with the brilliant hue.

Unfortunately, all of the hues in the flesh tone scale are not of the same intensity. Some are relatively bright, such as Stein's 3. Others are relatively grayed, such as Mehron's 11. Thus we must add a third color dimension to our classification. Again it is impossible to take into account every variation in intensity, but a division into three groups seems to work out reasonably well in practice. Figure 22 shows graphically where these are located. The brightest colors can be referred to as *clear* and the grayest ones as *grayed*. Since most of the colors we use fall in the middle group between these two, we may consider them as *normal*. For purposes of the numbering system the simplest procedure seems to be to add a *c* to the color number when it is clear or relatively high in intensity and a *g* when it is grayed or low in intensity. When the color falls in the "normal" group, we need not indicate the fact.

Thus, an O8 would fall in the center segment, while an O8c would be brighter or clearer than O8, and an O8g would be grayer. The hue and the value would remain the same.

If you will study the double color cone, Figure 20, and the color triangle, Figure 21, you will see that while medium tones of various hues may be relatively far apart and thus easily distinguishable as to hue, colors as they approach white or black automatically draw closer and closer together. This means simply that while an O8 is quite clearly different from an RO8, an O1 and an RO1 may be rather difficult to separate and to the untrained eye will probably look just alike. The same is true with the deep shades such as O15 and RO15. Both are very dark brown, and the RO15 is only slightly more red.

It should be reiterated here for the benefit of those who have not previously studied color that the color brown is in reality a low value of orange. In other words, if you add black to orange, the result will be brown—light or dark depending on the relative amount of each color used. A yellow-orange will produce a yellower brown, and a red-orange will produce a redder brown. The color rust, for example, could be produced by a mixture of red-orange and black. The deepest shades of yellow produce a color which is close to an olive green.

Now we have a method for indicating with reasonable accuracy the hue, value, and intensity of any makeup foundation color. For example, an O8 is a medium orange. O5 is of the same hue but lighter, and O8g is of the same value but grayer. O5g is both lighter and grayer, and O5c is lighter and clearer.

An R8 is of the same value as O8 but is redder. R10 is both redder and darker. R10g is redder, grayer, and darker.

Thus, the relationship between two colors can be seen at a glance. The color chart in Appendix H demonstrates this graphically. The colors are divided, first of all, according to value so that, for example, all colors in the O group are together, and all in the Y group. This will be obvious at a glance. Then within each hue group the colors are subdivided into three sections—one for the normal colors, one for the clear or brighter colors, and one for the grayed colors. Within each of those divisions the colors are arranged according to value from light to dark. Thus it is possible to see not only how the various groups of hues differ from each other but also the range in value within each hue and the effects of graying upon the colors.

It should be pointed out that a grayed color always appears darker than a bright color of the same value. Therefore, an RO6g, for example, will probably look darker to you than an RO6c or even an RO6. And since colors automatically become closer together as they approach gray at the center of the color cone, the grayed versions of the various hues will be much more nearly alike than the clear versions which are strongly differentiated.

Let us see, now, how to use the chart. Suppose we want to do a makeup for an active, healthy young man of about 25, perhaps somewhat sunburned. We would probably want a clear, bright, reddish color, a little darker than average. Since an O7 or O8 is generally considered as average for a man, we might use a 9 or 10 value in the RO group. And since it is to be relatively clear and bright, we will not want a g color. Our color, then, would be, say, an RO10c. We look in the chart under RO10c and find that we have a choice of Leichner's greasepaint 9, Stein's 9, or Mehron's foundation 12 or cake 12B. These colors may not be exactly the same, but they are close enough for practical purposes in stage makeup. If we wish to use Factor's makeup, we can select a slightly less clear shade, RO10, and use Factor's Pan-Stik 7A.

Shading colors. As you will notice, the chart also includes shading or lining colors (more intense hues used for modeling, rouging, and accenting) organized under a similar but not identical system. Again the hues are separated from each other and progress in the order of the spectrum from red (specifically, in this case, purple-red) to purple. It would be possible to give each hue a number (as has been done in previous editions of the book), but that involves memorizing numbers, and experience has shown that the numbers are seldom used. Since these intense colors are in actual makeup practice usually referred to by the hue (such as "red" or "blue"), it has seemed best to designate them in that way. Keep in mind that in such designations as purple-red, orange-red, blue-green, and green-blue the last color named gives the basic hue and the first color modifies it. In other words, blue-green, for example, is more green than green-blue, and blue-violet is more violet than violet-blue.

It might be well to point out here that the color designated in the color chart as "violet-blue" will be considered blue by most people. But, then, so will the color which is called "blue." There is, unfortunately, too little discrimination in daily usage among the various shades of blue and green in particular. It is astonishing how often a clearly discernible green is referred to as blue and a definite blue is called green. The subtleties of the blue-greens and the green-blues seem to be beyond the average person who has no technical knowledge of or special interest in color. Color names, such as turquoise or aquamarine, come more easily, but they are unfortunately imprecise. In the case of the reds, the colors called "purple-red," "red," "orange-red," and even "red-orange" will to many people appear to be simply slight variations of what they call "red." As for the tints and shades, particularly among the greens-blues-violets and the purples-reds-oranges, they come even closer together. But careful examination will reveal significant differences.

Within most of the hue groups there is some variation in value, though much less than in the foundation color groups. Five gradations from light to dark are sufficient for classification, and these can be numbered from 1 (very light) to 5 (very dark). 3 is the medium tone. Thus, for example, a *Red 3* is a medium red; *Orange-Red 1* is a very light orange-red; and *Gray 4* is a dark gray. This seems somewhat simpler, especially in writing, than using such terms as "Medium Red" and "Very Light Orange-Red." And the simplicity of a 1–5 value scale can hardly cause any difficulty. However, if you prefer to say "Very Light Red" rather than "Red 1," there is no reason why you shouldn't. The meaning is the same.

White and black obviously require no value number since they are constants. The gray group follows the usual 1–5 labeling system. An occasional color which is lighter than the #1 value shown in the chart can be designated as *Pale*, as for example Mehron's foundation 19—*Pale Blue*.

To avoid any possible confusion, perhaps it should be pointed out that the colors yellow, yellow-orange, orange, red-orange, red, and purple-red also appear in the foundation color group. But the shading colors are far more intense (less grayed) than the same hues in the foundation group and are neither identical to nor interchangeable with the foundation colors. A glance at Figure 22 should make this clear. All shading colors are located in the shaded area labeled "Bright," the medium value being at the middle point of the triangle. Thus, red and orange shading colors are brighter than the brightest of the foundation colors, which are labeled "Clear."

Occasionally, foundation colors which happen to duplicate shading colors (such as white or black) will be labeled like shading colors. Or shading colors such as the various browns (which are not pure spectral hues but are low values of orange) will be labeled under the appropriate number in the foundation group. Since the primary objective in the two systems is to separate the two types of colors, not the two types of paint, such overlapping is of no importance.

There may be some tendency at first to confuse the flesh tones of the foundation color group with the reds, yellows, and oranges of the shading color group. This confusion can be avoided entirely if the foundation colors are always referred to by letter (Y, OY, YO, O, RO, R, P) and the shading colors by name (as Yellow, Yellow-Orange, Orange). In other words, we refer to a specific foundation as Y3 or as being in the Y group, whereas the more brilliant shading color is referred to as Yellow 3. It should be noted, however, that the 3 in the two cases does not have the same meaning since the value scale for foundation colors (1–15) has much greater range than the scale for the shading colors (1–5). Although both refer to value, each must be interpreted in relation to the group (foundation or shading color) in which it is being used. Once the distinction between the two types of paint and the systems used to designate them is thoroughly understood, there should be no possibility of confusing them.

Use of the color system. In order to make the best possible use of this organization of colors, it would be well to label all of your own base and shading colors in accordance with the color chart in this book. Then you will be able to decide which number of paint you want and select it from your makeup kit immediately without consulting the chart. Unless this is done, you will be unable to select colors without consulting the chart each time.

If you need a color you don't have, you can find out from the chart from which company to obtain it. This will save much time and will make possible a more accurate color selection than would be possible from manufacturers' descriptive labels.

But suppose you are confronted with a more trying, yet not uncommon, situation. You have always used Stein's makeup. But upon a particular occasion you are handed a large kit of Factor's makeup, including, among other things, about 15 tubes of base and 10 shading colors. You can, of course, open each tube, peek through the tiny hole, and guess what the paint would look like on your face. But if you have the color analysis available, your task will be greatly simplified and will require less trial and error experimentation. You need only decide upon the approximate number of base, shadow, highlight, and rouge that you need, then consult the chart where you will find the corresponding number in Factor's paints.

Or perhaps a friend has a Factor's Pan-Stik 2A, which is exactly the color you want, but you are using Mehron's makeup. By consulting the table of equivalents in Appendix H, you will find that Factor's Pan-Stik 2A is RO6. Then merely turn to RO6 in the color chart, and you will find that Mehron's foundation 6½ and cake 6½B are RO6 and therefore essentially the same as Factor's Pan-Stik 2A.

In using the charts in this book, it would be well to keep in mind that no system of makeup color classification can be completely accurate for two reasons. In the first place, the colors as we refer to them should look as they do on the skin, which is almost never the same as the color in the tube, stick, or cake, and the precise color on the skin varies with the individual. In the second place, and this is even more aggravating, makeup colors are inconsistent and vary from batch to batch.

I have before me, for example, two cakes of Stein's 32. One is a medium warm brown, the other is an extremely dark brownish gray, almost black. It is difficult to be sure which is *supposed* to be the correct shade for 32, and it is obvious that in buying 32 you can't be sure what color you're actually going to get.

I have also bought Factor cakes at different times and found similar, if less dramatic, variations. I have two cakes of 31, for example, and find that one is approximately four shades lighter than the other. There are similar variations in greasepaint in hue, value, and intensity, and there are, of course, comparable variations in rouge and shading colors. Fortunately, these wide variations are the exception, but some variation seems to be commonplace. This cannot be blamed entirely on the manufacturers, though certainly greater vigilance would prevent too wide a departure from the established colors. Much of the trouble arises from the color pigments used in the makeup. Even though exactly the same amount of pigment is used in every batch of makeup, the pigment itself sometimes varies, and this variation will be reflected in the color of the product.

Despite these unavoidable variations in color, for stage makeup (much more than for film or television makeup) a reasonably satisfactory grouping can be made. The aim in the classification has been to achieve as high a degree of accuracy as possible without sacrificing relative simplicity and practicality.

In referring to colors in the chart, two facts should be kept in mind:

1. The color analysis is based on specific tubes or cakes of paint which may vary slightly from the established color. So long as the actor is aware of this possibility, however, it should not prove excessively troublesome.

2. The fact that several makeup paints are listed under one color does not mean that they are *exactly* the same. It does mean that they are close enough in color to be used interchangeably for stage purposes.

At first reading the classification system may seem complex. Once the few basic points of classification are understood, however, the grouping will seem simple and logical. In any case, it must be apparent that some system is vital in organizing the many available colors. Some of the advantages of such organization are listed below:

1. The best colors and materials from various companies can be used together without confusion.

2. The artist can determine the number of the color he wishes to use without consulting a chart, examining numerous tubes or boxes, or having memorized colors and the meaningless numbers and descriptive terms attached to them.

3. The artist can change from one brand of makeup to another without being forced to memorize a completely new set of numbers.

4. The artist can see at a glance what colors are available in the various brands of makeup without being forced to rely upon vague descriptive terms.

5. For purposes of this textbook, colors can be mentioned much more specifically and with less confusion than would otherwise be possible.

The purpose of this long discussion is simply to help familiarize you with the workings of the system of color designation to be used throughout this book and to try to convince you that its purpose is not further complication but really simplification of the work which is to come.

If you become thoroughly familiar with this color classification, you will approach the problems of makeup with a great deal more confidence than you otherwise could, for your solution to practical problems will be based upon thorough understanding rather than superficial knowledge.

COLOR MIXING

After deciding upon the exact color that you need for a particular makeup, you may discover that you don't have such a color in your kit. It would be impractical for even a very large and complete makeup kit to contain every color made. In fact, for reasons of economy of both money and space, the individual kit should contain as few colors as possible. From these few colors any other color can be obtained by mixing. Before approaching the problem of mixing greasepaints, however, suppose we consider the basic principles of color mixing applicable to any pigment color.

Mixing pure hues and neutrals. The Prang system of color arrangement is based on the theory that there are three primary hues from which any other hue can be obtained by mixing. These three hues are red, yellow, and blue. (See location on color wheel, Figure 19.) They can be mixed to achieve three secondary hues—orange, green, and violet. These hues will not, however, be as brilliant when obtained by mixing as when compounded directly from their sources in nature. Mixed colors always lose some intensity. A glance at the color wheel will show why. Blue-green, for example, lies midway on a straight line between blue and green since it is obtained by mixing those two colors. Obviously, that brings it nearer to gray in the center of the wheel than if it were placed on the periphery as are the primary and secondary colors. If the orange on the color wheel were obtained by mixing red and yellow, it too would fall nearer the center.

The three primaries cannot be obtained by mixing. However, those three can be used to mix any other hue desired. A mixture of red and yellow will produce orange; yellow and blue will produce green; and blue and red will produce violet. The hues can be varied by varying the proportions of primaries used.

Colors falling opposite each other on the color wheel are called complements and when mixed will produce a neutral gray, as indicated on the color wheel. Blue and orange, for example, can be mixed to produce gray. However, if only a little blue is added to the orange, the result is a burnt orange. Still more blue will give varying intensities of brown.

The same result can be obtained by mixing black and white with the brilliant hue. Any color imaginable can be obtained by mixing three pigments—a brilliant hue, black and white. An examination of the color triangle in Figure 21 will show how that is true. This triangle should be imagined as a paper-thin slice cut vertically from the outside of the cone to the center. Since the triangle bounds the complete range of any one hue, a mixture of hue, black, and white at the three points can provide a color at any point within the triangle.

Pink, for example, can be obtained by mixing white with red. Mixing black with red will give maroon. In order to achieve a dusty rose, both black and white must be added. Figure 23 shows where various tints, tones, and shades of red fall on the color triangle.

Mixing color in makeup. Exactly the same principles apply to mixing

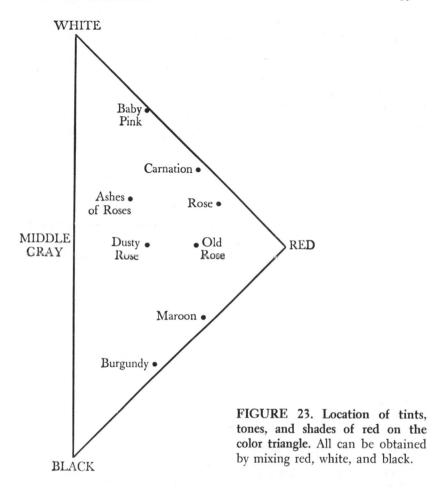

FIGURE 23. Location of tints, tones, and shades of red on the color triangle. All can be obtained by mixing red, white, and black.

makeup colors except that you are seldom dealing with brilliant hues. And usually instead of black and white, you will use other colored paints which are light or dark.

Suppose, for example, that you decide you need an O6 base color. You have no O6, but you do have an O3 and an O9. Obviously, a mixture of the two will produce what you need. But suppose you have nothing at all in the O group. Then you might use a Y6 and an R6 since both are of the same value but of hues which will produce orange when mixed. Or a Y9 and an R3 might do. There you would be mixing both values and hues. The amount of each paint to be used must be determined experimentally.

A further method of simplifying your makeup kit is to use only a few flesh colors and modify them with the more intense colors used in shading.

Suppose you have an O6 but find it isn't red enough. Merely add a little red. If it is too dark, add some white. If the red makes it too brilliant, add some gray (black and white). Provided you have red, yellow, blue, black, and white in your kit, you need never worry about not having the color you need.

In summary, then, color has three characteristics—hue (the name by which we know it), value (the relative lightness or darkness), and intensity (the relative grayness). All hues can be produced by mixing the three primary colors—red, yellow, and blue; all variations in these hues can be produced by additions of black and white. And finally, the system of color designation used in this book provides a practical means of selecting makeup colors through the use of a numbering system which is both logical and meaningful. A complete comprehension of this system is essential to an understanding of all discussions of color throughout the book.

PROBLEMS

1. Translate the following very general color descriptions as well as you can into terms of hue, value, and intensity: vivid pink, dull grayish green, royal purple, very pale yellow, burgundy, powder blue, magenta, steel blue, rose, burnt orange, apple green, aqua, coral, chocolate, peach, rust, mustard, lilac, buff.

2. Without consulting the chart in Appendix H, indicate the approximate hue and value (such as light red, dark brown, medium yellow) of each of the following numbers:

R5	Y1	R7c	RO4	Blue 2	Green-Blue 2
RO9	O8g	O15g	P2	Gray 5	Blue-Green 3
Y7	OY9g	RO6g	Red 3	Orange 1	Orange-Red 4

3. Following the principle of complements, what hue would you use to gray each of the following: red-orange, blue-violet, peacock blue, slightly reddish orange, bluish green, blue-violet, greenish yellow, green. Assume that all colors are of medium value and of maximum intensity.

4. Select five or six foundation paints from your kit. Then, using only makeup paints Red 3 (or Purple-Red 3), Yellow 3, Blue 3, White, and Black,* try to duplicate each of the colors.

---

* If your black paint is not a true black (not completely neutral, that is), it will throw off the color of the mixture. Most black paints in makeup tend slightly toward the blue. To find out whether or not you have a true black, mix a little with some white to make a medium gray. If the gray is entirely neutral, you have a true black, but if it seems to have a cast of any specific color (such as blue), it needs to be adjusted.

5. Using foundation color O7 plus Red 3 (or Purple-Red 3), Yellow 3, Blue 3, White, and Black, mix in the palm of your hand an approximation of each of the following listed makeup colors, as shown in the color chart in Appendix H: O3, O7, O12, O15, O15g, YO5, RO8, RO8c, R5, P3, R9g, O6g. In judging the colors, always spread the paint very thinly on your skin.

6. If you are working in a class, mix several samples of paint; then trade samples with another student, and match his sample exactly without knowing what colors he used to mix it. This should be done until you have trained your eye to judge colors accurately. Until you can match samples your knowledge of color is inadequate for truly effective work in makeup. If you are working alone rather than with a group, mix several colors at random without paying any particular attention to the ingredients. Then go back and try to duplicate them, not by random trial and error but by first analyzing as well as you can the colors to be matched.

This can be done by adding a tiny bit of the complementary color to the black. For example, if the gray appears bluish, add a very small amount of the darkest orange you have to the black and test again by mixing with white. If this is not done, and if the black is not true, you will be puzzled by the results of all mixing in which black is involved.

7

COLOR IN MAKEUP

In Chapter 2 we proposed a method of analyzing a character as a basis for deciding, among other things, what makeup colors should be used, and in Chapter 6 we discussed the general characteristics of color and the principles of color mixing and developed a system of meaningful symbols to be used in designating specific colors in makeup. Now we must correlate those discussions in selecting a specific color of makeup for a specific character. This can be done in relation to the various uses for color in makeup—that is, in foundation (or base), rouge, shadows, and highlights.

FOUNDATION

There are two reasons for changing the color of an actor's skin with a foundation paint. One is, as we have said, to suggest character. The other is to counteract the effect of stage lights and stage distance. An actor who looks perfectly healthy off stage may look ghostly on stage unless he happens to have dark skin. If the actor's skin is dark enough to project and is of the correct color for the character, then there is usually no need for a base. Such a situation is, however, rare.

In view of the great number of available foundation colors and the variety of factors which determine the color of the skin, the problem of choosing the right color for the right character seems rather appalling at first. Since characters are individuals, no set rules can be given, but if the problem is broken down into its component parts, the solution is simplified.

We know that color has three characteristics—hue, value, and intensity—and that our system of color designation is based on those three characteristics. The obvious procedure, therefore, is to analyze the character on the basis of those same characteristics. Decide, first of all, what basic hue his skin is—Y, OY, YO, O, RO, R, or P—basing your judgment on your analysis of the various factors such as health, heredity, and environment which are responsible for the skin color. Then decide whether his skin would be light or dark, choosing a number between 1 and 15 to indicate the value. In this connection it should be pointed out that men's skin coloring is usually darker than women's. A 7, which is average for men, will look dark on women, and a 5, which is average for women, will seem pale on men. This average value (5 or 6 for women and 7 or 8 for men) is the one most frequently employed in corrective makeup. However, in character makeup it should be used primarily as a point of departure.

After you have decided on the value and the hue, you have your base number—provided you think the skin would be normally clear. However, if you think it would be grayed, add a g. If you want an unusually bright color, add a c.

The actor's own skin coloring will also have some effect on the color selected. A given color of makeup will not look the same on a deeply tanned skin as on a pale pink one. This is always one of the elements to be considered in selecting the makeup color.

In this chapter, since we are analyzing color rather than characters, we shall discuss the various base colors and indicate how they may be used and in general what effects they give. These suggestions must not be regarded as infallible rules but merely as guides which you may retain or discard as you become more experienced in makeup.

In making up characters of other races or nationalities, refer to the chart in Appendix E.

Y group. This color group is rarely used except to mix with other base colors for a more sallow effect or for Oriental skin coloring. The greasepaints labeled "Mikado" and falling in the Y group should never be used for realistic Oriental makeup unless blended with a tan or an olive paint. Conceivably they might be used in a stylized production. A yellowish flesh color for Caucasians suggests poor circulation and an indoor life with little exposure to the sun. It gives a distinctly unhealthy look.

OY and YO groups. The lighter values are useful for pale, sallow complexions. The darker ones, especially in the YO group, provide a clear tan color with less warmth than the O group and are useful for various racial types.

O group. This is one of the most frequently used groups, especially for healthy young men and women. O1–3 are pale colors and are used largely as highlights. O10 gives quite a deep suntan. The average for women is about O5 or O6 and for men O7 and O8. This group, being neither particularly red nor particularly yellow serves as a good basic color to which other colors may be added for slight variation.

RO group. This also gives a normal, healthy coloring and is an extremely useful group. When used for young men and women, it usually suggests a somewhat more active life or more time in the sun. Other factors may be involved too. Values from 4 to 10 may be used for youth. RO4 is light without being pale (though it would, of course, look pale on men), while RO9 and RO10 give a very definite sunburned effect, at least under average lighting. Under strong amber lights the deeper colors may look quite normal. RO6 and RO7 are good healthy, warm colors.

Later in life redder complexions may indicate frequent exposure to the sun, but they are also associated with a rather volatile temper and sometimes, of course, with drinking. Falstaff would be quite red, and so might Harry Brock in *Born Yesterday.* The deeper values, especially RO8 and RO9, are usually used in connection with age. Often they may be mixed with colors in other groups.

R and P groups. Neither of these groups contains a great many colors, but occasionally it is desirable to use a base even redder than those found in the RO group. These reds, of course, have less of an orange cast and may be quite useful in certain healthy middle-age effects. The high values in both groups are very useful, particularly for women of all ages and sometimes for healthy, well-scrubbed, middle-aged men who take very good care of themselves but don't get much sun. These would be the deeper pinks, of course.

Pink is a fragile color, especially in its lighter values. It is particularly useful for women during certain periods of history (such as Sheridan's) when a pink and white complexion was greatly admired. Women never let the sun touch their skin for fear of reddening or tanning, and frequently it was whitened with makeup. P1 or P2 is excellent for this white effect and should be used rather than pure white, which would seem too clown-like. This, of course, is an environmental influence. Pale pink can also be used for modern young women who do not lead a very active life, but it would seldom be used for young men.

In middle age in both men and women, pink is usually associated with plumpness. Gaunt faces are usually pale or sallow, whereas plump or jowly ones may often be pink. The disposition must be considered too—

there are pink dispositions, for example, as well as red dispositions and murky yellow ones.

Pink is used less often for elderly people and usually in the lighter values to suggest extreme frailty not accompanied by ill health.

The very lightest values give an effect of whiteness and should be used cautiously, for the effect is rather striking. Such whiteness might come from either extreme frailty or from deliberate makeup by the character. Lavender foundation gives an even more striking effect of whiteness and is sometimes useful for extremely frail old ladies, a supernatural character like the White-Faced Girl in *Will o' the Wisp*, or in combination with heavy lip and eye makeup for such a character as the prostitute in *Escape*.

Clear colors. The very clear or bright colors are usually used only when an exceptionally strong color effect is desired, as, for example, for a fresh (and presumably painful) sunburn. The brightest colors are used much less frequently in the modern theater than they used to be, but they may sometimes be desirable with certain lighting. The "normal" colors are quite suitable to represent a clear, healthy skin, and the effect is usually more realistic than that achieved by using overly bright colors.

Grayed colors. There are grayed colors in most of the hue groups, and they are extremely useful. In the upper and middle values they have a definitely sallow effect for age or sickness in average stage use, though lighting and the rest of the makeup can change that. In the middle and lower values they begin to run from the sallow into the tan and then brown—the Creoles, the Egyptians, the Negroes. These tans and browns differ from the normal (middle-intensity) tans and browns in that they are much softer and less sharp and, of course, closer to gray. For this reason the tan effect appears at a higher value than it does in the middle-intensity colors. The grayed colors are used for the majority of racial groups other than the Caucasian and are used frequently for Southern European and Asian peoples, infrequently for Northern. (See table in Appendix E.)

Suppose, now, we apply some of our generalizations to specific characters. *The Silver Whistle* has an interesting aggregation of characters, old and young, requiring a variety of base colors. Miss Hoadley, for example, is an elderly alcoholic, very jovial and very well upholstered. She would no doubt fall somewhere in the R or RO group. Mrs. Sampler, on the other hand, is a sweet, coy old lady and a bit of a flirt. A pale pink would be appropriate. Mrs. Hanmer, who is sitting around waiting to die and probably won't for a long time, is a cynic with an acid tongue. A yellowish base might do for her.

Miss Tripp is an active, good-natured young woman and would certainly require a base in the middle O or RO group (O6, for example). Her fiancé, the Reverend Watson, is much less active—O5 or O6 might do. Since men tend to be darker in general than women, the same color of base is likely to appear lighter on men. Emmett is a young tramp who spends all of his time in the open—O8 or O9 would be right for him. The Bishop might be either yellow or pink, and Father Shay could be rather reddish. A yellow pallor might be good for the undertaker. These are, of course, only general suggestions which would be modified by the actor's interpretation and his own general coloring and physical appearance. But they do give an idea of the wide variety of skin colorings which may be found even within one racial group.

Choose your base color carefully, for it has a great deal to do with the immediate reaction of the audience to the character and their ultimate acceptance of the validity of the actor's characterization. And be sure to base your choice on all of the factors in the character's life which may affect the color of his skin, not on only one or two. It is obviously impossible for you to say definitely exactly what total effect will result from a combination of such factors, but you can decide on the effect which will be of greatest significance for the character and will reveal as much as possible about that character to the audience.

ROUGE

The coloring of cheeks and lips is dependent upon the same factors which affect the basic skin color. For women, however, there is far greater opportunity to suggest temperamental differences since stage makeup represents natural coloring plus street makeup.

In suggesting natural color, the Red and Purple-Red groups are most often used. One of the most natural moist rouges available, however, is Red-Orange 1, which works equally well for men and women. For brand numbers see the color chart in Appendix H and the discussion under *moist rouge* in Appendix A.

A deep reddish base (such as R10 or especially RO10) can be used for men and is easier to apply than the intense colors, or a little greasepaint foundation can be mixed with an Orange-Red rouge. Brownish red rouges (RO13c and Red-Orange 4 and 5) are also available.

In representing street makeup for women, decide what colors the character might normally wear, then from those colors choose the one which best fits in with the general coloring and with the costume.

Orange 3 is obviously a color which many women would not wear.

So is Purple-Red 2. But suppose you are making up a character who might be willing to use either. If she is wearing a flame colored dress or accessories in that color, Orange 3 will be excellent and the Red-Purple 4 impossible, unless, of course, you want to indicate that she would normally wear the wrong color. The whole problem, in other words, must be considered entirely from the point of view of the character since it is, after all, a problem over which she has complete control. But remember one thing above all—if the woman would not be wearing street makeup, don't make her look as if she is. The touching and otherwise believable picture of Mama down on her knees scrubbing the floor in the Broadway production of *I Remember Mama* was somewhat marred by scarlet lips, bright blue eyeshadow, and false eyelashes. The performance itself was admirable, but the makeup strained one's credulity.

The misuse of lipstick and eye makeup is one of the most aggravating faults of makeup in the professional theater. Too many actresses are willing to sacrifice validity of character to personal vanity. Such cases occur occasionally in the nonprofessional theater but much less frequently—due, no doubt, to the fact that there are more young actresses struggling to look older than aging ones using all of their art to appear young.

EYE MAKEUP

Eye makeup includes eyeshadow, mascara, artificial eyelashes, and pencil for brows and accents, all used for the purpose of beautifying and projecting the eyes. Black is normally used for lashes and black or brown for the brows and accents, depending upon the color of the hair and on whether or not the brows are supposed to look made up.

Eyeshadow may be used both to beautify and to project the eye and to suggest character. When the person would definitely not be using eyeshadow, a conservative color, such as blue, blue-gray, blue-green, or especially brown, is safest. For corrective eye makeup for men, brown is always used.

For young women who would be wearing conservative makeup use a color which, within the limits imposed by the character's personality, either matches the costume or looks well with it. Blue-green, for example, is good with turquoise and many other colors, gray-blue or blue with gray, and so on. Be careful with violet. It may tend to age the character or give the effect of weeping. Nearly any color can be used provided it is subtle enough. But avoid brilliant, conspicuous colors.

For more dramatic characters, young or old, who would wear eye-

shadow with a dash, more brilliant colors are effective. The hue will depend largely on the color in the costume. Eyeshadow which clashes with
the costume color is rather jarring and should be used only when that
effect is intended.

SHADOWS

It is possible to be somewhat more specific about colors for shadows
used in modeling, though they must also be determined on the basis of
character analysis. The following principles may be used as a guide:

1. Shadow color must be related to the foundation color. A single
effective color for universal application does not exist. This is not an
arbitrary rule. It follows naturally from observation of the laws of nature.
A shadow in nature is not a superimposed patch. It is merely the normal
color of an object (or a face) as it appears to the eye when receiving relatively little light. An object which receives no light obviously can reflect
none and so appears black. But when there is any light at all present, even
though none of it falls directly on the object in question, a few rays are
almost sure to be scattered by reflection from other surfaces and thus
eventually to reach the object we are trying to see and again be reflected to
the eye. But the lack of intensity in the light will result in a comparable
lack of intensity in the color as we see it. Thus, all objects which are in
relative shadow will appear as a grayed version of their natural color—or
they would if all light rays from a source of white light were reflected from
white surfaces and so arrived at the object as white light of low intensity.

But in nature this seldom happens. The rays which the object receives
may very well have been reflected from a colored surface. Thus certain colors of light rays may predominate over others. This is something we cannot
usually take into account in makeup, but it must be understood in order
to explain why a simple addition of gray or black or a complementary
color to the foundation color is not always sufficient or desirable. It is,
however, usually a good way to start and considerably safer than using the
so-called shadow colors.

This is a relatively simple problem of mixing when greasepaint is
being used. With cake makeup, however, it is necessary to select another
cake of the correct color. This should be a cake of the same hue, at least
three shades darker (for subtle shadows), usually more. And since
shadowed areas are usually grayer as well as darker, it is often (though not
always) best to use a grayer color—in other words, a color with a g in the
number. For example, with an RO7 base an RO9g might be used as a

shadow. A still deeper color, such as P13g might be used for the darkest part of the shadow. However, a fairly deep color, such as O12, being closer to neutral gray as well as to black, is automatically grayer than a light or middle-value color, such as O7, and can therefore serve effectively as a shadow.

It is not always necessary to use exactly the same hue in the shadow as in the base. For example, an ROg or an Rg shadow would do very well with an O base since both are somewhat warmer than the base. But it is seldom wise to use a shadow color cooler than the base. An OYg or a YOg shadow with an RO base, for example, would look gray and dirty and would seem to be superimposed rather than representative of a natural lack of light on flesh.

Rather than trying to remember rules, the important thing to keep in mind is the natural effect of lights and shadows you are trying to duplicate.

2. It is usually necessary to use two values of the shadow color in most shadows—a medium dark and a dark, depending, of course, on the depth of the shadow to be created. Often it is more effective to use two different hues. The basic shadow should be lower in value and intensity than the foundation color, but of the same basic hue. The second shadow color, or *accent*, as it may be called, should be of still lower value but may in some cases be of a different hue. For example, the basic shadow color might be RO9g. The accent could be P13g. You may even wish to go into the violets and greens for accents. Since the accent color usually covers a very small area, it is ordinarily not observable at stage distance as a separate color but merely serves to deepen the shadow. The use of another color tends to give the shadow greater transparency and third dimension. The greater the stage distance involved, the greater this color contrast may be. The precise color chosen for the accent will depend on the flesh tone, the shadow, and the surrounding colors (set or costume, for example) which might reflect light into the shadow.

3. It is sometimes possible and desirable to relate the shadow or the accent color to the color of the costume. Any strong color in the clothing is always reflected to some extent in the natural shadows of the face. In other words, when a woman is wearing a red dress, the rays of light from whatever light source is being used will fall upon both the face and the dress. Certain areas of the face which are not in direct light will, since they receive little light to reflect, appear dark to us. The dark will be a low intensity and often a low value of the basic skin color. However, the light rays falling on the red dress will be reflected not only directly to the eye of the viewer but also back up to the face. That part of the face in strong,

direct light will show little effect from these additional red rays because they are relatively weak in comparison to the direct rays. But the areas of the face which receive little direct light—the shadows, that is—will in turn reflect some of those reflected red rays to the eye, making the shadow look slightly red. This is a natural phenomenon in no way dependent upon makeup, and through years of experience the human mind has come to expect this phenomenon of color reflection in shadows. In fact, it is so much a part of our experience that we are seldom actually aware of the true color of a shadow. Instead, we see it as our mind tells us it would be without the reflection of the colored rays.

Naturally, those shadow areas which would normally receive the greatest reflection from below (that is, under the chin, the nose, the cheekbones, and the eyebrows) will in the makeup require the most red. Other areas (such as the temples) will require little or none. Probably the most satisfactory way to add the necessary color is to use the color of the costume as the accent. The cheek shadow, for example, could be applied in the usual way, and the underside of the cheekbone, which is always the darkest part of the shadow, could be deepened with a maroon or lake (in the case of a red costume). There is no need to give rules for this—the areas which are in direct line to receive reflected light from below can always be determined from observation.

Again let me point out that this relating of shadow color to the costume cannot and should not always be done. The color of the foundation paint is of first importance, and more often than not the same costume will not be worn throughout the play, thus making any color relationship impractical. However, it is a point to be kept in mind on the few occasions when it can help the makeup.

A similar phenomenon may take place when the set reflects a strong color. A green set, for example, might be the determining factor in choosing green accents, or a red or pink set might incline one to lake or even violet accents. The color of the set, like the color of the costume, should not be of primary concern, but either or both may be considered when there is some doubt as to what accent color would be most effective.

We have already indicated that the shadow color should usually be of the same or nearly the same hue as the base but of lower value and intensity. This is a good general principle to observe. However, it may be useful to list specifically the colors which are usually used for shading. The following comments refer only to the various colors used to represent natural facial shadows. They do not apply to the same colors when used as eyeshadow.

Brown group. This includes the low values of all base colors except the P series, in which the low values are maroon. Naturally, the Y series will produce a yellowish brown—almost greenish, in fact, and the R series will produce a very reddish brown; but all are recognizably brown, and all are useful as shadow colors in connection with foundation colors in their own or in neighboring series. Accents may also come from this group. Following is a list of specific makeup shades which are very frequently used as shadows. But one should not develop the habit of using them exclusively. It is always better to choose exactly the right color to go with a particular makeup than to fall back on one of the conventional shadow colors.

GREASE:

    Factor— Shading (Lining) Colors 21 (YO12), 22 (RO13c)

    Leichner—Liners 28 (YO15), 30 (Orange 5); Greasepaint 7 (RO14), 11 (YO15g), 16 (O15g)

    Mehron— Shado-liners 8 (YO13), 8½ (RO14c)

    Stein— Shading (Soft Lining) Colors 1 (O13c), 2 (RO14c), 6 (YO12), 7 (O15), 22 (RO13)

CAKE:

    Factor— Light Egyptian (O7g), Dark Egyptian (O11g), Indian (O9g)

    Mehron— 11B (R9g), 37 (R14), 38 (P13g), Red Brown (R12)

    Stein— 39 (RO7g), 37 (O13), 32 (O15), 50 (RO9g)

PENCILS:

    Factor— Brown (YO15g), Light Brown (Y15g), Maroon (RO14)

    Leichner—Light Brown (O14c), Dark Brown (O15g)

    Mehron— Light Brown (YO14), Dark Brown (O15g), Auburn (O12c)

    Stein— Brown (YO15g), Maroon (Orange-Red 5)

Red group. The maroon or lake colors are extremely useful in shadowing, especially if the base is at all ruddy. They may be used as accents to give more life to shadows which look too gray or muddy or to represent red reflected from costume or set. The great majority of makeups can be improved by the use of a good deal of red in the shadows. Stein used to have an excellent maroon shadow in cake (#9). Unfortunately, the color now being sold as #9 is so unlike the original as to be quite useless. Mehron's Red-Brown is similar but less red. In grease it is usually well to mix one of the dark reds (moist rouge or lip rouge) with a dark brown shading color. So-called maroon pencils for quick touch-up of accents are available, but the color is seldom maroon.

Violet group. Violet and purple shadows are useful with pink or pale lavender flesh tones when an effect of delicacy or frailty is desired. As accents they may sometimes be used with lake or even brown shadows but rarely when an effect of strength or robustness is required. Violet and purple are frequently useful in stylized makeups—as, for example, ballet, sprites, fairies, and statuary. There are several good violets and purples available in grease. Mehron's cakes 11B and 38 and Stein's cake 50 have a gray-violet cast. These are the most generally useful cake shadows available.

Green group. Green should rarely be used as a shadow color in realistic makeups. It may, however, occasionally be used as an accent color, particularly if there is a good deal of green in the set or costume. Even then it tends to work well only with pale or yellowish makeups. In stylized makeups it can be very useful for such characters as witches, elves, sprites, and trolls. There are several shades of green available in grease, and Stein makes a green cake. Mehron has a green pencil which may sometimes be useful.

Gray group. Gray shadows should usually be used in realistic makeup only to indicate extreme illness or death or occasionally a dirty face. In nature, a pure gray shadow would be found only on a white or gray surface receiving reflected white rays. Since flesh is never chalk white or neutral gray, a gray shadow is not appropriate. The gray may, however, be mixed with the base color or with one of the shadow colors to give a grayish effect. The violet you take from the tin or jar, for example, may be too intense for use as a shadow color. If so, it can be mixed with gray to tone it down. Or the red-brown or maroon color you find in the tin or mix in your hand may seem too intense. It too can be toned down with gray. Gray is sometimes useful in stylized makeups—*Blithe Spirit*, for example—but is seldom suitable for realistic effects unless mixed with another color. Gray is available in grease, cake, and pencils.

HIGHLIGHTS

The safest rule is always to use white for grease highlights and Y1, O1–3, RO1–3, R2, or P2 for cake or Pan-Stik. When grease highlights are applied over grease base, a little of the base color is certain to mix with them, giving them the approximate tone you would choose anyway. Furthermore, the white of the highlights will be toned down somewhat with powder so that they will blend with the whole makeup. If your highlights are well blended, there is little danger of their being too light.

Skillful use of color is essential to effective makeup, yet rarely is color used to its fullest advantage. Clean characters with dirty faces, healthy characters with deathly pallors, and dying characters who seem bursting with health—all represent careless use of color. If you have mastered or at least begun to master the technique of choosing effective colors, you have solved one of the most difficult problems in makeup.

PROBLEMS

1. Carefully observe a number of people of various ages in regard to skin color. Decide in each case how you would achieve that color with makeup, then jot down the color number along with a few remarks on the person's age, apparent health, temperament, and so on. Keep these notes and analyze them, drawing any conclusions which seem warranted concerning the effects of heredity, environment, and age.

2. Choose makeup colors for three or four of the following named characters and, if you are in a class, discuss these choices: King Lear, Cordelia, Macbeth, Orlando, Hamlet, Ophelia, Juliet, Bottom, Starveling, Richard II, Richard III, Falstaff, Sir Andrew Aguecheek, Petruchio, Katherina, Shylock.

8

APPLICATION OF
MAKEUP

Since the problems and procedures involved in the application of greasepaint and of cake makeup are quite different, they will be discussed separately. Which type of makeup you choose is a matter of personal preference. The advantages and disadvantages of each are discussed, along with the characteristics of both types of paint, in Appendix A. For lack of a better all-inclusive term, "greasepaint" will include Pan-Stik, Velvet Stick, and Mehron's foundation paint, none of which has a grease base. But all are used in essentially the same way. It also includes the more intense shading colors in all brands.

GREASEPAINT

Foundation. Whether you are using grease or cake makeup, the first step is to apply your foundation (base) in order to achieve the color of skin which you have decided is appropriate. Probably the most common fault in the application of greasepaint is the tendency to use two or three times too much, the result of which is a greasy makeup which does not take shadows well, rubs off easily, induces a great deal of perspiration, requires an abnormally heavy coating of powder, and creates a masklike effect. Always apply your base sparingly.

If you are using stick paint (this form of greasepaint is outmoded but is still used by some actors), you must first apply a thin layer of cold cream over the entire face and neck, then wipe it off, leaving only a very thin film. Secondly, rub the stick in streaks across the face and neck—about two on each cheek, two on the forehead, one down the nose, one under the nose, one across the chin, and several on the neck. Then blend the paint with your fingertips to make a completely smooth foundation.

In using soft paint, *never use cold cream first!* Don't even use it to remove street makeup if you can avoid it. Since the paint itself is of just the right consistency to spread easily and cover well, the addition of any cream will disturb the consistency and will result in an excessively greasy makeup with poor covering ability.

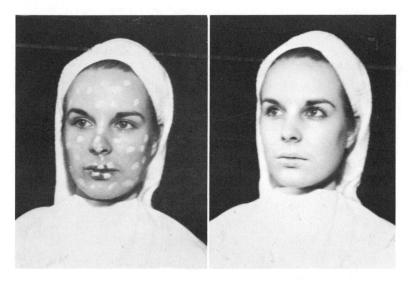

FIGURES 24, 25. Application of greasepaint. Paint is applied from tube in dots, then blended with the fingertips dipped in cold water.

The paint can be taken directly from the tube on your finger tip and applied in small dots evenly over the face, neck, and ears (Figure 24). If you are mixing paints, however, mix them in your hand first to obtain the correct color, then apply the mixed paint in dots. When you have spotted the face with paint, dip your finger tips into cold water and blend the base thoroughly, making sure that every exposed part of the flesh is covered, *including the back of the neck!* (Figure 25.) Blend it into the hairline so that no line of demarcation is visible, but be careful not to get makeup into the hair. Use very little paint. The thinner the base is, the better. The purpose of greasepaint foundation is to color the face, not to mask it.

When you have finished, rub a clean finger lightly across your face. If it leaves a mark or if a noticeable amount of paint comes off on the finger, you have used too much paint and should wipe some off. The skin should feel moist and soft to the touch but not slippery. You can also test the foundation by blotting very lightly with tissue. If a noticeable amount comes off onto the tissue, the paint is too heavy.

For most makeups it is desirable that the foundation color be very smoothly blended to form a completely even film of color over the skin. There are occasions, however, as in age makeups, when a smooth skin texture is not desirable. It is usually helpful to use two (or even three) different colors of base and juxtapose spots of the different colors on the face. Then when you blend the paint, work very carefully so that the colors are *not* completely mixed but leave a slightly splotched effect. Be sure, though, that the effect is splotchy, not patchy. Naturally, the colors should not be so different that the technique becomes obvious to the viewer. And ordinarily you will not use this over the entire face. The cheeks, jowls, neck, and hands are the most likely places for it.

It is also possible to apply a stipple of colors over the completed makeup, using a brush or a red rubber sponge. Ordinarily the colors you are using in the shadows can be repeated along with a little highlight color. Even a light red can be worked in effectively in areas where there might be a little color. The colors can then be softened slightly with a clean brush, if it seems necessary, and powdered.

For a more thorough stippling technique, combining greasepaint and cake makeup, see Figures 46 and 47 and the accompanying text.

Rouge. When the base is blended, you will apply your rouge. This is done by first applying a small spot of it to the part of the face where you want the most intense color, then blending it out carefully in all directions with short, quick, straight strokes, not with a circular motion, unless you are deliberately attempting to create an effect of roundness in the cheeks. Always use a very light touch in blending rouge and work gradually, applying only a little at a time. When the first application has been thoroughly blended, more small spots can be applied in the same place and blended as before until the desired intensity is reached. There should never be a line of demarcation between the rouge and the base color unless you are deliberately making the rouge obvious for the purpose of characterization.

If you prefer to use a brush-on cake rouge instead of a moist rouge, it must be applied *after* the base has been powdered. A soft, round brush usually comes with the cake. Draw it gently across the cake, picking up a small amount of color, then dust the brush lightly over the area to be tinted. Keep adding color until you have the desired effect. For final blending, blow the remaining color off the brush and dust the clean brush over the cheeks. This is a particularly good technique for men or for any makeup which must appear completely natural.

Shading colors. After you have blended the moist rouge (if that is the type you are using), model the face with highlights and shadows (Figures 28–30). Apply the shadows first, using fingers or a brush, depending on the size and type of shadow. A ⅜-inch flat shading brush is suitable for the larger areas and a ³⁄₁₆-inch brush for wrinkles. It is extremely important in applying the shadow color, as in applying rouge, to use a light touch. Never pull at the face with the fingers, but touch it gently—just enough to spread the color. Until you develop a lightness of touch, you will never be able to use shadow colors effectively. Then highlight the shadows. Detailed tech niques for modeling will be described in Chapter 12.

Powder. When you have completed the modeling, set the whole makeup with face powder by patting it on with a puff, not rubbing or stroking. The excess can be dusted off with a powder brush. Ordinary face powders will affect the hue and intensity of the makeup paint. The safest rule is to use a fairly light powder, which will have much less effect on the makeup than a dark powder. If there are highlights, a light powder is essential, for any powder darker than the highlights will tend to obliterate them. The most satisfactory solution to the problem lies in a neutral, translucent powder which sets the makeup without seriously affecting the color. All makeup companies have such a powder, and it should replace the variety of colored powders found in most makeup kits.

Cream stick. This term covers both Pan-Stik (Factor) and Velvet Stick (Stein). It is usually transferred from the stick to the face with the fingers or with a brush. It can be blended with the fingers (or with a rubber sponge if you prefer), but the fingers should not be moistened. As with any grease base, use only a thin film, just enough to color the skin and conceal minor blemishes. Then dust the base very lightly with a neutral powder and go over the whole makeup lightly with a damp sponge. This removes excess powder and sets the makeup.

Moist rouge and shading colors, as well as cake makeup, can be combined with cream stick. Moist rouge is normally applied over the cream stick base. It is quite possible to apply dry rouge (with a damp sponge) over the powdered makeup, but brush-on rouge is preferable.

Shading can be done in several ways:

1. A deeper shade of cream stick under the base; light cream stick over the base for highlights.

2. Both light and dark cream stick over the base.

3. Dark and light cake makeup over the powdered cream stick base.

4. Dark cake makeup over the powdered base with highlights of light cream stick.

5. Light cake makeup highlights over powdered base and shadows of cream stick.

You will no doubt be able to work out other combinations of your own. There are no rules about what may or may not be done with any kind of makeup. Anything which works is legitimate.

Removal. Both grease and cream stick makeup can be removed with any cream or liquid cleanser (see *Makeup removers* in Appendix A). For cake or liquid makeup some actors prefer to use just soap and water.

CAKE MAKEUP

Foundation. Both cake and liquid greaseless makeup are applied with a sponge for large areas and a brush for small ones. A round natural silk sponge is usually best for the base color and either a flat cellulose type or the natural silk for shading. For use with liquid makeup, the sponge should be dampened first to soften it, but no water should be retained. For cake makeup the sponge should be damp but not wet. If the makeup does not come off on the sponge easily, you are not using enough water. If it seems to be thick and heavy on the face, you are using too much water. Only by experimentation will you be able to judge the necessary degree of dampness. It would be well to note too that in some brands of cake makeup the color comes off the cake much more readily than in others. If you use more than one brand of makeup, this may require some adjustment.

The makeup is taken on the sponge, then stroked lightly across the face until the whole area is covered smoothly (Figure 27). As with grease-paint, the base should be very thin. Its purpose is only to color the face. Cake makeup requires no powder.

Rouge. Occasionally, water soluble makeup is combined with a certain amount of grease makeup. Moist rouge or under rouge may be applied directly to the skin (which may require a very light coating of cold cream for moist rouge but not for under rouge) rather more heavily than is customary, then the cake makeup applied over it. The technique of application here is to pat the makeup over the grease first in order not to smear it, then to smooth it out very lightly. The amount of base you use over the rouge will determine how much of it shows through. The direct method of rouge application—that is, from a dry rouge cake using a damp sponge—is easier and usually preferable. This is done on top of the base, and no powder is necessary. Special care must be taken to blend the edges of the rouge thoroughly with a clean sponge. Brush-on rouge works best of all.

Shading colors. Shadows and highlights are applied with brushes and appropriate dark and light cake colors, as illustrated in Figures 26–33. Although a sponge can be used for larger areas, the paint can be more easily controlled with the brushes. For larger areas, a ⅜-inch flat sable brush works very well (Figure 30). For smaller areas and most wrinkles, a ³⁄₁₆-inch brush is best (Figure 28). A pointed Chinese brush (Figure 29), an eye-liner brush, or a ⅛-inch flat sable brush can be used for small details. The precise method of handling the brushes is described under *nasolabial folds* in Chapter 12. It should perhaps be mentioned here, however, that in general the technique is first to lay on color in the darkest area of the shadow or the lightest area of the highlight, then clean the brush and blend the edges of the shadow or highlight with the damp brush until they blend imperceptibly into the foundation. Using separate brushes for shadows and highlights is a great time-saver.

If you do wish to shade with a sponge, hold it so that only a small section of it touches the face. When using a flat sponge, you can use one corner. Apply the color directly to the face only in the area which is to be most strongly shadowed or highlighted. Then with a clean section of the dampened sponge, using a very light touch, blend the color out over the entire area to be covered, letting it fade out as you go until it blends into the base color. It may be helpful to run a clean section of the sponge very lightly over the edge of the shadow or the highlight where it meets the base in order to help merge the two.

Whether you are using a sponge or a brush, it is always best to build up a shadow or a highlight with several applications, just as you do rouge, rather than trying to get just the right amount the first time. It is much easier to add color than it is to subtract it. If a shadow does become too dark, it should be lightened by lifting the color with a clean damp sponge. *Never try to lighten a shadow in either cake or grease by covering it with a highlight.* The result will be a muddy and probable splotchy color. Shadows and highlights can also be toned down or softened by stippling lightly with your sponge, using the base color.

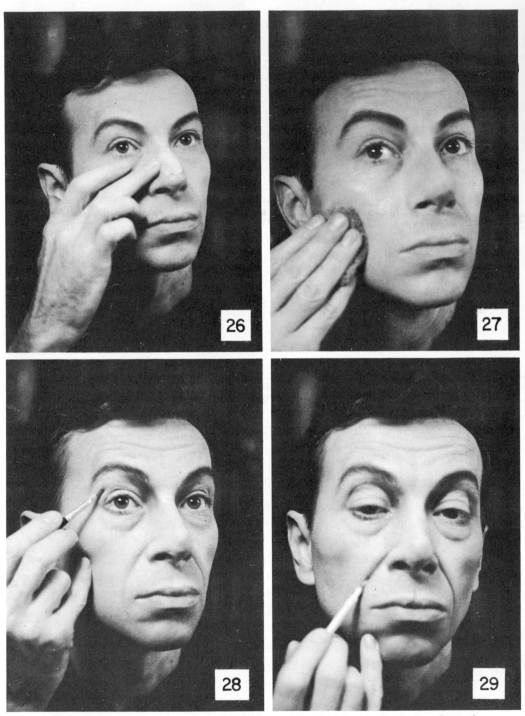

FIGURES 26–33. The Mad Hatter from *Alice in Wonderland*. Based on the
Tenniel illustrations (see Figure 222). Nose is first built up with putty-wax.
Then the entire face is covered with cake base (RO3g), shaded with RO9g,
accented with P13g, and highlighted with O1. (Note the various brushes

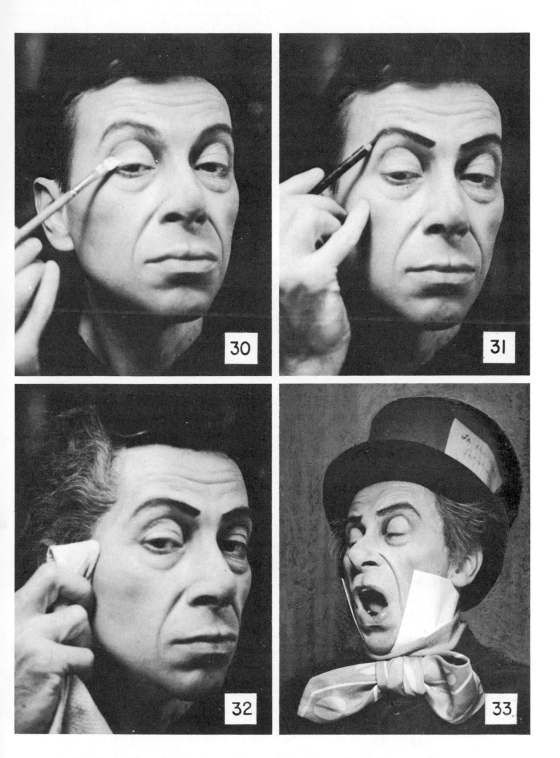

used.) Lips and eyebrows are made up, hair pieces glued down, and costume added. As always, the effectiveness of the final makeup depends to a great extent on the actor underneath.

Stippling. A stippling technique is also useful to suggest a rougher skin texture. It is particularly effective in counteracting the excessive smoothness of youthful skin when you are trying to age it. A red rubber sponge is best, though a natural silk one can be used. When the makeup is completed (usually a trifle lighter than you would normally make it), take up some shadow color from the cake on a slightly damp sponge and touch the sponge lightly to the skin so that the pattern of the sponge holes is left on the face. This can be done over areas which are too obviously smooth or which are too light and need toning down. It is also possible to lighten too-dark areas by using the same technique with a light color. Or you can stipple with more than one color—perhaps the shadow color first, then a light rouge (concentrating on the areas which should be most red), then a highlight. This must naturally be done with great care in order to avoid unsightly splotches. Overzealousness in applying the stipple can be rather difficult to correct. (See also the discussion of grease stippling in connection with Figures 46 and 47.)

GREASE AND CAKE MAKEUP COMBINED

Frequently it is advantageous to use both grease and cake in the same makeup. The most obvious need arises when you wish to use cake makeup but need the covering power of grease in blocking out eyebrows. The powdered grease can be easily covered with cake and the makeup finished in the usual way. But ordinarily the advantages are more subtle and the technique chosen a matter of personal choice. Here are a few of the possible techniques. It would be a good idea to try all of them in order to discover for yourself the advantages of each. As you work, you will undoubtedly develop your own modifications.

Method 1. With this method the cake is used only for the base color. All shadows and highlights are made with grease shaders or cream stick. After the rouge is blended, model the entire face (again having used a very little cold cream if necessary) with heavy shadows, rather reddish in hue to counteract the effect of the cake base. These should be done with exactly the same techniques used for shadows over greasepaint except for exaggeration of depth. Secondly, highlight the shadows with white grease shading color (Figure 36). Then pat on the greaseless cake or liquid makeup and smooth it over (Figure 37). This method is useful for very subtle aging. It would not be successful, however, in achieving the strong three-dimensional effect shown in Figure 49.

Method 2. This method is as follows: (1) Model the face with heavy

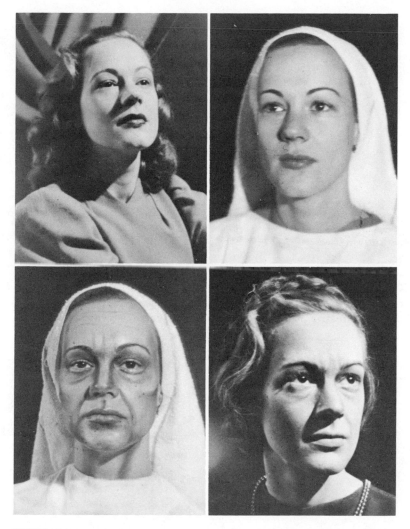

FIGURES 34, 35, 36, 37. Technique for using greaseless liquid makeup in suggesting middle age. The technique is fully explained in the text. The model (Figure 34) is shown first with street makeup removed (Figure 35), then with grease shadows and highlights applied directly to the skin (Figure 36), and finally with liquid base sponged over the shadows and highlights for the character of Mrs. Alving in *Ghosts* (Figure 37). Compare this series with Figures 26–33 and 38–45.

FIGURE 38. The model who posed for the following photographs, shown in corrective makeup.

FIGURE 39. The model as Mrs. Keeney in Eugene O'Neill's *Ile*. Compare with Figure 45.

FIGURE 40. Excess street makeup has been removed. The color remaining on the lips will be covered later.

FIGURE 41. Major areas shadowed with RO14 grease. This shading is usually done with the fingertips.

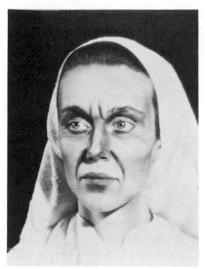

FIGURE 42. Detailed lowlights and wrinkles added with shading brush.

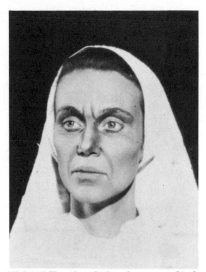

FIGURE 43. Cake base applied with sponge over entire face and neck.

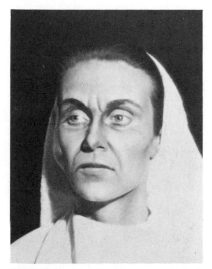

FIGURE 44. Shadows accented with P13g cake and highlighted with O3 cake. Eyebrows and lips made up.

FIGURE 45. Completed grease and cake makeup for Demetria in *On Borrowed Time*. Hair grayed with whitener.

grease or cake shadows, using no foundation. (2) Pat on the cake base and smooth it over. (3) Highlight the shadows, using white grease shading color or, preferably, light cream stick over the cake base. (4) Set the high-lights by patting on a neutral powder. (5) Accent the deepest parts of the wrinkles with a dark cake shader, preferably of a different color, as suggested in Chapter 7. This technique permits a much greater three-dimensional effect than is possible with Method 1.

Method 3. This procedure, illustrated in Figures 38–45, follows Method 2 fairly closely. (1) Apply grease shadows heavily (Figures 41, 42). (2) Pat on the cake base and smooth it over (Figure 43). (3) Accent and highlight the shadows with light and dark cake makeup (Figure 44). The advantage of not using any grease over the cake makeup is that there is no necessity for using powder.

Stippling. An effective stippling technique combining grease and cake makeup is illustrated in Figure 47. The stippling is done with grease (shading colors, rouge) or cream stick applied with a firm, flat sponge. Although for most stippling a red rubber sponge is used, an ordinary cellulose household sponge works very well for this technique. It can be cut into small pieces (Figure 46), dampened with water, then squeezed dry. The sponges illustrated are about 1¼ by 2 inches. They can be of any size or shape you find convenient—even circular if you wish. You will need, in addition, a smooth, flat, easily cleaned surface on which to spread the paint. Glass is fine, but the flat top of a plastic cake-makeup container (Figure 46-D) does very well and is easily available in the kit. This is the procedure:

1. Select three colors for stippling. Which ones you choose will depend on the effect you want—healthy, sickly, tanned, sunburned, sallow. Keep in mind that colors used for men are usually darker' than those used for women. The first one should be quite dark—a dark brown is good. Even black is sometimes possible. The second should usually be some shade of red—a light moist rouge, for example. The third should be very light, the hue depending on whether you wish to aim for a yellow, pink, tan, or purple-sallow effect. It is a good idea to start with white and tint it by adding a tiny bit of another color. Or you may wish to use pure white.

2. Spread a small amount of your first stipple color on the smooth, flat surface you have chosen for a palette, then press your sponge lightly onto the paint, as has been done in Figure 46-A. Be sure you do not have too much paint on the sponge. Then keep pressing the sponge against the face (Figure 47-A) until you have covered all exposed areas. If you wish, you may give the skin a base coat of cake makeup first, but this is not necessary. Since you are stippling with a very dark color, be careful not to use

FIGURE 46. Materials for stippling. Cellulose sponges cut
into small pieces with paints used for the makeup in Figure
47. A separate sponge is used for each color—dark brown
(A), light red (B), and pale yellowish flesh tone (C).
The paint is spread on a flat surface, such as glass or a
plastic cake makeup container (D), from which the sponge
can pick it up evenly.

too much. Avoid smearing the stipple or leaving dark blotches of paint.
You may set this first stipple with translucent powder or wait until you
have finished all three coats, as you wish.

3. Follow the same procedure with your second stipple color. If this is
a red stipple, you can make it heavier on areas which you wish to appear
more red in the final makeup. The amount you use will depend on how
healthy the character is to be. Again, powdering is optional.

4. Apply your third stipple (Figure 47-B). With this you can control
the overall lightness or darkness of the final effect. Set the grease stippling
with translucent powder, pressing the powder into the makeup very carefully so as not to smear it. The slightest smear must be retouched by stippling with a small brush (an eye-liner brush does very well). Now your
base coat is finished, and you may proceed with the modeling, using cake
makeup or cream stick, if you prefer.

5. Apply the shadows with a brush. This must be done with extreme
care since mistakes require painstaking repairs in the stippling. Highlight
by stippling with a light cake or cream stick, using a small sponge or a
brush. (See Figure 47-C.)

6. Add detailed wrinkles with Chinese brushes or eye-liners in order
to break up large highlighted areas such as the cheekbones and the forehead (Figure 47-D). If you have used cream stick for shadows and highlights, you will need to powder again; otherwise, you will not.

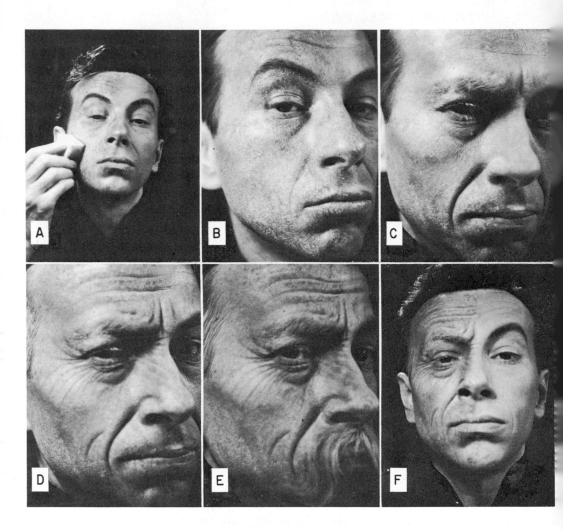

FIGURE 47. Stippling for age. The skin (with or without a cake base) is stippled first with dark brown grease or cream stick (A), then with a light moist rouge, and finally with a light base (B). After the makeup is set with translucent powder, cake shadows (R9g, R12, and P13g) are carefully laid in with sable brushes, highlights stippled on with Y1 cake, and eyebrows grayed with white cake (C). Detailed wrinkles are added with a Chinese brush and cake shadows and highlighted with an eye-liner brush (D). Mustache is added and makeup touched up (E). The final photograph (F) shows the stippled makeup on half the face, flat cake makeup on the other.

7. Complete your makeup with grayed eyebrows, beard, wig, or whatever else is required.

It is possible to shadow and highlight the face strongly with cake before applying your stipple, then merely to strengthen shadows and highlights after you have finished stippling. There is probably some advantage in this, particularly for the inexperienced makeup artist, since it is possible to place the shadows correctly without ruining three coats of stippling. For the final touching up you can then follow the original pattern.

These are merely suggestions for stippling techniques. There are many more possibilities. But for young actors especially, some method must be used to break up areas of smooth skin if an age makeup is to be effective. (See Hal Holbrook's Mark Twain makeup, Figures 179–184.)

If you are to be thoroughly proficient, it is important that you be able to cope with all forms of makeup, partly because you never know when you may be required to use a kind of makeup other than that which you usually use, and partly because until you have learned to use all of them, you will not know for sure which kind you prefer. Familiarizing yourself with a technique does not mean trying it once and discarding it, however. It is important that you be able to do a good makeup with grease (including cream stick), cake, or a combination of both.

PROBLEMS

1. Choose three base colors differing in hue, value, and intensity. Apply each of these in turn to your entire face, including the lips; then check to be sure you haven't used too much. In each case look at yourself from a little distance if possible. Decide what effect the color gives, what it seems to suggest about health, age, temperament, and so on. Think of two or three characters for which you might use each of the different bases. Then, if you're working in a class, let other members of the class look at you and discuss the effects and possible characters for which each base might be used. File notes in your morgue on all conclusions.

2. Apply a medium base (O6, O5g, RO5g). Using a medium or dark shading color (RO9g, R9g, R14, P13g), shade all the hollows of the face (refer to Figures 9 and 10), blending the edges carefully. Now highlight all of the bones with a light base (O1, RO1, white). If you are using grease, powder with a neutral powder. If you are using cake, stipple lightly with the base color. Shadows and highlights can be applied with a brush, sponge, or your fingers, as you choose. The purpose is not to make a skull or an age makeup, but merely to locate accurately the bones of your face

and to apply highlights and shadows to emphasize them. Study your makeup carefully. Do the shadows look like patches of paint instead of depressions in the flesh? If so, can you tell why? Try to improve the makeup as much as you can. After working on Chapter 12, you will probably understand more clearly why your makeup may not have been so successful as it might be.

3. Repeat the same makeup using one of the other techniques (grease or greaseless) described in this chapter.

9

ADAPTING THE
MAKEUP

Thus far we have discussed makeup in terms of the ideal—analyzing the character the playwright has created and trying to build up a physical image which will satisfy that conception as well as contribute to the actor's interpretation. But before we begin actually making up, we must be aware of the practical necessity of adapting our ideal conception to the face of the individual actor. Naturally, the more nearly suited the actor is to the role physically, the easier this will be, but there are nearly always some compromises to be made.

Probably the only way to present the character visually exactly as we imagine him is to have the actor wear a mask. This, in rare instances, can be done, but since increasing the amount of makeup always decreases the actor's facial expressiveness and in the case of even a rubber mask renders his face practically immobile, this is obviously an undesirable solution and should be resorted to only in cases where an actor must go from youth to extreme age in a matter of minutes or for such stylized characters as Death or the Duchess in *Alice in Wonderland*. In most instances we must accept the actor's basic bone structure and make what illusory changes we can with paint, along with simple three-dimensional changes (particularly in the shape of the nose) and either simple or elaborate changes in the hair. The objective is always to help the actor develop his character without inhibiting his facial expression.

LIMITATIONS OF MAKEUP

It follows quite naturally from our premise that there are certain changes which cannot be made with makeup. Actors, as we know, are of all shapes and dimensions. It should ordinarily be the problem of the director to fit the actor to the part as nearly as possible, relying on the makeup artist for relatively minor changes. It would be unwise, for example, for a director to cast a very thin actor as Falstaff since there is really no choice but for Falstaff to be fat. If however, it must be done for one reason or another, it is usually possible to change the thin actor into a reasonably fat Falstaff (Figure 48) with varying degrees of success.

FIGURES 48, 49. Falstaff and Iago. The illusion of width for Falstaff is achieved by carrying the light base from ear to ear and pulling hair and beard out horizontally. In the Iago makeup, the sides of the face are shadowed and the nose lengthened. The heavy nasolabial folds also help to lengthen the face. Cake makeup was used for both, with putty-wax for the noses, real hair beards on lace, wigs, and crepe hair for Falstaff's eyebrows. The model is shown in Figure 7.

Now suppose the director in casting *The Barretts of Wimpole Street* wishes to use the young actor in Figure 7. The problem of aging him and adding whiskers is not a particularly difficult one. But suppose the director has cast a fat actor in the part even though he really pictures Mr. Barrett as being rather slender? Obviously, there is nothing the makeup artist can do but transform the fat actor into a fat Mr. Barrett. And provided both director and actor are willing to admit that Mr. Barrett might be fat, the solution is quite a happy one. In other words, it is up to the director either to cast an actor who physically fits his conception of a particular part or to revise his conception of the part to fit the actor whom he desires to cast.

OPTICAL ILLUSIONS

In trying to bring the actor's face closer to the mental picture we have of the character, we must more often than not make use of optical illusions. Observe, for example, the two faces in Figures 48 and 49. One appears to be very broad and the other longer and narrower. Yet both faces

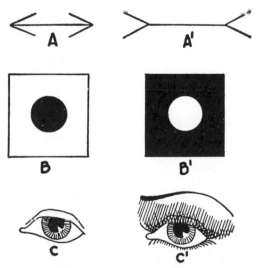

FIGURE 50. Optical illusions.

are actually the same since both belong to the actor in Figure 7. The apparent difference is an optical illusion.

There are two types of illusion applicable to makeup—those relating to the length of a given line and those relating to the size of a given area. Lines A and A′ in Figure 50 are of exactly the same length, but A′ appears to be somewhat longer because of the extensions. The circles in B and B′ are of exactly the same size, but the white surrounded by black appears slightly larger than the black surrounded by white because black is a recessive color—that is, it seems to go away from the eye and thus appears

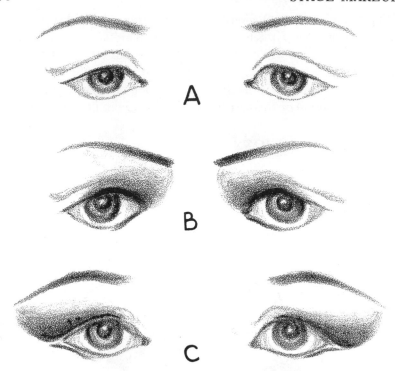

FIGURE 51. Optical illusions in eye makeup. All three pairs of eyes are exactly the same distance apart, but in B they are made to seem closer together and in C farther apart by the application of principles of optical illusion, which are used in both corrective and character makeup.

smaller than it actually is, while white tends to come toward the eye and appears larger than it is.

Both of these illusions can be applied to eye makeup, for example. If the eyeshadow is extended outward from the eye, the eye itself appears to be wider than it actually is, while confining the shadow to a small area or blending it in toward the center of the lid gives the impression of a smaller eye. Long, dark eyelashes give a similar illusion. C and C′ demonstrate a combination of these illusions.

Also, an eye without shadow or, better yet, surrounded by light base (in other words, a dark spot surrounded by light, as in Figure 50-C) will seem smaller than an eye with shadow (a light spot—the white of the eye, that is—surrounded by dark, as in Figure 50-C′).

Figure 51 shows how optical illusions can be used to make normal eyes

(A) seem closer together (B) or farther apart (C). If you will measure these pairs of eyes, you will find that all are of exactly the same size and are exactly the same distance apart. But in B the eyebrows are brought closer together and the shadow is concentrated toward the nose, making the eyes appear somewhat closer together. In C the brows and the shadow are kept outward and far apart, giving the illusion of widely spaced eyes. This effect is extremely useful in both character and corrective makeup.

The principle of the light spot appearing larger than the dark one can also be applied to the whole face, as in Figures 48 and 49. A light base (Figure 48) will give the impression of a wider face than a dark base (Figure 49). This may be confined just to the cheeks, chin, forehead, and nose or applied to the entire area. Long, heavy nasolabial folds and frown wrinkles between the eyebrows will, of course, give the illusion of a longer nose (Figure 45).

In Figure 48 the bushy hair on the sides of the head, the wide beard, the wide nose, the light base—all give the illusion of width, whereas in Figure 49 the heavy vertical folds, the high forehead, the long narrow nose, the shadows on the sides of the face—all contribute to the illusion of length.

It is well to be familiar with the principles of such illusions not only in order to use them to advantage but to avoid them when they are not desirable.

Whether we are correcting an actor's features to make them more pleasing or changing them to fit a specific character, it is always necessary to relate the makeup to the individual actor's face, compromising with the ideal physical picture to obtain useful, workable results.

10

CORRECTIVE
MAKEUP

We have been discussing general problems and means of adapting the makeup to the actor for purposes of developing a character. There is one additional problem, and it is with this specific problem, since it is a relatively simple one, that we should begin our practical work in makeup.

Quite often we have a problem of the actor who is to look like himself on stage, but better. This happens when an actor is actually to appear as himself (as in platform performances, lectures, photographs) or when it is assumed that he looks essentially right for the character but must be made as attractive as possible. This may mean slight adjustments such as changing the shape of the mouth or the curve of the eyebrows, lowering the forehead, or shortening the nose. In the professional theater it frequently means making the actor look younger.

FACIAL PROPORTIONS

The first problem in corrective makeup is to observe in what ways the actor's face departs from the ideal. Although there are different basic facial shapes, there are standard proportions which are considered pleasing.

As we learned in our clay modeling, the ideal face can be divided horizontally into three equal parts: (1) from the hairline to the eyebrows, (2) from the eyebrows to the bottom of the nose, and (3) from the bottom of the nose to the tip of the chin. If these three sections are not equal, an effort should be made to make them appear as nearly equal as possible. This can be done in the following ways:

1. If the forehead is too high, it can be darkened near the hairline with a fairly wide stripe of color two or three shades darker than the rest of the base. This can be blended downward very gradually so that it disappears imperceptibly into the foundation. There must be no line of demarcation. This follows the principle discussed in the previous chapter that a dark spot seems smaller than a light spot of equal size. Following the same principle, a forehead which is too low can be raised by means of a color two or three shades lighter than the base applied at the hairline as before.

2. If the nose is too long, it can be shortened by applying a deeper color under the tip and blending it up over the tip (Figure 64-G). If the nose is too short, a highlight (two or three shades lighter than the base) can be carried down over and under the tip (Figure 64-C-6).

3. If the chin is too long, the lower part can be shadowed; if it is too short, it can be highlighted in the usual way, always being carefully blended.

If the two sides of the face are sufficiently different to appear obviously asymmetrical, the less attractive side should be made up to match the more pleasing one. Which side is the more attractive can usually be judged by covering first one half of the face with a sheet of paper, then the other. An even more effective, though more elaborate, technique is to make a full-face photograph, then take a reverse print. Both the normal print and the reverse one can be cut vertically in half and the halves switched and pasted together. You will then have two photographs of the face with both sides matching. But one will be based on the right side, the other on the left. The less appealing face will indicate the side which is to be corrected. It is essential, of course, that the photograph be taken absolutely straight on or else the technique will not work.

FOREHEAD

We have already seen how a forehead can be raised or lowered. It can be narrowed or widened in exactly the same way by shadows or highlights at the temples blending onto the front plane of the forehead. As always, there should be a difference of only two or three shades between the shadows and the base since deeper shadows at the temples tend to age the face. If the frontal lobes are too prominent, tone them down with a shadow and bring the depression between the frontal lobes and the superciliary arch forward with a highlight. If the temples seem sunken, they should be highlighted.

NOSE

In addition to lengthening or shortening the nose, it may be desirable to change the apparent width. In order to widen a nose which is too sharp and narrow, run a broad highlight down the center (Figure 64-E). You may also wish to highlight the wings of the nostrils. To make a broad nose narrower, shadow the nostrils and the sides of the nose and run a very narrow highlight down the center (Figure 64-B-6). If the nose is too bulbous at the tip, shadow the tip on either side of the highlight. If the nose is crooked, run a fairly narrow highlight down the nose, bending it slightly in the opposite direction from the real bend and shadow it on either side. Be sure all shadows and highlights are carefully blended. Normally in corrective makeup, shadows and highlights are only two or three shades darker than the base. But in making up the nose it is often possible and sometimes necessary to use stronger contrasts to achieve the desired effect. This you will have to determine by using your own judgment in individual cases. Remember that the greater the contrast, the more careful the blending must be.

JAW LINE AND CHIN

If the jaw line is too square or too prominent, shadow the part which needs to be rounded off or toned down, carrying the shadow both under and over the jawbone and blend carefully into the foundation. If the chin is too prominent, shadow the whole chin. If it recedes, highlight it. If it is too square, round off the corners with shadows. If it is too pointed, flatten the point with a square shadow. A double chin can be minimized by shadowing it.

WRINKLES

Wrinkles cannot be blotted out completely any more than a double chin, but they too can be minimized by brushing in a highlight where you normally find a shadow and shadowing the prominent part of the wrinkle which normally catches a highlight. This will tend to flatten the wrinkle out. This applies also, of course, to circles or bags under the eyes (see Figures 52 and 53).

EYES

The basic problem in all corrective eye makeup is to add emphasis to the eye. This is done by means of colored eyeshadow, eye lining, mascara, and sometimes false eyelashes. In Figure 53 the eyes have been accented without the use of false eyelashes.

Eyeshadow. We have already discussed the choice of color for eye-shadow. Normally the shadow is placed on the eyelid only (the upper one, never the lower) and is heaviest next to the eye. It should not extend up to the eyebrow. If the eyes are too close together (they should be the width of an eye apart), they can be made to seem farther apart by

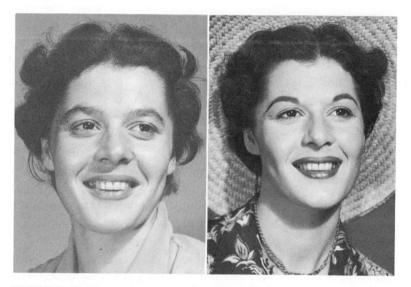

FIGURE 52, 53. Corrective makeup. By student Bert Roth. Observe the effect of the smooth foundation, highlighting to counteract shadows under the eyes, shaping of the eyebrows and the lips, accenting the eyes, and the neater hairdo.

moving the eyeshadow outward as shown in Figure 51-C. The eyes illustrated are normally spaced rather than being too close, but the principle is the same. You can see how this application of a principle of optical illusion seems to spread the eyes apart. If the eyes are too far apart, they can be brought together by moving the eyeshadow in toward the nose, as shown in Figure 51-B. Occasionally the eyelid is highlighted instead of shadowed in order to make the eyes more prominent. The method usually used is described in detail on page 129 in the discussion of highlighting the lids for glamor makeup.

A touch of rouge on the bone just below the outer end of the eyebrow will add a youthful sparkle to the eye. The red dot often placed at the tear duct is supposed to do the same thing but contributes little or nothing.

Accents. Eyes are further emphasized by what is unfortunately called eye lining (see Figure 53). With a brush or a sharp eyebrow pencil (brown or black) a line is drawn along the upper lid close to the lashes. This line should start about two-thirds of the way in toward the nose or, unless the eyes are too close together, at the tear duct. The line follows the lashes and extends about a quarter of an inch beyond the outer corner of the eye. It should end in a graceful curve, not a straight line, and it must fade out, not end abruptly.

A similar line is drawn on the lower lid from about a third of the way in from the outer corner outward toward the top line. This line should fade out before it quite meets the top line. Then both lines should be softened by running the finger lightly over them so that they really become narrow shadows and not lines at all. If they are referred to as eye *accents*, there may be less of a tendency to leave them as lines. Their purpose is to enlarge the eye slightly as well as to emphasize it. They must *never* completely surround the eye. Sometimes a small amount of white is brushed or penciled in below the outer quarter inch of the top line.

If the eyes are too close together, the accents are made strongest at the outer ends and are carried farther beyond the corner of the eye than usual (Figure 51-C). If the eyes are too far apart, the accents are shifted to the inner corners and do not extend to the outer corners at all (Figure 51-B).

Eyelashes. Women's eyelashes are always darkened with mascara (Figure 53), usually black, though blue and green may occasionally be effective. If men's eyelashes are very light or very sparse, brown or black mascara will be helpful in defining the eye. False eyelashes can be used for women if the eyes need additional definition. Normally, one false eyelash is cut in two and the hairs cut on the bias so that when the eyelashes are applied, they are longer at the outer end than in the center of the eye. Be sure to cut the two halves of the lash in reverse so that you will have one left and one right lash. The lashes are applied with a special eyelash adhesive or with surgical adhesive. If the eyes are to be made wider apart, the lashes can be extended farther beyond the corner of the eye. Mascara should be applied or false eyelashes put on after the makeup has been powdered. Be very careful not to get mascara into the eyes, as it can be very painful.

EYEBROWS

It is not necessary in corrective makeup to make the eyebrows fit one single pattern, but they should be made as flattering as possible to the eye and to the face in general. This means that the line of the eyebrow must follow that of the eye, as in Figure 51-A or 14-F. Eyebrows which are too straight or too arched or too slanted or too thick or too thin or too shaggy or too close together or too far apart are less attractive than they should be and need to be corrected. Look at the page of eyes, Figure 65. Only A is a normal, attractive brow. The others do wonders in suggesting character but nothing to beautify the eye, which is the problem which faces us now.

If the brow is well formed and well placed, it can be darkened (if that is necessary) with black or brown eyebrow pencil, using short, quick, light strokes, following the direction of the hair. Eyebrows should not be darkened by drawing a hard, heavy line. The object is to darken the hairs, not the skin underneath, unless, of course, the natural brow needs to be filled out. Always strive for a natural look in both men and women. In many cases men's eyebrows will not need darkening; but if they are very light, brown or black eyebrow pencil, depending on the color of the hair, should be used. It is also possible to darken the brows with mascara if you prefer. In fact, this is sometimes preferable, especially for men, since there is less danger of achieving an undesirable painted effect.

If there are unnecessary hairs between the eyebrows, pluck them out. Except for these hairs, men's eyebrows should almost never be plucked. If women's eyebrows are much too heavy or if there are stray hairs, they should be plucked (Figures 52-3), but beware of plucking too much. If the eyes (and the eyebrows) are too close together, the inner ends can be plucked and the outer ends extended with pencil (Figure 51-C). If they are too far apart, they can be penciled in toward the center (Figure 51-B).

If the line of the brow is not good (too straight or too slanted, for example,) it can often be reshaped somewhat by plucking. If this is insufficient, further reshaping can be done with the pencil. It may not be possible to achieve an ideal, classic brow (and this is really not necessary), but the best should be made of the one which is there. It is possible, of course, to block out the natural brows if that is absolutely necessary (see Chapter 12) and to draw on new ones, but that is not usually done for corrective makeup. In correcting any eyebrow, keep in mind that it should express the individual—but his or her most attractive qualities.

CHEEKS

If the cheeks are too round, the part of the cheek to be made less prominent should be shaded with a base two or three shades darker than that used on the rest of the face. It is important, as always, to blend this lowlight imperceptibly into the lighter base. If the cheeks are too hollowed or sunken, the procedure can be reversed by using a base two or three shades lighter than normal. This will counteract the shadows which betray the sunken cheeks.

We have already discussed selecting the color of rouge and the technique of application. The problem in corrective makeup is one of placement. The rouge should be placed on the cheekbone, not usually low on the cheek, though occasionally it may prove effective in glamorizing the face to use the rouge as a shadow below the cheekbone in order to sink in the cheeks. This may sometimes work in individual cases but is not recommended for the usual corrective makeup. In any case, experiment with it before deciding definitely to use it.

Rouge should not be placed too near the eye or the nose. A good rule to follow is never to let it come nearer the nose than an imaginary line dropped vertically from the center of the eye. If the face is too narrow, it should be kept even further from the nose and placed nearer the ears. If the face is too wide, keep the rouge away from the ears and apply it in a more or less vertical rather than horizontal pattern. It should never be a round spot, and it must always be applied with subtlety.

Rouge is not always used for men. There is no hard and fast rule. But for corrective makeup if the actor has the sort of complexion and coloring which is usually associated with color in the cheeks, rouge may be used. (This would mean that, in general, blonds are more likely to require rouge than brunets.) Or if he seems to require a little color in order to look healthier, it may be used. But if it is used, it must be applied with great subtlety, and it should ordinarily be spread over a wider area than for women, even into the temples if the face is narrow. But above all, it must look completely natural. In case of doubt, use none.

LIPS

The shape of the lips should not be made to conform to a set pattern. Rather, they should be shaped to complement the individual face. But there is ordinarily some room for improvement in the natural shape. This can be done in various ways. Figure 54 shows a number of lips needing

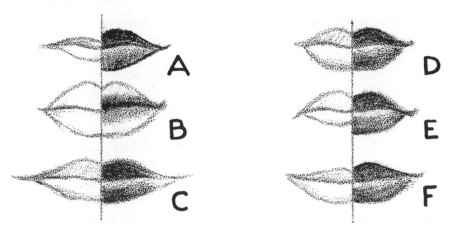

FIGURE 54. Corrective lip makeup. The left half of each pair of lips shows the natural size and shape and the right half what can be done to improve them with makeup.

and receiving corrective treatment. The left half of the lip in each case represents the actor's own, while the right half shows at least one possibility for improving it with makeup.

Thin lips (A) can usually be corrected for women by overpainting—that is, drawing on new lips of the shape and size you want. This is more difficult for men. If it is really important to make the mouth fuller, be sure to use a natural color (this may need to be mixed—usually a brownish or orange-red mixed with the base color will do it), and always make the lower lip lighter than the upper. A highlight over the upper lip may help, and an artificial shadow below the center part of the lower lip can be used to suggest the normal overhang of the lip.

The most difficult problem of all is presented by thick lips (B). Since the edges are nearly always very definite, it is almost impossible to conceal them. But they can be minimized by covering the lips with base, then using color only toward the inside of the lips and fading it outward into the base color.

For too-wide lips (C) keep the color toward the center of the lips and cover the outer corners with base.

If the mouth is too narrow (D), carry the color to the extreme corners. Ordinarily, it is not possible to carry the color beyond the natural corners of the mouth with any degree of success. The artifice becomes apparent as soon as the mouth is opened.

In the case of a mouth with a heavy upper lip, a thin lower one, and the corners turned down (E), the solution is to overpaint the lower lip to match the upper one and to turn up the corners with paint.

For a mouth with a thin upper lip (F), the upper lip must be overpainted to match the lower.

Normally it is best not to carry the color to the extreme corners of the mouth except for purposes of widening it. Lips should always be drawn with a narrow flat brush and blotted with tissue.

It is frequently helpful, especially when overpainting, to define the lips by outlining them with a brown or, better yet, a dark red pencil. This should not be left as a line, however, but should be blended with your brush toward the center of the lip. It is also possible to do the outline with the brush and a darker shade of red than you have used on the lips.

For men, especially when no lipstick is used at all, the outline can be done very subtly with a brown pencil and then blended. Further definition is often possible by deepening the natural shadow immediately below the center of the lower lip. If the lip is naturally protruding or overhanging, this will not be necessary; but if the natural shadow is slight, it may be helpful.

NECK

If the neck shows age, it can be improved somewhat by shadowing the prominent muscles and highlighting the depressions. Even a sagging neckline can be minimized by shadowing, at least when viewed from the front. The shadow should be strongest just under the jaw line and can blend gradually into the foundation, which can be of a darker shade than that used on the face. The shadow must never be allowed to come up over the jaw line. The jaw line itself can be defined with a highlight which will tend to strengthen it and take the attention away from the neck.

When the neck is seen in profile, however, no amount of paint will be completely effective. The best solution, especially for women, is actually to tighten the skin under the jaw by pulling the skin in front of the ears upward. This can be done by the use of *facial lifts*, constructed and applied as follows:

(1) Cut 2 rectangles about 4 inches by ½ inch of mousseline de soie or other very thin, tough fabric. The edges may be pinked if you find that preferable.

(2) Fold over about ½ inch of the fabric at one end to strengthen it, and sew or staple it to a length (about 8 inches) of cotton elastic band ½ inch wide. This should be done for both pieces of the mousseline. After

the mousseline is attached to the face, the elastic will go over the top of the head. A dressmaker's hook should be sewn to the free end of one tape and two or three eyes to the other so that the two ends can be hooked together at just the right tension. If you prefer, you can make the elastic slightly shorter, fold over the ends to make loops, and tie ordinary string to each loop. Then the string can be tied on top of the head to make exactly the desired tension. Whatever method is used, the construction should be completed in advance so that in making up the actor for the performance, it will be necessary only to attach the pieces.

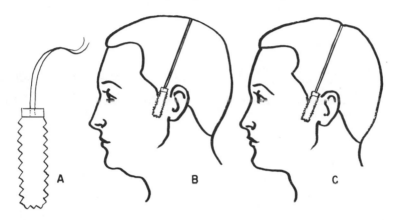

FIGURE 55. Facial lift. The lift (A), made of mousseline de soie, is attached with spirit gum to the skin in front of the ear (B), then pulled tight over the top of the head (C). The tape over the head can be concealed with a wig or sometimes with the natural hair, carefully combed. In the latter case, the tape should more or less match the color of the hair.

(3) The two pieces of mousseline should be attached to the dry skin, vertically in front of the ears and below the sideburns, with spirit gum.

(4) In order to conceal the edges of the fabric, stipple with Duo adhesive (or Mehron's Flexol) and allow it to dry along with the spirit gum.

(5) Attach the elastic over the head and adjust the tension. Too-great tension will result in obvious wrinkles or creases in the skin and must, of course, be avoided.

(6) Cover the lifts with sealer and allow it to dry. In some cases a heavy application of greasepaint or rubber mask grease may suffice. If you plan to use a cake or Pan-Stik makeup, powder the grease before proceeding.

(7) If cake makeup is used, a brand with exceptionally good covering power (such as Mehron's) is preferable. A greasepaint makeup is likely to prove more satisfactory, however, especially since it will also help to conceal fine wrinkles and skin irregularities.

(8) If the natural hair is to be used, it can be combed over the elastic to conceal it. This, however, is exceedingly difficult if not impossible for men. If a wig or a toupee is not to be worn, it may be necessary to wear false sideburns. These should be constructed on hairlace. Crepe hair ones would hardly prove satisfactory. If a wig is to be used, for either men or women, the elastic will be covered automatically.

Be sure that the top of the lift, where the elastic is attached to the mousseline, is high enough so that it can be concealed by the hair. It must never, of course, fall below the natural side hair.

This is not the only method of constructing facial lifts, but it will serve to illustrate the general principle. Each makeup artist has his own preference as to materials and exact technique of construction.

TEETH

Dark or discolored teeth can be lightened with tooth enamel. There are several shades of white and cream available. Certain irregularities (such as very long front teeth) can be corrected by shortening the teeth with black tooth enamel, black wax, or black eyebrow pencil. More serious deficiencies, such as broken, missing, or extremely irregular teeth, require the services of a dentist. This can be very expensive, but for the professional actor, unless he is doing only character roles, it is important to have the most attractive teeth possible.

HAIR

The actor's normal hair style should be considered carefully in relation to the shape of the face, and if it is not flattering, it should be restyled. This can be done merely by recombing in various ways and checking in the mirror. A change in hair style can often do wonders for a woman's appearance. There is less opportunity for change in men, but the basic silhouette is still important and can often be improved.

If the face is too long, obviously a hairdo high on the head will only make things worse. Try to keep the hair flat on top and wider at the sides. If the face is too short and wide, exactly the reverse will apply. If the face is too round, a round hairdo following the shape of the face will emphasize the deficiency. If the features are too sharp, the hairdo should be soft around the face, not sleek.

If a man's hairline is receding slightly, it can often be corrected with eyebrow pencil of the appropriate color on the scalp. This should be softened and blurred with the finger so that there is no definite line. It is best to use short strokes of the pencil following the direction of the hair. Never draw a hard, horizontal line. Darkening the base color at the hairline will help too. Don Lee Scalp Masque (see Appendix A and Chapter 16) is excellent for bald spots which have not gone too far and can also be used with some success on the hairline. Black or brown cake makeup is also effective. If the hair has receded beyond the point where it can be corrected with paint, the actor should procure a good toupee. This must be made to order and is expensive, but it can make an actor appear years younger and far more attractive. For suggestions on procuring toupees, see Appendix A; for instructions on wearing and caring for them, see Chapter 16.

PROBLEMS

1. Make your face thinner, then rounder, and observe the results critically in the mirror. If you are working on someone else, look at the effect from a distance, under lights if possible.

2. Make your forehead wider and lower, then higher and narrower.

3. Using only paint, change the shape of your nose, making it (*a*) longer, (*b*) shorter and broader, (*c*) flatter, (*d*) crooked.

4. Make your forehead more prominent and your chin less prominent, then you chin more prominent and your forehead less prominent.

5. Lengthen your entire face, then shorten it.

6. Make your eyes (*a*) larger (*b*) smaller, (*c*) farther apart, (*d*) closer together.

7. Change the shape of your eyebrows as much as you can without blocking them out.

8. Make your mouth (*a*) wider, (*b*) narrower, (*c*) thicker, (*d*) thinner.

9. Analyze to the best of your ability your own face—that is, specify its general shape, prominent bones, size of eyes, nose, mouth, and chin, height of forehead, and the like. Specify which are your best features and which are the ones that could be improved upon.

10. Do a complete corrective makeup on yourself, following your analysis.

11

LIGHT AND SHADE

We have now learned to color the face with various shades of paint, and we have learned how to use optical illusions to change to some degree its apparent shape in order to beautify the actor. Now we must turn to the vastly more complex problem of helping the actor become a character, of using the same paints to create the illusion of the person who first took shape in the mind of a playwright and who must now be brought to life.

This is essentially the problem the portrait painter faces except that he is working on a flat, white canvas while we have a three-dimensional head to begin with. This is not necessarily an advantage, for it means that we are limited in the effects we can achieve whereas the portrait painter can create any illusion he wants. The portrait painter has an additional advantage of considerable importance. He can determine his source of light and go ahead, secure in the knowledge that once the painting is complete, his imaginary light source will never change. On the stage it changes constantly.

But in spite of these differences, the basic problem remains the same, and, not unreasonably, the solution to the problem is essentially the same for us as for the portrait painter. We both observe in life what happens when light falls on an object. We see the patterns of light and shade (another name for an absence of light) which reveal to the eye the real shape of an object. Then with colored paints of varying degrees of lightness and darkness, of brightness and grayness, we recreate the *effect*; and if we are sufficiently skillful, the observer will be misled by the effect into believing he is seeing the real thing. This is not strictly true in the case of portraits, for one is always aware that he is seeing a picture. In fact, it is not, or should not be, the aim of the painter to imitate reality so closely that his work becomes photographic. But in a sense that is what the makeup artist must do. Although he can and should be considerably more selective than the photographer, it is really only in stylized makeup that his art should be permitted to reveal itself. In the usual realistic makeup his objective, from a strictly technical point of view, should be to deceive the audience.

Suppose we look at the oil painting in Figure 56. The painting creates the illusion of reality without for a moment fooling us into believing that it is real. We are aware of brush strokes and of simplifications and heightened contrasts which are expected in painting, but at the same time a three-dimensional figure has been created on a flat canvas merely by careful juxtaposition of light and dark paint.

It is perhaps worth pointing out that this particular painting was se-

FIGURE 56. Oil painting of Asmodeus from the monodrama *Journey to Rages*. Techniques used in the painting are the same as those required for makeup.

lected because it was done by a makeup artist, not a professional painter, using the same techniques of modeling in light and shade that he uses in makeup. A makeup of an actor as the character in the portrait would involve the use of exactly the same principles, but they would have to be applied somewhat more realistically. The technique would not need to be slavishly photographic, but it should be convincingly realistic. The makeup artist can eliminate nonessentials and select details which will contribute to the desired effect. But we must not be aware of his materials or his means. In Figure 57 we see an attempt to duplicate a painting on an actor's face, using essentially the same techniques employed by the painter.

You are undoubtedly familiar with the kind of makeup one sees all too frequently in both the professional and the nonprofessional theater—makeup in which the actor appears to have drawn a diagram of his face with a black pencil and made a few careless smudges here and there in the process. Compare that sort of makeup with the makeups in Figures

FIGURE 57. Student makeup copied from a fifteenth-century painting. Improvised costume. Makeup by Alja Hurnen on herself.

57 and 63 in which the same paint has been carefully applied in accordance with long-established principles of light and shade.

For whatever encouragement it may give, it should be pointed out that these makeups were done by a student, not by a professional makeup artist. Compare them with the ones on and by the same student in Figures 159, 160, and 168.

Since the basis of actual makeup technique, then, lies in understanding and applying the principles of chiaroscuro or light and shade, which have been used by painters for centuries, our next step is to study these principles in theory, to observe them in life, then to apply them in monochromatic drawing.

FLAT AND CURVED SURFACES

How are we able to tell by sight alone whether a surface is flat or curved? The general outline of the object may provide a fairly reliable clue. But suppose we are trying to distinguish between a cylinder and a 4-sided tube of approximately the same size. If we cover up the ends, the outline will be exactly the same. But we will still have no difficulty in determining which is which simply because the patterns of light and shade will be completely different, as illustrated in Figure 58. What, then, is *chiaroscuro* or *light and shade?*

Perhaps the simplest way to approach it is to imagine the two forms in Figure 58 in total darkness, which means that both are completely black. In other words, there is a total absence of light, which, after all, provides the only means of our seeing these or any other objects. Now we turn on a light in the position of the double arrow F. The light hits the objects and is reflected from them to our eyes, enabling us to see them. But observe that the light does not illuminate the entire object in either case. Only those surfaces upon which the rays of light fall directly are fully visible because only they receive light rays to reflect to the eye. Surfaces which are situated away from the light source remain in darkness. This is what enables us to determine in what direction the surface planes of an object lie and whether they are flat, curved, or irregular. This information automatically tells us the shape of the object.

HARD AND SOFT EDGES

In both of the forms in Figure 58 part of the form is lighted, and part remains in darkness. But the shift from the lighted plane to the nonlighted or shadowed plane is entirely different in the two. In one there is a gradual shift from light through semilight (or gray) to dark. In the other the shift is abrupt and knife-sharp. Thus we know that one object has a rounded surface, the other has flat, angular ones. The sharp division between the two flat surfaces is known as a *hard edge*, while the gradual change between planes on the curved surface, though technically not an edge at all, is known as a *soft edge*. This is a principle which is basic to all makeup and which you will be called upon to apply repeatedly.

Observe, for example, wrinkles in the face. The largest and the easiest to analyze is the nasolabial fold, which, as the name suggests, extends from the nostrils to the mouth. If your own are not yet developed, observe someone else's. There is usually a definite crease in the flesh, which, unfortunately, is too often represented on the stage with a flat stripe of black or brown paint. But this crease is not a stripe. It is an edge, a hard edge— or at least it becomes one when light falls upon the wrinkle from above, lighting the top of the fold as if it were a cylinder, then fading off into shadow (a soft edge). But instead of continuing around, as a cylinder would, the flesh changes direction abruptly at the crease and moves into another plane, giving the effect of a hard edge. Unless we understand the principle of hard and soft edges and know how to create them with lights and darks, we shall never be able to achieve a convincing makeup.

Figure 60 shows fairly clearly the comparison between a cylinder and a nasolabial fold. Study also the nasolabial folds in Figures 49, 63, 75, 101, 140 and 213. You might also pick out some of the hard and soft edges in the drawings of eyes in Figure 65. In the oil painting in Figure 56 we see how the painter uses the same principles of lights and darks, hard and soft edges, to create a three-dimensional effect. Notice how the lights and darks of the cylinder are used in painting the turban, for example, and also the folds of material in the costume.

Remember, then, that sharp corners result in strong lights and darks being placed next to each other (Figure 58-A'-B'), giving us so-called hard edges, whereas curved surfaces result in lights and darks being joined by an infinite number of intermediate shades (A and B), giving us soft edges.

DRAWING IN LIGHT AND SHADE

Now, in order to be sure that we understand the principle and can apply it, suppose we draw some simple objects, such as a cylinder and a box. Anyone can draw with a little practice. You may not have the particular type of talent necessary to become a great or even a very skillful artist, but you can become proficient enough to use the principles of light and

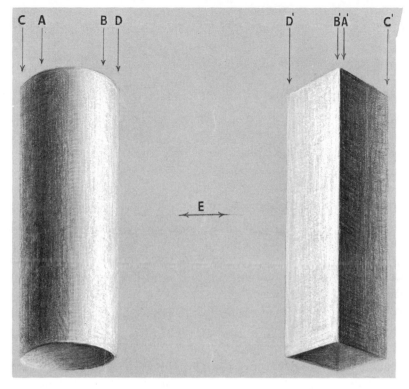

FIGURE 58. Technique of modeling curved and angular surfaces.

shade to make recognizable objects. Remember that unless you can draw a wrinkle on paper, you can hardly expect to be able to draw one on the face.

The simplest way to begin is probably to reproduce the drawing in Figure 58. It might be to your advantage at first to try to do the drawing without looking at the book, then check your mistakes. You might also do the same objects with the light from a different source.

In any event, before beginning your own drawing, pay particular attention to the areas indicated by the arrows. Arrow A indicates the darkest area on the cylinder and B, the lightest. You will observe that neither of these areas is precisely at the edge of the cylinder. The edge of the dark side (C) is slightly lighter than the darkest part, while the light edge (D) is somewhat darker than the highlight (B). The reason for this is simply that on the dark side a small amount of reflected light is always seen at the extreme edge, and on the light side the surface of the edge is curving away from us so abruptly that it seems to be less brightly lighted. Try drawing a cylinder with maximum light and dark areas at the extreme edges and notice the result. The cylinder will probably seem to stop abruptly at the edges instead of continuing around to complete itself.

The source of light has been arbitrarily considered for this drawing to be in the position of the arrow E. Thus the right side of the cylinder is in direct light, resulting in a strong highlight and a gradual diminution of light from this highlight to the darkest part of the lowlight on the opposite side of the cylinder. No matter from which direction the light is coming, it will cause a highlight upon the part of the object nearest it and leave a lowlight on the opposite side. Thus there can be no shadow, or lowlight, without a corresponding highlight—a principle which must be carefully observed by the makeup artist.

This principle of light and shade holds true no matter what the shape of an object may be. In Figure 58, for example, we have a rectangular object illuminated from the left. Since there is a sudden change in the plane of the surface rather than a gradual one, there is a correspondingly sharp contrast in light areas, which gives us, as we have already explained, a hard edge where the surface changes direction. This hard edge is intensified in drawing by placing the lightest light next to the darkest dark. In other words, both the strongest highlight and the deepest shadow are at the edge of the rectangle nearest the eye. It is by means of this intensification of contrasts that the artist imparts solidity and third dimension to such an object. According to the principle of aerial perspective, the centralization of color value and of intensity is inversely proportional to the nearness of the color to the eye. In relation to chiaroscuro, this principle means simply that with distance both black and white become more gray— less strongly differentiated, in other words. You have undoubtedly observed this effect in distant mountains or tall buildings or even in cars or houses at a considerable distance. Thus the near edge of the rectangle is made to appear closer by intensification of its color, no matter what the hue and value may be. The far edges are made to recede by means of a decrease in color intensity and centralization of value.

Perhaps, in passing, we should mention cast shadows. The type of shadow about which we have been studying is known as a real or true shadow. The term *lowlight* is frequently used to refer to it. However, when unidirectional light falls upon an object, it not only leaves part of the object itself in shadow, but it also casts a shadow of the object on any area around it from which the light is cut off. In other words, when an object intercepts the light, it casts a shadow. This shadow is known as a *cast* shadow and is never used in makeup because of the constant movement

FIGURE 59. Drapery study in charcoal and chalk, showing technique of modeling hard and soft edges.

of the actor and the resultant directional changes in light. A cast shadow always has a hard edge, it follows the shape of the object upon which it falls, and it is darkest at the outer edge. Observe the cast shadows of the drapery in Figure 59 and of the hand in Figure 56. Remember that cast shadows have no function whatever in makeup. They are merely mentioned for the sake of completeness and to enlighten any who might be confused about their classification.

You would do well to spend considerable time in practicing relatively simple charcoal sketches. Figure 60 should be helpful in learning methods of procedure and blending techniques. Since the flat-sided figure is easier, that should probably be done first. Start with your darkest dark at what is to be the hard edge, and blend it gradually out toward the outer edge, allowing it to become slightly lighter as you go. This can be done by applying the charcoal directly as carefully as you can, then blending with the fingers or with a paper stump to achieve smooth transitions. It is quite possible to achieve the transition without blending merely by using the charcoal carefully, allowing the strokes to become lighter as you recede from the hard edge. This has been done in Figures 58 and 59. The drawings in Figure 60 have been blended with the fingers. What technique

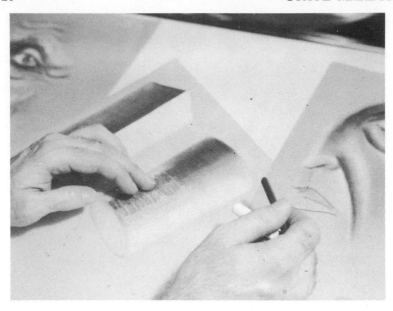

FIGURE 60. Drawing in charcoal and chalk. The charcoal strokes are being blended with the finger to soften the edges.

you use is of little importance so long as you achieve the results. When the dark side is completed, do the light side in the same way, starting heavily with the chalk at the hard edge next to the black.

The cylinder is somewhat more difficult because of the necessity for making gradual transitions from light to dark. Figure 60 shows how the dark can be applied (in either horizontal or vertical strokes) and then blended. The light can be approached in the same way. However, try to let the gray paper serve as the middle tone between the light and the dark. In other words, the charcoal and the chalk should never quite meet since the gray of the paper is approximately halfway between and can serve as a transitional tone.

If you get along well with your first drawings and want to try something more difficult, set up a simple drapery study with a single light source and sketch it. Figure 59 illustrates such a study. Do not copy this one, however. You will learn far more by sketching from life.

Figure 81 illustrates a third basic shape, the sphere, and one of its applications to makeup. Notice how the principle is used in painting the cheek in Figure 56. In the sphere all shadows and highlights fall in a circular pattern.

Try also drawing eyes, mouths, noses, ears, and complete heads. You should be familiar with their construction from your work in clay modeling. Now see if you can create a three-dimensional illusion with charcoal and chalk. Figures 14, 51, 64, 65, and the portraits in Appendix F may be helpful, but again draw from life as much as you can.

Remember that whenever a single light falls on a three-dimensional object, those parts of the object not in the direct line of light will remain in shadow. Conversely, wherever there is a lowlight or shadow, there is a corresponding highlight. When the surface changes direction abruptly, the shadow and the highlight are immediately adjacent. But when the surface changes direction gradually, shadow and highlight are separated by a gradation of intermediate shades.

PROBLEMS

1. With charcoal and chalk on gray charcoal paper (obtainable from your local art dealer or stationery store) sketch a number of cylinders in various positions, determining each time the direction from which the light is coming. An actual cylinder should be used as a model if possible.

2. Repeat Problem 1 for cubes and spheres.

3. Now attempt to draw a few simple objects, such as vases, books, boxes, and bottles, employing the principles of light and shade you have learned.

4. Pick out the hard and soft edges in the drapery study, Figure 59.

5. Set up a very simple drapery study, and try to sketch it. Since this is often difficult for the beginner, do not be discouraged, but keep practicing, striving for accuracy of modeling and the appearance of third dimension.

6. Pick out the hard and soft edges in Figure 56 and in the face in Figure 63. Remember that hard edges are always very sharply defined.

7. Sketch a large number of eyes, noses, mouths, and ears of various sizes and shapes in various positions. Also, attempt a complete head or two.

Note: Adequate time should be spent with the problems above, for proficiency in simple sketching in light and shade will be found to save a great deal of time in experimentation with makeup.

12

MODELING WITH PAINT

When the sculptor creates a head, he actually models it in three dimensions. When the painter, on the other hand, models a head, he must create the illusion of three dimensions while using only two. The makeup artist uses both methods, usually in combination. But since the greater part of his work will be done in two dimensions, we shall begin by discussing the technique of modeling with paint.

We have already studied the general construction of the face. Now, in order to simplify our discussion of the problem of remodeling it, suppose we divide the face into five general areas—forehead, eyes, nose, cheeks, and front jaws. These area divisions are shown in Figure 61. Each area will then be subdivided into planes for more detailed analysis. The discussions of each area will indicate the various possible treatments of that area, and it will be up to you to apply those techniques to a specific character.

Since colors for shadow, highlight, rouge, and eyeshadow have been discussed in Chapter 7, we will be concerned here only with the technique for modeling, assuming that the appropriate colors will be used.

AREA 1: FOREHEAD

This area is divided into five planes as shown in Figure 62. Planes A and C are the frontal and superciliary arches, D the temporal hollow, and B the slight depression between the two prominences.

Far too often in attempts to represent age the forehead is covered with transverse wrinkles. That may be a reasonably effective means of aging provided they really look like wrinkles, but they seldom do. If you feel you must have wrinkles, then be sure not only that your shadows are adequately blended and accented with one soft and one hard edge, but that each shadow is adequately highlighted. The highlights, too, must each have one hard and one soft edge. They will help more than anything else to avoid the lined or dirty look that usually characterizes attempts at making wrinkled foreheads. (See Figures 57, 63, 64-C-D, 128, 197-F-G, 198-A-C-I, 199-C-E-F, 200-L.)

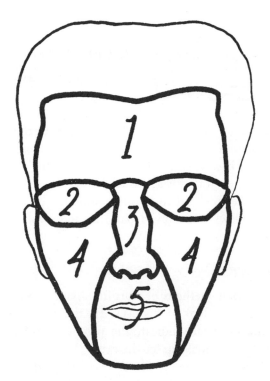

FIGURE 61. Division of the face into areas
for detailed analysis of modeling techniques.

A simpler method of aging the forehead, and one more effective in most cases, is to utilize the concept of planes. The two prominences, A and C, Figure 62, catch the light and so should be highlighted (Figure 64-B-3-4); the depression, B, falling between them, may be slightly shadowed (Figure 64-B-2). Be careful, however, not to emphasize the transverse shadow too strongly or a skull-like appearance will result. Sometimes this depression can merely be left the base color while the adjacent areas are highlighted. (See also Figure 205.)

The temples, D, are always shadowed for age (Figures 8, 41, 47, 49, 64-B-1, 205), the depth of the shadow depending upon the state of preservation of the individual. These shadows are often barely perceptible in early middle age and are usually quite pronounced in old age (Figure 8-G-K). Be sure that they are always carried to the hairline. They tend to be more intense at the inner edge and to lighten as they approach the hair.

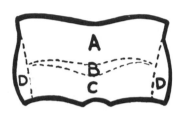

FIGURE 62. Area 1: Forehead.

All edges in area 1 must be soft. That, of course, refers only to planes of light and shade, not to wrinkles. For old age, the forehead is likely to be lighter than the base color, and sometimes instead of being wrinkled, the skin may be stretched tightly across the skull.

If you want the forehead to be more rounded or bulging, apply the highlights and shadows in a curved pattern, as shown in Figure 81-B-C (6, 7, 14, 15).

AREA 2: EYES

One of the easiest methods of learning about a person's disposition, health, and so on, is to look at his eyes. By the same token, one of the surest ways of making a face indicate the precise characteristics you want it to is to concentrate on makeup for the eyes.

In Figure 65 we see a page of fifteen eyes. All of the eye openings, the irises, and the pupils are of the same size and shape. In fact, all were traced from one drawing so as to make them as nearly identical as possible. This page, then, can represent the right eye of a single actor, and everything we can read in these eyes about the character has in this instance been created with charcoal and chalk and on the actor would be created with makeup.

Eyes A, B, C, and D are identical except for the eyebrows. In all other eyes there is modeling in light and shade in addition to changes in the eyebrows. All of these effects can be achieved with paint (and sometimes crepe hair), with the exception of O which requires tape, rubber, or plastic

FIGURE 63. Student makeup in improvised costume. By Alja Hurnen. Observe the careful modeling
with highlights and shadows to emphasize bone
structure and create wrinkles. Compare with other
makeups of Mrs. Hurnen in Figures 57, 159, 160,
and 168.

to cut across part of the eye opening. Figure 67 shows similar changes
achieved with makeup.

In Chapter 10 we discussed principles of corrective eye makeup and
the use of optical illusions. You might refer again to Figure 51. Now we
shall discuss methods of changing the eye to help project the character.

Fortunately for the makeup artist, the eye responds more effectively
to modeling with paint than nearly any other part of the face. But since
the great variety of possibilities for changing the eye may cause confusion,
suppose we study the orbital area bit by bit instead of trying to consider
it as a whole.

Figure 66 indicates the six logical divisions of planes in this area.

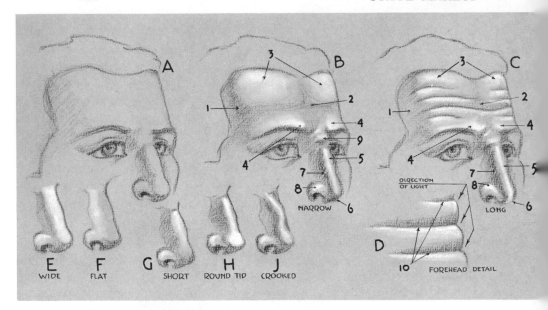

FIGURE 64. Modeling the features with highlights and shadows. Aging the forehead and changing the apparent shape of the nose.

Though the exact shape of each will vary from person to person, the six planes can always be found and treated individually. Since both color and shading can vary within a single plane, you can readily see how many effects are possible from the combination of the six planes.

Plane A (see also Figure 14-E-1) extends forward from the eye to the bridge of the nose and is invariably shadowed for age. The center of this plane is usually one of the darkest parts of the whole orbital area. (See Figures 8, 28–33, 57, 65-E-F-G-K-L-N-O-P, 67-B-C-D-F.) The lower edge fades into the shadow on the side of the nose. The outer edge is a soft one which turns into a highlight on the bridge of the nose. The inner edge is also always soft, fading into plane B. In general, the greater the age, the deeper this shadow. Shadowing plane A tends to make the eye recede, thus aging it, without giving any particular effect of dissipation. (See Figure 214.)

Plane B is a transition area which is either left the base color or included with A. In the latter case, the shadow of A is usually lightened as it crosses B and approaches C.

Plane C (see also Figure 14-E-2, 3) is a very important one in indicating age. Frequently the skin there sags and actually covers a part of the open eye (Figures 67-D, 117, 128, 178, 197-I, 198-B, 199-B, 200-O). Although we

cannot do that with paint, we can approach the effect by strongly highlighting C_1 with white and shadowing the lower edge of C_2 (Figures 35,
65-F-K-L). The deepest part of the shadow is at the bottom of the area,
and it turns very gradually into a highlight as it approaches C_1. The dotted
line indicates only a general division of the whole plane, not a definite
one. The inner edge of plane C is a very definite division, however, and
should be heavily shadowed if sagging flesh is to be indicated (Figures 57,
65-F). If not, then again the transition to B is a gradual one.

It is usually wise to use two colors for the narrow shadow which creates the impression of a fold of flesh. A shadow can be drawn with the
basic shading color along the division between B and C and blended
carefully to form two soft edges. Then the simulated crease can be deepened with another color in accordance with the suggestions given under
"Shadows" in Chapter 7. The accent should also be lightly blended.

The lightest part of the highlight is always nearest the eyebrow—in
other words, on the superciliary bone where it forms the outer edge of the
eye socket. It gradually recedes into a soft shadow as it approaches the
B-C division whether or not a fold is to be made (Figure 65-E-J-K).

Usually when there is to be a fold, it falls a little nearer the nose
than the division indicated in the diagram. That is, the fold has its inception very near the inner end of the eyebrow (Figures 65-F, 117).

If the whole orbital area is to appear sunken, then plane C may be
shadowed rather than highlighted (Figure 65-H-N). This, however, tends
to give a rather skull-like appearance and is usually done only to indicate
extreme illness or emaciation or for characters who are supposed to inspire
fear or horror. Frequently, wrinkles cut across the outer edge of plane C_2
(Figures 65-F-G-K-N-P, 197-A-G, 198-C-I, 199 B E F). These are commonly known as crow's-feet. If you use them, be sure to make them true
wrinkles, not lines (see discussion of forehead wrinkles at the beginning
of this chapter).

Plane D (see also Figure 14-E-4) is the eyelid itself and may be either
highlighted or shadowed. If the whole eye is to appear sunken, D must
be shadowed (Figure 65-E-H). But frequently in age the eyeball itself
protrudes, while the skin sinks in around it. In that case D must be highlighted and the upper division between it and the other areas deeply shadowed in the same manner as suggested for the B-C division in making a
fold. (See Figures 8-F-G-J-K, 30–33, 47, 65-G-J, 67-F, 204, 212, 214.) When
D is highlighted, C_1 is usually highlighted too (Figures 30–33, 47, 65-F-G-J-
K, 204, 212, 218), although there must be a deep shadow between the
areas.

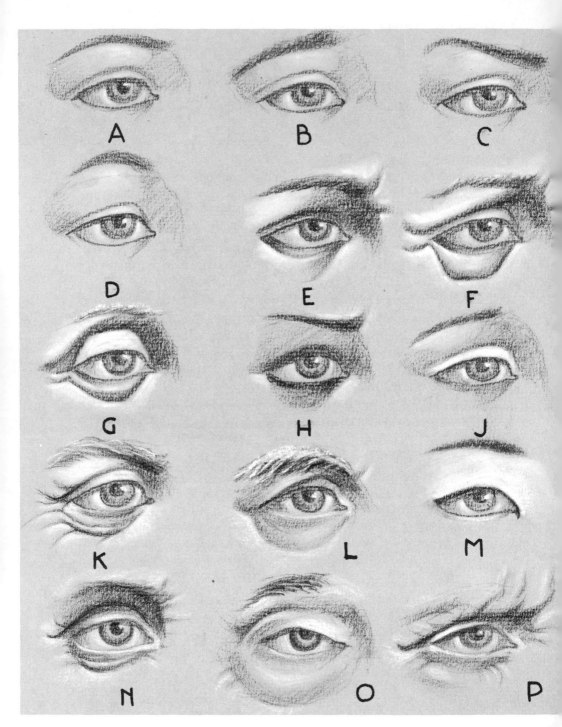

FIGURE 65. Eyes and eyebrows. All of the eye openings above are the same size and shape. Changes have been made with highlighting and shadowing and by reshaping the eyebrows. In one case (O) a prosthetic piece would have to be added to make the change and possibly also in M. In A, B, C, and D only the eyebrows are different.

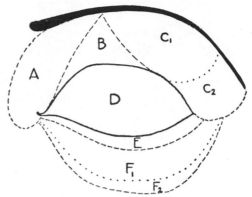

FIGURE 66. Division of the orbital area into planes for shadowing and highlighting.

Plane D is also sometimes highlighted in the same way for glamor makeups with the colored eyeshadow used only on the lower part close to the eye. Frequently, for either age or glamor, the actor will want to create the effect of a more prominent lid than he has naturally. This can often be faked quite successfully with paint (Figures 26–33, 67-F) even when the actor's own lids completely disappear under unusually prominent and overhanging A, B, and C areas. With a dark brown or a maroon pencil or with a brush and your deepest shadow color, draw on the enlarged lid in approximately the pattern shown in Figure 65-G. Then shadow upward toward the eyebrow, just as you would if there were a natural crease, and strongly highlight the entire false lid (Figure 30). The secret of modeling this false eyelid convincingly is to make the shadow edge extremely dark so that it gives the effect of a deep crease. As always, using different colors for the larger shadowed area and a deep accent color is helpful.

To indicate weak eyes, which often accompany extreme old age, rouge the lower part of D with red. Using red in all of the eye shadows tends to give an effect of age, whereas cool shadows may often suggest dissipation or evil. Figure 65-O shows a very old and weak eye which, as we have already indicated, cannot be achieved with paint. A prosthetic piece of rubber or tape is necessary.

Plane E (see also Figure 14-E-5) is nearly always shadowed for age, although usually not heavily, and is almost never highlighted (Figures 8-E-G-J, 45, 49, 65-E-F-G-H-K-L-N-O-P, 67-B-C-D-F, 88, 151, 199-E-F, 204, 217). The shadow is usually deepest at the outer end, away from the nose (Figures 8-G, 65-E-N). The division between E and F is usually blended into a soft edge (65-H), though it may upon rare occasions be fairly hard (65-E-F). A strong shadow in E tends to give the eyes a rather piercing, evil quality (Figures 65-H, 156, 163, 164). It would always be appropriate for Richard

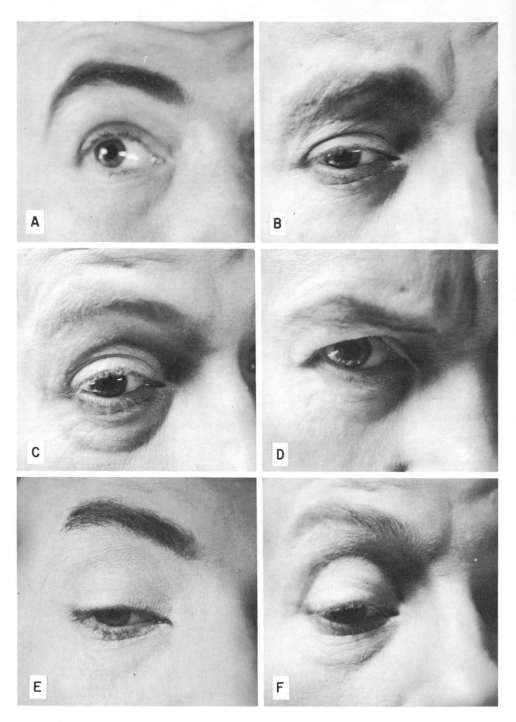

FIGURE 67. **Character through eye makeup.** All six eyes belong to the actor in Figure 7. Changes were made with cake makeup—RO9g and R12 for shadows, P13g for accents, and O1 for highlights. The natural eyebrow was used in all cases. In E the outer end of the brow was blocked out with spirit gum.

III and probably for Macbeth but not for Jacques or Duncan, for example.

Since this shadow tends to strengthen the eye, it should usually not be too pronounced in old age (Figures 8-G, 65-L-O, 198-G-H). Rouging E helps weaken the eyes and age them.

Plane F may be shadowed in its entirety, though never very heavily (Figure 65-H), or the shadow may be begun at the inner corner, then blended out along the lower edge, never being allowed to reach the outer corner (Figures 65-J, 67-B-D, 213).

EYE POUCHES

The third possibility for Plane F is that of a pouch (Figures 8-E-G-K, 65-F-G-K-L-N-O, 67-C, 68, 101, 151, 198-C-E-F-G, 199-B-F, 200-H-L-K-O), in which case F_1 is highlighted and F_2 is shadowed. The entire lower edge of F_2 must be hard, with a rather heavy shadow which blends up across F_2 and turns into a strong highlight at the bottom edge of F_1. In other words, the division between F_1 and F_2 must always be a soft edge. The strong highlight decreases somewhat as it approaches the E-F division.

One of the secrets of making a convincing pouch is to keep the shadow heaviest at the bottom, where the fold of skin naturally falls and to let it become very thin and almost fade out as it rises to the corner of the eye (Figure 68-D). The fact that these subtle variations must be made in an extremely small area makes pouches somewhat challenging, and they should be attempted only after careful practice. Always use both a shadow color and an accent (see Chapter 7). And make sure the pouches look rounded at the bottom where the sagging skin turns under. A flatly painted shadow will look exactly like paint, not like a pouch.

The following is the step-by-step technique for modeling a pouch with paint, as illustrated in Figure 68:

1. With your shadow color, lightly outline the pouch, then pull the shadow upward to give it thickness along the bottom (A). If you have the beginnings of a natural pouch of your own, it will be easy to determine the correct size and shape. If you do not, then you will have to decide on the basis of what seems to fit in best with your eye and what will be easiest to model convincingly. Be very precise about the outside edge, keeping it sharp and clean. Use whichever brush seems to work best for you. The whole pouch can be done with a flat $\frac{3}{16}$-inch brush; however, you may prefer a narrower one and you will probably find a pointed Chinese brush very useful as well.

2. With your accent color and your pointed brush, if you have one,

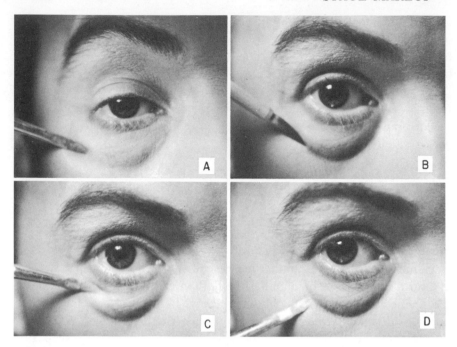

FIGURE 68. Modeling a pouch with shadows and highlights. RO9g cake shadow is applied with a ³⁄₁₆-inch flat brush (A), deepened and accented with a Chinese brush, using P13g cake (B), then highlighted above (C) and below (D) with O1 cake. For a very slight sagging effect, A alone would be sufficient.

deepen just the bottom edge of the pouch, then pull the paint upward to soften the upper edge (B).

3. Highlight the inside of the pouch (C), being very careful not to mix the highlight with the shadow and to make both edges of the highlight soft in order to give a gradual transition—as if you were modeling a tiny, slightly bent cylinder.

4. Very carefully highlight the outside edge of the pouch (D), keeping the edge of the highlight next to the pouch very sharp and clean and softening the lower edge so that it disappears into the base color.

This is the procedure for a strong, well-defined pouch. It can be modified according to how thick and heavy you want the pouch and how well-defined it is to be. A pouch which is just beginning to form will obviously be less dark and less sharp. The best procedure is to check pouches in your morgue or in Appendix F and then adapt one of them to your own eye. Any eye can be given some kind of pouch, but not every kind of pouch is suitable for every eye. Try always to make the kind of pouch the actor is likely one day to develop naturally.

Also, the procedure suggested is for the simplest kind of pouch. You may wish, for example, to break the pouch with wrinkles or to make a sort of double pouch, both shown in Figure 67-C. A variety of possibilities can be seen in Appendix F. But perhaps most important of all, remember that all people do not develop pouches with age. Check the various illustrations in this book and in your own morgue for aged eyes without pouches.

Plane F is the area of dissipation. Be careful not to shadow it too heavily unless you are attempting to show the ravages of a dissipated life or lack of sleep or illness (Figure 65-H). The cooler colors are best for this purpose. Pouches, however, can be used with less danger on that score.

The whole F plane is sometimes rather wrinkled (Figures 67-C, 209), and very often diagonal wrinkles cut across the lower edge of F_2 on the side away from the nose (Figures 47-E, 65-K-N-P, 197-A-G, 198-C-G-I, 199-B-E-F). These, as well as the ones above in Plane C_2, are commonly called crow's-feet. See Figure 184 for some very skillfully painted ones.

After you have the orbital planes clarified in your mind, remember that the secret of shading them effectively lies in a constant variation in intensity of shadow and highlight and in some variation in color. Not one of these areas should ever be flatly shadowed or flatly highlighted. You should start your shading at the point of maximum intensity, then decrease it gradually in other parts of the area. As suggested in Chapter 7, the use of at least two colors in the shadow is usually the most effective means for achieving a three-dimensional effect.

Oriental eyes. Since Oriental eyes require very special treatment, it will be more practical to consider them apart from the Caucasian eye. An examination of photographs of Oriental eyes will show that they are slanted much less often than Caucasians are led to believe. Therefore, the exaggerated and artificial slanted eye lining which is not infrequently used for Oriental makeups should be avoided.

In the Oriental eye the lid itself ordinarily disappears completely under a fold of flesh which is really an extension of planes A, B, and C, Figure 66, downward to the actual eye opening. This fold overlaps the lower lid slightly at both the tear duct and the outer corner of the eye (Figures 196-C-G-K-Q, 197-D).

One of the most striking characteristics of the Oriental eye is the flatness of the orbital area. Since the eye itself is prominent and the bridge of the nose is not built up, the dip between the two (plane A) is likely to be very slight. It is here particularly that the makeup must counteract the normal conformation of the Caucasian eye.

If the Oriental eye is to be achieved with paint alone, it is necessary to highlight the entire orbital area quite strongly, especially plane A, in

order to bring the eye forward and counteract the natural shadows. Sometimes there is a slightly puffy effect in plane E (Figures 196-G-H, 197-C). If
you wish to create this effect, you can model it as a pouch or a transverse
wrinkle with the usual shadow and highlight.

In addition to the highlighting, two small shadows are necessary.
These can be seen in Figure 65-M. One is a crescent-shaped shadow at the
tear duct which gives the illusion of what is called the epicanthic fold—
an extension of the upper eyelid which slightly covers the lower one. This
shadow must be precisely placed, as shown in Figures 65-M and 67-E. The
second shadow is placed on the outer third of the upper lid (Figure 65-M)
and does not extend beyond the eye. It can be somewhat heavier than the
usual eye accent used in corrective makeup.

The eyebrows may be slightly slanted or rather short and straight (Figures 65-M, 67-E, 196-C-G-H-K). They should not follow the eye downward in a graceful curve as is customary for youthful brows in Caucasians.
They taper off quite abruptly at the ends. The acutely slanted brow for
Orientals is a stage convention which should be avoided in realistic makeups. It is on a par with yellow greasepaint. Figure 8-D shows some rather
unusual eyebrows for an elderly Oriental.

In aging the Oriental eye, pouches are very effective, and sometimes,
especially in old age, there can be a deep crease around Plane D, as shown
in Figure 8-D.

For many eyes this painting technique is effective. However, for eyes
which do not adapt easily, three-dimensional makeup (Chapter 13) may
be required.

EYEBROWS

We have already discussed in the chapter on corrective makeup the
problem of beautifying the brows. But besides being an adornment, they
offer a great opportunity for characterization. Too frequently they are left
in their natural state or merely whitened a little to suggest age. As a result,
the whole makeup is rendered completely unconvincing. The eyebrows in
Figures 33, 47-E, 48, 49, 77, 155, and 156 show some of the variety possible
in adapting the actor's natural eyebrows (Figure 7) to specific characters.

But unless your eyebrows or those of your subject are unusually
adaptable, you would do well to add hair to them (Figure 184), cover
them completely with additional hair (Figures 157, 158, 166, 167), or block
them out with soap and greasepaint, spirit gum (Figures 140, 151), spirit
gum and gauze (Figure 69), derma wax and sealer, or by other methods

which you may devise. Rubber pieces can also be used (Figures 117, 128), as explained in Chapter 14.

Blocking out with soap. In soaping, rub a moistened bar of soap repeatedly over the brows, which must be free of grease, until they are flattened down. When they are dry, cover them with a heavy coat of base or with alternate layers of base and powder if necessary. If they are heavy, a coat of sealer or flexible collodion can be applied over the dried soap with a brush or with the fingers. Be sure to spread the sealer beyond the soaped area for firm adhesion. Then apply the makeup over the dried sealer. Unless the brows are very light, soaping is probably the least satisfactory method of covering them since the hairs are almost sure to loosen during a performance, allowing the brows to become visible.

Blocking out with spirit gum. A more effective method is to glue down the hairs with spirit gum. The gum should be brushed well into the brows. Then when it is very tacky, the brows can be pressed down with a damp cloth. In pressing them down, try to spread the hairs out so that there will not be a solid lump, and see that the surface is as smooth as possible. When the spirit gum is dry, you may wish to cover it with sealer, but this is not usually necessary. Makeup can be applied over the brow as usual; but if the brow is dark, it may require several coats with powdering between. Cake makeup may or may not cover the gummed brow satisfactorily. If it does not, a little Pan-Stik or greasepaint of the same shade can be used first and powdered. The spirit gum can be removed with alcohol or acetone. Be very careful, however, not to let either one run down into the eyes. The safest procedure is to dampen a towel with the remover, then bend over so that the eyebrow is lower than the eye.

Blocking out with derma wax. If the brows are very heavy, you may wish to mat them down with derma wax, then cover the wax with sealer, collodion, or spirit gum. This also helps to solve the color problem since the hairs will be largely covered with the opaque wax. It is wise to brush on a light coat of spirit gum and let it dry before applying the wax since the wax may tend to bubble and loosen through perspiration or movement of the muscles. After the sealer is dry, makeup can be applied. The sealer should be peeled off with the fingers, the wax can be massaged out with cream, and the spirit gum can be dissolved with acetone or alcohol. Figures 157–158 show makeups for which the eyebrows have been blocked out with derma wax.

Blocking out with gauze. In order to cover the brow more completely, it is possible to paint it first with spirit gum (Figure 69-A), then to lay over the sticky gum a piece of gauze bandage trimmed only slightly larger

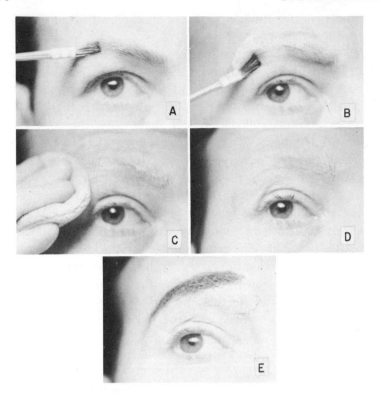

FIGURE 69. Blocking out eyebrows with gauze. (A) Spirit gum applied over brow; (B) shaped gauze attached to brow with more spirit gum; (C) gauze powdered; (D) gauze covered with Pan-Stik or grease, powdered again, then covered with base color; (E) crepe hair eyebrow attached with spirit gum.

than the brow. The gauze can be painted with spirit gum, flexible collodion, or sealer (Figure 69-B). The greatest problem with this method is to avoid surface irregularities. It is possible to do the same thing with cleansing tissues, but the tissues, being very thin, do not really tone down the color much. Organza de soie, which is much tougher and has greater covering ability, can be used in the same way. Then the gauze is powdered (Figure 69-C) and covered with makeup (Figure 69-D).

Figure 65-A shows a normal eye and eyebrow. B, C, and D show the same eye with nothing changed but the eyebrow. You can easily observe the striking change in character. These changes would require complete or partial blocking out of the natural brows. If a part of the natural brow can be used, it need not be blocked out, of course.

Changing the eyebrows. Figures 123–125 show an interesting contrast

in eyebrows on the same face. In 123 the natural brows have been minimized with paint, in 124 they have been covered completely with hair, and
in 125 crepe hair has been added but does not entirely obliterate the
natural brow. In Figures 111–112 the eyebrows (again it is the same face)
have been blocked out and new ones added. In Figure 67 we see six
treatments of the natural brow.

If you are adding new eyebrows with crepe hair, it may often be wise
to attach the new brows before the old ones have been covered with
makeup. Since the makeup must usually be heavy over the old brows,
chances are the spirit gum may not stick very well. But it is a simple matter
to attach them immediately after the old brows have been matted down
(especially if spirit gum is being used in the construction) and to do the
makeup after the new brows are firmly anchored.

Sometimes you may need no eyebrows at all—that gives a remarkable
effect of extreme age (Figure 65-P). Very light brows may sometimes be
penciled in, but ordinarily, unless the character would have penciled-on
eyebrows, they should be constructed of crepe hair, which will be discussed in Chapter 15.

The brows may take a wide variety of forms. They may be very sparse
and irregular (Figures 8-A-D, 198-H) or bushy and overhanging (Figures
8-G-K, 65-L, 197-H, 198-G, 200-H). They may be very thick (Figures
65-K, 118, 197-A-F, 200-L) or moderately thin (Figures 65-F-G-J, 199-E).
But in suggesting age they must never looked plucked, unless that is appropriate for the character (Figure 151), and they are seldom as long as in
youth. Avoid the gentle arch in age, and make the brows more angular
(Figures 65-F, 67-D, 101, 197-G, 198-A). But never hesitate to cover up
your own eyebrows and start afresh. Figure 65 and those in Appendix F
should serve as source material for a number of possible variations in eyebrow treatment.

Eyebrows can be aged quickly, when that is necessary, by running
white stick liner or white Pan-Stick through them against the direction of
hair growth (Figure 47). This can also be done with regular greasepaint,
clown white, or even cake makeup. This should be strictly an emergency
measure, however, since only occasionally will it achieve exactly the right
kind of eyebrow for the character.

AREA 3: NOSE

This area has seven planes (Figure 70). For youthful makeups the
nose is not usually modeled. However, if it tends to flatten out under lights
or if it is to be altered in apparent conformation for either corrective or

character purposes, then certain of the principles of modeling may be applied.

Plane A is the very small depression usually found between the superciliary arch and the nose. In the classic nose it is not present, of course. It is shadowed for age and usually contains one to three vertical wrinkles (Figures 47-E, 63, 67-D-F, 197-G). The two appearing at the inner ends of the eyebrows have their inception down in plane A of the eyesocket (area 2) and become narrower as they continue upward (Figures 65-E-F, 67-F, 197-A-B-F). The center wrinkle is likely to be narrow at both ends and wider in the middle (Figure 197-G). These wrinkles must not stop abruptly but must narrow to a point and disappear. Like all facial wrinkles, they must follow the actor's natural ones. In order to avoid conflict between the real and the painted, wrinkles must never be drawn where they do not naturally occur, unless, of course, the actor is too young to be able to produce natural wrinkles by the usual facial contortions. Each of these

FIGURE 70. Planes of the nose.

wrinkles consists of a shadow with one hard and one soft edge bounded by two highlights—one with one hard and one soft edge, the other with two soft edges. These are the wrinkles of frowning and when made rather deep will lend severity to the facial expression. If this is to be avoided, then the plane may be shadowed and the wrinkles either eliminated or toned down considerably.

Plane B (see also Figure 14-C-1, 2) is the prominent part of the nose and is highlighted both in indicating age and in sharpening and narrowing the nose (Figure 64-B-5, C-5). If the nose is too long, the lower end of the plane may be left the base color or slightly shadowed (Figure 64-G). The width of the highlight will largely determine the apparent width of the nose. (See Figure 64-B-E. Also compare Figures 48 and 49.) If the nose is too sharp and needs to be broadened or flattened, plane B can be left the base color or lightly shadowed (Figure 64-F). If the tip is to be broadened or rounded slightly without the use of prosthesis, it can be done by rounding and broadening the highlight (Figure 64-H). The effect of a broken nose can be achieved with a crooked highlight rather heavily shadowed on each side (Figure 64-J). Conversely, a real broken nose can be straightened by reversing the procedure, as explained in Chapter 10.

Plane C (see also 14-C-5) is nearly always shadowed for age (Figures 35, 45, 49, 64-C-7, 97, 140, 151). The edges between planes B and C must always be soft as well as the outer edges of plane C. If the nose tends to flatten out under light, as it sometimes does in youthful makeups, plane C may be subtly shadowed to give the nose greater depth.

Plane D (see also Figure 14-C-4) may be shadowed with plane C, especially if the nostrils are too wide, but usually a touch of highlight will give the nose more form. To widen the nostrils, highlight plane D (Figures 48, 64, 163, 167).

Plane E (see also Figure 14-C-3) is always shadowed for age (Figure 45), but the fact that it receives only reflected light from the floor and sometimes a little from the footlights means that it is automatically in natural shadow. Carrying the highlight from plane B down into E will help give the nose a droopy effect (Figure 64-C-6).

AREA 4: CHEEKS

This area (Figure 72) is subjected to more mistreatment than nearly any other, especially in age makeups. Treatment of the cheeks involves both coloring and modeling.

In order to suggest age, the rouge should ordinarily be concentrated in plane B and occasionally allowed to spread into plane C. Remember that for most healthy persons, young or old, some rouge is usually necessary. A general roundness of the rouge area is not ordinarily desirable but may be used to help round the face in either youth or age.

In modeling the cheeks for age or to achieve the effect of prominent cheekbones in youth, the cheekbone (Figure 71-A-1) must be highlighted, and the hollow below it must be made to sink in with a shadow (Figures 35, 47, 49, 57, 73).

As you have already discovered in your study of facial anatomy and in your clay modeling, the cheekbone is rounded so that when light is coming from above (as we have to assume it is in makeup for the stage), the upper part of the bone receives strong light, while the lower part, which curves downward and inward, does not receive direct light and therefore appears considerably darker. Although there is no right or wrong method for doing this highlighting and shadowing in makeup, this particular area causes so much trouble that I should like to suggest a specific procedure

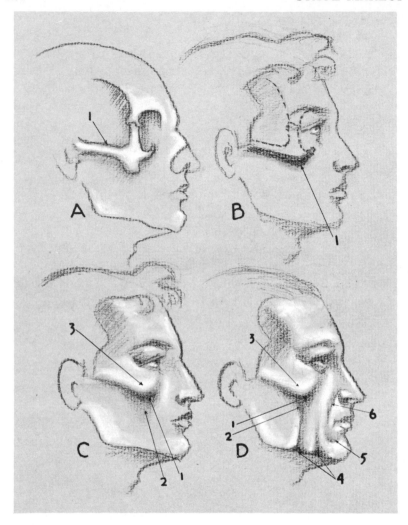

FIGURE 71. Shadowing and highlighting the cheekbone. A shows the form of the bone itself, B the placement of the shadow, and C the blending of the shadow and addition of the highlight. D shows additional shadowing and highlighting for age without changing the profile or the jaw line.

which may help avoid some of the difficulty. Once you have learned what the final effect should be, you may use any method you prefer of achieving it.

1. The first step is to prod the bone (as you have done before in the study of anatomy) to find the lower part of the bone which curves back

in and does not receive direct light. Then with the finger (or a sponge or a brush if you are using cake makeup) lay on the shadow color along the lower half of the cheekbone (Figures 71-B-1, 73-A). This is Plane A₂ in the cheek diagram, Figure 72.

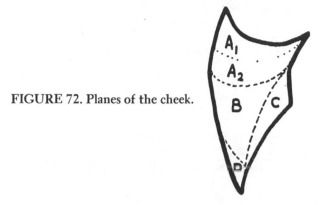

FIGURE 72. Planes of the cheek.

2. With a clean finger, a clean brush, or a clean sponge very carefully soften the upper edge of the shadow, but do not carry it to the top part of the bone (Figure 73-C). Then in the same way blend the lower edge down into the soft hollow of the cheek, letting it become increasingly lighter as it goes down (Figures 71-C-2, 73-B). The shadow is now extending into Plane B of the diagram.

3. With a finger, brush, or sponge lay on a strip of highlight along the top of the bone, making sure that at no point does it touch the shadow (Figure 73-D). With a clean finger, brush, or sponge, blend the upper edge out so that it disappears into the foundation (Figure 73-F), and very carefully soften the lower edge so that there is a gradual transition from the light to the dark (Figures 71-C-3, 73-E). There must not be a definite line between the two. Now you have your completely modeled cheekbone.

How much the cheek sinks in and how prominent the bone is will depend on the intensity of your shadow and your highlight. For youthful makeups this modeling will need to be very subtle. If you are trying to create the effect of puffy cheeks, you will not model the cheekbone except very slightly in some cases for age but usually only at the back part near the ears (Figure 81-C-13). In some cases the shadow may connect with other shadows, as in Figures 8-K and 71-D. If the actor's face is very full, it is not usually wise to try to model the cheekbone to give the effect of sunken cheeks. It is better to accept the roundness of the cheeks and age him on that basis. The method will be discussed later in the chapter.

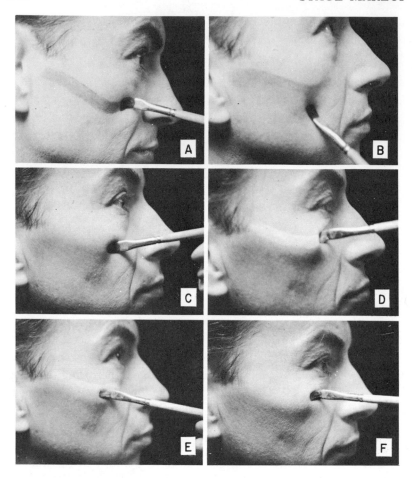

FIGURE 73. Modeling the cheekbone with cake makeup. Steps in emphasizing the cheekbone and sinking in the cheek with shadows and highlights, using a ⅜-inch brush. The makeup could have been applied with a sponge instead of a brush and blended with a sponge or with the fingers—or a combination of all three. For detailed instructions see text.

NASOLABIAL FOLDS

Plane C includes the *nasolabial folds* (Figures 71-D-6, 82-J). These are the wrinkles running from either side of the nose downward to the mouth. These folds are nearly always present to some degree in middle age and old age, though the extent and exact form vary considerably.

The most important thing to understand about them is that each has one hard edge and one soft edge. Wherever there is a crease in the flesh,

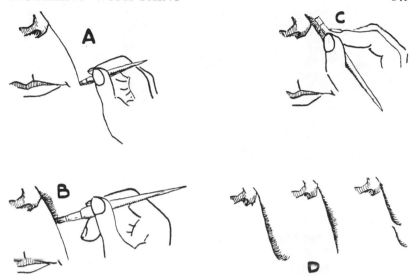

FIGURE 74. Technique of modeling nasolabial folds with a $\frac{3}{16}$-inch flat brush. D indicates common variations in the folds.

as there is in the nasolabial fold, a hard edge is automatically formed. Outward from this crease the shadow lightens and turns gradually into a highlight as the crest of the fold is reached. (Observe the conformation of the folds in Figures 8, 49, 63, 101, 140, 200-H-L-O.) Here is one possible technique of application:

Using a $\frac{3}{16}$-inch flat makeup brush and a basic shadow color, hold the brush at right angles to the face (Figures 74-A, 75-A). With the edge of it, make a thin, dark line, as shown in Figure 76-A. This should coincide with the natural crease in the flesh formed when one smiles or sneers. Secondly, without adding any color, hold the brush as shown in 74-B and 75-B and brush outward from the line, letting the shadow narrow down to nothing at the lower end (Figure 76-B). Thirdly, wipe the brush clean and holding it as in 74-C, brush lightly downward over the outer edge of the shadow in order to blend it more thoroughly (Figure 76-C).

This should make a good fold except that the crease will probably not seem deep enough. So, using the accent color, follow the same technique as indicated in A. Then with the technique shown in B, brush this color out slightly, but do not carry it out the full width of the shadow—merely enough to avoid leaving a line of color in the crease. This should give the fold an effect of much greater depth and third dimension (Figure 75-F). If you prefer, you may put in this accent with a Chinese brush or a makeup

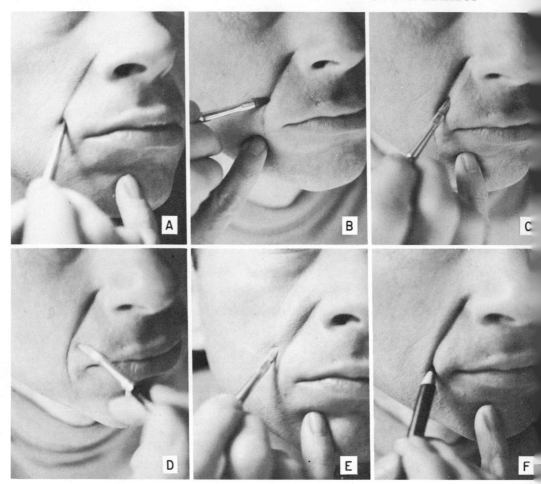

FIGURE 75. Modeling nasolabial folds with cake makeup. Successive steps in painting and blending cake shadows and highlights with a ³⁄₁₆-inch flat brush and accenting with a makeup pencil. Accenting can also be done with a brush and a deep shadow color.

pencil (as in Figure 75-F). Whether you put in the accent before or after the highlight is a matter of choice.

A highlight is necessary to add the final touch. Without it the most carefully drawn wrinkle will look flat and unreal.

The highlight in this case is not a thin line, but a wide stripe starting about halfway between the eye socket and the nostril and following the wrinkle down (Figures 75-E, 76-E). It is also wide at the top and narrow at the bottom. Leave a little space between the outer edge of the shadow

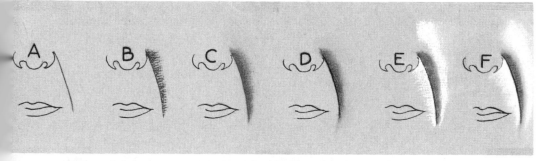

FIGURE 76. **Modeling a nasolabial fold with paint.** Successive steps in painting on, and then blending, the shadow and the highlight.

and the highlight; then blend the highlight carefully on both sides with a clean brush (Figure 76-F). The brush, in making the highlight, should be held as in 74-C and 75-E. Figure 49 shows this highlight clearly.

Another highlight on the inside of the fold will help. Using the 74-A technique, draw a line on the inner edge of the shadow, barely touching the first shadow line. Be careful not to smear the shadow, however. Then, using the B technique, blend out the highlight in the reverse direction from that of the shadow (Figure 76-E, 75-D). It can be carried much farther away from the crease than the shadow and can be blended imperceptibly in the foundation color (Figure 76-F). Figures 63 and 166 show such a highlight after blending.

A little practice with this brush technique should improve nasolabial folds considerably and thus the whole makeup. Figure 74-D shows various forms of the nasolabial fold. Observe people and photographs to see what kind of effect each gives. Pay particular attention to the nasolabial folds in Figures 49, 63, 101, 140, 201.

Further examples will be found in Appendix F.

JAW LINE

Plane D of area 4 (Figure 72) is the mandible or jawbone, which is highlighted for age. One of the best means of indicating age is to emphasize the sagging *depressor anguli oris* muscles which cross the jawbone just beyond the chin (Figure 82-E). These sagging muscles, when they become rather prominent, are often referred to as jowls.

It is not possible to create real jowls (Figure 8) with paint, but the sagging can be suggested, as shown in Figures 78 and 82.

Figure 82-F is the normal youthful jaw line. If you will examine the face to the right closely, you will see that it is exactly the same in outline, including a firm straight jaw line. The sagging effect (Figure 82-H) has been created entirely with lights and shadows. Instead of having the highlighted flesh sag below the jaw line, a triangular shadow cuts up over the jaw line so that highlights on either side will give the effect of flesh sagging around it. The correct placement of this shadow can usually be determined by squeezing the flesh of the jaw between the fingers to see where it creases naturally, or by having the actor pull back his chin and turn his head in various ways until the crease appears. On an extremely youthful, firm jaw it may well be impossible to find the natural location of the muscular sag, in which case you can estimate the correct position from photographs in your morgue. (Note especially Figures 214 and 215.)

A small triangular shadow should first be drawn with a brush, then the edges softened with a clean brush. The center of this triangle (Figure 82-H) should then be darkened with your accent color. Unless the deepest part of this shadow is very dark, it will look flat and painted. It is important, of course, to carry the shadow under the jaw and blend it out so that the audience will not see a sudden end to the shadow at the jaw line.

The sagging flesh can then be simulated with a highlight, as in 82-H. This must have two soft edges, blending gradually into the shadow on the bottom and into the foundation at the top. There will also be a highlight on the other side of the shadow, as shown in Figure 82, and on the masseter muscle, Figure 82-D and I.

It is often extremely helpful in aging the jaw line, especially with youthful actors, to work from within as well as without. A small bit of sponge (either foam rubber or natural silk) can be placed between the lower jaw and the cheek to make the cheek protrude (Figure 77). Absorbent cotton or cleansing tissues can also be used. Naturally, the sponge must be sanitary. A new sponge or a sponge which is reserved for this purpose and for one individual should be used, and whether new or not should be sterilized before use. The exact size and shape to be used can be determined by experimentation, starting with a slightly oversize piece and cutting it down. Once the pieces are cut to the right size, they can be preserved for future use. They should be thoroughly washed and dried after each wearing and kept in a tightly covered box or jar.

Although the sponges will not fill out the jowls in quite the way you want them to, they will, when assisted by painted shadows and highlights, create a more convincing effect than paint alone. But the particular type of effect they create will not be appropriate for every age makeup. You will

FIGURES 77, 78. **Aging the jaw line.** In Figure 77 the aging has been done with sponges in the cheeks and cake shadows and highlights. In Figure 78 the effect of sagging flesh is being created with cake makeup alone, the modeling being done with a ⅜-inch flat sable brush. Model for both is shown in Figure 7.

need to experiment to see whether or not they are suitable. (See Figures 140 and 151.)

Although the actor may object at first to sponges in his mouth, they are usually no great problem. They do not interfere with articulation or projection, though they may change the quality of the voice slightly. This is frequently an aid in making the voice sound older.

For a greater effect of puffiness in the cheeks as well as the jowls (as for the aged Victoria, for example), a large piece of sponge can be used. It would be well to start with an entire small or medium-sized sponge and then cut it down as much as necessary. The larger the sponge, of course, the more uncomfortable it is likely to become and the more difficulty it is likely to cause for the actor. If sponges are to be used at all, they must be used for a number of rehearsals to enable the actor to become accustomed to them. No actor can be expected to go through a dress rehearsal, let alone a performance, with a mouth unexpectedly full of sponges.

With faces which tend to be muscular rather than soft and flabby, there are frequently deep vertical creases cutting up from the jaw line across the cheek. These vary according to the individual, but Figure 71 shows how they can be suggested with paint. The youthful jawline is represented by C; the same straight jaw line is shadowed in D to suggest the sagging flesh and creases. These creases are difficult to suggest convincingly unless there are the beginnings of natural ones which can be followed and deepened. The same little triangular shadow we discussed above is shown by D-4. Study people and photographs so that you will understand exactly how these folds are formed. Modeling them in clay will also help. (See Figures 201-K and 203.)

AREA 5: MOUTH AND CHIN

This area includes seven planes (Figure 79). When there are naso-labial folds, the outer edge of plane A is always hard. The highlight decreases in intensity as it approaches plane B, which is usually shadowed.

The lips can be treated in various ways. In youth they should be shaped with lipstick to suggest character as much as possible. Unfortunately, this is seldom done. Too often an actress will try to beautify her own lips, regardless of the character being played. However, you should

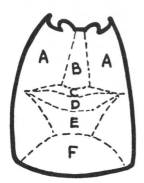

FIGURE 79. Planes of the upper and lower jaws.

have already decided in your analysis what shape your character's lips would be and the color of lipstick to use. If the actor's lips do not conform to those needed for the character, simply cover them with base and reshape them, using the techniques suggested in Chapter 10 (see Figure 54). For men use the lipstick sparingly or not at all and avoid a definite cupid's bow. For women it is often wise to make the lower lip slightly lighter than the upper. This gives the mouth more form and helps prevent its looking like a blob of red paint on the face.

If the lips are to be aged, they can be covered with base and redrawn thinner, or they can be left completely colorless. The latter is often the most effective solution to the mouth problem. Sometimes the upper lip, plane C, is shadowed and the lower lip, plane D, highlighted or left the base color. (See Figures 45, 63, 77, 88, 94, 97, and 178.) As age increases, the two planes narrow (Figure 8-G-K), and in extreme old age both planes are usually cut by vertical wrinkles (Figures 8-G, 201-A-C-E).

If a warm red-brown shadow is used, then lip rouge will not usually be necessary in old age. In middle age a little more color may be used, though both cases, as you know, depend also on other factors in your character analysis. If the character would be wearing lipstick, regardless of age, apply it just as the character would. It's an excellent means of expressing temperament or personality. Remember, however, to make it conform to the character's general lip formation, not the actor's.

Plane E (Figure 79) is always at least partially shadowed for age (Figures 63, 88, 97, 140, 151, 178), and plane F (Figure 79) is highlighted (Figure 82-L), the strongest parts of the shadow and of the highlight being at the division, which is a semihard edge. (See Figures 63, 77, 140, 151.)

In age, the corners of the mouth usually sag (Figures 8, 45, 57, 63, 88,

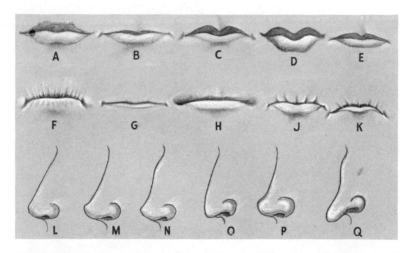

FIGURE 80. **Types of mouths and noses.** The shape of the mouth can be changed with paint; the shape of the nose, with putty or wax. F, G, H, J, and K show types of mouths common in middle and old age.

94, 140, 201-A-E-J-K). A narrow shadow is drawn downward from the corners of the mouth. This usually has two soft edges, but sometimes the lower edge may be creased, resulting in a hard edge (Figure 63). There is a highlight above and to the outside of this which is usually a continuation of the highlight from the nasolabial fold, as in Figures 63, 178, and 201-A-D. There is also a strong highlight below and to the inside. The inside edge of this highlight (toward the center of the mouth) is always soft and must be faded very gradually into the foundation. It is usually a fairly wide highlight (Figures 178, 201-G-J).

The preceding analysis, remember, includes only the face. Other exposed parts of the body must be made up with equal care. Less concentration on superficial details, such as wrinkles, and more on shadowing and highlighting planes of the face will result in makeups which are not only more convincing on close inspection but which will carry to the back of the house. Remember that it's not the painted details which make the Parthenon the most nearly perfect building the world has ever known, but the basic plan. The same principle applies to painting the face to represent the natural chiaroscuro which would result from certain peculiarities of construction.

THE ROUND FACE

Thus far we have been discussing the normal face and the problems of aging to represent a general sagging and sinking in. Sometimes, however, we are faced also with the problem of what to do with a round face and how to make a normal face more round.

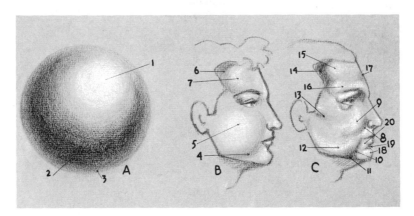

FIGURE 81. The principle of the sphere applied to the face. Drawing of a sphere in charcoal and chalk, then the same principles of drawing applied to the youthful and to the aged face.

In rounding a youthful face (and keeping it youthful) we must use the principle of the sphere, Figure 81. Drawing A shows the shading and highlighting for a sphere, and drawing B in outline is a normal youthful face—the same one shown in Figure 71. But the effect of roundness is achieved by carrying a thin, crescent-shaped shadow in an arc from close to the eye, past the nostrils and mouth, and around to the back of the jaw, as shown in Figure 81-B-4. The highlight, 5, is made in a round pattern in about the center of the cheek. All edges must be very soft, and the shadow must be very subtle. This will not work on a thin face with prominent cheekbones and sunken cheeks. The best you can do in such a case is to reverse the normal shadows and highlights in order to counteract the real ones which are being formed.

As has been mentioned previously, rouging the face in a round pattern (approximately where the highlight, 81-B-5, is located) will be helpful in rounding the face.

Figure 81-C shows how a normal face (again exactly the same face in outline, though the hair has been flattened to age it) can be aged to suggest roundness and puffiness instead of emaciation. Observe the roundness of the forehead shadows and highlights (14, 15), the arc of the nasolabial fold (9), which has become more of a shadow than a wrinkle, and the lower jaw modeling (10, 11, 12), which again follows the shape of the sphere. There is only the suggestion of a shadow under the cheekbone (13).

A round face cannot be made thin, but it can be thinned somewhat by highlighting the cheekbones and shading the whole cheek with a color two or three shades darker than the base. If a round face is to be aged, the principles illustrated in Figure 81-C should usually be used rather than those in 71-D. It may, however, be possible or desirable to use the type of nasolabial fold shown in 82-J, which is the most common one, instead of the type which will increase the roundness of the face. Everything depends on the actor's face and on the effect you are trying to create. Obviously 81-C suggests a happier, jollier character than 82-J. This, in fact, is something which should always be kept in mind. A roundness and an upsweep to the nasolabial fold (as to any shadow or wrinkle) suggests a happier disposition than a long droop, which tends to lengthen and sag the face. Compare Figures 8-A and 8-H.

It is sometimes possible to use sponges or absorbent cotton in the cheeks to fill them out, as suggested earlier under the discussion of modeling jowls for age. The technique is the same (often using an entire small or medium sponge), but the modeling with paint will suggest fullness or roundness rather than age. The modeling will, of course, be the same as without the use of sponges. The sponges will merely help the illusion. This technique is suggested only as a possibility and is not recommended as an ideal solution to every problem of making an actor's face rounded.

NECK

The neck is just as important to the whole makeup as the face and can spoil the effect completely if it is not skillfully made up. We have already mentioned that both front and back of the neck must be covered with base. For juveniles, nothing else is necessary. But for age the neck must be modeled.

There are three prominences in the neck important in makeup—the laryngeal protuberance down the center and the sterno-cleido-mastoid muscles, which extended from each ear in a V-shape down to the sternum at the top and center of the rib cage (Figure 82-A-G). These are sometimes referred to as the "bonnet-string muscles." The depression between each of the muscles and the larynx should be shadowed (Figures 36 and 42) as well as the opposite side of each muscle. Then the muscles and the larynx can be highlighted. This gives a thin, scrawny neck (Figures 82 and 83).

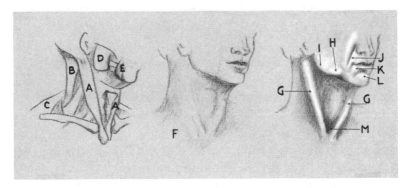

FIGURE 82. Planes and muscles of the neck and jaw shown diagrammatically, then in youth and in age.

It is also possible and extremely effective, particularly for old age, to model the numerous wrinkles which form around the neck and extend diagonally up toward the ears. Figure 184 shows quite clearly how this is done and how it succeeds in breaking up the smooth, youthful neck and jaw line. But it is essential that every wrinkle be carefully modeled with highlights and shadows. To determine the correct placement of the wrinkles, it is usually necessary to twist and turn the head until natural wrinkles are formed. For plumper characters, these transverse wrinkles are always used, but they are wider and fewer in number.

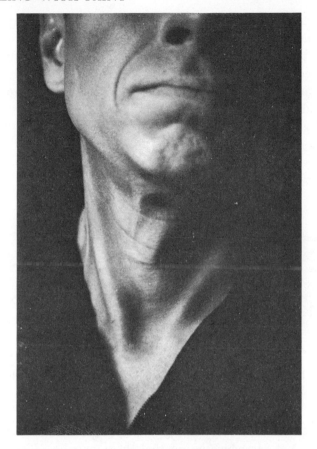

FIGURE 83. Neck aged with cake makeup. Shadows and highlights applied with ¾₆-inch, ⅜-inch, and eye-liner sable brushes. Model in Figure 7.

The neck is often a little darker than the face in age. Darkening the back of the neck is a particularly good technique for dark-skinned individuals, especially outdoor people with leathery skin.

HANDS

In representing youth, the hands need only be given a coat of base color to match the face, but that base coat is very important. If you have ever seen an actor raise a ghostly white hand to a rosy face, the reason will be obvious.

For age a certain amount of modeling is necessary. Usually, unless the character tends to be quite pudgy, the bones in the hands become much more prominent and the veins begin to stand out (Figures 84, 85, and 202). The bones, both in the back of the hand and in the fingers, should be shadowed along either side and highlighted on top. Often the joints may swell and redden. The swelling can be suggested by narrow crescent-shaped shadows around the joints and rounded highlights on top. A little rouge will give the color.

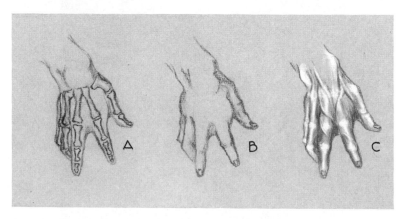

FIGURE 84. Bones of the hand and shadowing and highlighting for age.

Veins can be drawn in with pale blue. They must, however, be three-dimensional, not flat, which means that there must be a highlight on top of every vein and a shadow along the side. They must be treated as elongated cylinders. Their roundness will be particularly pronounced as they cross over bones; at other times they may be no more than a faint bluish shadow under the skin. But they are always irregular, often forking out and meandering across the hand. If the actor's natural veins are visible, they can be followed; and if his veins are prominent, they *should* be followed. Otherwise, it is possible to place the veins wherever they appear to be most effective. Be careful, however, not to use too many. A few veins carefully placed and convincingly painted will be far more effective than a complicated network.

The color of the veins will depend on the type and color of the hand. A pale, delicate, fine-skinned hand will naturally reveal much more blue in the veins than a rough, deeply tanned one, on which the veins may not appear blue at all and can be modeled with the normal shadow and highlight colors.

If the hand is to be delicate and not rough or reddened, it can usually best be aged with paint. If, however, it is to be rough textured, it should usually be stippled or, better yet, given a three-dimensional skin texture, as described in Chapter 13. The hand can also be painted to represent the blotched skin which usually accompanies age. This is especially useful when the hand is to be pudgy rather than bony, though it can be done for both.

Fingernail polish should be removed for aged hands unless the character would be wearing it. Although this seems like an obvious thing to do, very few nonprofessional actresses remember to remove nail polish before going to the theatre. Should that happen, the acetone in the kit will remove it quickly.

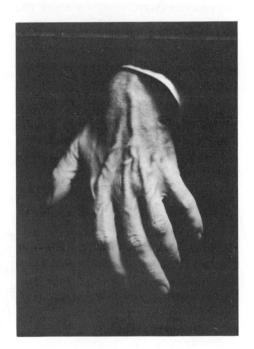

FIGURE 85. Hand aged with cake makeup. Notice how the veins become more prominent as they cross the bones. See Figure 98 for the same hand aged with spirit gum and tissue.

TEETH

A good set of flashing white teeth can ruin an otherwise effective age makeup. They can be darkened with a fairly dark tooth enamel and chipped or even removed entirely with black tooth enamel or black wax (see Appendix A). The treatment of the teeth in age will vary greatly with the character. In some, they will be perfect and in others, slowly rotting away.

If the teeth are not so white as they should be for juvenile characters, they can be whitened with light tooth enamel. Black eyebrow pencil is a possible substitute for black enamel in blocking out teeth. The teeth must be perfectly dry in order to take the pencil, and they may have to be touched up occasionally.

If the teeth are uneven, the lower edges of the longer ones can be blocked out. Or if they are too even, the process can be reversed. Pointed fangs can be made in the same way.

These, then, are suggested techniques for modeling with paint in order to develop character, indicating not only age but the varied effects of environment, temperament, health, and heredity as well. Once these techniques have been mastered, they can be applied to any character of any age in order to create whatever effect you may have in mind.

PROBLEMS

1. Make up yourself or someone else as one of the following pairs of characters. All of the characters are youthful, but the pairs have been selected to show definite contrast which must be indicated in the makeup.

Portia and Juliet; Katherina and Bianca; Olivia and Maria; Barbara and Sarah (*Major Barbara*); Ruth and Eileen (*My Sister Eileen*); Ophelia and Audrey; Sally and Natalia (*I Am a Camera*); Eliza Doolittle (*Pygmalion*, Acts 1 and 5); Gigi (*Gigi*) and Bessie Watty (*The Corn is Green*); Laurie and Ado Annie (*Oklahoma*); Romaine and The Other Woman (*Witness for the Prosecution*); Canina and Colomba (*Volpone*); St. Joan and Billie Dawn (*Born Yesterday*); Rosalie (*Oh Dad, Poor Dad, Mamma's Hung You In the Closet and I'm Feelin' So Sad*) and Ophelia (*Hamlet*); Lili (*Carnival*) and Electra (*Electra*); Joan (*St. Joan*) and Hypatia (*Misalliance*); Nancy Jones (*The Knack*) and Desdemona (*Othello*); Frankie (*The Member of the Wedding*) and Alma (*Summer and Smoke*); Alice (*The Killing of Sister George*) and Carol (*Black Comedy*).

Charles Lomax and Bill Walker (*Major Barbara*); Danny and Hubert (*Night Must Fall*); Antonio and Launcelot Gobbo; Orlando and Touchstone; Romeo and Hamlet; Oswald (*Ghosts*) and Bo Decker (*Bus Stop*); Desmonde and Alfred (*The Happy Time*); Dauphin (*St. Joan*) and Mosca (*Volpone*); Billy Bigelow (*Carousel*) and Leo (*The Little Foxes*); Lt. Cable (*South Pacific*) and Albert (*Ladies in Retirement*); Stanley Kowalski and A Young Collector (*A Streetcar Named Desire*); the two Gareths (*Philadelphia, Here I Come*); Jerry (*The Zoo Story*) and Jonathan (*Oh Dad, Poor Dad*); Albert Amundson (*A Thousand Clowns*) and Colin (*The Knack*); Bentley (*Misalliance*) and Dromio (*Comedy of Errors*); Frank and Tom (*White Lies*); Joey (*The Homecoming*) and Brindsley (*Black Comedy*).

2. Choose at least five character photographs from your morgue and analyze each face according to the plan of areas and planes used in this chapter. Indicate whether each plane would be shadowed or highlighted.

3. Model your own cheekbones with highlights and shadows according to the instructions in the chapter, taking care to follow your own bone structure precisely and to keep the shadow darkest on the under side of the bone. If you are using cake, you may want to stipple with the base color after you have finished. The most common difficulties encountered in making cheek shadows are failing to follow the natural bone structure, placing the shadow too low on the cheek (below the bone, that is, instead of on the under side of it), and making the shadow flat and patch-like instead of varying from dark to light.

4. Following the specific instructions in the chapter, practice doing nasolabial folds until you can do them convincingly. If you have trouble making them three-dimensional, model the folds on your clay head and study the conformation you are trying to suggest with paint. The most common difficulties encountered are failure to follow the natural crease precisely and to keep the crease very sharp, failure to carry the shadow up along the nostril, failure to taper the shadow and highlight at the end, failure to keep the shadow and the highlights separated, giving a blurred, dirty effect, and failure to use a second shadow color as an accent to deepen and sharpen the crease.

5. Choose several different kinds of nasolabial folds from your file of photographs or from Appendix F and produce them with makeup.

6. Choose at least three eyes from Figures 197–200 or from your own morgue and reproduce them with makeup. Block out the natural eyebrows whenever necessary. In modeling pouches, most difficulties arise from failure to round the bottom of the pouch like a cylinder, using strong darks and lights, and from making the upper ends of the pouch too thick.

7. Do Oriental eyes, using as a model a photograph from your morgue or from Figure 197.

8. Repeat Problem 5, using photographs of mouths from Figures 199–201 or from your own morgue.

9. Age your forehead, using only highlights and shadows rather than wrinkles.

10. Add wrinkles to the above, following your natural ones and model-

ing each wrinkle with extreme care, using shadows, accents, and highlights and making sure that each one has a hard edge and a soft one. Forehead wrinkles are extremely difficult to do convincingly and require a great deal of practice. Most difficulties arise from making the shadows too flat so that they look like stripes of paint, from leaving them blunt on the ends instead of tapering them, from failing to keep a sharp edge, from the use of unnatural colors in the shadows, and from reversing shadows and highlights through failure to consider the direction of light.

11. Age your neck and jaw line in two different ways, using photographs in Appendix F or your own morgue and the drawings in this chapter as guides.

12. Age your hands, deciding first what kind of character they are for. Would they be plump or bony, pale or dark, smooth or wrinkled, fine or coarse?

13. Make up yourself or someone else as at least two of the following characters: Pastor Manders (*Ghosts*); Harry Sims (*The Twelve Pound Look*); Doc Gibbs (*Our Town*); Morrell (*Candida*); Tyson, Tappercoom (*The Lady's Not For Burning*); Mr. Collins (*Pride and Prejudice*); Sir Robert Morton (*The Winslow Boy*); Harry Brock (*Born Yesterday*); Oscar, Horace, Ben (*The Little Foxes*); Sir Andrew (*Major Barbara*); Androcles (*Androcles and the Lion*); Papa (*The Happy Time*); Gooper (*Cat on a Hot Tin Roof*); Morgenhall, Fowle (*The Dock Brief*); Cajetan (*Luther*); S. B. O'Donnell, Canon O'Byrne, Con Sweeney (*Philadelphia, Here I Come*); Willy Loman (*Death of a Salesman*); Mr. Bumble (*Oliver*); Doc (*Come Back, Little Sheba*); George (*Who's Afraid of Virginia Woolf*); Harry (*The Collection*); Harold Gorringe (*Black Comedy*).

Alice More (*A Man for All Seasons*); Madame Rosepettle (*Oh Dad, Poor Dad*); Maxine, Hannah, Frau Fahrenkopf (*The Night of the Iguana*); Clytemnestra (*Electra*); Dolly Levi (*The Matchmaker, Dolly*); Lizzy Sweeney (*Philadelphia, Here I Come*); Linda (*Death of a Salesman*); Blanche (*A Streetcar Named Desire*); Lola (*Come Back, Little Sheba*); Martha (*Who's Afraid of Virginia Woolf*); Medea (*Medea*); Miss Holroyd (*Bell, Book, and Candle*); Violet, Nell (*How's the World Treating You?*); George, Mrs. Mercy Croft (*The Killing of Sister George*); Elizabeth Barrett; Lady Capulet, the Nurse; Kate, Mrs. Sims (*The Twelve Pound Look*); Madame Popov (*The Boor*); Penny (*You Can't Take It With You*); Christine (*Mourning Becomes Electra*); Mrs. Bennet, Lady Lucas, Lady Catherine (*Pride and Prejudice*); Birdie, Regina (*The Little Foxes*); Mrs. Eynsford-Hill (*Pygmalion*); Mrs. Craig, Mrs. Harold (*Craig's Wife*); Mrs. Erlynne (*Lady Windemere's Fan*); Lady Bracknell (*The*

Importance of Being Earnest); Vinnie (*Life With Father*); Countess Aurelia, Mme. Constance, Mlle. Gabrielle, Mme. Joséphine (*The Madwoman of Chaillot*); Miss Madrigal (*The Chalk Garden*); Margaret (*The Lady's Not For Burning*); Arkadina (*The Sea Gull*); Mme. St. Pé (*Waltz of the Toreadors*); Lady Macbeth; Queen Gertrude; Sophie (*White Lies*).

14. Choose from your morgue three good photographs of very old people. Analyze all of the factors which make them look old rather than middle-aged. Look at them from a distance, and pick out the most prominent effects of old age.

15. Make up yourself or someone else as at least two of the following characters: Queen Margaret (*Richard III*); Mrs. Hanmer, Miss Hoadley, Mrs. Gross, Mrs. Sampler (*The Silver Whistle*); Lavinia (*The Heiress*); Duchess of Berwick (*Lady Windemere's Fan*); Flora Van Huysen (*The Matchmaker*); Dowager Empress (*Anastasia*); Mrs. St. Maugham (*The Chalk Garden*); Abby, Martha (*Arsenic and Old Lace*); Mrs. Midget (*Outward Bound*); Mrs. Coade (*Dear Brutus*); Mrs. Bramson (*Night Must Fall*); Miss Nellie (*On Borrowed Time*); Victoria Regina (last scene); Ase (*Peer Gynt*); Clara, Gertrude (*Save Me a Place at Forest Lawn*); Grandma (*The American Dream*); She (*The Chinese Prime Minister*); Anfisa (*Three Sisters*); Avdotya Nazarovna (*Ivanov*); Marina (*Uncle Vanya*).

Nonno (*The Night of the Iguana*); Bent (*The Chinese Prime Minister*); Friar Laurence (*Romeo and Juliet*); Lob (*Dear Brutus*); Luka (*The Boor*); Duke Senior (*As You Like It*); Martin Vanderhoff (*You Can't Take It With You*); Old Werle (*The Wild Duck*); Gramps (*On Borrowed Time*); Mr. Witherspoon (*Arsenic and Old Lace*); Mr. Beebe (*The Silver Whistle*); Archbishop of Rheims (*St. Joan*); The Chaplain (*The Lady's Not For Burning*); Corbaccio (*Volpone*).

13

THREE-DIMENSIONAL MAKEUP

In the preceding chapter we discussed a method of doing makeup by means of chiaroscuro with the aid of various hues and values of paint. We did not try actually to change the natural shape of the actor's features but attempted merely to give the impression that such changes had been made. There are times, however, when a painted makeup may not be entirely convincing and a three-dimensional makeup is required. By this is meant the actual building up of the features with some substance which can be molded into any desired shape. Nose putty and derma wax are the two commonly used materials (see Appendix A). Other combinations of materials can also be used and will be described in this chapter.

Three-dimensional makeup presents great opportunity for an active imagination and skilled fingers. The slightest change in the shape of the nose can make a tremendous difference in the appearance of a character. Yet, the average actor is content to assume that the nose of nearly every character he plays will be exactly like his own, thus throwing away one of his most valuable means of characterization through makeup.

NOSE PUTTY

Nose putty is the most generally useful material for direct, three-dimensional constructions. It is used primarily for changing the shape of the nose, but after considerable practice it can often be used effectively on the cheekbones, chin, forehead, and ears—that is, on any bony or cartilaginous structure. It is seldom possible to apply it to parts of the face in which there is much movement of the muscles, for bubbles will appear in the surface of the putty and ruin the effect.

The use of putty should not be restricted to fantastic noses or even very striking ones. There are minor changes which can be made in order to give the actor a nose unlike his own and suitable for the character. Such changes are simple to make (Figures 86, 87). The less putty you need to use, the less difficulty you are likely to have with shaping and blending. Once the technique of building up the nose is mastered, other constructions will seem less difficult.

Building up the nose. The first step in building up the nose should be to make a profile sketch of the shape you want, bearing in mind that no matter what the shape or size of the addition, it must appear to be an integral, living part of the face, not something stuck on. This means that the basic structure of the nose must give the impression of being supported by bone and cartilage and not look like a large wad of discarded chewing gum. It also means that the false nose must be so carefully blended into

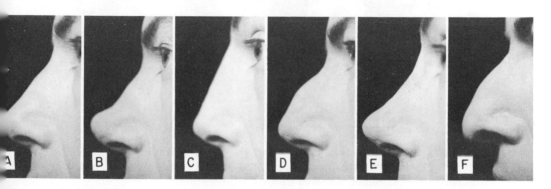

FIGURE 86. Changing the shape of the nose. Five of the noses above (B-F) have been reshaped with small additions of nose putty. A minimum of putty was used, and it was confined to the area being built up. After careful modeling, the putty additions were given simulated skin texture and covered with makeup.

the natural skin that it is impossible to tell where the real leaves off and the false begins.

Once you have a clear plan firmly in mind and know exactly what you intend to do, applying and shaping the nose putty is not a particularly difficult problem—provided you observe a few simple rules:

1. Keep your sketch in front of you and have available two mirrors to give you a profile view of the nose as you work.

2. Make sure the skin is free of all grease and makeup before applying the putty.

3. Cream your fingers *lightly* to keep the putty from sticking to them. Then separate a small piece of putty from the mass and knead it with the fingers until it is very pliable. If the putty should be too stiff and the heat of the hand does not soften it sufficiently, immerse it in hot water for a few minutes or place it near a radiator or some other heat source. Although it is possible to soften putty by the addition of a small amount of cold cream, the method is not recommended. The tendency to add too much cream makes the putty soft and mushy and quite unmanageable.

4. Stick the softened ball of putty on the part of the nose which is to be built up most (Figure 87-A), pressing it into the skin for good adhesion. If it does not seem to be securely attached, paint the nose with spirit gum and let it dry before applying the putty.

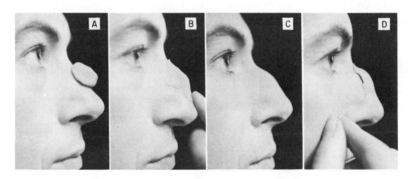

FIGURE 87. **Modeling a putty nose.** Ball of putty is pressed onto the nose, spread with the fingers, smoothed out with cream, covered with makeup, and, finally, removed with a thread.

5. Carefully blend the edges of the putty into the skin, shaping the nose as you work. Always confine the putty to as small an area as possible, being especially careful to keep it off the cheeks and the nasolabial folds. In blending the edges, there is always a tendency to keep pulling the putty outward until it has spread well away from the actual construction. In order to avoid this, it is helpful to model it toward the center of the nose as well as away from the center.

6. When the blending is finished, you can make final adjustments in the shape. Using your sketch as a guide and your mirror to check the nose

from all angles, keep pressing and prodding the putty lightly until you have precisely the shape you want, always keeping in mind the image of flesh and skin over bone and cartilage. Rubbing lightly with a little cold cream will help to eliminate unintentional cracks and bumps and give a completely smooth surface. Remove as much of the cream as possible before applying the base.

When the surface of the putty nose is smooth and the edges perfectly blended, apply the base, covering the false nose with makeup along with the rest of the skin. If the putty is too greasy, press powder into it before applying the base. If you use greasepaint on the nose, do not blend it with water. Be careful not to change the shape of the nose when you spread the paint. When the foundation is completely blended, make sure that the nose is the same shade as the rest of the skin and that it blends into the foundation.

If the putty is considerably lighter than the natural skin, give it a light coat of rouge or light brown shading color before applying the base.

Cream stick or cake makeup can usually be used successfully over putty, though the cake may not always dry the same color on the putty as on the natural skin. In using cake makeup over putty, powder the putty first, then press the sponge onto the putty—do not rub. If it doesn't take well, give the putty a light coat of grease and powder first.

Then complete the makeup in the usual way. For illustrations of the use of nose putty, see Figures 57, 63, and 86. Figure 80 illustrates several types of noses. Many more can be found in Appendix F, especially in Figures 199 and 200.

Removal of putty. After cleaning off the foundation paint with cleansing cream, remove the putty. A simple way is by means of a thread. Starting at either the base of the nose or at the bridge, pull the thread tight with both hands and run it along the nose under the putty (Figure 87-D). The putty which is thus removed can usually be saved for one or two more makeups. The putty remaining on the nose can be removed by massaging with cleansing cream until soft enough to be wiped off with tissues. In order to avoid irritation, this should always be done gently.

Building up the chin. Nose putty can be used fairly successfully on the chin if it is confined to the bony part, but it is difficult to keep the putty from spreading to the softer areas, where it will develop wrinkles and bubbles because of the movement of the muscles underneath. When using putty on the chin, as on all areas other than the nose, it is advisable to cover the area with spirit gum first. Then stick the ball of putty on the tip of the chin and carefully work it outward in all directions until you have the desired shape. Then cover the chin with makeup.

Crepe hair can be applied to such a chin without the aid of spirit gum. Simply press one end of the hair very carefully into the putty and construct the goatee, as described in Chapter 15. It is possible to use spirit gum over the putty for attaching the hair if you prefer.

Building up other areas. Other areas of the face and hands can be built up with nose putty in much the same way. If the area to be covered is very large, however, or if there is no solid bone structure underneath, the use of other constructions (to be described later in the chapter) is more practical.

DERMA WAX

Derma wax (see Appendix A) is softer than nose putty and not so readily adhesive. It can be shaped and blended far more easily but is less stable during a performance. Before using derma wax, always apply a coat of spirit gum to the skin and let it dry. This will help keep perspiration from loosening the wax. When the wax construction is completed, paint it with a sealer (Appendix A). When this is dry, it will form a tough film which will help the wax to maintain its shape and serve as a foundation for the makeup. If the wax is very light in color, it is wise to press a medium dark powder or cake makeup into the surface before applying the sealer. This will make it easier to cover with the makeup foundation.

The wax itself will take cake makeup quite well but when covered with a sealer, it will not. When using a sealer, cover first with greasepaint or cream stick makeup, then powder and apply the cake.

In working with wax, dip the fingers into cold water. Do *not* cream them. This will only soften the wax. Firm wax should be used for building up bony parts of the face. Soft wax is more suitable for blocking out eyebrows (see Chapter 12) and for other techniques discussed on the following pages.

For close work you may wish to blend the edges of the wax into the skin with alcohol and a soft brush. You may also wish to give the wax a semblance of skin texture, which can be done by pressing the finished nose gently with a piece of grapefruit rind, with a latex piece made for this purpose by painting several coats of latex on grapefruit rind and then peeling the dried latex off, or with a firm, fine-textured rubber sponge. If you apply sealer and it smooths out the skin texture, then press again when it's dry.

FIGURE 88. The Queen of Hearts from *Alice in Wonderland*. Based on the Tenniel drawings. Nose built up with firm derma wax and eyebrows blocked out with soft derma wax. Hairlace wig. Cake makeup. Model in Figure 7.

PUTTY-WAX

A half-and-half mixture of nose putty and derma wax eliminates some of the disadvantages of each. They can be mixed manually if the putty is soft enough. It is recommended, however, that the mixture (which will henceforth be referred to simply as putty-wax) be made up a can or a box at a time by melting the two together in a double boiler. It can then be poured into a container, cooled, and used as needed. If you are mixing only a small amount, it's simpler to remove half the contents of a metal box of derma wax, add a piece of nose putty to the remaining half, and place the box in a shallow pan of simmering water. When the wax and the putty are both melted, they can be stirred thoroughly, then cooled.

LATEX

In the next chapter the technique for using liquid latex in casting prosthetic pieces of rubber is discussed. It is also possible to use latex directly. Information about the material itself can be found in Appendix A.

One of the great problems in aging a young face is overcoming the natural smoothness of the skin. Methods of giving the effect of a rougher texture using only cake makeup or greasepaint have already been suggested in Chapter 8. Direct application of latex provides a simple method of creating a three-dimensional skin texture:

First, do a complete age makeup. If you use grease, use as little as possible and set it with translucent powder. If you use cake (a water-soluble paint which tends to mix with latex), you will need to be very careful not to smear the makeup.

Working on one area of the face at a time, pull the skin tight with the fingers and stipple or brush on clear latex (Paramount calls this Vultex). If you are using cake makeup, stippling works better than painting. When each area is dry, dust it with powder, then release. The skin will form a great many fine wrinkles. When the entire face has been covered, the makeup can be touched up with grease or cream stick if necessary. Cake makeup does not take well over latex.

If you prefer, you can use the latex technique directly on the dry skin, then add any makeup which seems necessary. For this method you may wish to use a flesh-colored latex in order to provide a suitable foundation color.

This is a very useful technique for arena theatres or any sort of closeup work. The techniques described on the following pages are likely to prove more satisfactory, however, for large theatres, where greater projection is necessary.

LATEX AND TISSUE

This technique involves the use of liquid latex and cleansing tissue or a good quality of paper toweling (Masslinn towels are considered the best for this work). The toweling will give much deeper wrinkles than the tissues (Figure 89). You can cover the entire face or only a part of it—around the eyes, mouth, or jaw line, for example. This is the technique:

1. Be sure the skin is clean and dry and free of grease. Then paint the area to be covered with liquid latex. A rather dark shade is preferable unless the finished makeup is to be very light.

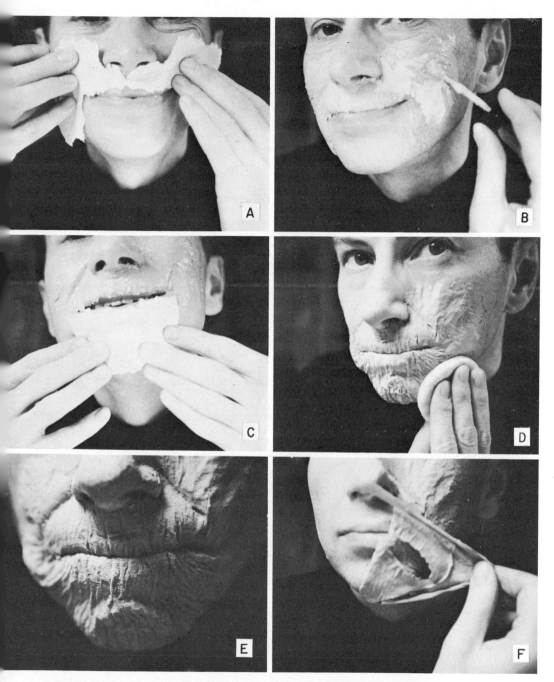

FIGURE 89. Skin texture with latex and paper toweling. (A) Paper towel is torn to shape of mouth with broad smile and is pressed into wet latex. (B) Additional coat of latex is brushed or sponged over toweling. (C) Section of toweling is pressed into wet latex on chin. (D) When dry, latex is powdered. Relaxing the smile forms the wrinkles. (E) Toweling is covered with Pan-Stik base, lightly shadowed and highlighted, then powdered. Nose has been stippled with latex to give the skin a slightly roughened texture. (F) Latex and toweling removed by pulling.

2. Tear (do not cut) a single thickness of tissue or toweling to the approximate size and shape of the area to be covered (Figure 89-A), pull the skin tight with one hand, and with the other apply the tissue to the area covered with wet latex. In the case of the area around the mouth, a broad smile will take the place of pulling the skin with the hand (Figure 89-A-B). For best results work on only a small area at a time.

3. Paint another layer of latex over the tissue or towel (Figure 89-B), and let it dry or force-dry it with a hair drier.

4. Release the skin and powder the latex (Figure 89-D). Natural wrinkles will form.

5. When all of the latex work is finished, cover the whole face with whatever type of makeup you are using. If you have used a dark latex, apply your base (which will probably be lighter) carefully and lightly over the latex-covered tissue or toweling. Normally, there should be sufficient texture to catch the base only on top, leaving the dark latex showing through in the creases or tiny depressions. This will emphasize the texture as well as any wrinkles which may have formed. It is also possible to use a medium base over a light latex.

6. Complete the makeup as usual with shadows and highlights (Figure 89-E). In order to take advantage of the texture, keep the shading very subtle.

The latex can be peeled off quite easily after the performance (Figure 89-F). Be very careful, however, not to get any into the hair, eyebrows, or eyelashes. If the eyebrows are to be covered, block them out first by one of the methods suggested in Chapter 12 so that there are no free hairs. Then they can safely be covered with latex.

If you wish to build up parts of the face in connection with this method, it can be done with either derma wax, putty-wax, or cotton, preferably keeping the addition as small as possible. Great care must be taken that it blends naturally into the skin. In using cotton, modify the basic method as follows:

1. Shape the cotton carefully and apply it to the wet latex on the face. This works particularly well for eye pouches.

2. Immediately apply the single layer of tissue, covering the dry cotton.

3. Apply the second layer of latex over the entire layer of tissue, and complete the makeup as usual.

In using putty-wax, the method is as follows:

1. Apply a coat of liquid adhesive or latex first, wrinkling the face. Let it dry.

2. Add small amounts of the putty-wax for jowls, nasolabial folds, and the like. Be sure you make a good blend.

3. Brush at least two layers of latex over the putty-wax.

4. Use rubber mask grease as your makeup foundation, then model the putty constructions gently with a modeling tool until they are as nearly perfect as you can make them.

5. Stipple the makeup with a coarse brush and powder lightly.

Use as little wax as possible around the mouth. The latex-tissue technique should be used around the neck. Do not try to remove the putty-wax with cream first. Instead, peel off as much of the latex as you can, and wash with soap and water.

It is recommended that in using this technique you begin with small areas and experiment with the effects you can obtain. In using cotton or putty, keep the constructions very small and very simple, especially at first. The more complex you try to make them, the less likely you are to succeed.

Latex should never be used for a performance unless it has first been tried for a full rehearsal. It has a tendency to work loose from the skin, especially if the actor perspires very much or if there is considerable movement of the muscles underneath. If it does, it can usually be pasted down with spirit gum. Also, it may irritate sensitive skin, leaving it reddened for an hour or so after the latex is removed. If there are problems in any of these areas, it would be wise to avoid latex and use another method.

The same technique can be followed using a sealer (see Appendix A) instead of latex. In removing the makeup, you will probably be able to peel off most of it first, then dissolve the rest with acetone.

LATEX, COTTON, AND SPIRIT GUM

An effective method of achieving a leathery, wrinkled, weatherbeaten skin texture is to use latex, cotton, and spirit gum, as illustrated in Figures 90–95. This is the technique:

1. Paint the skin with spirit gum. If you are going to do the whole face, it is best to work a section at a time. The mouth and chin area is a good place to start. The eyes should probably be done last. If you cover the eyebrows, flatten them out first with derma wax so that they will not get stuck in the latex.

2. When the gum is tacky, lay on absorbent cotton (Figure 90) and let the gum dry. Be sure the fibers follow the direction you wish the wrinkles to go—that is, vertically over the mouth, almost vertically down the cheeks, and horizontally on the forehead. Figure 90 shows only the mouth and cheeks with cotton. The rest of the face was done later.

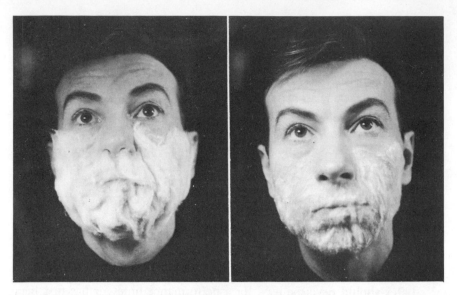

FIGURES 90, 91, 92, 93. Latex, cotton, and spirit gum technique. Cotton is stuck to the skin with spirit gum and the excess pulled off. The remaining cotton is covered with latex and dried with the skin pulled taut. When the skin is

FIGURE 94. Finished makeup showing three-dimensional texture effect. Very little shading and highlighting used. Eyebrows trimmed.

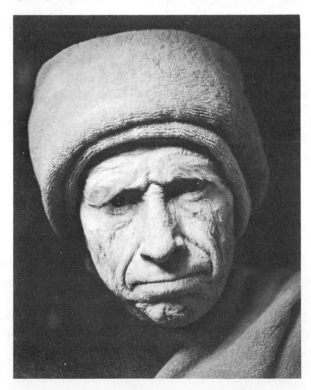

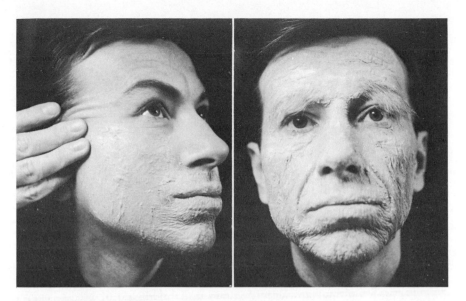

released, the latex falls into a pattern of wrinkles. Figure 93 shows the makeup with untrimmed crepe hair eyebrows but no paint. The nose has been covered with latex and cornmeal for texture.

FIGURE 95. Latex makeup being pulled off. Because of the undercoat of spirit gum, the latex does not pull off so easily as usual.

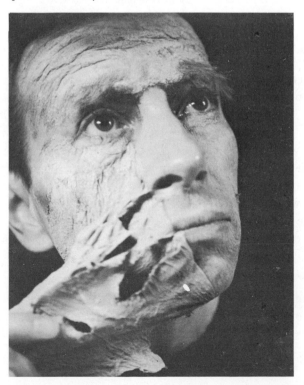

3. Pull off most of the cotton (Figure 91). The less you leave on, the more subtle the effect will be.

4. Cover the cotton with latex, using your finger or a brush. This should be done with the skin stretched as tight as possible (Figure 92). Only one section of the face should be done at a time. The mouth can be stretched simply with a broad smile, which must be held till the latex is dry. The skin of the cheeks must be pulled taut with the fingers. A hair drier should be used to speed the drying. When the latex is dry and the skin relaxed, it will fall naturally into wrinkles (Figure 93).

5. If the eyebrows are covered, crepe hair brows can be attached with latex, as they have been in Figure 93. The nose in this makeup has been covered with latex and cornmeal (see below).

6. Give the entire face a base coat of rubber mask grease or grease-paint of the appropriate shade, and powder with neutral face powder.

7. Finish the makeup with shadows and highlights of grease, cream stick makeup, or cake (Figure 94).

8. Most of the makeup can be peeled off (Figure 95), but because of the undercoat of spirit gum, it will peel less easily than latex usually does. The remainder of the gum will have to be cleaned from the skin with alcohol or acetone. In both pulling the latex off and using acetone, be very careful around the eyes and eyebrows. In order to avoid pulling hairs out of the brows, pull very slowly and brush in a little alcohol or acetone as you go.

LATEX AND CORNMEAL

In order to give the skin a rough texture, with or without wrinkling, cornmeal (or very fine bread crumbs, if you prefer) can be used with the latex. It is possible either to mix the cornmeal with the latex before applying it (Figure 96) or to apply cornmeal to a wet coating of latex, then cover with another layer of latex, as was done for the nose in Figure 94. You then make up with rubber mask grease or greasepaint in the usual way.

If you wish also to wrinkle the skin, simply apply the latex and corn-meal to the stretched skin and do not release the skin until the latex is completely dry. A hair drier should be used for drying in this case.

SYRUP AND TISSUE

For quick changes in which an age makeup is needed for the first scene and must be quickly removed for a subsequent scene, Karo syrup (either dark or light) provides a good adhesive which can be removed

FIGURE 96. Latex and corn-meal. The two are mixed together before being applied, the proportions depending on the roughness of texture wanted. Useful for representing rough stone, mummified flesh, skin diseases, or miscellaneous monster effects.

quickly and easily with soap and water. The procedure, much the same as for latex and tissue, is illustrated in Figure 97.

1. Using a stiff-bristled brush (a glue or paste brush will do nicely), apply the syrup to a section of the skin (Figure 97-A).

2. Lay on a single thickness of peach-colored tissue (or orchid for frail old ladies), torn to the approximate size and shape of the area you are starting with (Figure 97-B).

3. Follow the same procedure until you have covered as much of the skin as you wish (Figure 97-C). Eyebrows can be covered or not, as you choose. If you are covering most of the face, you should usually cover the neck also, particularly on a young actor.

4. You may wish to cover all the tissue with more syrup. If you do, then let it dry or force-dry it with an electric drier and press powder into it to eliminate any stickiness.

5. Cover both the tissue and all exposed skin with cream-stick makeup or greasepaint (Figure 97-D). If, however, the peach-colored tissue blends with the skin tone and gives a suitable color, then you may be able to get along without any base—a great convenience for quick changes. It is also possible to use the syrup and colored tissue over a cake makeup. This is often done when the tissue is to be used on only part of the face (under the eyes, for example) or when there is a quick change involved.

6. With brush and fingers, add grease or cream-stick shadows and highlights (Figure 97-E). This step may or may not be necessary, depending on the amount of projection required. For arena theater particularly, the tissue alone, with or without base, may be quite sufficient. For greater projection without using shadows and highlights, simply make deeper wrinkles in the tissue.

7. Powder the makeup with neutral powder and touch up if necessary (Figure 97-F).

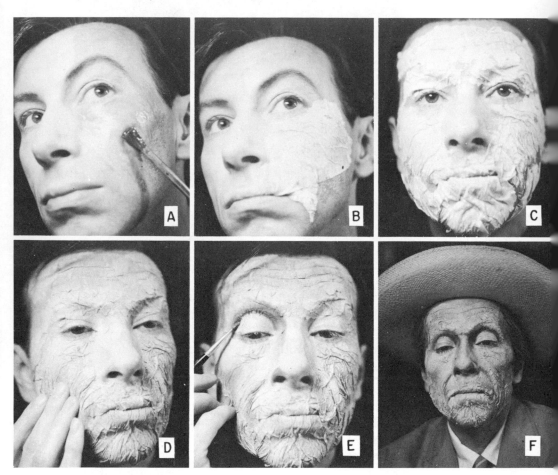

FIGURE 97. Skin texture with tissue and syrup. (A) Karo syrup is applied to the skin with a stiff-bristled brush, a section at a time; (B) a single thickness of tissue is stuck to the syrup and wrinkled; (C) most of the face is covered with tissue, including the eyebrows; (D) Pan-Stik is applied with the fingers; (E) shadows and highlights are added with brush and fingers; (F) makeup is powdered and wig added.

Although the makeup is fairly stable for short periods, it will be loosened by excessive perspiration, which will dissolve the syrup. Other things being equal, the less active the muscles under the makeup, the longer it will adhere to the skin. It can be used on the hands as well as on the face and neck.

SPIRIT GUM AND TISSUE

We have already discussed one method of achieving wrinkled skin texture with latex and tissue. Essentially the same method can be used with spirit gum and either facial or bathroom tissue. This is particularly successful in aging the hands (Figure 98). The method is as follows:

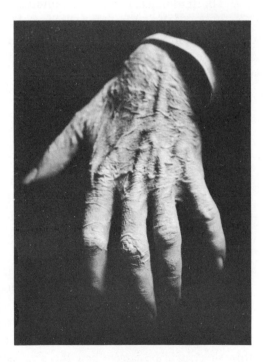

FIGURE 98. Hand aged with spirit gum and tissue. See Figure 85 for the same hand aged with paint.

1. Double the hand into a tight fist, and paint with spirit gum.

2. Place the tissue on the spirit gum, which should be fairly wet, and push it into wrinkles.

3. Let the spirit gum dry or force-dry it.

4. Open the hand and apply the foundation paint.

5. The hand should be stippled with a sponge to represent the mottled

effect common to old age. This can be done by applying a base first, then stippling on another color, by stippling on two colors with no initial application of base, or stippling on one color and letting some of the natural color show through.

6. Additional shadowing and highlighting of bones and veins can be done with a brush before powdering or with cake makeup and blue, gray, and white pencils after powdering.

The textured makeup should be carried up under the sleeve of the costume. The fingers can be done individually after the basic coat of spirit gum has dried and the fist is opened out.

COTTON AND COLLODION

The traditional method of building up large areas on the face is by means of cotton and flexible collodion. This is not a very satisfactory technique at best and should be replaced whenever possible by rubber prosthesis (see Chapter 14) or one of the other methods described in this chapter. For those who may need to use it at some time, however, here is the technique:

1. Coat with spirit gum the entire area to be covered by the construction. Before attaching any cotton, allow the gum to dry slightly.

2. Then stick a tuft of cotton, which, when crushed, will almost equal the thickness of the construction, on the area at the point of maximum thickness. If there is to be more than one thick place, of course, several tufts of cotton will need to be used. All edges of the tuft should be frayed so that they will blend fairly smoothly into the foundation. If you are planning to remove the construction after the performance and use it again, soak this bottom layer of cotton with spirit gum or collodion; otherwise, leave it dry.

If there are to be two identical constructions, do them as nearly simultaneously as possible. That is, build up both as you go along rather than completing one and then starting on the other.

3. Cut or tear off a piece of cotton which, when opened into a fairly thin sheet, will be larger than the area covered by the tuft now on the face. Carefully mold this into the shape required—usually roughly circular. The piece should be of fairly even thickness throughout. Then dampen the cotton—preferably all but the extreme edges. The water should be squeezed into the cotton so that it becomes a thin, tenuous sheet. Then pull all edges of the cotton sheet lightly so that any excess dry cotton is

removed, leaving a thin fringe on all sides. This fringe is very important in blending the construction into the foundation. After you have prepared this sheet of cotton, place it on a warm light bulb to dry while preparing a similar one for the twin construction.

4. When the cotton has dried somewhat, place it on the face so that it overlaps on all sides the tuft of cotton already there. Unless the spirit gum is too dry, the cotton will probably stick very readily.

5. If this makes a large enough construction, brush over the whole sheet very lightly with spirit gum. The gum should be brushed on from the center out, always following the line of the imaginary radii of the circle. Special care should be taken to blend the edges very smoothly so that no join will be visible. Also, be especially careful not to roughen the surface of the cotton.

6. When the spirit gum is nearly dry, the process can be repeated, this time with flexible collodion (diluted to nearly half with alcohol or acetone) or with a plastic sealer (see Appendix A). If no sealer or collodion is available, brush cold water over the construction while the gum is still wet. This will help to form a hard shell-like surface.

In case this first sheet of cotton should not build up the face as much as desired, continue adding dampened cotton prepared in the same manner. Be sure, however, that each new piece completely overlaps the preceding one. The under pieces may or may not be soaked with spirit gum, as you prefer. Usually gum and sealer are used only on the top layer. Derma wax can be used over the cotton construction to give it smoothness. If this is done, another layer of sealer should be painted over it.

Painting the cotton construction. After the sealer or collodion is completely dry, paint the construction carefully and lightly with a very dark shade of base in order to counteract the effect of the white cotton. This can be done with a brush or with the fingers. Then apply the base coat to be used for the character to the skin and to all constructions. In doing this, always be very careful of the cotton applications. Complete the makeup in the usual way.

Types of cotton constructions. The best criterion of what can be done with cotton and collodion is your own ingenuity. If you are both skillful and imaginative, the range of possibilities is wide. Cheekbones, chin, forehead, cheeks, and lips can all be enlarged or remodeled. Jowls and double chins can sometimes be constructed. Such makeups are seldom effective, however, except in large theaters, where the audience is at some distance from the actor, or for certain nonrealistic makeups.

SPECIAL CONSTRUCTIONS

The following reference list presents a few special constructions which you may have occasion to use. Many of these can be done more effectively with rubber makeup, as described in the next chapter. Direct methods however, are quicker.

Blindness. The actor can usually suggest blindness by keeping the eyes nearly closed or by a constant stare, especially if both eyes are to be blind. Blindness in one eye is considerably more difficult. A blind eye can be constructed from filmed silk. An oval piece, with three or four protruding tabs, can be cut from the silk and painted to represent a staring eye, a missing one, a badly disfigured one, or a partly closed eyelid. The piece should be large enough to cover the eye opening and the upper and lower lids. It should overlap the corners of the eye opening slightly. It can be attached by sticking the tabs down with spirit gum. A little cotton can be used to pad it if desired. A rubber piece (see Chapter 14) provides an even simpler solution.

A strip of fishskin can also be placed vertically over the opening to cover the iris and the pupil. It should be attached just below the lower lid and above the upper one.

The thin, translucent skin of an egg can be used under the lid to cover the eyeball itself.

Burns. Minor burns can be simulated by stippling the skin with red greasepaint or shading color applied with a red rubber sponge. For deeper burns, coat the skin with latex, which can be pulled loose and allowed to hang if you want that effect. A single layer of cleansing tissue placed over the latex and then covered with another layer of latex will give more body to the hanging skin for stage work. Cotton can be used with the latex for burnt flesh. Makeup can be applied over the latex. For close work you might wish to drop candle wax on the latex to give the effect of blisters.

Cuts. See *Welts and warts.*

Ears. It is sometimes necessary to make pointed ears for sprites, leprechauns, devils, and the like. Rubber constructions are ideal but somewhat difficult to make. Here is a simple, direct method which is satisfactory for distance work:

1. Cut a paper pattern the exact size and shape of the tip to be added.

2. Cut a small square of muslin and trace the ear pattern onto it. Cut out around this about ¼ inch beyond the edge on all sides. You will need four of these pieces.

3. Stitch two of the pieces of muslin together on the penciled line, leaving the bottom open.

4. Turn this double piece inside out, insert a bent pipe cleaner, and shape it to the pointed tip, cutting it off a fraction of an inch above the bottom of the ear construction. Two pipe cleaners can be used for a thicker piece.

5. Stitch along the inner side of the pipe cleaner to hold it in place. Then trim the bottom of the piece to fit the real ear.

6. Attach the muslin or gauze to the ear with spirit gum. Be sure to let the gum become tacky before trying to attach the piece. Both front and back of the upper curve of the ear should be painted with gum so that the two layers of muslin can encase the ear.

7. When the gum is thoroughly dry, cover the pieces with greasepaint along with the rest of the ear. Touching the tip and the lobe with rouge will give a more lifelike quality. The tip can be removed with acetone and used a number of times.

A very small tip can be built up with putty. But the putty must be covered with sealer so as not to get stuck in the hair. Since in hot weather on a hot stage it may not hold its shape, and since it must be made up fresh for every performance, it is much less satisfactory than a rubber piece or a construction of the type suggested above.

Oriental eye. If the eye is sufficiently deepset to make it difficult or impossible to create the effect of an Oriental eye with paint and if a rubber eyelid (Chapter 14) is not practicable, a satisfactory effect can usually be achieved with adhesive tape. This is one method:

1. Tear or cut slightly over 2 inches of tape from a roll 1-inch wide. This is represented by the broken line (A) in Figure 99.

2. Mark and cut as shown by the heavy lines (99-B). This forms the eye opening and rounds off the upper edges so that the tape will be easier to conceal.

3. Cover the area indicated by 99-C with greasepaint on the *back* of the tape. This gives a nonsticky area over the actor's own eyelid.

4. Attach the tape (usually slightly on the diagonal) so that the top falls just below the natural brow and covers the downward sweep of the outer end (Figure 100-A). In order to prevent the eyebrow's appearing to be cut off too abruptly, lift a few hairs from under the tape and let them fall on the outside. Stipple the edges of the tape with latex cream adhesive (Duo or Flexol) to help conceal them.

5. When the adhesive is dry, cover the tape and the skin with base (Figure 100-B), and finish the makeup. If you are using a cake foundation,

cover the tape and a little of the skin around it with grease or Pan-Stik
first; powder; then apply the cake makeup. In order to counteract the
flatness of the tape, shadow the lower edge and highlight the center to give
a puffy effect (Figure 100-C).

The cutting of the tape can be greatly simplified by cutting 4 inches
instead of 2, folding it double, sticky sides together, marking and cutting
either side, then separating the two pieces. This will insure both eyes' being exactly alike. If you place a piece of waxed paper between the two
sticky sides, you will have no trouble getting them apart. Be sure the tape
is not uncomfortable, that it does not interfere with the normal action
of the eyelid, and that the actor can see without difficulty.

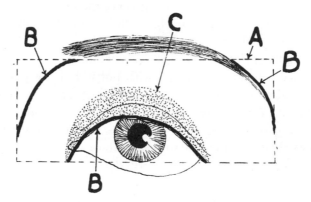

FIGURE 99. Diagram of Oriental eyelid made with
adhesive tape.

A simpler tape construction can be used with equal effectiveness on
certain eyes. This consists of a crescent-shaped piece of adhesive tape,
the outer edge of which is attached to the side of the nose and under the
inner end of the eyebrow. The inner edge of the crescent (which should
be very nearly a half moon) hangs free. The purpose of the piece is only
to conceal the deep depressions (plane A, Figure 66) which are normal
to the Caucasian eye. Plane A in the drawing represents almost exactly
the shape and position of the tape.

Fingernails. Long fingernails can be cut out of used photographic film
and glued onto the natural nails with spirit gum or liquid adhesive. They
can be colored with nail polish or paint. The false fingernails available at
cosmetic counters, if they are long enough, provide a much simpler solution to the problem, however.

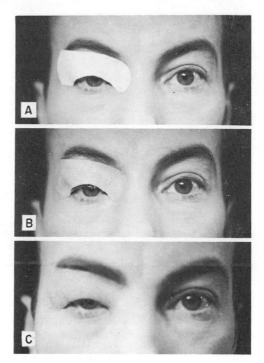

FIGURE 100. Oriental eyelid made with adhesive tape. Tape is cut to fit the eye and stuck on, the edges are stippled with latex and the tape darkened with grease or Pan-Stik, and finally the makeup is completed with eyebrow pencil and cake base, shadows, and highlights. Notice particularly how the flat tape is slightly rounded with shadowing.

Scars. Although scars can be suggested effectively with paint, they can be made more realistic by the use of three-dimensional makeup. One method is relatively simple. The area to be scarred can be painted with nonflexible collodion before any greasepaint is applied. As the collodion dries, it will wrinkle and draw the skin. If the scar thus formed is not deep enough, successive coats can be applied. Every coat should be allowed to dry completely before another is added. The makeup is then applied as usual. The scar may be accented with red, purple, brown, pink, ivory, white, or other colors. Avoid using collodion close to the eye. The scars can be peeled off or removed with acetone. If collodion irritates the skin, this method should not be used. Latex scars, which can be pasted on with spirit gum, are also effective (see Chapter 14).

Interesting scar effects can be achieved by using cleansing tissue or absorbent cotton with latex. The latex (or spirit gum, if you prefer) is applied first, then a very thin piece of cotton or tissue, then more latex. The area can be roughened as much as you like by pulling up bits of cotton. Makeup is applied as usual. Coloring should be fairly subtle in order not to lose the three-dimensional effect.

Another method is to pour or brush latex onto glass and with a

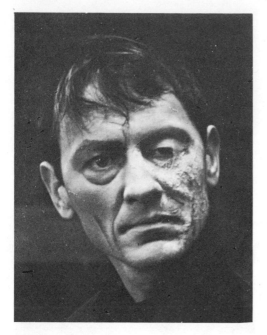

FIGURE 101. Scar tissue. Make-up by University of North Carolina graduate student Bill Smith. Left eye is partially covered with adhesive tape and the left side of the face with layers of latex. Base, shadows, and highlights done with cake makeup. For pictures of Mr. Smith in other makeups, see Figures 151–153.

palette knife or an orangewood stick swirl it and shape it into the size and kind of scar you want. Then allow it to dry or force-dry it, peel it off the glass, and apply it to the skin with spirit gum. Then make up in the usual way, coloring the scar appropriately. This is a variation of the molded latex scars or welts described in Chapter 14. It is an excellent technique where closeups are involved and is perhaps more useful for arena staging than for the normal theater situation, in which the audience is at a considerable distance. For greater projection, combine the latex with cotton or tissue as suggested above (see Figure 102).

Teeth. The method of blocking out teeth is described in Chapter 12. Enlarged or protruding teeth can be constructed from pink dental wax and ivory inlay wax (both obtainable from dental supply houses). The pink wax comes in sheets. It can be softened over heat and pressed around the teeth and the excess carved off. Then the false teeth can be molded out of ivory inlay wax, which can also be softened by heating. After the tooth is molded, it can be heated slightly and stuck to the pink wax. The pink and the ivory colors are excellent for gums and teeth, and no further coloring is necessary. Before putting in the set of false teeth, you can sprinkle a little adhesive powder for false teeth on the inside of the wax construction. (See Figures 103 and 165.)

Welts and warts. Welts are, so to speak, scars in reverse. They can be

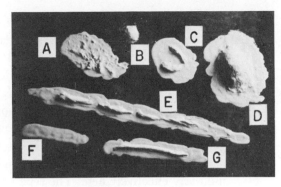

FIGURE 102. Scars, welts, warts, and wens. These are made on glass with latex and tissue (C, E), cotton (A, B, D), and string (G). These are three-dimensional enough to carry for some distance. For close work they would have to be more subtle.

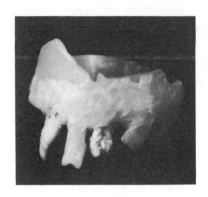

FIGURE 103. False teeth. Constructed of pink dental wax and ivory inlay wax. One tooth is real. Made by Bert Roth, ABC-TV. (See also Figure 165.)

FIGURE 104. Scar and fresh wound. The latex scar is cut from the piece shown in Figure 102–E, and the wound is made with derma wax cut with a palette knife.

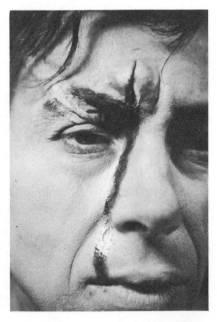

constructed of nose putty or wax and appropriately painted. If a cut is desired, the welt should be constructed in the usual way, then cut with a
palette knife (Figure 104). The inside of the cut can be painted red. If
it's to be a very fresh cut, a few drops or even a stream of artificial blood
can be added. Sealer can be painted on after the cut is made but before
any blood is added. The same technique can be used for making a scar if
you wish.

The latex-tissue-cotton-on-glass method described under *Scars* can be
used very effectively here. The type of welt shown in Figure 102-E (latex
and tissue) was used in the Broadway production of William Inge's
Natural Affection, in which a character had to display a number of ugly
welts from whip lashes across his back. The latex welts were made in long
strips, cut into appropriate lengths, applied with spirit gum, and painted.
After the first application, the makeup on the latex had to be touched up
only slightly.

Warts (see Figures 166 and 168) can be made in the same way as
welts, of either wax or putty. Hairs from wool crepe braids can be stuck
into the putty if desired. When wax is used, spirit gum must always be
used on the skin first, and the wax should be covered with a sealer. Both
warts and welts can also be made of molded latex (Chapter 14) or directly,
as described above. Figure 102 shows a wart (B) and a large wen (D)
made of latex and cotton.

PROBLEMS

1. Model three noses in putty, derma wax, and putty-wax following
sketches N, O, and P in Figure 80. Be sure the noses are well constructed,
smooth, and carefully blended. Make up each nose and then observe it
carefully under a good light to be sure that it looks real. You should take
as much time as necessary to do these noses well.

2. Model a fourth nose from figures 199–200 or from your own
morgue.

3. Experiment in building up some areas of the face other than the
nose by one of the alternative methods suggested in this chapter.

4. Experiment on a small area of the face or hand with each of the
suggested methods for creating a wrinkled skin effect.

5. Using the clay head you modeled previously, age the head to represent one of the characters in Problems 13 and 15, Chapter 12, using photographs from your morgue as guides in modeling.

6. Duplicate the clay features on your own face as nearly as possible, using three-dimensional constructions and paint.

7. Choose three other characters in Problems 13 and 15 and make rough sketches of simple constructions you would ordinarily use in making up that character.

8. Remodel your clay head to represent one of the characters in the following list. Then try to duplicate the remodeled head with makeup: Puck (*Midsummer Night's Dream*); Caliban (*The Tempest*); the Trolls (*Peer Gynt*); Evil (*Everyman*); Falstaff; Sir Toby Belch; Lob (*Dear Brutus*); the Witches (*Macbeth*); Mephistopheles (*Faust*); Bardolph (*Merry Wives of Windsor*); Dr. Pinch (*Comedy of Errors*); Duchess, Cook, Red Queen, White Queen (*Alice in Wonderland*); Og (*Finian's Rainbow*); Cyrano de Bergerac; Corbaccio (*Volpone*).

14

RUBBER PROSTHESIS

The most satisfactory and professional method of building up the face is through the use of rubber prosthesis. The rubber pieces, which can be used to build up any part of the face, neck, or hands, are stiff enough in the central portions to make them hold their shape and thin enough at the edges, where they are attached to the skin, to blend imperceptibly into the foundation. The rubber construction is not a solid piece of rubber but a rubber shell, light in weight and not uncomfortable to wear. It can be made up in any color and can have a simulated skin texture which is quite convincing in closeups, as in Figure 124, for example. Figure 110 shows several rubber pieces and the plaster molds from which they were cast.

The advantage of rubber makeup is considerable: (1) It can provide three-dimensional additions to the face impossible to achieve with nose putty and derma wax or other direct constructions. (2) Rubber pieces are in appearance much more like the skin than putty or wax. (3) They are more carefully modeled than putty and wax usually are and, of course, they need not be modeled on the face, which always poses a difficult problem in side views for the actor who is doing his own makeup. (4) Rubber pieces are light and cause no discomfort to the actor, and there is little danger of their coming off once they are securely pasted down. (5) They can be quickly applied and quickly removed. (6) And, what is often very important, they can be used again and again. The rubber will not last indefinitely, but it should hold up for quite a long period of time if it is kept clean and in a box where it is not likely to be pressed out of shape. The liquid latex itself is relatively inexpensive, but the labor involved in making it up is considerable.

Complete rubber masks are possible, but they allow for almost no change in expression and so are undesirable except for very special characters, such as the Troll King in *Peer Gynt*. Even then a few rubber pieces will allow more freedom.

CASTING FOR PROSTHESIS

The first step in rubber prosthesis is to reproduce the actor's own face or some part of his face in plaster. In order to do that, a negative mold must be made. This negative mold can be made with plaster, but a substance called *moulage* (see Appendix A) is far more satisfactory.

Preparing the subject. If the whole face is being cast, it is best to have the subject lie at about a 30 to 40 degree angle rather than flat in order to prevent distortion of the jaw and neck area. A barber's chair is ideal. A cardboard mask should be cut out to fit around the neck in order to catch drippings from the moulage (see Figure 105). A plastic makeup cape (Figures 105–107) is about the best way to protect the clothing. The hardened moulage can easily be removed from the cape later. Any sort of rubber or plastic cap can be used to protect the hair (Figure 105).

The face requires no special preparation, but psychologically the subject usually does. It must be made clear to him that there is no danger. If for any reason the moulage interferes with his breathing, he need only expel his breath forcefully, open his mouth and break the moulage mold, or remove the moulage from his nose or mouth with his hands. Most subjects, once they have been given confidence in the operator, find the process rather pleasant and relaxing.

It is important that the facial muscles not be moved while the mold is being made. A smile or the raise of an eyebrow can ruin the mold. Always arrange with the subject about signals for "yes" and "no" so that he will be able to answer questions such as "Is the moulage too warm?" "Can you breathe easily?" "Are you comfortable?" It is a good idea, especially with nervous subjects, to let them watch a mold being made on someone else first and also to explain to them as you go along exactly what you're doing. It is usually best to work in a private room where there is not a great deal of noise or activity and where the subject does not feel he is being watched by a number of people. If others are watching, it is essential that they understand from the start that they must be quiet except for any questions which they may have. Any remarks or noises which disturb the subject or tend to make him smile must not be permitted. If a good mold is to be made, the complete co-operation of the subject and any observers is essential.

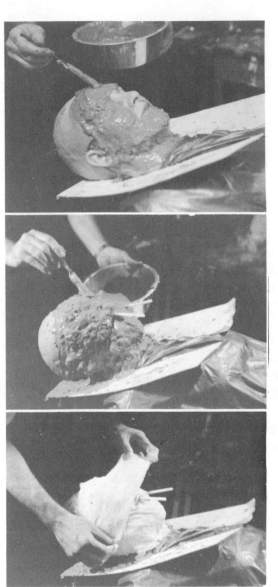

FIGURES 105, 106, 107, 108. Casting a plaster head with moulage. At the top left the warm moulage is shown being applied with a brush. The head is covered with a rubber cap. The model breathes through the straws. Plaster-impregnated bandages are then added to give the mold rigidity. After the moulage mold has hardened, it is removed and filled with wet plaster.

Negative moulage mold. To prepare the moulage for use, add 1 cup of water for each can and heat in the top of a double boiler until it is in liquid form. Then, as soon as it is cool enough to touch, brush it quickly over the face or the facial area being cast with a large brush, making sure there is a fairly thick layer (½–1 inch) at all points. If the nose is being cast, it is possible to insert straws or rolls of paper into the nostrils first to permit breathing (Figure 106). Derma wax around the straw will hold it in the nostril and make it impossible for the moulage to seep in. It is generally considered preferable, however, not to use straws since they may distort the shape of the nostril. When straws are not used, ask the subject to take a deep breath and hold it, brush moulage quickly over the nose, then ask him to expel air forcefully through the nose. This will remove moulage from the nostrils. Thereafter, you can work around this area carefully and fill in the holes after the mold has been removed. You can explain to the subject that if moulage should cover the holes accidentally, again he need only expel his breath forcefully to remove it.

The eyes should be kept closed, of course. Cotton may be stuffed into the ear opening if you wish. When the moulage has solidified (usually from 15 to 30 minutes is necessary unless you force-dry it with a hair drier or cold cloths), ask the subject to move his facial muscles in order to loosen the mold. Then it can easily be removed. It is best to loosen it first near the ear to let in the air. The moulage does not stick to skin nor hair, which is one of its greatest advantages over plaster.

If the whole face is being cast, then some sort of rigid construction must be set into the moulage to make the mold strong enough to hold its shape. The perforated metal strips found in Erector sets make good braces when bent in a curve to follow the general shape of the face. They may be bolted together, or they may simply be laid into the moulage separately. An adjustable wire mask form is even better. Or you can make up a form with wire clothes hangers. In either case, the strengtheners must be placed on the moulage before you are completely finished so that they will actually be built into the mold. Before placing them on the mold, it is well to draw them through the warm moulage. Then continue adding moulage until the metal pieces are embedded. This must be done very quickly, however, because the warm liquid moulage will not stick to moulage which has already hardened. So work rapidly, keeping the entire surface soft until you have finished. In working with ears, be very careful of undercuts so that you will not break the mold as you remove it.

Another method of strengthening the mold is to lay strips of plaster bandage (available from surgical supply companies) over the moulage

(Figure 107). When the plaster hardens, it will provide a rigid form to hold the shape of the moulage.

When the negative mold is finished, the positive plaster cast should be made immediately in order to prevent the possibility of shrinkage of the moulage as it loses its moisture.

Positive plaster cast. In preparing the plaster, first put 2 or 3 cups of water in a pan or a dish, then slowly sift in plaster of Paris until it is just barely below the surface of the water. Let the mixture stand *without stirring* until it begins to thicken. When it approaches a suitable consistency for pouring, it can be stirred very gently. It will then begin to harden quickly. After the plaster has been stirred, the pan should be hit a few times on the bottom with the palm of the hand in order to force air bubbles to the surface.

Although plaster can be poured when it is thin and watery or as thick as mayonnaise, an in-between consistency (say, that of heavy cream) usually works best. If it is too thin, it will be hard to manage and will take longer to harden; if it is too thick, it may not conform to the shape of the mold. It should be pointed out, however, that thin plaster results in a harder, more durable cast than thick plaster.

The wet plaster can be either poured slowly and gently or spooned into a negative mold. In filling the mold, be sure it is adequately supported so that the shape will not be distorted. Having someone hold it in his lap with his hands cupped around it for support (Figure 108) works very well.

If you plan to hang the cast on a wall for storage, form a loop from a length of wire (part of a coat hanger will do) and embed the ends in the plaster before it hardens, leaving the loop outside and near the top of the cast. This can prove to be a great convenience.

When the plaster is thoroughly hardened in the mold, the moulage can be broken off and saved for future use. The plaster cast should be allowed to dry thoroughly before being used. This may take as much as a week. Then give the cast one or two coats of white shellac. You now have a reproduction of the actor's face (Figure 110), on which you can model in clay the features you want to reproduce in latex.

Clay models. The modeling of individual features is done with artists' modeling clay, which requires no special technique. You will do it largely with your fingers, though a clay modeling tool (Figure 109) may be helpful for details. Be sure the clay is perfectly smooth, completely blended at the edges, and in general exactly the way you want the rubber piece to be. You can simulate skin texture by dotting the clay with tiny depressions to represent pores. Remember that the slightest mark on the clay will be reproduced on the rubber.

FIGURE 109. Casting eye pouches. Right eye shows modeled clay pouch with clay fence to hold in plaster. Plaster has been poured over the left eye. To the right is the bowl of wet plaster and the modeling tool.

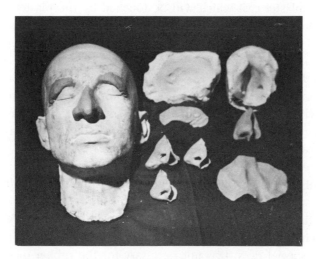

FIGURE 110. Positive plaster cast of the head of the actor in Figure 7. Nose and sagging eyelids have been modeled in clay. At top center is the negative plaster cast of the left eyelid made directly from the clay model on the head. Below it is the finished rubber eyelid made by painting liquid rubber on the negative cast. Top right is a similar plaster cast of the nose and below it the finished rubber nose. Both pieces were used for the Shylock makeup, Figure 117. At lower center are three rubber noses for Cyrano, Disraeli, and Mr. Puff. At lower right is a sagging neck piece.

A useful trick for making skin texture quickly is to make a rubber negative of grapefruit skin, as suggested in Chapter 13. This is done by painting liquid latex onto a section of the outside of a grapefruit—preferably one which is not too smooth. At least four or five coats will be necessary. When the latex is thoroughly dry, remove it from the grapefruit, powder it, and you will have a textured piece which can be pressed into clay, transferring the texture. All clay models should be textured—except for eyelids—so that the natural smoothness of the rubber piece will not contrast with the skin which is textured by pores. Observe the texture of the nose in Figure 124.

Negative plaster cast. The next step is to make a negative cast of the clay feature just as you made a negative cast of the actor's face. This, however, must be done with plaster rather than moulage.

First, with some extra clay build up a sort of fence or dam around the modeled feature to prevent the plaster from spilling over the cast (Figure 109). Then, using cold cream, mineral oil, or vaseline, grease all exposed parts of the plaster cast which will be touched by the plaster mold to be poured. When the cast is greased, make up your plaster just as before and pour it over the new feature, giving plenty of thickness so that the cast will not break when you remove it.

When the plaster is hard, pull off the clay fence and maneuver the new cast around until it can be easily slipped off. Now you have a negative cast from which you can make any number of rubber pieces (Figure 110). If by chance air bubbles have left little holes anywhere in the cast, fill them up with plaster before making the rubber pieces.

Positive rubber cast. There are two techniques for making the final rubber prosthetic pieces from the plaster casts. One is a *painting* method, the other a *slush* method.

For either method, liquid latex is used (see Appendix A). The latex can be purchased in a few flesh tones. It can also be tinted with food coloring or with special dyes. It is not necessary for the rubber piece to match the base color, but if it is too light, it will be more difficult to cover. The solidified rubber will always be considerably darker than the liquid latex.

The main requirement is to make the central parts of the piece thick enough to hold their shape and the edges thin enough to blend into the skin without an obvious line. In the brush technique a layer of latex is painted into the negative plaster mold (which requires no surface preparation). The type of brush used is a matter of choice. A soft bristle lets the latex flow on more easily, but it is also very difficult to clean, and unless extreme care is taken, it will probably not last very long. A stiff bristle is easier to clean but doesn't give as smooth a coat of latex. A flat, medium stiff bristle is perhaps the most generally practical. Inexpensive brushes should be used. Brushes in use should be kept in soapy water and washed out thoroughly with soap the moment you have finished with them. Once the latex has solidified, it cannot be removed from the brush.

Before painting in the first coat, it would be well to estimate about where you want the edge of the piece to be and mark that with a pencil on the plaster. Then you can be sure to keep the latex thin along that line. On the first coat you should overlap the line slightly to allow for trimming.

Subsequent coats are painted in after the first coat is completely dry. In fact, each coat must dry thoroughly before another is added. Each subsequent coat can begin a little farther from the edge to provide a gradual thinning. The number of coats needed depends on the thickness of the coats. You will probably need a minimum of six and in most cases more. This you will have to learn by experience.

In using the slush method, some of the latex is poured into the mold and gently sloshed around to build up layers of the latex. This is done by holding the plaster mold in the hand and moving or rocking it so that the latex runs first up to and just beyond the proposed edge, as marked with a pencil. Subsequent movements should carry the latex farther and farther from the edge. Then when you think you have built up enough thickness, drain off the excess latex or, if you like, leave a tiny bit in to dry and give a little additional rigidity.

Before removing the rubber piece, be sure it is completely dry. In deep molds, such as noses, this may sometimes take several hours. Then dust the surface of the latex with face powder or talcum to prevent sticking. Once it has been dusted, it will never stick again, even if you should wash the powder off immediately. Then loosen the rubber at a spot along the edge and carefully lift it away from the plaster. As you do so, dust more talcum inside to keep that surface of the rubber from sticking. Sometimes the rubber comes away easily, sometimes it has to be pulled, but it will come. If you do have to pull hard, however, be sure not to pull it by the tissue-thin edge, which is likely to tear. As soon as you are able to loosen a little more of the piece, grasp it farther down to pull out the remainder. Tweezers are sometimes helpful.

When the piece is out, trim any rough edges and try it on. If further trimming seems necessary, mark the desired edge with a pencil, then trim.

However, make sure you do not trim the piece in too far and thus lose the thin edge. If your first piece is not entirely successful, you will learn from the mistakes you make on that one how to approach the second.

TYPES OF PROSTHETIC PIECES

Noses. There are three basic criteria for a useful, workable rubber nose—it must be rigid enough to hold its shape without wrinkling or sagging, the blending edges must be tissue-thin, and the blend should take place on a solid, rather than a flexible, foundation (on the actor's nose, that is, not on his cheeks or his nasolabial folds).

The first two of these criteria depend on the distribution of latex in the plaster cast and have already been discussed. The third requires careful placement of the clay used in building up the nose of the plaster cast. The actual modeling of the clay corresponds closely to the modeling of a putty nose—the accurate following of natural nose structure, the careful blending of edges, the limiting of the clay addition to as small an area as possible, and the final addition of skin texture, which is more important for a latex addition than for a putty one.

The principle difference is one of degree. Whereas putty may, if necessary, cover the sides of the nose completely, clay should not do so but should stop far enough short of the outer boundaries of the sides of the nose to allow for a blending edge of latex beyond the section which is being built up. The greater the latitude given for this blend, the better.

The latex piece need not cover the entire nose. On the contrary, the smaller the area it covers, the more successful it is likely to be. A tilted tip or a small hump, for example, does not require modeling and casting a complete nose. If the piece you make involves the nostrils, they will have to be cut out of the piece after it has been cast.

Since the final rubber piece can be no better than the clay nose from which it was cast, considerable time and care should be spent in meticulous modeling. Once the model is perfected and cast, achieving an effective rubber piece is merely a matter of careful manipulation of the liquid latex in the cast. Rubber noses were used for the makeups in Figures 117, 124, 128, and 168.

Eyelids. The most obvious use for rubber eyelids is in Oriental makeup (Figures 111, 112). In modeling them, be sure to give the clay sufficient thickness over the center of the eyeball so that the movement of the real eyelids will not be impeded. Before trying to model Oriental lids, collect several good photographs of Orientals and follow them carefully. Also, study the Oriental eyes in Figures 196 and 197.

Drooping eyelids for age (Figures 117, 128) are extremely useful and

FIGURES 111, 112. Youthful and aged Oriental makeup. By student Jan Vidra. Oriental eyelids of rubber. For other makeups of Mr. Vidra see Figures 123–125, 161, and 162.

can do wonders in aging youthful eyes. Figure 110 shows a pair of drooping eyelids modeled in clay on a plaster head as well as one of the negative molds and the positive rubber piece made from it. There is no standard form for such lids. It is essential to work from photographs of older people—preferably from a number of them, combining the most useful and adaptable features of each. There are many kinds of drooping lids, and you must choose the one most appropriate for the character. (See Figures 197–200.)

Although the Oriental rubber eyelids usually come just to the eyebrow, it is better in general to let the sagging ones cover the natural brow completely. This gets rid of the youthful brow, which is often a detriment, and makes it possible to put an aged brow onto the rubber piece itself. This can be done with crepe hair and latex or, if you prefer, by ventilating real hair into the rubber (see Chapter 15). Remember that only the edges which are to be attached to the skin must be thin. The edge which falls diagonally across the eye is naturally free and should be quite thick.

Eye pouches. These are invaluable aids to aging and are probably the simplest kind of piece you can make (Figures 117, 128). Again you should work from photographs of real people (see Figures 197–200). Some pouches will be fairly smooth and definitely pouchlike. Others will be fairly flat and a mass of fine wrinkles. There are endless variations. If there is a definite line of demarcation to the pouch you wish to make, then you will not have to leave a thin edge on the bottom of the rubber piece,

FIGURE 113. Plaster mold and latex ear for Abraham Lincoln. Made for Hal Holbrook for *Abe Lincoln in Illinois*. Above is the closed mold into which latex is poured; below is the opened mold and untrimmed ear which has been removed from the mold.

but there will have to be one at the top. As usual, remember the skin texture.

Ears. Rubber cauliflower ears can be slipped over the actor's real ears very simply. Or rubber tips can be used for such characters as the leprechaun in *Finian's Rainbow* and Puck. Small ears can become large ears too, but unfortunately the process can't be reversed.

In making ears, partial or complete, it is necessary to make a "shell" that will fit over the natural ear. This requires a *split mold*. After you have modeled the clay ear on the plaster cast of the actor's natural ear and built your clay fence, place the cast so that the ear is horizontal. Then pour plaster up to the middle of the rim of the ear. It's a good idea to let the surface of the plaster be somewhat uneven. If the plaster is fairly thick, this will happen automatically, giving a bumpy or undulating surface. When the plaster is dry, grease the surface with vaseline or cold cream and pour in more plaster, covering the ear. When this plaster is dry, remove the clay fence, as usual, then very carefully pry the two sections of plaster apart and remove both from the clay ear.

You can then fit the two sections back together. If the surface is uneven, this will be no problem, for there will be only one way they will fit. This will give you a deep mold with a crevice (Figure 113), into which you can pour the latex and slosh it around to cover all the surfaces of the negative mold. Excess can be poured back out. It is better to build the ear up with several coats rather than trying to do the whole thing at once. Be sure to keep the latex thin at the edges, which will be glued to the natural ear, and thick around the rim so that the ears will hold their shape.

When you are sure the latex is dry (it's a good idea to force dry it with a hair drier), powder the inside, then carefully pry the mold apart, powdering as you do so. The ear will then have to be trimmed around the edges. Figure 113 shows an untrimmed ear with the separated mold. After the latex ear has been slipped over the natural one and glued down, it should be made up to match the face. Shadows and highlights can be added, if necessary, to increase the third dimension.

In painting the cast with latex, you may have difficulty in deciding how far out to bring the latex. After you have made and trimmed your first ear, you will be able to see where the boundaries should be. Then you can mark these boundaries on the plaster cast with a pencil to serve as guide lines for all future ears. This will make it possible to keep the latex thin at all edges which are to be glued down.

Chin. Weak chins can be built up or normal ones made to protrude, round chins can be made more square or more pointed, or any chin can be aged by being made more irregular. Goatees can be pasted on the rubber chins as easily as on real ones and will not need to be remade for each performance. Frequently a chin can be combined in the same piece with a scrawny or a fat neck.

Neck. It is possible to age the neck slightly with paint, but the profile is difficult to change. A firm chin and a youthful neck will look firm and youthful no matter how much paint you put on it. But a rubber piece will quickly produce an old neck from any angle. You can have prominent muscles and sagging flesh or transverse rolls of fat. Necks are, however, difficult to do and not entirely satisfactory except when a foamed rubber process is used (see end of chapter).

Welts and warts. These are extremely simple to make and can be pasted on quickly like any other rubber piece. They can be cast, of course, without having a cast of a face or even a feature to work on.

Bald caps. The best solution to the problem of a completely bald head or even of a partially bald one is a rubber cap. This can be worn plain, or hair can be added (see Chapter 16). Since it adapts itself to the shape of the head and fits snugly, and since it can be constructed with a very thin edge, it is considerably more satisfactory than the usual bald wig.

Ideally, the latex should be slushed or painted (a combination of the two is most satisfactory) into a negative plaster head mold. This can be made from a wig block or millinery form. If the surface of the form is smooth, it may be possible to cast the plaster directly from the form after the usual greasing. If there is doubt about the surface, however, a thin layer of modeling clay can be used over it. If the clay is used, some reshaping can be done if that seems desirable. The normal hairline should be marked on the form with a pencil or crayon that will transfer to the plaster in order to simplify painting in the latex later. The usual clay dikes are built up and the plaster poured over the form.

Obviously, since the top of the form is larger than the bottom, it cannot be removed from the plaster cast. There are two possible solutions to this. One is to cut the plaster cast in two with a thread while it is still soft. The two halves are allowed to dry, then removed and put back together again. The join can be smoothed out and touched up with additional plaster.

A better method, if you have the right kind of form, is to slice the form into sections vertically. If you cut it twice each way, you will have nine sections, including a center one which will be in contact with the cast only for a few square inches on the top. A balsa wood form is best for this purpose since it is easily cut. Once the pieces have been cut, they are put back together, tied firmly at the base, and the form is covered with clay for a smooth surface. Then when the plaster is dry, the center section is removed from the bottom, releasing the other pieces so that they too can be pulled out.

In making the cap in the negative mold, it is probably easiest to pour in a quantity of latex and slosh it around, gradually building up layers of rubber. In order to have the thin front edge of the cap correctly shaped, that area should be painted in with a brush, using only one or two coats at the very edge. The back of the cap should be left long so that it will cover all of the neck hair and can be tucked into the collar. If this back tab is not needed, it can be cut off later.

It is also possible to make a bald cap by painting the latex directly onto the form. This has several obvious disadvantages, but it can be done, though never with really high quality results. In the first place, the surface of the form must be suitable for taking the latex. If the cap is to be used shiny side out, as made, the surface must be very smooth, which is not easy to achieve. Even if the surface is not uneven, it will not take makeup well. The cap can be used inside out, but this means that the form must be free of ridges or imperfections which will be transferred to the cap.

Whatever method you use, the bald cap should prove a very useful item. Probably it will take several tries before you find out exactly how much latex to use and exactly where the thin edge should come. In wearing the cap, paste down the edge and stipple it as for any rubber prosthetic piece. In making it up, use rubber mask grease. (See also, *Plastic Caps* in Appendix A.)

Hands. One of the most dramatic uses of rubber is for hands. Wrinkled and veined hands can be made up in the form of gloves which can be slipped on and off easily (Figure 117). These are invaluable for quick changes. Rubber pieces to be pasted on the backs of the hands are, of course, less difficult to make. It is also possible to buy thin, snug rubber gloves and build them up directly with latex, paste on veins, knuckles, etc., or a combination of the two.

APPLICATION OF PROSTHETIC PIECES

Rubber pieces must be attached to the dry skin before any cream or makeup has been used. They can be attached with either liquid latex, latex cream adhesive, or spirit gum. The latex is likely to become loosened during the performance, however, and it has the added disadvantage of building up on the rubber piece itself, thickening the edge. Spirit gum is far more reliable as an adhesive, unless the piece is to be used for a very short scene without too much facial activity. When the gum has become tacky, the edges of the piece can be pressed into it until they adhere snugly. Be sure that the edges are smooth and free from wrinkles.

The edges of the latex piece should be stippled with latex cream adhesive (Duo or Flexol), which should then be allowed to dry before the makeup is applied. This will help to conceal the edge.

Greasepaint should not be used on rubber since it will cause it to deteriorate. Mehron's rubber mask grease (see Appendix A) can be used instead. If cake makeup is used, either use rubber mask grease first, powder, and go over it with cake makeup or before applying the cake, rub

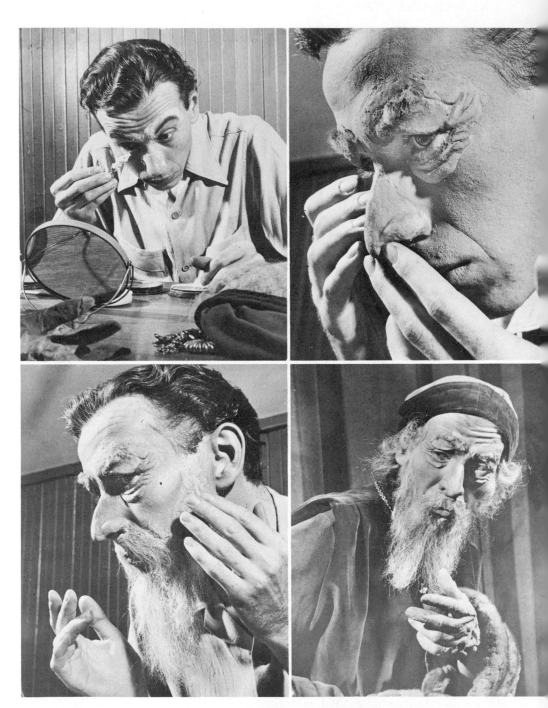

FIGURES 114, 115, 116, 117. Makeup for Shylock using rubber nose, eye pouches, eyelids, and hands. Crepe hair eyebrows attached to the rubber pieces with latex. Beard and mustache on latex.

castor oil into the rubber. The castor oil will not entirely prevent the makeup's looking a bit lighter on the rubber than on the skin, but it will help considerably. The rest of the makeup is completed in the usual way. Figures 114–117 show a makeup of Shylock being done with rubber nose, eyelids, and hands. The pieces are being applied with latex instead of spirit gum. Figure 110 shows some of the pieces used.

The rubber pieces can be removed by merely pulling them off. If adhesive has been used, it should be removed from the rubber piece immediately if it is possible to do so. It can usually be pulled or rolled off with the fingers. If gum has been used, the rubber piece should be cleaned thoroughly with alcohol or acetone. It is also wise to remove makeup from the piece with alcohol or acetone.

In addition to the great practical convenience to professional actors who repeat the same makeup night after night, the use of a few good rubber pieces can make a tremendous difference in the appearance of a character makeup. This is particularly important in the nonprofessional theater where young people often play older parts. The three-dimensional rubber pieces, when carefully applied and covered with paint, are undetectable. Drooping lids with appropriate brows combined with a sagging neckline will age an actor by many years without so much as one painted wrinkle. The use of rubber makes it possible to concentrate on a few telling features rather than on a myriad of painted details which are often lost before they cross the footlights.

FOAMED LATEX

Although the hollow, shell like latex pieces just described work well on bony parts of the face, their hollowness is likely to become apparent on softer areas where there is much movement. This problem can be overcome through the use of foamed latex, with which it is possible to make three-dimensional, spongy jowls and sagging necks which look and move like natural flesh. The process is a complicated one, but for those who wish to experiment with it, the following abbreviated instructions are included.

Closed molds. Previously we have used open molds into which the liquid latex has been painted or slushed to form a shell. For foamed pieces it is necessary to use two molds—a positive and a negative. The positive mold duplicates the actor's own feature to be built up (as, for example, a nose), whereas the negative mold is taken of the projected changed feature and corresponds to the single mold used for painted-in latex pieces. The two molds reproduce the actor's own feature and the altered feature. When these two molds are fitted together, the space between will correspond precisely to the clay addition which has been built up on the plaster cast. This space is then filled with foamed latex, giving a spongy, three-dimensional piece which can be attached to the face. The casting is done with stone (see Appendix A), which is harder, less porous, and more durable than plaster. Following is the procedure for making the closed mold:

1. Make a negative cast of the actor's nose (or any other feature) in the usual way. This may be of plaster. Then make two ½-inch balls of clay and cut them in half. This will give you four half spheres, which should be placed on the negative plaster cast, surrounding the nose. These will serve as keys or guides later in fitting the two molds together.

2. Build up high clay dikes around the cast, grease the cast, and pour in the stone mixture (which is handled like plaster) to make a positive cast. When the stone has hardened, pull away the clay dikes, and separate the positive stone cast from the plaster negative.

3. Now proceed as for any latex piece, modeling the character nose in clay on the stone positive, including skin texture as usual.

4. Build up a high clay dike on the positive mold; grease the cast and the clay nose; then pour in stone to make a negative cast. This negative will be of the character nose.

5. When the stone has hardened, remove the dikes, and separate the casts. Remove the clay nose from the positive cast, and clean both casts thoroughly. Now you have two tight-fitting casts with semispherical keys to insure an exact fit. The air space between the positive and the negative nose will be filled with foamed latex to form the prosthetic nose.

Foaming the latex. Various companies which supply latex have developed their own formulae for foaming latex. The following is recommended by UniRoyal Chemical (see Appendix B) for use with their latex foam sponge compound (LOTOL L–7176), which is furnished in four parts, as follows:

Part A is the base latex compound—LOTOL L–7176 (171 grams).

Part B is the sulfur dispersion—NX–762–B (4 grams).

Part C is the zinc oxide dispersion—NX–935 (9 grams).

Part D is the gelling agent—P–4934 (5 grams), which is diluted with water (5 grams) before being added.

The three additives are normally supplied with the base compound. The amounts given above should produce about a quart of wet foam, depending on the density of foam desired. Smaller or larger quantities can be mixed using the same proportions. Following is the mixing and foaming procedure:

1. Mix parts A, B, and C by stirring together, but do not mix more than you will use in one day. Then add any concentrated, water-soluble dye for flesh color. This can be obtained in red, yellow, and blue, which can be mixed to achieve any desired color. Exact amounts will have to be determined by experimentation. For flesh tones you will need the greatest amount of yellow and red (usually more yellow unless the color is to be very pink) and only a very small amount of blue (probably a maximum of 1 or 2 drops), even for sallow tones. The total amount of dye will probably not exceed 10 drops. Proceed cautiously, and note carefully each time how many drops of each color you use and the approximate color which results so that you will have the information for future use. Since dyes vary, no exact formulae can be given here. As with any latex, remember that the color when dry is several shades darker than when wet.

2. Whip the compound at high speed to approximately 5 volumes. This should take only a minute or so. The bowl in which you whip should be marked for 5 volumes in advance. For a firmer sponge decrease the volume and for a softer one increase it.

3. While the material is still frothing, reduce speed slightly and add Part D (diluted with water, as indicated). Mix for 30 seconds, then reduce the speed still further and continue to whip for a minute or so in order to refine the foam.

4. Pour the compound immediately into the well-greased mold, which should be closed and allowed to stand for about 6–8 minutes. The mold can be greased with castor oil (preferably mixed with zinc stearate) or with rubber mask grease. The latter will color the sponge slightly.

5. Place the mold in a 300° F. oven (preferably air-circulated) for 20–30 minutes. The mold should be allowed to cool slowly in the oven.

6. When the mold is cool, carefully separate the two halves and remove the foamed piece. Trim the ragged edges but not too closely nor too evenly. They should be very thin and somewhat irregular.

Application. The foamed latex pieces can be attached with spirit gum, latex, or Duo adhesive and stippled with Duo adhesive to blend the edges (see Figure 192-C-E-F). For areas in which there is a great deal of muscular activity, Slomon's Medico Adhesive, though more difficult to use, provides greater security. Rubber mask grease should be applied to the pieces with a sponge (Figure 192-L). You may then wish to adjust the color generally or locally (as with rouge, for example) by stippling on additional color with a coarse sponge. This tends to add texture and relieve the flatness of the rubber mask grease base. Then press a generous amount of powder into the makeup to set it and remove all shine. To suggest even greater texture and color variation (as for broken blood vessels), use a coarse sponge or a brush to stipple additional colors over the powdered makeup—red-brown, grayed purple, dull brick red, rose, gray, lavender, creamy yellow, or whatever colors seem appropriate. (See Chapter 8.) This stippling should then be lightly powdered. If you wish the makeup to have a slight natural sheen (as you might for a bald head, for example), simply apply a light coating of K-Y lubricating jelly and allow it to dry or force-dry it with a hair drier. For the application of a complete makeup using foamed latex, study the series of photographs of the TV makeup for Hal Holbrook's Mark Twain in Figure 192.

The procedure in print looks long and complex, but once you have followed it in actual practice, you will find it relatively simple. It is the making of the closed molds which is the most time-consuming, but if you have already mastered the casting of open molds, you should have no difficulty. The molds can, of course, be reused many times. As for the foaming, if you have the necessary equipment and materials and follow directions carefully, you should have good results on your first try. The foamed pieces are well worth the extra time they require.

15

BEARDS AND
MUSTACHES

The first step in making a beard or a mustache is to make a rough sketch of what you have in mind. Drawings and photographs in this book and in your morgue should be helpful. The style you choose will, of course, depend upon the period of the play and on the personality of the character.

You can make or buy beards or mustaches, usually of real hair, which can be used again and again. This type is the quickest to apply, the most comfortable to wear, and the most convincing. It is also the most expensive. If you will be using a beard or a mustache for only a few performances and if your budget is limited, crepe hair is the answer.

CREPE HAIR

Wool crepe is relatively inexpensive and, if it is skillfully manipulated, quite effective (see Figures 118 and 153). It is indispensable for last minute jobs and for any beard or mustache which will not be used more than a few times. It can be used for beards, goatees, mustaches, sideburns, eyebrows, and occasionally to add to the natural hair. However, it is not usually satisfactory for movie or television closeups.

Color. A number of shades of hair are available. The one chosen should usually be somewhat lighter than the natural hair or the wig, both because hair on the face often is lighter and because the lack of sheen of the crepe hair makes it appear somewhat darker than it is. It is best to mix several shades by straightening both, then combing them together.

205

FIGURE 118. **Student makeup.** Beard, mustache, and eyebrows of crepe hair. Eye pouches of rubber. Makeup by Bert Roth.

This will give a far more realistic effect than a flat color. Pure black or pure white crepe hair should seldom be used except for burlesque purposes. Black needs some gray or brown; and white, some gray, brown, or blond to make it convincingly real.

Since combing wool crepe, even with a wide-toothed comb, tends to waste a good deal of hair, mixing can be accomplished more economically by first cutting the various shades of hair into whatever lengths you are going to need (Figure 120). Then you can proceed in one of two ways—either take strands of hair of each color and gradually put them together until all the hair is assembled into one pile or put your lengths of the

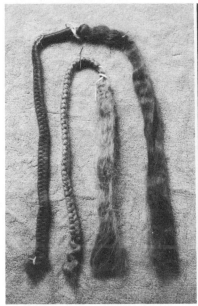
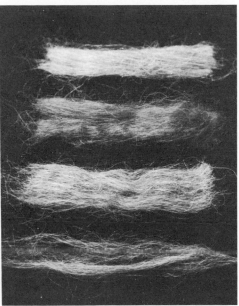

FIGURES 119, 120. Crepe hair. Figure 119 shows two braids of wool crepe with the ends straightened. The three top lengths of straightened hair in Figure 120 are laid out, ready for mixing. At the bottom is a mixture of a strand of each—light brown, medium brown, and gray. An even more subtle mixture could be made by using smaller strands.

various shades of hair together and keep pulling them apart and putting them back together until they are adequately mixed. The principle, though not the technique, is the same as for shuffling cards.

The first method will give you a more even mixture, particularly if you work with only a few hairs at a time. For realistic beards you will ordinarily want to choose colors which are not too strongly contrasting in hue or value. Shades of gray and brown mix well and give a soft, natural effect. Black, white, and red, for example, would be exceedingly difficult to blend successfully. You can use as few or as many shades of hair as you wish.

Colors can also be mixed as you apply the beard, with the darker shades underneath and the lighter ones along the hairline, where the beard blends into the skin. Both methods were used for the beard in Figure 153.

Preparation. Crepe hair comes in braids of very kinky, wooly strands, which usually need to be straightened before the hair is applied. This is done by cutting the string which holds the braids together, then wetting the amount of hair that is to be used. The portion of the hair that has been dampened should then be straightened by stretching it between the legs or arms of a chair, two clothes hooks, or any other solid objects not too far apart. Both ends of the stretched hair are tied with string to whatever moorings are being used and permitted to dry.

It is possible to straighten the damp hair more quickly by pressing it with an electric iron, but one must be careful not to scorch the hair. Pressing under a damp cloth may be found preferable.

After the hair is dry, it should be carefully combed with a wide-toothed comb, then cut in lengths as needed. A great deal of the hair will probably be combed out of the braid. This should be removed from the comb, gathered in bunches, and recombed as often as necessary. It can be used for mustaches and for the shorter lengths of hair needed in making beards. In combing, always begin near the end of the braid and work in, combing gently. Otherwise you will tear the braid apart.

In case slightly wavy hair is desired, it should be stretched less tightly while drying. Often it need only be moistened and allowed to dry without stretching. It is also possible to use straightened hair, then to curl it with an electric curling iron after it has been properly trimmed.

Occasionally it is possible to use the hair without straightening at all if a very thin, fluffy kind of beard is needed. To prepare the hair for use in this way, pull out the braid as far as it will go without cutting the string, grasp the braid with one hand, the loose end of the hair with the other, and pull in sharp jerks until a section of the hair is detached from the braid. The hair can then be spread out and manipulated with the fingers in various ways until it is quite fluffy. One method is to pull at both ends. Half of the hair will go with the left hand, half with the right. The two strands can then be put back together and the process repeated until there are no dark spots where the hair is thick and heavy. The curl is thus shuffled around so that it is no longer recognizable as a definite wave. If the hair is then too fluffy, it can be rolled briskly between the palms of the hands. This is nearly always necessary for mustaches. This technique is particularly useful when skin should show through the beard in spots, as sometimes happens on the chin. It can be used in an emergency if there is no straightened hair and no time to do it, but ordinarily it should be used only when a fluffy, semitransparent effect is desired.

Application. The hair is commonly applied with spirit gum over the completed makeup. If grease base is applied in a very thin coat, as it should always be, and well powdered, the gum should stick. Over cake makeup there is no problem.

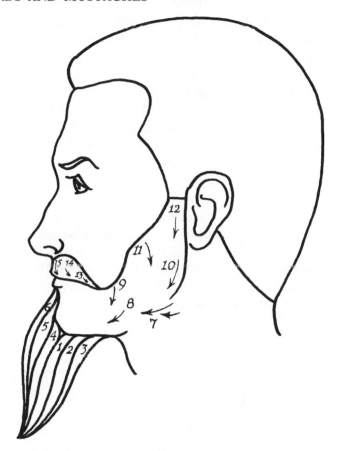

FIGURE 121. Diagram for applying crepe hair beard.
Layers of hair are applied in the order indicated by
the numbers. Arrows indicate the general direction
of growth of hair.

You will already have determined the shape of beard you want. In
applying the hair, you must always be aware of the natural line and
direction of growth, as shown in the diagram in Figure 121. The numbers
indicate the order of application. The procedure is as follows:

1. Paint the area to be covered by hair with spirit gum and allow the
gum to become quite sticky. Lightly tapping the gum repeatedly with the
tip of a finger will speed up the process. It's a good idea to have some
powder handy to dust on the fingers or on the scissors when they get
sticky. Both can be cleaned with acetone occasionally.

2. When the gum is tacky, apply the hair first to the underside of the
chin (Figure 122-A), keeping in mind that the hair there grows forward.
Usually this should be in three layers. Press the first layer into the gum

under the chin, about ½ or ¾ of an inch back from the tip (#1 in Figure 121). Press with the scissors, a towel, or a damp chamois for a few seconds (Figure 122-B), then add a second and a third layer (#2 and #3), the latter starting from the lowest point on the neck where the hair grows naturally. The hair along the edge of this line should be very thinly spread. If you are making a full beard, the hair should be carried up to the highest point at which the beard grows on the underside of the jaw.

3. Then apply the hair to the front of the chin. The hair can first be attached in a roughly semicircular pattern, following the line of the tip of the chin (#4 in Figure 121). Then add thinner layers of hair (#5 and #6), following the line of the beard as outlined by the spirit gum. For full beards the hair should be built up gradually, starting at the chin and proceeding to the sideburns (Figures 121, #7–12 and 122-C). Since the hair is usually not so heavy on the sides of the face, a few applications will be sufficient. One application of hair should always be pressed and allowed to dry slightly before another is made. Remember that ordinarily the thin layer of hair at the edge of the beard will be slightly lighter in color than the hair underneath.

4. When you have completed the application and have allowed the spirit gum time to dry, gently pull all of the hair in the beard in order to remove all stray hairs which are not firmly anchored. A beard which will not resist this gentle pulling is not secure enough to wear onstage.

5. Trim and shape the beard with barbers' shears according to the style required. If the beard is to be straggly, little or no trimming may be required; but a neat beard needs careful shaping. Use a hand mirror for a good profile view.

6. Usually you will want to spray the beard with hair lacquer so that it will hold its shape. An unkempt beard may not require this, but on the other hand, you may wish to use the spray to maintain the disorder.

Mustaches should not be stuck on in two pieces (except for distance work in which accurate detail is not necessary) but built up in the same manner as beards, starting at either end and working toward the center, always letting the hair fall in the natural direction of growth (Figure 121, #13–15). One end of each hair should always be free. The ends of the mustache may be waxed or creamed to make them hold their shape. Better yet, the whole mustache can be sprayed with diluted spirit gum (see *Atomizer*, Appendix A), hair lacquer, or spray-on bandage (Appendix A).

In making sideburns, either separately or as part of a beard, the join with the natural sideburn is frequently a problem. It is sometimes possible, if the actor's hair is long and his sideburns are not neatly trimmed, to undercut the natural sideburns so that at least a quarter inch of real hair can be made to overlap the false hair. However, it is usually more practical to continue the front edge of the false sideburn upward slightly in front of the real sideburn to a point somewhat above the eyebrow. There is nearly always a natural angle where the hair grows forward on the temple, then recedes. The artificial hairs can then be combed into the natural sideburn, and there will be no obvious join.

Latex base. If you need the hair construction for more than one performance, the practical thing to do is to make it up on a latex base rather than directly on the skin. Following is the procedure for making a mustache. Beards and sideburns would be done in the same way.

1. Paint the entire mustache area with liquid latex, carrying it just a little beyond the limits of the mustache. If the character is to be aged, carry the latex application partially over the upper lip until the lip is as thin as you want it to be. When the first application is dry, add at least three successive applications until the rubber seems thick enough to form a firm base.

2. Then when your crepe hair is ready to attach, paint on a final coat of latex and immediately push the ends of the hair into the latex. Never press the hair down with a towel. It will be firmly anchored when the latex dries. Since the latex dries quickly, it is wise to do only one small area at a time.

3. Pull out all loose hairs and trim the mustache.

The mustache may be anchored solidly enough to leave for the first performance. But if there is much movement around the mouth or excessive perspiration, the latex may loosen and pull away from the skin. It is safer, therefore, to remove it immediately and reattach it with spirit gum. This can be done simply by lifting one edge of the latex with the fingernail and pulling the mustache off. The back of the latex should be powdered immediately to prevent its sticking to itself. Rough edges should be trimmed before putting the mustache back on. But in the trimming be sure to leave as thin a blending edge as possible.

In reattaching the mustache, apply the spirit gum to the back of the latex, but only around the edges—unless there is to be so much movement that you would feel more secure with a greater area of adhesion. Let the gum become slightly tacky before attaching the piece to the skin. In removing the mustache, apply alcohol or spirit gum remover (with a brush or a cloth) around the edges of the latex to loosen it. Do not try to pull it off without first loosening the gum. When the mustache has been removed, clean all the gum from the back of the latex with your remover.

When you are going to the trouble of making a hair construction, it

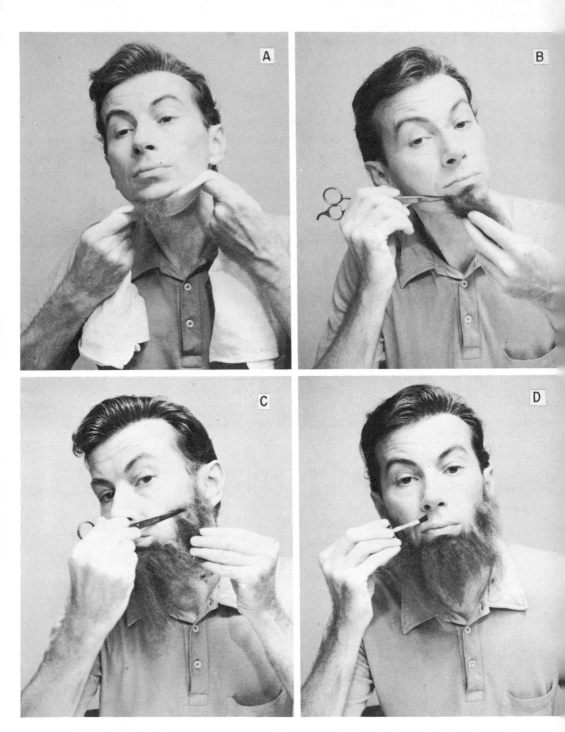

FIGURE 122. Constructing a beard with crepe hair and spirit gum. Straightened hair is built up gradually in layers, using at least two shades of hair. All loose

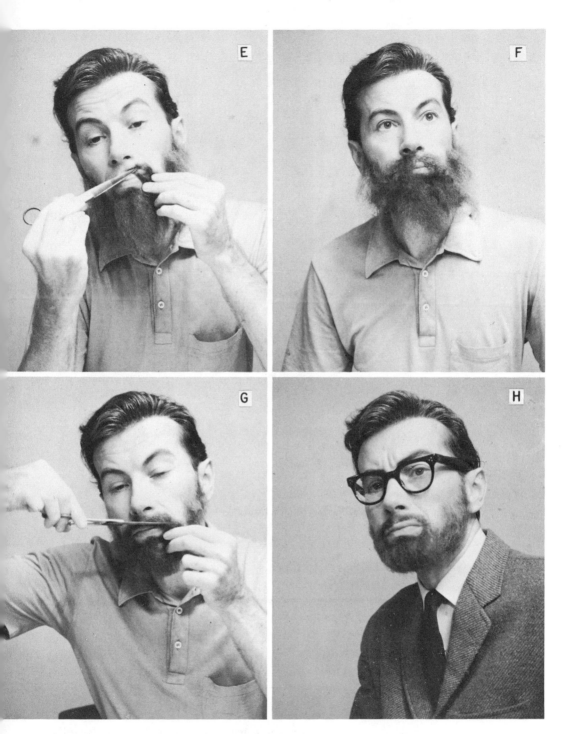

hairs should be pulled out before the final trimming.

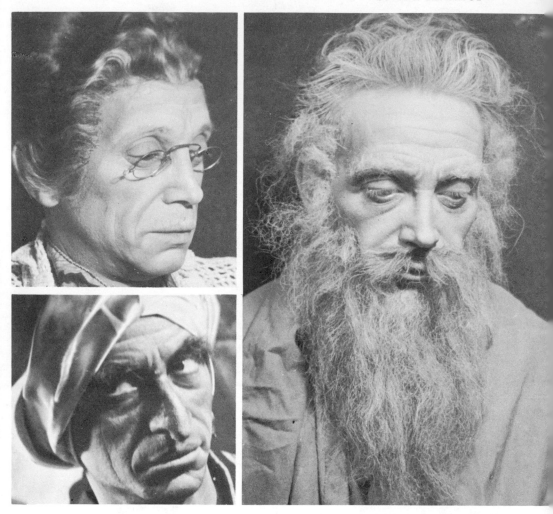

FIGURES 123, 124, 125. Three student makeups using crepe hair, wigs, and rubber prosthesis. By Jan Vidra. Observe the careful modeling with highlights and shadows and the effectiveness of the eye makeup, especially the eyebrows, in suggesting character. Wig on net in Figure 123. Eyebrows of crepe hair and nose of rubber in 124. Natural hair in 125 with crepe hair beard, mustache, and eyebrows. Costumes improvised in class. Compare these with other makeups of Mr. Vidra in Figures 111, 112, 161, and 162.

would seem reasonable to make it up in a form that can be saved whether you plan to use it again immediately or not. And you should find the latex construction no more difficult—in some way less so—than one with spirit gum.

Crepe hair takes time and practice for successful application but is indispensable for a great many character makeups. Numerous types of beards and mustaches are illustrated in Figures 47, 48, 49, 117, 118, 125, 128, 133, 153, 173, 174, 176, and in Appendices F and G.

Eyebrows. Crepe hair can be used to supplement the natural brows, or it can be used to make completely new ones, as suggested in Chapter 12. In adding to the natural brows, it is possible to attach the crepe hair to the skin over the brow and comb it into the brow or to stick tufts of crepe hair into the brow. Which method is used will depend on the form and thickness of the natural brow and of the proposed artificial brow. Crepe hair brows are shown in Figures 94, 118, 124, 125, 140, 158, 163, 164, 166, 167 and 168.

Sometimes it is necessary to block out the eyebrow completely (see Chapter 12 for details) and build new ones with crepe hair and spirit gum or latex (Figures 111, 112, 140, 158). In using latex around the eyebrows, be very careful not to get it into the brows. It will probably be impossible to remove it without removing the hairs too. But once the hairs have been matted down with spirit gum, wax, or sealer, it is safe to apply latex over them.

VENTILATED PIECES

In many instances crepe hair beards and mustaches are not satisfactory. For movie and television closeups they are not sufficiently realistic, and for long-run plays they are a nuisance. The most realistic and convenient beards and mustaches are made of real or synthetic hairs individually knotted onto a net foundation. This knotting process is usually known as *ventilating*, though it is sometimes referred to as *working* or *knotting* the hair. Even in closeups the hair appears to be actually growing out of the skin, and the piece can be attached with very little trouble and removed even more easily. And with proper care it will last a long time.

Materials. Foundations may be of silk net, treated silk lace (plastic coated), nylon net, hairlace, cotton net, silk gauze, or a combination of gauze and net. The gauze is a somewhat stiff, thin, tough, closely woven fabric. The better nets are also thin, fairly stiff, and somewhat transparent so that when they are glued to the skin, they become invisible from a short distance. For many years hairlace was considered the finest type of net available, but it has now been largely replaced with silk or nylon net. Throughout our discussion the terms *lace* and *net* will be used interchangeably. Frequently beards and sometimes even mustaches are constructed of silk gauze for the body of the piece and edged with lace for the blend into the skin. The mustache in Figure 180 was ventilated onto silk gauze and the ones in Figures 128, 133, 153, 157, 158, 173, and 176 onto net.

Human hair is usually used, though in some instances, when greater stiffness is desired, yak hair (Figure 126) is substituted. The yak hair is

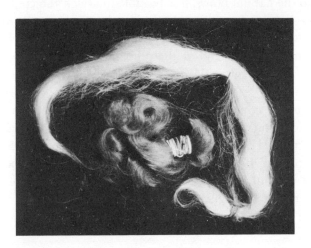

FIGURE 126. Real hair. White yak hair shown on the outside, human hair in the center. The root ends are tightly bound with string.

less expensive. The beard and mustache in Figure 128 are made of white yak hair on net. Yak hair does not mat, and it does not snarl as readily as human hair does. The finest human hair comes largely from European women who let it grow long for the specific purpose of selling it. All colors are available. Coarser, cheaper hair is obtainable from the Chinese. The hair comes in hanks of various lengths, tightly bound with string at the cut end, and waved. Hair is purchased by weight. The price depends on the quality and the color. Grays are usually the most expensive.

Synthetic hair is also available in a number of colors. There is a nylon-saran hair which has a high sheen, giving it a somewhat artificial look. It can, however, be effective for certain stylized characters. It is more like yak hair than real hair, though finer than yak. The nylon-saran-dynel with human hair (NSD-H) has less sheen and is much closer in appearance to real hair. It is excellent for ventilated beards and mustaches. It is not recommended for direct application with spirit gum, but it can be used somewhat more easily with a latex base. Real hair is waved. Synthetic hair is straight. For sources of all types of hair see Appendix A.

FIGURES 127, 128. Actor Mitchell Erickson as King Lear. Beard and mustache of white yak hair on net. Wig also of white yak hair. Rubber nose, eye pouches, and sagging flesh over eyes. Natural eyebrows are covered by the rubber pieces, into which white yak hair eyebrows have been ventilated.

Construction. The first step in constructing a beard or a mustache is to draw the outline of the proposed piece on the face with an eyebrow pencil. This means, of course, the area from which the hair would normally be growing, not the entire extent of the hair. In other words, a long handle-bar mustache may grow from the same basic area as a short clipped mustache. The only difference is that the hair itself is longer.

After the area is marked on the skin, lay on a piece of thin white translucent paper and trace the outline onto the paper. Then cut out along the traced lines. This will give you an excellent paper pattern. For mustaches this is a very simple process, but for beards there is obviously a complication since the hair grows both over and under the jawbone. The solution is to take a few tucks in the paper and crease it so that it fits the chin and jaw snugly. Then cut with the tucks in it.

The third step is to pin the pattern to a wig block (Figures 131–132), beard block (Figure 146-A), or other solid foundation and lay a piece of net over it. The net should be at least a half inch longer and wider than the pattern. It will be trimmed later. In Figure 130 the solid line represents the pattern of a mustache showing through the gauze. The net should be pinned down with large-headed or special T-shaped pins if you are using a canvas-covered, sawdust-filled block or with thumb tacks on a wooden block. Be sure the net is secured firmly, with the head of the pin or tack resting tightly against it so that it is not pulled out of shape in the knotting process. Better yet, secure it with masking tape instead of tacks or pins (146-A).

The ventilating needle is shown in Figure 129. It consists of a handle about 3 inches long into which the needle is inserted. The needle is about 1½ inches long and curved with a sharp fishhook at the end. The size of this hook regulates the number of hairs which will automatically be drawn from the hank when the needle is inserted. For example, a #1 needle should draw 1 hair, a #6 needle, 6 hairs. For the body of a wig or a mustache a fairly large needle is used. Obviously, the larger the needle, the faster the work will go. But for the edges a small needle must be used so that the knots will not show. Large needles should be used only where the knots are covered by subsequent layers of hair. It is wiser not to use larger than a #4 for mustaches. A #1 or #2 should be used for the top few rows.

Figure 129 illustrates the ventilating technique. Practice this on a piece of scrap netting before you try to work on a mustache. A little practice should make you reasonably expert. This is the procedure:

A. Remove a very small bit of hair from the hank, and double it about a third of the way from the root end. Assuming you are righthanded,

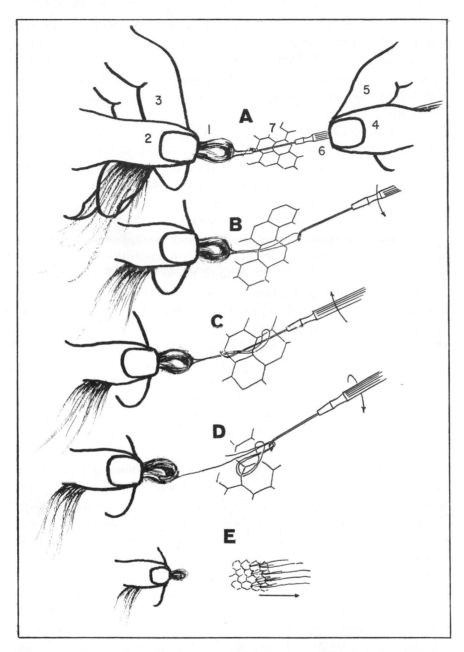

FIGURE 129. Ventilating hair onto lace. Progressive positions of the needle in relation to the hair and the lace. Size of the lace is greatly magnified.

grasp this loop (1) between the thumb (2) and the forefinger (3) of your left hand. With the thumb (4) and the forefinger (5) of your right hand hold the needle (6), and slip it under one strand of the net (7). In the drawing the size of the net is greatly exaggerated for clarity. Then thrust the hook of the needle into the hair. The hook should be pointing toward you or slightly upward.

B. With the thumb and finger of the right hand twist the needle counterclockwise, as indicated by the arrow, in order to turn the hook of the needle down so that it will not catch on the net as you draw it back. Draw back, as illustrated, but only far enough to clear the net. If you draw it too far, you will pull out the short end of the hair. Until the knot is made, you must have a double hair to work with.

C. Move the needle toward the left hand, hook it under the double hair, and give it a half-turn clockwise in order to catch the hair.

D. Continue the clockwise turn until the hook is pointing downward and draw the needle back through the loop. Continue to draw it to the right until the entire length of the hair is through. Pull the knot tight. Until you learn to do this as you pull the hair through with the needle, it may be necessary to pull it tight with the fingers.

E. The hairs will then lie in one direction, moving away from the left hand. Always move the right hand in the direction you wish the hairs to lie. Along the visible edges of your mustache you will probably place a hair in each tiny opening of the net, but when you are using a larger needle, you will space the knots in order to give you the thickness of hair you wish.

Since single knots may sometimes loosen, permitting hairs to be combed out of the piece, a double knotting process can be used for added security. In section D above, after the needle has been drawn back through the loop, but before the ends have been drawn through, the needle is once again hooked around the stems of the hair. Then the needle is drawn back through the second loop which has been formed, and the ends are pulled through and the hair pulled tight as usual.

This knotting sounds like a difficult and complex process, but it really is not. Once you have mastered the needle technique, you will make the necessary movements automatically and proceed quite rapidly. A whole wig requires a great deal of time to make, but a mustache can be done fairly quickly.

In making a mustache, always begin at the outer corners and work along the bottom and upward (Figure 130). The top hair should always be the last to be knotted in. When the hair is in, trim the net about a quarter

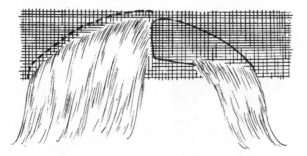

FIGURE 130. Ventilating a mustache on net or gauze. The solid line represents the outline of the mustache, which is always drawn on paper underneath the net or, if gauze is used, on the gauze itself. The dotted line represents where the gauze or net will be trimmed.

inch beyond the hair, as shown by the dotted line in Figure 130. Since the cut edges will eventually ravel and have to be cut down further, the wider the net edge is at first, the longer the mustache will last. But at the same time, the wider net will be more visible to the audience.

You will undoubtedly want to do some preliminary trimming of the mustache before trying it on, for when you finish the ventilating, the hair will probably be as long as that in Figure 131. Cut carefully with a good pair of barber's shears, a little at a time. Then try on the mustache before doing the final trimming.

For both beards and mustaches, though it is especially important for beards, you should usually use more than one shade of hair. Facial hair is usually darker underneath, lighter on top and along the edges. The lighter hair along the edge, being nearer the color of the skin, is extremely helpful in making a subtle, realistic blend. With gray hair, the differences in color are especially marked. There can sometimes be dark brown or even black hairs underneath and white ones above. This can be done very subtly in ventilating since the hairs are put in individually. A few red or auburn hairs will frequently give a gray beard added life. Observe real beards—gray ones are rarely, if ever, the same throughout. Frequently there are very marked streaks, but notice where and how these usually fall. Three colors of hair were used for the mustache in Figure 131.

One additional note is necessary in regard to beards. When the general outline of the net is cut before beginning the beard, open out the pattern and cut the net flat. Then place the pattern on a form (such as a plaster cast of the head) so that the original tucks can be taken. Identical

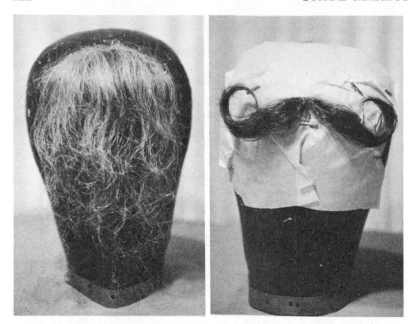

FIGURES 131, 132. Ventilated mustaches on wig blocks. Made by students Bill Smith and Mike Carrington. The gray mustache has not yet been trimmed and dressed. For the finished mustache see Figure 153. The dark mustache has been sprayed with Safeguard bandage.

tucks can be taken in the net. These can be folded down, and you may secure them with thread if you like. However, after a little practice, you will find that you can secure these tucks simply by ventilating through the three thicknesses of net so that you are actually tying in the tucks with strands of hair.

If you wish to make the body of the beard foundation with gauze, simply lay the gauze over the beard pattern as you would the net, only trim it down ⅜ to ½ inch below the upper outline of the beard. The gauze should, of course, not show when the beard is finished. Then lay on a strip of net along the edge, overlapping the gauze about ½ inch and, of course, overlapping the edge of the pattern also. Then the hair can be ventilated through both net and gauze, tying them together.

Since the gauze is closely woven, ventilating is much more difficult, and great care must be taken in withdrawing the hook to prevent its catching on the gauze.

Application. In order that any ventilated piece with a net edge, whether wig, beard, or mustache, look natural, it must be carefully applied.

This is the technique:

1. Place the piece on your face in exactly the right position. If you have a beard or a mustache with a partial gauze foundation, you can secure it to the skin with double-faced toupee tape. If you are using a mustache with no gauze, hold it with the left hand (if you are right-handed) or else set it on the face and then observe very carefully where it goes so that you can estimate where to place the spirit gum.

2. Brush a thin coat of spirit gum onto the dry skin (no makeup) beneath the lace edge. Do not apply it to the lace. *Do not use latex!*

3. Let the spirit gum become slightly tacky. The time required varies with the brand of spirit gum, but it is short in any case. As in applying crepe hair, it can be speeded up by tapping repeatedly with one finger over the gummed area. Then press the lace edge into the gum with a clean, white, lintless towel or a damp chamois, being careful to press the lace straight down without letting it slide on the skin, thus stretching it and making unsightly corrugations or ripples. Use a clean section of the towel each time you press. When you have pressed the lace until there is no more shine to the spirit gum and the towel does not stick to the face, pat a damp towel over the area. Then with a toothbrush, a dye brush, or an eyebrow brush, lift any hairs along the edge which may have accidentally been stuck down by the gum.

Dressing. When the beard or the mustache is securely attached, it can be combed with a wide-toothed comb. However, in combing any hair piece, always hold the comb at an angle so that there is no possibility that the teeth will dig into the net foundation and tear it. This means holding it at the reverse angle from the one usually used in combing your own hair. This is very difficult to get used to but very important. Also, when the hair is fairly long, always begin combing at the ends and work toward the roots. Human hair in hairpieces of any kind becomes matted and tangled much more easily than the same hair would while growing on the head for the simple reason that half of the hair is going in the wrong direction. In other words, the hair is knotted somewhere near the middle, and the roots, as well as the ends, are extended outward. A human hair is not quite the simple, smooth filament it appears to be. There are little scalelike projections, all going in the same direction. You can usually feel the difference by running a hair quickly between your thumb and your forefinger in the right direction and then reversing it. When hairs are not all going in the same direction, these tiny scales catch onto each other and cause matting. Therefore, special care is needed in combing hairpieces of any kind. Synthetic hair does not mat.

If the hair does not fall just as you would like it to naturally, comb it with water, set it, and let it dry before recombing it. You can push it into waves or even make pin curls (on the ends of beards or mustaches, for example). When the hair is dry, spray it with brilliantine or hair lacquer and comb or, if you prefer, dip the comb into brilliantine. If you want the hair to look dry or unhealthy or dirty, you will, naturally, omit the brilliantine.

The hair can also be curled with a curling iron if you prefer. However, heat should be used with great care, if at all, on synthetic hair. Water waving is much preferable. In order to maintain the wave in synthetic hair, it may be necessary to spray it with hair lacquer.

Removing and cleaning. To remove the beard or the mustache, dip a stiff brush into acetone and press the bristles into the lace edge. Do not scrub and do not pull up the lace by force. Keep flooding it with acetone until the spirit gum is softened and the lace comes up by itself. Any good lace or net is very delicate, and great care must be taken not to stretch or tear it. Then dip the lace edge into a dish of acetone to remove all traces of spirit gum and makeup. The lace must be kept absolutely clean if it is to remain invisible on the skin. It may be desirable occasionally (perhaps once a week during regular performances) to soak the whole piece in acetone for a few minutes. The hair can best be cleaned by dipping in carbon tetrachloride, naphtha, or benzine. This does not affect any wave which may be in the hair.

Beards and mustaches should be carefully stored so that they will be kept clean and the lace will not be damaged. It is best to keep each beard individually in a box sufficiently large that it will not be pressed flat.

Measuring for beards. If you wish to order a beard by mail, the following are the necessary measurements. Letters refer to those in Figure 154. The heavy dotted lines represent beard measurements; the light broken line is the beard line.

A. From sideburn to sideburn under chin
B. From lip to end of beard line under chin
C. Width across the front (average measurement, 3 inches)
D. Corner of lip to back of jawbone

If you are ordering a ready-made beard, all of these measurements may not be necessary, especially if you should be renting it. But better too many than not enough.

Adapting beards. One great advantage of ventilated pieces is that they can be restyled, often merely by combing, for a variety of characters. With this in mind, it is not a bad idea to make a full beard in three pieces—one center and two side sections—with, of course, a separate mustache (see

FIGURE 133. A versatile beard. Late nineteenth-century beard styles made by combining the four ventilated hair pieces shown in Figure 134. The same hair-lace wig was used throughout and recombed. Model shown in Figure 7.

FIGURE 134. Full beard in sections. Sideburns, mustache, and beard made of real hair ventilated into nylon net. These pieces can be recombed, straightened, or curled and used in various combinations, as shown in Figure 133.

Figure 134). Then the pieces can be used singly or in any combination, as shown in Figure 133, in which all eight makeups are done with a single wig and the four pieces shown in Figure 134. This is only a sampling of the variety which could be obtained by combining pieces and recombing. The same pieces and, in fact, the same wig were used for the stylized Gothic makeup in Figure 155, for which the beard, mustache, and front hair of the wig were curled with an iron.

It is most useful for an actor or any theatre group to build up a stock of ventilated beards and mustaches, particularly such versatile ones as those in Figure 134. Real hair should be used when possible since it can be recombed and restyled much more easily than synthetic hair. The color can be changed if necessary, though it's always better to have several colors on hand. The best way to build up a stock of hair pieces is to make whatever is required for each character you do instead of using crepe hair. Then the pieces can be saved and used in the future. This takes more time initially but pays off in the end, giving you a stock of realistic beards and mustaches to choose from.

PROBLEMS

1. Make it a point during the next few days to observe facial hair. Make sketches and notes for your file of as many types of mustaches and beards as you can find. Notice where partially grayed beards are the light-

est and where the darkest in a number of individual cases, and make any generalizations which seem warranted.

2. With crepe hair, duplicate one or two beards from your morgue or from styles illustrated in Appendix F or G. If you have time, complete the makeup or use the beard for one of the characters in Problem 3 for which it would be appropriate.

3. Using suitable hair applications, make up yourself or someone else as one of the characters in each of the following groups:

a. Davies (*The Caretaker*); Horace Vandergelder (*The Matchmaker*); Engstrand (*Ghosts*); Helmer (*A Doll's House*); Constable Warren (*Our Town*); Robert Browning (*The Barretts of Wimpole Street*); Sergius (*Arms and the Man*); Alfred Doolittle, Colonel Pickering (*Pygmalion, My Fair Lady*); Mr. Wickham (*Pride and Prejudice*); Father (*Life With Father*); Sewer Man (*The Madwoman of Chaillot*).

b. Iago; King Richard II; Dr. Rank (*A Doll's House*); Gustave Rosenberg (*Kind Lady*); Dr. Sloper (*The Heiress*); Creon (*Antigone*); Trigorin (*The Sea Gull*); Dr. Stockmann (*An Enemy of the People*); Kolenkov (*You Can't Take It With You*); Solinus (*Comedy of Errors*); Ulric Brendel (*Rosmersholm*); Macbeth; Gremio (*Taming of the Shrew*); King of Hearts (*Alice in Wonderland*); Volpone; General St. Pé (*Waltz of the Toreadors*); Astroff (*Uncle Vanya*); Firs (*The Cherry Orchard*); Fagin (*Oliver*).

c. Agmar (*The Gods of the Mountain*); King Henry IV; Baptista, Vincentio (*Taming of the Shrew*); Falstaff; King Lear; Duncan (*Macbeth*); Claudius, Polonius (*Hamlet*); Prospero (*The Tempest*); Shylock, Old Gobbo (*Merchant of Venice*); Kalchas (*Daughters of Atreus*); Teiresias (*Antigone*); The Grandfather (*The Intruder*); Angelo, Ageon (*Comedy of Errors*); Captain Shotover (*Heartbreak House*); Kublai Khan, Chu-Yin (*Marco Millions*); Gandalf (*Lord of the Rings*).

16

HAIR AND WIGS

The hair is an extremely important part of any makeup and is invaluable in suggesting period, personality, age, and health. A simple rearrangement of the hair can often transform the actor into an entirely different person. Conversely, failure to make the hair suit the character can ruin an otherwise skillful makeup.

NATURAL HAIR

More often than not the actor's own hair can be used for the character he is playing, as in Figure 125. This is the simplest and most economical solution to the hair problem and is always preferable to using a poor wig. It is important, unless a complete wig is to be worn, to caution actors at the start of the rehearsal period not to have their hair cut. Not only does short hair tend to look still shorter onstage, but it is inappropriate for a great many characters and it mitigates the illusion of age, which may be necessary for the character.

Restyling. Although one is limited by the length of the actor's own hair, within such limitations great variety can be achieved by a change in style for men as well as for women. Observe, for example, the hair in Figures 1, 3, 4, 6, and 175. It is in every case the hair of the actor in Figure 7. The same head of hair can be parted on the side, in the middle, or not at all. It can be combed straight back or straight forward. It can be well combed or mussed. It can be straight or waved, close to the head or fluffed out. All of these transformations, unless the hair is very unmanageable, can be made with the aid of a comb and a brush, hair spray or hair dressing, and water.

For both men and women it is possible to wave the hair, if it is naturally straight, by setting it with pin curls or on rollers or by curling it with a curling iron. If the hair is to look well groomed, it can be sprayed with brilliantine or a commercial hair spray, or a hair dressing can be applied with the fingers and combed through the hair, just as it would be for street wear. A lacquer spray for keeping the hair in place is sometimes desirable, depending on how manageable the natural hair is and how well it stays combed.

For characters whose hair would be expected to look dull and lifeless, no hair dressing should be used. If the hair naturally has a sheen, a little face powder the color of the hair can be dusted on or a little cake makeup of the correct shade can be applied with sponge to dull the hair. If the hair is to look stiff and matted, it can be heavily sprayed with a liquid hair set and shaped with the fingers rather than with a comb or a brush.

Coloring and graying. The most satisfactory method of coloring or graying the hair is by the use of a temporary spray which can be washed out (see Appendix A for suggestions). It is available in aerosol spray cans or in glass bottles to be used with an atomizer. Both are available in gold, silver, black, and a wide variety of colors including blue, pink, and chartreuse. The silver is excellent for graying. The entire head can be sprayed or the hair can be streaked with gray or with color. It is even possible to use more than one color. For example, blond hair can be changed to brown streaked with gray merely by spraying first with the brown, then when it is thoroughly dry, with silver. Black hair can be made blonde, but it is recommended that it first be sprayed with red, then with blond since the blond spray would not cover adequately.

One must be extremely careful in using such a spray to keep it off the face and to avoid patchiness. The best way to keep it off the skin is to cut a piece of paper to match the hairline and hold it over the forehead as the front of the hair is being sprayed. This cutout can be kept in the makeup kit for future use. In partial graying, the gray should be combed in after spraying.

If the silvery effect is inappropriate (as, for example, for a Bowery bum), there are many other methods of graying possible. White Pan-Stik can be used quickly and easily and does not leave a flat, dull finish. It will rub off, but it is probably preferable to white greasepaint, which is sometimes used.

White cake makeup, liquid white mascara, and liquid hair whitener are all possible products for graying the hair. For a complete graying (when the silvery effect will not do), liquid hair whitener is the most satisfactory.

Cake makeup and mascara are fine for streaking or touching up. If the effect of these whiteners is too dull or flat, a little brilliantine can be sprayed on or combed in.

White powder or cornstarch should be used only in an emergency or for quick changes, for the effect is usually quite unnatural and any unusual activity on the part of the actor sends up a cloud of white dust. Aluminum powder is undesirable for the reasons given in Appendix A. White grease-paint and even shoe polish are sometimes used, but they have no advantage over mascara, and the desirability of using shoe polish on the scalp is certainly questionable.

In emergencies if a colored hair spray is not available or if a very dull, lifeless effect is desired, the hair can be colored with liquid base, cake makeup, or even colored face powder. But these methods are seldom very satisfactory.

For men whose hair is thin at the crown, Scalp Masque (see Appendix A) is an excellent preparation for touching up. The liquid, which comes in various shades, is applied with an attached dauber, then rubbed with cotton or a clean cloth. Provided the spot is not completely bald, the result is usually effective enough to be used for street wear. Cake makeup of the correct color is a good substitute. In an emergency, eyebrow pencil, greasepaint, or Pan-Stik can be used for the same purpose, but they have the disadvantage of a shine.

WIGS AND HAIRPIECES

If it is not possible to change the actor's own hair to achieve the effect needed for the character, a wig or a hairpiece is necessary. *Wigs* cover the entire hair area, whereas *hairpieces* are used to supplement the natural hair. Hairpieces can be divided into two kinds—*toupees*, which supply a front hairline and cover part or all of the top of the head and blend into the natural hair at the back and on the sides, and *falls*, which are attached to the natural hair, usually near the crown, in order to lengthen it in back. The natural hair is then combed over the edge of the fall and into the false hair. The fall is extremely useful for period styles, especially for men. The result is far less expensive than a wig would be and frequently more effective. The front hairline, which is always the greatest problem in a wig, is natural; the fall provides the necessary length. In Appendix G some of the illustrated hair styles which would be particularly well suited to the use of the fall are Plates 9*t*, 14*j-n-o-q*, and 17*b*.

Switches are used by women to extend the hair when it is possible to pin it to the natural hair without a blend, as in Plates 8a-c-i-g-k-l-n-p, for example.

Wigs can be classified by the type of construction, type of hair, and length of hair. Naturally, in choosing a particular wig, the color will also be an essential factor.

The construction of a wig involves both the type of foundation material to be used and the method by which the hair is to be added. Both of these depend to some extent on the direction in which the hair is to lie.

Foundations may be of cotton or imitation silk net, treated silk lace (plastic coated), nylon net, hairlace, silk gauze, or a combination of these.

Probably the simplest form of wig is that made entirely of cotton net edged and strengthened with a cotton webbing and made to hug the head by means of short lengths of steel spring or whalebone sewn into the foundation. These are curved slightly in order to press the edges of the foundation against the skin and are used at critical spots at which the foundation might tend to pull away from the head—normally at the front center, in front of the ears, and behind the ears at the very bottom of the foundation. There should be an elastic across the back of the neck to pull the foundation as snug as possible.

This type of wig makes no provision for a part and does not provide a realistic hairline in front, but it is quite suitable for wigs which are representing wigs and not natural hair—for example, the wigs normally worn by the upper classes in the eighteenth century (see Appendix G). This type of foundation could have a silk gauze insert to make a parting possible. When the hair is to be separated in any way to expose the scalp, silk gauze must be used unless (as is the case with toupees) there is actually a bare scalp underneath the wig, in which case silk or nylon net is preferable. For close inspection a *drawn parting* is necessary. This is a painstaking and delicate technique by which the hair is knotted into gauze, then the hairs are drawn individually through another piece of gauze so that no knots will be visible and the hair will seem to be growing directly out of the scalp. The effect is extremely realistic but is never necessary for stage work. It is used primarily for women's wigs for street wear.

If the hair is to be combed away from the face, revealing a natural looking hairline, the best solution is a section of nylon net or hairlace in the front of the wig (Figure 135). The rest of the wig may be of silk gauze, caul netting, or a combination of the two. The nylon net should extend for at least half an inch beyond the hair so that it can be glued to the skin with spirit gum. Eventually it will ravel and will have to be trimmed closer. The wider it is originally, the longer the wig will last but the more difficult it

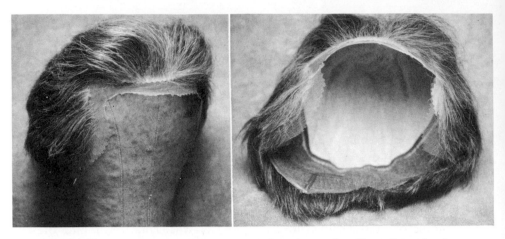

FIGURES 135, 136. Ventilated wig with lace front. Outside and inside views.

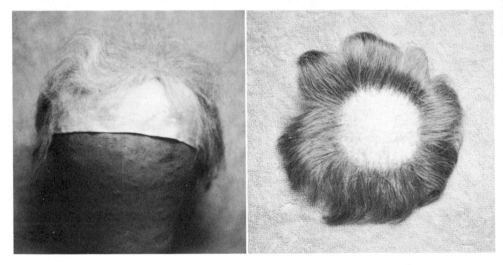

FIGURES 137, 138. Blender wig and monk's tonsure. In the blender wig gray hair is sparsely ventilated into the fabric on top. The blender must be made up to match the actor's flesh tone. The tonsure is a small ventilated piece made for Albert Finney for *Luther*, with the hair matching Mr. Finney's own.

will be to conceal the net, as we learned in our work with ventilated beards. Figure 123 shows a wig in which the lace front is not entirely glued down and is detectable in the photograph.

If the hairline of the wig is to be farther back than the actor's own hairline, a *blender* will be necessary to cover the natural hair in front (see Figures 137 and 183). This extends down onto the forehead where the line of the blender must theoretically be rendered invisible with makeup. This is not always possible, but suggestions will be included under "Wearing the Wig."

If the hair is to be combed forward (as in Figure 140 and Appendix G—Plate 2a-b-d-h, etc.), there is no hairline problem, and a simple net foundation can be used. Such a wig will naturally be less expensive to buy and simpler to make.

PERIOD HAIR STYLES

It is essential in period plays that the hair style match the costume in period. Women's hair can frequently be restyled to fit the period, but men usually need a wig or a fall to achieve the correct period feeling.

The drawings in Appendix G illustrate representative hair styles for men and women from the early Egyptian to the present. These drawings by no means include all of the variations in style of any given period but merely show a few specific hair styles (most of them taken from paintings, sculpture, or photographs of the period) which seem to be fairly representative. All of the drawings represent styles worn during the period indicated but not necessarily at the height of fashion. They are intended to provide a handy makeup guide rather than an exhaustive historical study. For such a study see *Fashions in Hair—The First Five Thousand Years,* from which these drawings were taken.

In referring to the drawings it is well to note the general style and basic silhouette of the period and adapt the characteristics of that style to the individual character, making such variations as seem appropriate or expedient. In any period it will be found that social class is reflected in the hair style as well as the dress. When you see an elaborate hair style illustrated (such as Plates 1e, 3f, 12t, 13b, 15k-n-o-p, and 16a-b-c) you may be sure it was worn by a person of high social standing. Obviously, such styles would be out of place on peasants or servants. The simpler styles which require little time or care in dressing are naturally more appropriate for those people who have less interest in fashion and less time and money to indulge in it.

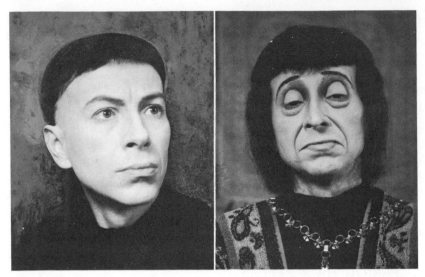

FIGURES 139, 140. Henry V and the Prince of Arragon. Hair styles fashionable at the beginning (left) and at the end (right) of the fifteenth century. For Henry V the sideburns were blocked out with spirit gum, powder, cream stick, and cake makeup. For the Prince of Arragon (from *The Merchant of Venice*) the eyebrows were blocked out with spirit gum and derma wax. All shadowing and highlighting was done with cake makeup. Model shown in Figure 7.

This does not mean that all simple styles (such as Plates 2*j*, 5*a*, 8*r*, and 21*p*) are to be used for peasant classes only. Simple styles are frequently fashionable, but they are carefully planned.

Of course, social standing and adherence to fashion are not always synonymous. An emperor's wife may be a very simple person with simple tastes, and this will be reflected in her hair style. But chances are that her hair, though not fashionably styled, will be carefully dressed. The personality must always be considered. This is particularly true in our present society. It is no longer true that women who work at ordinary jobs on a relatively low social level do not have the time or the money to spend on their hair. In fact, some of the most elaborate hair styles to be seen today may be on shopgirls, whereas the wealthy and the socially elite may dress their hair very simply—carefully and no doubt expensively, but still simply. It is largely a matter of taste.

Age is a factor too. Sometimes older people will tend to dress their hair in a style which they have worn for many years and which may once have been fashionable. This is more true in the past than in the present, and of course it does not apply to older women who are fashion-conscious. However, even if older women do follow the fashion of the moment, they will ordinarily not adopt the extreme fashions, which are usually more suitable for younger women. Plates 19e-f-m and 21g-j-m, for example, are obviously inappropriate for a woman of seventy. As with the rest of the makeup, you must exercise your own judgment in helping the actor to reveal the character.

With the plates of drawings in Appendix G there are included in the captions brief comments on each period, indicating general characteristics of the hair styles.

CONSTRUCTING THE WIG

When the wig has been designed, you must either buy or make a foundation and then attach the hair to the foundation. For a full wig you would do well to buy a net wig cap if it can possibly be adapted to the type of wig you need. Such a cap is shown in Figures 143–145. These are relatively inexpensive cotton foundations and quite adequate for many types of wigs. They are usually available in white, gray, brown, and black. Choose the color nearest that of the hair you plan to use. Wigs in Figures 63, 128, 140, 151, 152, and 168 are constructed on such a foundation, and wigs from most of the styles in Plate 7, for example, could be. There are stays which hold the wig fairly snugly to the head and an elastic at the nape of the neck to pull it tight. If there is to be a natural looking front hairline, however, such a cap cannot be used, at least in its original form. Individually fitted wigs with a natural hairline are expensive and require a much better quality foundation cap, as illustrated in the Bob Kelly wig in process of construction, Figure 146-C.

Ventilating. The technique of ventilating a wig is the same as for mustaches and beards. Since this was discussed thoroughly in the last chapter, we shall not repeat the instructions. Double knotting, except at the visible front edges, is usually desirable though not necessary. As with beards and mustaches, we always begin with the hair which is to be underneath and finish with that which is to be on top. This means beginning at the nape of the neck and working upward toward the crown as shown in Figures 143 and 144. If you are right-handed, the wig block will be held in the lap as shown in Figure 144. Be sure to include occasional hairs of a different shade. If you like, use darker hair at the back and lighter toward the front.

If the hair is to be combed back, you simply proceed forward until you

FIGURE 141. Eighteenth-century wigmaker's tools. These include hackles (K, Q), powder bag, puff, and cone (G, H, I), curl papers (C), razors (g), barber's basin (a), and a machine for binding pigtails (MNO).

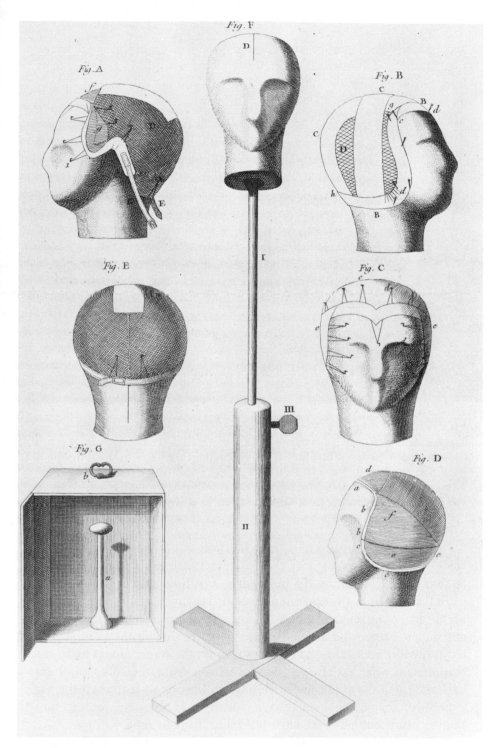

FIGURE 142. French eighteenth-century wig blocks and foundations. In the lower left-hand corner is a wig carrying case.

approach the front hairline, always pulling the hair toward the back of the wig. Brushing or combing it occasionally as you work will keep stray hairs from getting in your way. The amount of hair you use will depend entirely on how thick you want the hair to be. Ordinarily, it is desirable to keep the wig as light in weight as possible within the limits set by the effect you are trying to achieve. The hair can be knotted into the binding tapes as well as through the net, as shown in Figures 143 and 144.

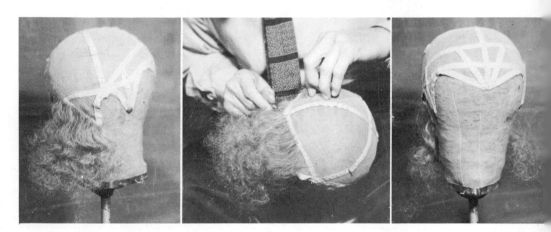

FIGURES 143, 144, 145. Ventilating a wig. This is an inexpensive cotton net foundation which can be purchased ready-made. The center picture shows a common position for ventilating. The ventilating needle is held in the right hand and the hair in the left. Real hair is being used. Notice the wave which forms naturally in the hair. Wig block is the canvas covered type, shown both on and off the wig stand.

When you approach the front hairline, use a smaller needle, and space your hair closer and very evenly. In fact, it is usually not a bad idea to stop ½ to 1 inch from the front edge, turn the wig block around, and work the hair from the opposite direction, beginning at the edge and leting the hair hang down as if over the face. Then when you reach the previous stopping place and all the hair is in, you can comb the front section back. It will then tend to stand up away from the forehead and make the hairline somewhat less obvious. Be sure that in ventilating along the front edge you catch the needle under the edge sufficiently so that when the wig is finished, none of the binding tape will show. If necessary, you can turn the wig inside out later and add a few hairs at the hairline.

If the hair is to be combed away from the crown in all directions

(Plate 7b-c-e-f-h-i, etc.) you will proceed from the outer edges of the cap upward in an ever-narrowing circle so that the final hairs are knotted in at the crown. Always ventilate the hair in the direction in which it is to lie except when you deliberately reverse direction in order to make the hair stand up rather than lie flat. This must be kept in mind constantly as you work.

Weaving. A simple wig, such as the one just described, can be made much more quickly and easily by sewing on rows of weft, particularly across the back, and ventilating only the front section. In fact, the entire wig can be made in this way provided the hair is to be combed back, but a much better hairline can be achieved by ventilating the front of the wig.

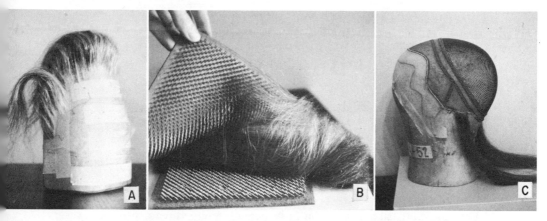

FIGURE 146. **Wig-making equipment.** (A) Wooden beard block (beard is upside down), (B) drawing mats with hair, (C) wooden wig block with high quality fitted wig foundation. Nylon net will be added to the foundation where the front hairline is pencilled in.

The weft (which is made of lengths of hair woven on two, three, or four silk strands) is sewn to the wig cap, starting at the back and moving forward over the top of the head. The lengths of weft are usually about an inch apart but may be more or less. The closer they are, the heavier the hair will be. If they are too far apart, the foundation may show through. A wig made of weft is heavier to wear and much less versatile since the style of the wig can be changed very little, whereas a ventilated wig is extremely light to wear and can be recombed in many ways.

Figure 147 illustrates the technique for making weft. A table or bench with an overlapping edge is necessary. Two weaving sticks are clamped to it, as shown in A. You can buy weaving sticks and clamps, or you can rig

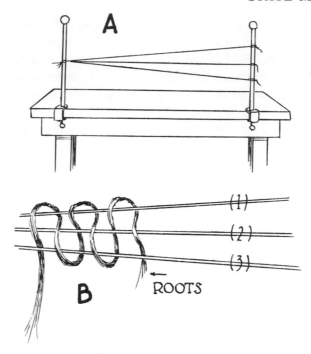

FIGURE 147. **Weaving hair.** (A) Shows how the weaving sticks are set up, and (B) shows the threading of the hair.

up your own. The essential elements are the three threads tied as shown. For fine weft, silk is used; but any heavy, strong thread, fishline, or very light cord will do. The threads or cords should be as strong as possible without being bulky.

If you are sufficiently serious about wigmaking to be weaving hair, then you should have a pair of drawing brushes or mats. The brushes have short stiff bristles. The mats, which are preferable for knotting and weaving, are made of two rectangles of tough leather into which are inserted short wires, all bent down parallel to the mat in the same direction (Figure 146-B). Hair which is to be woven is placed on one of the mats with the ends of the bent wires pointing toward the points (not the roots) of the hair. The root ends protrude slightly over the mat. The other mat is laid on top of the first one, wire side downward. The roots should be on the side of the mats facing the weaver and extending just enough so that they can be easily grasped. The amount of hair extending beyond the other side of the mats will depend entirely on the length of hair being used and is immaterial.

The purpose of the mats is, of course, to keep the hair firmly in place and to make it possible to draw out as many hairs as you wish without disturbing the remainder of the hair. Drawing mats should ideally be used in knotting as well as weaving. They have not been mentioned before since the additional equipment makes the process seem more complicated and more expensive, and it is possible to manage without them.

To weave, follow this procedure:

A. Draw a strand of hair from the braid (the more hairs you use, the heavier the weft will be), and hold it in your left hand with the root ends protruding upward.

B. Then, holding the strand of hair behind the threads, reach with the forefinger of your right hand between threads 2 and 3 (Figure 147-B), and pull the hair through and up over the top of 1.

C. Reach between 1 and 2; grasp the hair; pull it forward (toward you, that is) between 1 and 2.

D. Reach between 1 and 2 and grasp the hair from behind. Pull it away from you under 3, then forward between 1 and 2, and back over the top of 1.

E. Reach between 1 and 2 and grasp the hair. Pull it forward between 1 and 2.

F. Reach between 1 and 2 and pull the hair under 3, away from you, and up and out toward you between 1 and 2, then over the top.

G. Reach between 1 and 2, and pull the hair forward.

H. From behind, reach forward between 2 and 3 and pull the hair back.

I. Now, holding both ends of the hair, pull it close together and tight so that it seems to be hanging from a little knot. The root ends of the hair should be short—not much more than an inch hanging down. The other end will be long, of course.

Keep repeating this process, each time pushing the hair to the left and making sure it is as tight as you can make it. When you have the necessary length, cut the threads and tie both ends securely. Then the weft is ready to sew onto the wig foundation. There are numerous methods of weaving (see the eighteenth-century engraving in Figure 149), but this is one of the most common techniques for making weft to be used in wigs. It may seem complicated, perhaps even confusing at first glance, and you should be warned that it will almost certainly seem slow and awkward in the beginning. But a little practice makes it possible to weave very quickly and almost automatically.

Mixing hair. You may find that you need to mix two or more colors

FIGURE 148. French wig styles illustrated in Garsault's *Art du Perruquier*, 1767. (C) Knotted wig, (F) square wig, (D) abbot's wig, (A) bob wig, (B) bag wig, (G) brigadier wig, (H) pigtail wig, (E) natural wig.

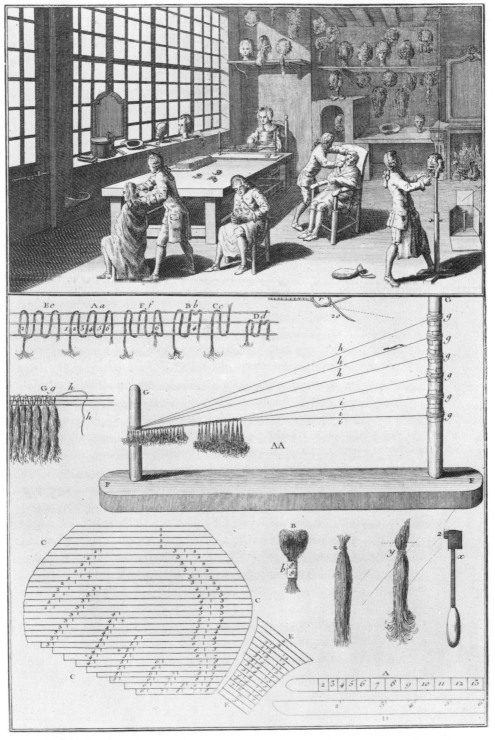

FIGURE 149. Eighteenth-century wig shop and (below) method of weaving hair. The diagram lower left is a white paper marked to indicate arrangement of hair on the wig.

of hair to achieve the effect you want. This requires the use of a hackle (or card), which is a wooden block from which project numerous sharp steel spikes. The spikes may be either vertical or slightly angled. The hackle has changed very little since the eighteenth century (see Figure 141-K). In using the hackle, you will need to secure it to a bench or a table with clamps.

Straight hair is more easily mixed than curly. In mixing, grasp in one hand and at the root ends the two hanks of hair to be mixed. Then slap the hair down onto the hackle and pull it through, mixing the two hanks with both hands as you pull. Keep repeating this process until the two colors are thoroughly blended. If you wish to add a third color, follow the same procedure. If you are not sure how much of a color you wish to add to the basic color, blend in a little at a time. The purpose of the hackle in this blending process is simply to keep the hair from tangling. Hair which is already tangled can be drawn through the hackle for untangling.

Remodeling the wig cap. If you need a natural hairline, the ready-made wig cap can still be used by cutting off the front portion (up to the second tape) and replacing it with hairlace or nylon net. As with beards and mustaches, a paper pattern of the desired hairline should be made first, then pinned to the wig block under the lace. The lace, remember, must extend at least ½ inch beyond the hairline, preferably more. It can always be trimmed, but it can't be extended. A #1 ventilating needle, which pulls out just one hair at a time, should be used for the last few rows along the front edge if you expect to have a natural looking hairline. If you use more than one hair at a time, the knots will be plainly visible. As before, you may ventliate either forward or backward, depending on whether you wish the hair to stand up slightly or lie flat.

It may sometimes be necessary to remove more of the foundation than just the front section. As you can see in Figure 143, there is a front tape and a small triangle of netting on the side which can easily be removed without disturbing the fit of the cap. If you need to go still farther back, you may have to resew one of the tapes so that the cap will hold its shape. When the hair is all in, trim the lace or net at the front no closer than ½ inch from the hairline.

If you need a part in the wig, insert a section of silk gauze about 1 inch wide and of whatever length is necessary at the spot where you wish the part. Then ventilate toward the part from each side, using a #1 needle on the gauze section. Tapes will have to be sewn on around the edges of the section of gauze to give firmness. The gauze part will, in most cases, be a continuation of a front section of lace at the hairline. If the wig is to be used over a bald head, nylon net can be used instead of gauze.

Occasionally, as in Plates 1*q* and 5*d-g-j*, for example, you may need a part in a wig in which the hairline does not show. You can then dispense with the netting and merely insert the section of gauze into the foundation.

Blenders. These are constructed of tightly woven, thin fabric which can be covered with greasepaint to match the foundation color on the skin. Several different fabrics are used. A high-grade shirting is satisfactory, or silk gauze can be used. Whatever fabric you use, the selvage and not a raw edge must cross the forehead and be used for the blend.

It is simplest to start with a ready-made wig foundation and remove the front and as much of the top as necessary, the exact amount depending on how far back the new hairline is to go. The blender must fit very tightly across the forehead and is attached to the side pieces of the wig foundation. Be particularly careful at the temples to prevent wrinkling which, of course, ruins the entire effect. The hair is ventilated into the gauze or shirting in the usual way, using a #1 needle for the first few rows or, if the hair is to be thin on top, for a number of rows. A good blender wig is difficult to make and must be very carefully fitted to be successful. A snug fit across the forehead is essential (see Figure 180).

Bald wigs. The most satisfactory method of constructing a bald wig is to make a snug rubber cap (see Chapter 14) or buy a plastic one and attach the necessary hair (real or crepe) with latex or spirit gum. Real hair can also be ventilated directly into the cap. Even when attaching the major part of the hair with latex the top few rows of the sparse hair which may be on top of the head should be ventilated for a more realistic effect. The edge of the cap is thin and gives a much better blend than the usual fabric blender.

Toupees and sideburns. A toupee is constructed of a silk gauze piece, bound with tape, slightly larger than the bald spot it is intended to cover. Good toupees have a lace front and, if there is to be a part, a lace insert for the parting. Toupees are frequently made without the lace front, and they usually look exactly like toupees. They are less expensive to have made and far simpler to put on and take off, and they last much longer; but they seldom fool anybody. A good toupee requires a lace front unless the hair is to be combed down over the forehead, concealing the hairline.

Making a convincing toupee for street wear is a job requiring great skill and long experience. Therefore, I think we can safely assume that you will not be interested in detailed instructions for fine wig or toupee work. Even a good stage toupee needs to be well made. There are occasions, however, when a satisfactory hairpiece (usually a very small one) can be made by the average actor or makeup artist.

In Figure 177, for example, we see an actor who is to be made up as Woodrow Wilson. Obviously his top hair is too sparse to be recombed in any way that would prove adequate. Therefore, a small hairpiece was made on nylon net (Figure 178). Since the hair was combed forward and only a fraction of an inch of the lace showed, great skill in wigmaking was not required, and the hairpiece proved quite satisfactory. Sometimes a pointed tuft of hair—a sort of widow's peak—is needed to change the actor's hairline. That can easily be made on lace in a few minutes. The technique is the same as for beards and mustaches. First draw the new hairline on the skin with eyebrow pencil, trace and cut a paper pattern and place the hairlace or nylon net over it on the wig block, leaving the usual ½ inch or more for pasting down. Then carefully selecting hair to match the color of the actor's own, work the hair with a small needle.

It is often necessary to conceal modern sharply cut sideburns, and this can easily be done with two small hairpieces with hair long enough to brush back over or behind the actor's ears and into his own hair. If he has let his hair grow long in back, these hairpieces will sometimes suffice. If not, he may need to combine the hairpieces with a fall pinned under his own hair in back. In Plates 9v-w and 14n, we can see hair styles which might require this treatment.

Again the pattern must be made and the net placed over it on the block. The new side hair may follow the actor's natural hairline, or it may extend farther onto the face. Naturally, it cannot go back of the actor's own.

As is always the case in making a natural looking hairline with dark hair, it is helpful to make the last row of a lighter shade of hair, partly to soften the line and partly to avoid having a row of dark knots which spoil the naturalness of the effect.

Falls. Falls, as we have already mentioned, are hairpieces used to lengthen the back hair while using the natural hair in front. This avoids the problem of creating a natural front hairline or of concealing the blender or the lace. Since the fall does not have a delicate lace edge, it will last far longer than a wig.

The fall can take many forms, depending on the use to which it is to be put. For a cascade of curls for women it can be constructed of weft in a sort of basket weave—that is, the rows of weft are laid out diagonally, about 1 inch apart, sewed together where they cross and stiffened with fine wire to give more body to the foundation. Usually, small loops are formed across the top of the piece for pinning to the natural hair. Or small combs can be sewed into the piece for attaching it. The fall is then attached and the front and top hair combed back over the join and blended with the false hair. If the fall takes the form of a mass of curls, it is not always necessary to comb the natural hair into it—it can be pinned on top of the natural hair.

The fall may also take the form of a Juliet cap with the front band across the top of the head from ear to ear (Figure 154, #3) and the bottom band around the nape of the neck. It is then constructed like the top and back of a wig. This is particularly useful for men or for women with short hair. In constructing such a piece, remember that the front of the fall must lie flat and not be too heavy.

An even smoother, flatter edge can be achieved by using a net front instead of the tape. A heavier, sturdier net can be used than would be suitable for blending at the forehead. In either case it will be necessary to pin the fall securely to the hair and then comb the natural front hair over and into it to make a perfect blend.

The great difficulty with using falls for men lies in camouflaging the modern short sideburns. Ideally, the actor should let his side hair grow so that it can be combed back over the ears. This is frequently impractical, however, necessitating either adding separate side pieces on lace (see preceding section on sideburns) or making such pieces part of the fall itself. If this is done, the side pieces, when glued to the skin, serve as additional support to hold the fall in place.

The hair in a fall can be of any length and can be dressed and redressed in any style. Since it is to be blended with the actor's own hair, it must always be made from real hair. It can be constructed entirely of weft, entirely ventilated, or a combination of the two.

DRESSING THE WIG

Whether you have made your own wig or rented or bought a good one, its effectiveness will depend to a great extent upon how skillfully it is dressed. A rented wig seldom looks the way you want it to, but you may be able to change that. Cheap mohair wigs on buckram (and other inexpensive wigs) cannot be changed and are usually a waste of money, but any human hair wig can be redressed, at least within the limits imposed by its particular construction. Although a rented wig must not be cut or damaged, there is no reason for its not being redressed.

The first step in dressing any wig is to pin or tack it to your wig block and brush and comb it out thoroughly. Bear in mind previous instructions for holding the comb in working with wigs or beards. If a very simple style is required and you are pressed for time, you can curl the ends with an electric curling iron.

You can do a more thorough job, however, by combing the hair with water until it is quite wet, then putting it up in pin curls (Figure 150-C) or on rollers (150-A). For those who do not already know, pin curls are made by forming a flat coil from a strand of hair and pinning it down flat to the head with a hairpin or a bobby pin. All pin curls in one row are usually coiled in the same direction, though they may be coiled in opposite directions on either side of a part. Frequently the direction of the coil is reversed in alternate rows. If you want the entire head of hair to be wavy, you will put it all up in flat pin curls, starting at the front hairline and moving back and down. Usually there will be some natural wave in the hair. This can be encouraged with a damp comb, and often the hair will need no further curling except at the ends.

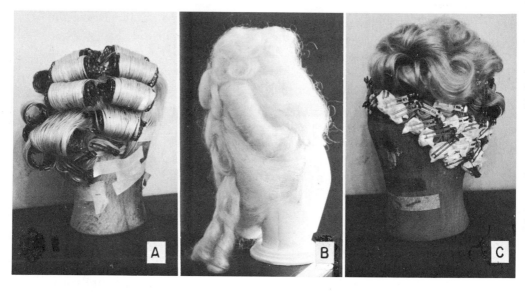

FIGURE 150. Dressing the wig. (A) Hair dressed on large rollers, (B) eighteenth-century wig of yak hair, (C) hair partially in pin curls and papers.

When the pin curls are thoroughly dry (the drying can be forced with a hair drier), comb them out. A little hair dressing may be necessary to provide a natural, healthy sheen. Then arrange the hair in waves or curls or puffs or whatever is required, combing it section by section as you go, and securing it with hairpins when necessary. Be sure the hairpins are inserted carefully so that they do not show. A rat-tail comb is often helpful in making rolls or curls. A hair lacquer spray may be used to set the hair after it has been dressed. The basic technique for dressing a wig is extremely simple, depending on the skill you have or can develop in handling hair.

WEARING THE WIG

Wigs must be handled carefully if they are to keep their shape and fit snugly. In putting on any full wig, grasp the lower back edge of the wig foundation with both hands; slide it up over the forehead until the hairline approaches within an inch or two of its proper position; then pull the wig down snugly over the head. Then with both hands resting on the wig move it back still further till the hairline is in the correct position. If the actor's own hair is long, it must be pulled up toward the top of the head first and pinned flat. A wide band around the head is frequently helpful in making sure that no stray hairs escape. (Figure 183 shows a wig being put on.)

FIGURES 151, 152, 153. The Madwoman of Chaillot, Chrétien de Neuvillette, and Captain Ahab. Student Bill Smith in his own makeups. (See also Figure 101.) The Madwoman's wig is of light gray hair ventilated on cotton net with no lace front. Eyebrows blocked out with spirit gum and wax, cotton in cheeks, cake makeup. Chrétien's wig is of light brown hair ventilated on cotton net with no lace front. Mustache and goatee are of crepe hair. Ahab's wig is ventilated on nylon net, giving a natural hairline. Beard is constructed of four colors of crepe hair (light gray, light gray-brown, blond, and medium gray) on latex. Mustache is of real hair ventilated on net (see Figure 131).

In removing the wig, grasp the back edge with both hands, and pull up and forward. Never remove the wig by pulling on the hair!

If the wig or toupee has a hairlace front, the procedure is the same as for applying beards on lace (see Chapter 15). Always paste down the lace edge to the dry skin before makeup is applied. Makeup should not be applied over the lace if it can be avoided. In removing any hairpiece with a lace edge, always dissolve the spirit gum with acetone until the lace comes away from the skin naturally. Never pull the lace off the skin.

If the wig has a blender, it should be put on in the same way, making sure that the blender covers the natural hairline and that it fits snugly against the skin. It should be pasted down with spirit gum. You may then wish to stipple the edge of the blender at the line where it meets the skin with latex cream adhesive. This can be done with the tube itself, dotting the edge so that the adhesive overlaps both blender and skin. This will help break the line across the forehead. This must be done when the skin is clean and dry and before any makeup has been applied. If the blender is too thick at the edge to be concealed by the adhesive, a small amount of derma wax or putty-wax (see Chapter 13) can be used as a filler. The skin should be coated with spirit gum and allowed to dry before the wax is applied. The wax can be coated with sealer and the makeup applied when the sealer is dry.

The filling in with wax should be done only if there is no alternative. If the blender is well made in the first place and the edge is kept clean, it will be thin enough to be concealed with adhesive and paint or, if you prefer, with paint alone. The secret of concealing the line is, first, to match the color of the blender perfectly to the color on the skin, bearing in mind that a given color of paint will not necessarily look the same on the fabric of the blender as it does on the skin. Secondly, it is essential to make up the blender as if it were the real forehead with the usual shadows and highlights and wrinkles. Ordinarily it should become lighter as it approaches the hairline, at least if the hairline is a receding one. Thirdly, the area in which the blender joins the skin must be so broken up with color that the line is lost. Shadows at the temples and highlights on the superciliary arch make a good start. A stippling technique (see Chapter 8) is almost essential. Ordinarily, grease or cream stick should be used rather than cake when a blender has to be concealed (see Figure 184).

When you remove the wig, it is not necessary to clean the entire blender each time, but you must clean the edge carefully and thoroughly with acetone. Any accumulation of adhesive and makeup will render a good blend impossible.

Toupees may have a lace front or they may not. If they do, the lace is attached with spirit gum; if they do not, the front is attached with toupee tape (Appendix A). The back can be attached to the scalp with tape or to the hair back of the crown with a French clip, which can be sewn onto the underside of the toupee.

In putting on a toupee with a lace front, place the toupee in position, then attach the lace front to the skin with spirit gum, being extremely careful to avoid corrugations in the lace. After pressing the gum dry, grasp the back edge of the toupee and gently but firmly pull it back so that it hugs the head, then press down, thus sticking the toupee tape to the skin. If a French clip is being used, it can be attached to a strand of hair about an inch wide. Since the clip makes a slight bump under the toupee (not noticeable except to the touch) and since the clip pulling on the hair may be slightly uncomfortable, the tape is preferable.

In removing the toupee, always soak the lace with acetone until it loosens, then clean it thoroughly with acetone after it is removed. Toupees without lace fronts are easier to put on and take off and require less care, but they rarely look as convincing.

When a wig is properly dressed before being worn, it should require little or no rearranging after it is on. For subsequent wearings, however, it may require some recombing. Check the wig carefully before each performance for styling and condition of the hair and do whatever redressing is necessary.

CARE OF THE WIG

Good wigs are expensive and should be given painstaking care. Any elaborately dressed wig or any wig with a lace front should be kept on a wig block between performances. At other times it should be stuffed with tissue paper and stored in an individual box.

Wigs to be effective must be kept clean. This can best be done by dipping them into carbon tetrachloride or naphtha. Observe the usual precautions about adequate ventilation and open flames. This type of cleaning does not materially affect the wave in the hair.

It is also possible to clean wigs by dipping them up and down in a detergent solution, then rinsing, but this removes all the wave, results in a good bit of tangling no matter how carefully the dipping is done, and is not recommended to the inexperienced. Never under any circumstances shampoo a wig. Any rubbing of the hair in water will result in hopeless matting and tangling, and the wig will be ruined.

RENTING OR BUYING WIGS

The usual means of obtaining wigs is to rent them if the play is to have only a few performances and to buy them if it is expected to have a longer run or to be repeated at intervals. Whether renting or buying, you should obtain the best wig you can afford, made of human or sometimes of yak hair. Wigs made of mohair are available at relatively low cost, but they are seldom satisfactory for realistic plays except in the case of judges' wigs, Egyptian styles, and some eighteenth-century styles. They frequently look wonderful in the catalogue but appalling on stage. Some of the synthetic-hair wigs are considerably better. They are discussed in Chapter 15 and in Appendix A. The wig in Figure 63 is obviously inadequate and detracts from an otherwise excellent makeup. However, the same inexpensive wig used on an unrealistic character (Figure 168) is quite effective.

It is not usually possible to rent wigs with lace fronts because they are too fragile and easily damaged. For the type of hairline ordinarily requiring a lace front, a blender is substituted.

In either renting or buying it is important, if ordering by mail, to send adequate measurements and to allow plenty of time for the wig to be dressed and sent through the mail. In some cases the wig may not be in stock and may have to be made up specially, in which case as much as three or four weeks' additional time may be required.

When possible it is preferable to buy a wig unless it is a very special style which you are unlikely to use again. This costs more for the particular play but saves money in the end—provided the wig is used for a number of subsequent productions.

For suggestions on where to obtain wigs, see Appendix A.

MEASURING FOR WIGS

If you are ordering a wig or a toupee, it is important to supply the wigmaker with accurate measurements. The numbers below refer to Figure 154, in which the heavy broken lines represent wig measurements. The first five measurements are the most important. The others are not always used.

1. Around the head (over the ears) from front hairline to nape of the neck and back. (The average measurement is 22 inches.)

2. From the front hairline to the nape of the neck over the top of the head. (The average measurement is 14 inches.)

3. From ear to ear over the top of the head. This is sometimes taken over the crown instead. (Average measurement, 12 inches.)

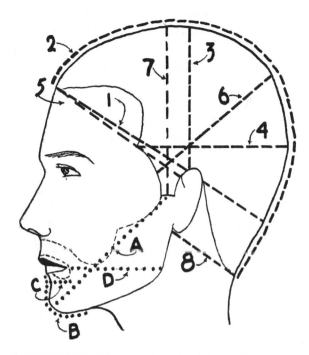

FIGURE 154. Diagram for wig and beard measurements. The heavy broken line represents wig measurements and the heavy dotted one, measurements for a beard.

4. Temple to temple around the back of the head. (Average measurement, 16 inches.)

5. Ear to ear across the forehead at the hairline.

6. Sideburn to sideburn over crown. (Infrequently used.)

7. Bottom of sideburn to bottom of sideburn over top. (Infrequently used.)

8. Bottom of ear to bottom of ear around back of neck. (Infrequently used.)

If there is to be a part, be sure to indicate how many inches from the center and on which side. If the wig or toupee is being made, it is also important to include an exact outline of hair at the temples.

ADAPTING WIGS

Fortunately, it is not necessary to have a different wig for every different hair style. As we have learned, any reasonably good wig can be redressed in various styles within the limitations set by the basic construction of the wig. The front hairline, the part or lack of one, and the length are crucial features. The color can be changed with sprays just as the natural hair can. Even the length need not always be a problem. If the hair is too short, a fall or a switch can sometimes be added to give the necessary length.

Length and color aside, we can classify wigs generally into the following groups:

1. Hair combed forward, concealing the hairline, as in Appendix G, Plate 7b-c-d-e-f. This is more often than not a male style. (See also Figures 139, 140, 155, 157, 176.)

2. Hair combed back, no parting, as in Plate 14a-b-c-d-g and Figures 123, 133-C, 135, 153, 173, 186, and 188. This ordinarily requires either a lace front or a blender except, for example, in the eighteenth-century styles which in many cases (though not all) represent wigs rather than real hair. Style a on Plate 14 is certainly a wig, but n is most probably natural hair.

3. Center part, as in Plate 6k-m-n-p-q.

4. Side part, as in Plate 17f-g-j-p.

5. Blender front, necessitated by a receding hairline or a hairline farther back than that of the actor who is to use the wig. Styles shown in Plate 9b-c-i-t, for example, would very likely require blenders. The hair may be combed as in 1, 2, 3, or 4 above; but since blender wigs are not usually interchangeable with other types, a separate listing is necessary.

6. Special styles, such as those with horizontal part (1q), double part (5g), or tonsure (5 p).

On the basis of this breakdown of types of wigs, it will be clear that many of the styles shown in the plates can with a little ingenuity and the use of supplementary falls and switches be achieved with a relatively small number of wigs. It is obvious, for example that Plates 2b-e, 5e-i-m, and 9a-d could be approximated with nothing more than a simple redressing of a single wig of type 1. Among the wigs with partings there are, perhaps, even more possibilities.

It must not be assumed, however, that *every* center-part style or *every* forward-combed style, for example, can be made from one specific center part or forward-combed wig with just the addition of hair. There are other elements which must be considered such as, for example, the thickness of the hair. Although sparse hair can be fluffed up somewhat and heavy hair can be sleeked down, the possibilities are not unlimited. But they are much greater than one would suspect at first glance. If you are working with a limited budget, adapting wigs to various styles is an important part of the makeup work. For one who is able to dress a wig skillfully, the problem of adapting it requires only a little additional ingenuity.

Learning to design hair styles and dress and care for wigs is as important a part of the makeup process as learning to make a good wrinkle. If you also know how to construct wigs, so much the better. In the professional theater, actors are not usually expected to design or to dress their own wigs, but they are expected to care for them and keep them looking fresh. Professional makeup artists need to have a thorough knowledge of wigs, but they do not have to make them and do not always have to dress them. In the nonprofessional theater, however, both actors and makeup artists need to acquire as many skills as possible. And every conceivable device must be used to keep expenses down. A thorough knowledge of how to deal with hair, real or false, will not only contribute greatly to the effectiveness of the makeup, but it can also help trim a significant part of the makeup budget. Whether for budgetary reasons or for lack of knowledge, the hair is far too often a sadly neglected part of the makeup; and yet it is frequently one of the simplest, most important, and most effective means we have of helping the actor become the character.

PROBLEMS

1. If you have the appropriate wigs available, make yourself up as two or three of the following:

Snake, Sir Peter Teazle, Sir Oliver Surface, Sir Benjamin Backbite (*The School for Scandal*); Dauphin, Archbishop of Rheims, Earl of Warwick (*St. Joan*); Tetzel, Staupitz, Lucas, Knight (*Luther*); Sir Fopling Flutter, Dorimant (*The Man of Mode*); Sir Novelty Fashion, Sir Tunbelly Clumsey (*The Relapse*); Mirabell, Petulant (*The Way of the World*); Peachum, Macheath, Macheath's gang (*The Beggar's Opera*); Captain Vere, John Claggart (*Billy Budd*); Richard II; Richard III; Henry IV.

Lady Sneerwell, Lady Teazle, Mrs. Candour, Maria (*The School for Scandal*); Mrs. Malaprop (*The Rivals*); Lady Wishfort, Mrs. Millament (*The Way of the World*); Polly Peachum, Lucy Locket (*The Beggar's Opera*); Mrs. Hardcastle (*She Stoops to Conquer*); Cleopatra, Ftatateeta (*Caesar and Cleopatra*).

17

NONREALISTIC MAKEUP

Now we turn to a phase of makeup in which the artist, be he actor or professional makeup man, can express unlimited ingenuity and creativity. Lon Chaney, Walt Disney, the great names in Hollywood makeup, and such painters and illustrators as Hieronymus Bosch and Sir John Tenniel stand as inspirational landmarks. The Frankenstein monster, the seven dwarfs, and Tenniel's *Alice in Wonderland* characters have become classics of visual characterization. From the medieval morality play to science fiction, opportunities for imaginative makeup abound, and Shakespeare alone has provided a wondrous array of beautiful, comic, and horrifying creatures.

Throughout the preceding chapters we have emphasized the importance of realism in makeup, of a constant reference to nature as our guide, in order to enhance the believability of the actor's characterization. There are occasions, however, when the makeup need not and should not be realistic. This may be dictated by the play itself and the nonrealistic characters in it or by a style of production chosen by the director and the designer.

But the fact that the play or the characters are nonrealistic does not mean that a completely new makeup technique will be required. There are many nonrealistic—or, at least, nonhuman—characters which will require a realistic treatment. Elves, trolls, fairies, witches, devils, angels, werewolves—all will frequently be presented realistically, even though they are nonhuman. Og in *Finian's Rainbow* may have pointed ears, but if the character is being presented realistically, the ears will require careful, realistic modeling. The fairy-creatures in *Midsummer Night's Dream* need

256

FIGURES 155, 156. Stylized makeups based on works of art. Mosaic makeup for stylized productions of medieval plays, pageants, or dances; bodyguard in *Arturo Ui*—makeup in the style of painter Karl Schmidt-Rottluff (see Figure 219).

to be as real in their own way as the human characters and usually require a realistic technique in the makeup. Although a Cyclops is a fictional character, you may wish to give him a very real eye in the middle of his forehead. Thus, there are vast areas of nonrealistic dramaturgy which might require precisely the sort of realism in technique we have been working for in earlier chapters.

On the other hand, there are production schemes which require, and plays or characters which permit, complete departure from reality, ranging from a caricature of essentially realistic detail (Figure 157–158) to complete stylization (Figure 155). In either case, the opportunity exists for striking use of creative imagination. Instead of aiming for realistic accuracy, we think in terms of using line, color, and form to heighten, to enliven, to clarify, to satirize, to amuse. Instead of consulting photographs for inspiration, we may consult works of art or go wherever our imagination leads us. Instead of using hair for wigs and beards, we may use rope, yarn, cloth, paper, wood shavings, feathers, plastic, or metal. Having let our imagination run free and having dreamed up a variety of possibilities for stylization, we must then co-ordinate those ideas suitable to the style of the production, selecting such elements as seem to make the greatest contribution to the overall conception.

FIGURES 157, 158. Two caricatures from a stylized production of *Johnny Johnson.* Cake makeup, eyebrows blocked out with derma wax. In Figure 157 the eyebrows, mustaches, and beard are actually three sets of mustaches. There are putty tips on both noses. Model in Figure 7.

The mosaic makeup in Figure 155 represents a striking use of stylization based on an art form. It would have to be used, however, in a play where it could logically reflect the subject matter, mood, and overall design. The makeup in Figure 156, based specifically on a German self-portrait of the 1930's (Figure 219), relates both in style and mood to Brecht's *Arturo Ui,* though other forms of stylization might be equally effective.

In addition to relating to the style of production and to the character, the makeup must also relate, in a very special way, to the audience. Although audiences are quite willing to go along with innovations in style, there are certain areas of resistance the makeup artist should be aware of. Our ideas about many nonrealistic characters—gnomes, trolls, fairies, elves—are somewhat vague, being based on a variety of illustrations and an equal variety of books and stories, and are thus open to fresh interpretation. But our ideas about some characters are not so flexible. *Alice in Wonderland* and *Through the Looking Glass* provide us with a good example.

Just as Gilbert Stuart determined for all time our image of George Washington, Sir John Tenniel created visual images of the characters in

Alice which are so widely known that they have come almost inviolable. Since we know and have known from childhood what the Duchess *really* looked like, any attempt to revise her image is likely to meet with firm resistance. She can be presented quite realistically (as are the Mad Hatter in Figure 33 and the Queen of Hearts in Figure 88), or she can be presented as a black and white drawing or a wooden marionette. But whatever the style of the makeup, she should probably look basically like the Duchess we know.

This is hardly a serious limitation. But in the Oriental theater such limitations can be much more severe. The beautifully decorative and colorful designs the actors paint on their faces look like a creative makeup artist's holiday. Actually, they are highly symbolic in both color and design and are never varied, no matter what actor is playing the part. But it is rare that the nonrealistic makeups we do will have such traditional strictures.

It is also possible to combine realistic makeups for nonrealistic characters with purely stylized makeups through the stylistic exaggeration of certain features in otherwise realistic makeups. Such exaggeration is frequently needed when the character depends entirely on physical movement rather than on speech or when the character, though human, symbolizes something greater than the individual human being. A single character representing Man or the Prodigal Son or the Earth Mother requires some heightening of his makeup, some telling exaggeration of detail. In the ballet *The Cage* the fact that human bodies are representing insect behavior must be reflected in the makeup.

In the ballet, as elsewhere, the style of the production, as well as the role, may determine the makeup. In the New York City Ballet production of *Firebird*, for example, the makeups were coordinated with the Chagall sets. Thus, combined stylization and realism range from a simple heightening of details for better definition and projection to strong exaggerations of line or color for dramatic effect. As in all nonrealistic makeup, our primary concern should be first to free the imagination, then to select those elements which make the most positive contribution to the projection of the character and to the overall design of the production.

Since the imagination often works better when offered a little stimulus, the following list of traditional character types is included. In referring to them, bear in mind that the descriptions are based largely on literature, art, and folklore. And though in many cases the characteristics of a type may be stated dogmatically, they represent only a convenient point of departure. It is up to you to vary them to suit your purpose.

Angels. First determine the style of the production and the sort of angel required. If an ethereal angel is called for, you may wish to work with pale lavenders, blues, greens, or whatever color best fits the production scheme. Hair and eyebrows might be of metallic gold or silver. The features will probably be idealized human ones. But if you are doing *The Green Pastures*, the angels can achieve the comedy effect required only by being completely real in a nonrealistic situation. For specific angels, such as Gabriel or Raphael, the makeup should contribute to the personality and to the function in the play. Angels come in all shapes and sizes and a variety of dispositions. Although an angel cannot be evil, he might, upon occasion, be avenging.

Animals. Papier maché heads can be used and sometimes must be; but if the style of the production permits, it may be more effective merely to suggest animal features on a human face (see Figure 160). This can be done in a completely stylized way with paint, or the paint can be combined with three-dimensional makeup. Crepe hair is nearly always essential. Split lips can be drawn on, giving a remarkably animal-like effect; nostrils can be flared and pointed; foreheads can be lowered. Real or painted whiskers alone can give a cat-like look to a face.

Clowns. Since the most successful clown makeups reflect individual characteristics, the first step is to decide what sort of clown you want—sad, happy, elegant, shy, brash, drunk, suspicious, ineffectual. Then design an exaggerated, stylized makeup to fit that conception. For a sad clown, for example, you will probably want to slant the eyebrows downward, as well as the corners of the mouth. If your clown is to be a tramp, you will need to think about an effect of beard stubble. For a clown with no particular personality you might paint geometric designs on the face. Sketching your design on paper first is likely to save time and result in a better makeup. There is no such thing as a standard clown. Make yours individual.

The base used is usually clown white (see Appendix A) or zinc oxide. All exposed areas of flesh should be evenly covered. Then with pencils, brushes, and shading colors you can duplicate your design. The hair should be treated in a style harmonious with the rest of the makeup. A skull cap or a wig is commonly used. Although professional clowns frequently do nothing to block out their eyebrows beyond covering them with clown white, the makeup is likely to be more effective if natural eyebrows are not visible through the makeup. Figure 162 shows a tramp-clown.

Death. Death is ordinarily pictured as having a skull for a head. You have already studied skull structure. The facial bones (Figure 9) should be modeled with white cake or greasepaint, lavender greasepaint, or clown white and shadowed with medium blue, gray, or violet. The

FIGURES 159, 160. Stylized doll and cat. By student Alja Hurnen. Observe the blocked out eyebrows and the frankly unrealistic painted details in both makeups. The hair for the doll is the student's own. Black crepe hair has been added to a wig for the cat makeup. Compare with other makeups of Mrs. Hurnen in Figures 57, 63, and 168.

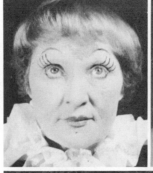 

FIGURE 161. Hsu Yen Chao, a Minister of State in the Sung Dynasty. By student Jan Vidra. Stylized makeup adapted from a Chinese mask. The small plaster mask upon which the makeup is based is shown on the top of the headdress. Colors are black, white, orange, and yellow. The beard is orange. The headdress is improvised out of paper and painted. For other makeups by and on Mr. Vidra see Figures 111, 112, 123–125, and 162.

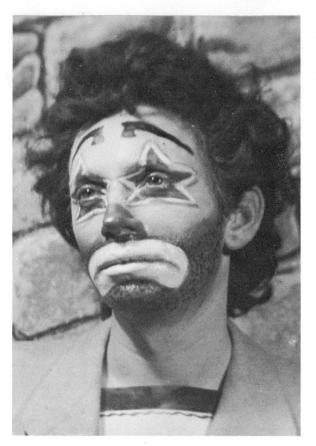

FIGURE 162. Tramp-clown makeup. By student Jan
Vidra. Compare with other makeups of Mr. Vidra
in Figures 111, 112, 123–125, and 161.

hollows should be filled in with black. If the head is to show, a white
skull cap must be worn. The cap should preferably be painted with the
same base as the face and the edges blended carefully into the foundation.
The cap should cover the ears. The eyebrows should always be blocked out
(see Chapter 12).

    If the makeup is to be luminous, the white paint can be dusted with
flourescent powder (see Appendix A) before the black is applied. Or
flourescent paint can be brushed over the completed makeup in the appropriate places. An ultraviolet ray must be used on a dark stage to cause
luminosity. Phosphorescent powder can be used without the ultraviolet
ray. Both liquid and pigment can be obtained for either type of paint.

The same technique can be used successfully for Death in *Death Takes a Holiday* in which the Count is occasionally called upon to appear according to our conventional idea of Death. However, a normal, though pale, makeup should be used instead of white and the flourescent paint or pigment applied only to the bones of the skull. Under normal stage lights the makeup will look normal, but under the ultraviolet ray the skull will appear. If the hands are to be seen, they must always be made up in harmony with the facial makeup. It is also possible to present Death much less conventionally—as a coldly beautiful woman, perhaps, or a black hooded figure with no face at all.

Devils. The conventional devil is often made up with a bright red foundation and a long face with sharp, pointed features. The cheekbones are prominent; nose and chin, long and pointed; eyes, narrow and dark; lips, thin and well defined; eyebrows, black, close together, and slanting upward; eye sockets, dark and sunken. A small, pointed mustache may be used and a rather delicate, long and pointed goatee. Long red, yellow, green, or black fingernails may be added. Horns are commonly used, set into a skull cap over the head.

For a three-dimensional makeup the nose and chin can be extended with putty. The natural eyebrows should be blocked out and false ones either made of crepe hair or painted on, depending on the degree of stylization. If the production is to be quite stylized, long, upward slanting extensions of the eye lining may be used with brightly colored or metallic eyeshadow. The eye sockets, cheeks, nose, and temples can be shadowed with a very dark brownish red and highlighted with light red, pink, or yellow. Dark red or green might be used on the lips.

The base need not be red. Bright pinks or foundation colors in the RO or R group might be used effectively. Green is also a possibility though perhaps not so logical a one as red. Blue or purple shadows and yellow highlights would be effective with a green base. A yellow base might also be used, or an extremely pale one of any tint with strong accents in black and bright colors. For that matter, there is no reason why a devil should not be made up with metallic gold if that fits the overall color scheme. Figures 163 and 164 show two versions of a stylized devil makeup.

Dolls. Dolls (china or porcelain ones, that is) should usually be made up with white, ivory, or pale pink foundations. The rouge, preferably of a pinkish or bluish pink variety, should be applied in a round spot in the center of each cheek, and the spot should be blended at the edges, but not perfectly. The lips should be small with a pronounced cupid's bow. The eyelashes should be blackened with mascara or cosmetic (or false ones

FIGURES 163, 164. Mephistopheles. Two stylized makeups. In Figure 163 the cake shadows and highlights are applied fairly flat with sharp edges. In Figure 164 these same shadows and highlights have been outlined with a black pencil, and a few decorative touches (over the eyes, for example) have been added. Any number of color combinations could be used.

used if possible), and the eyes outlined with brown or black and shadowed with blue or lavender. The eyes should be opened as wide as possible (see Figure 159). A wig may be desirable.

Although many dolls are fairly natural in facial coloring, the illusion of unreality can be projected more successfully by using the type of makeup suggested above.

Elves. An elf or brownie is considered to be a form of fairy sympathetic to man and living in the woods and fields. Elves are very small and have pointed, butterfly-shaped ears, small turned-up pug noses, and quite round, open eyes. They may wear caps which partially or completely cover the hair; however, the hair may show and be either short or long. It is usually not very carefully combed and is likely to fall over the forehead.

The skin may be of human flesh color, though the reddish shades should be avoided. They may have red cheeks and lips and should usually be cheerful and pleasant. The nose can be shaped with nose putty.

Fairies. Fairies include elves, sprites, gnomes, and the like; but here we shall consider only the variety represented by Titania and Oberon. Fairies may be tall yet should always be very slender and graceful unless otherwise specified for a particular character. The base color is usually ivory, light pink, or light orange, but it could as well be pale blue, green, lavender, or any color fitting into the general scheme. The red shades, being more human, should be avoided. Metallic flakes or sequins can be used with good effect on exposed parts of the body. The flakes should adhere to greasepaint, and the sequins can be attached with a latex adhesive or spirit gum.

The features should be delicate, well formed, mortal ones. The ears may be pointed or not. Some lip rouge should be used but no cheek rouge. The eyes should be as beautiful as possible. Blue, green, violet, gold, silver, or bronze eyeshadow might be used. Gold or bronze could also be used for the lips instead of pink or red. The women's hair is usually long and wavy and more often golden than dark.

Gnomes. Gnomes, goblins, and trolls are commonly thought of as living underground. They are always mischievous and nearly always unfriendly toward mortals. Usually they are grotesque and often very ugly, even deformed.

A long ugly nose, prominent cheekbones, prominent brow and receding forehead, pointed chin, receding chin, fat cheeks, sunken cheeks, large and wing-shaped ears, peculiarly shaped eyebrows, very bushy eyebrows, no eyebrows, pop eyes, small and beady eyes, and bulging forehead are some of the characteristics which may be considered in doing a makeup of this sort. Very long and flowing pointed beards are appropriate for older gnomes. The skin should be darker than for other types of fairies—possibly green, yellow, or other colors. The head may be entirely bald except for a tuft or two of hair, or else well supplied with unkempt hair.

Masks. Although any discussion of the design or making of masks is outside the province of this book, it should be pointed out that for some plays masks are requested by the playwright and for others the director and the designer may choose to use them, as, for example, in the Lincoln Center Repertory Theatre's production of *The Caucasian Chalk Circle*. Six of the masks used for that production are shown in Figures 223–228. Although a good deal is lost in black-and-white reproduction, the exaggeration of facial shapes, of planes of the face, and of expressions, as well as the use of feather mustaches to match the headdresses, serve as excellent examples of stylization which might well be adapted to certain makeups. The facial colors were exaggerations of natural ones, and the feather mustaches and goatees were in black, red, green, white, peach, co-ordinated with the costume. In order to blend the mask with the lower part of the actor's face, which was exposed, the mouth and chin were made up to match the colors and design of the mask. In previews at which some actors had done this and some had not, it was obvious how important the matching makeup was. The lack of such makeup for the photographs of the masks in Appendix F should also make this clear.

Monsters. This category covers a variety of creatures, from mechanical men to werewolves. If the monster is to be animalistic, the hair should grow low on the forehead, perhaps covering a good deal of the face. The nose usually needs to be widened and flattened. False teeth made to look like fangs will make the monster more terrifying. But if the creature is to appear in a children's play, it should be conceived with some discretion. Gory details, such as blood streaming from an open wound and eyes torn out of their sockets, might well be saved, if they are to be used at all, for

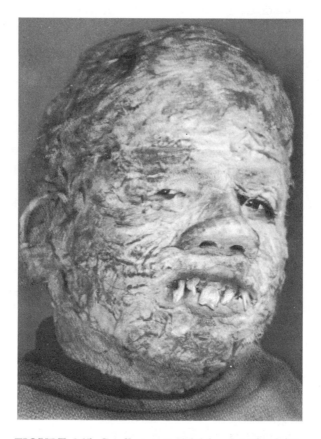

FIGURE 165. Small monster. Makeup with plastic cap and false teeth (see Figure 103), using Masslinn towels and Duo adhesive. Makeup by Bert Roth, ABC-TV.

adult horror plays. Foreheads can be raised and heads squared off, eyes re-arranged, teeth made large and protruding (Figure 165), and so on. Skin texture techniques can be used to good effect—towels or tissue with latex, tissue and spirit gum, latex and cornmeal. For mummies, toweling and latex or latex and cornmeal work very well. Cheekbones can be built up first with wax in order to give a better effect of caved-in cheeks.

Ogres. An ogre is usually conceived to be a hideous monster who feeds on human beings. Prosthetic applications will undoubtedly be needed. Consult the suggestions for a gnome makeup and then exaggerate them, making the entire effect as unpleasant as possible. The advisability of using a repulsive makeup, such as is required for Quasimodo, is questionable, but the monster can be made ugly and terrifying without being repulsive. Helpful pictures of ogres can be found in books of fairy tales.

Pierrot. Pierrot and Pierrette are often made up with clown white covering all exposed flesh. Ivory or very pale pink may be used if preferred and are, perhaps, more desirable. The lips should be small and quite red with a pronounced cupid's bow. The natural brows should be blocked out with soap and high arched ones painted on with black eyebrow pencil. Blue, green-blue, blue-gray, blue-violet, or violet eyeshadow may be used. The eyes should be well defined. Pierrette may have two small, well-blended dots of rouge. Her eyeshadow should usually be blue, lavender, or pale blue-green. A thoroughly stylized makeup is often even more effective. Rouge, lips, and eyebrows may all be in the shape of diamonds or other simple geometric figures. The design of the costume should harmonize.

Pirates. The typical pirate is dark-skinned (8–10 in the foundation colors) with strong, though often unattractive, features. The eyes should usually be heavily shadowed, and the cheekbones and jaw made more prominent. A well-placed scar and a few missing teeth are often helpful. The typical storybook pirate seems almost invariably to be minus one eye and occasionally a leg or an arm.

Santa Claus. Since the old gentleman is already so familiar, he hardly needs description. A fairly pink or ruddy complexion, plump red cheeks, a round pug nose, and a long white beard are the essentials. Because of the full beard, prosthetic applications are seldom necessary, though the shape of the nose often needs to be changed. A sharp or a hooked nose on Santa will ruin the whole effect.

But the script or the production may require a very realistic, hard-working Santa Claus with a matted beard and a grubby little face or a very elegant one with hair and beard of spun glass or silver foil. For comic effect your Santa may require just the reverse of the conventional image.

Statuary. All exposed flesh should ordinarily be white. Liquid white makeup is usually satisfactory; clown white is also good and sometimes preferable. If a slightly darker foundation, such as Y1, P1, or lavender, is used, white may be used as a highlight on the frontal bone, cheekbone, nose, lower lip, jaw, and chin. Lavender makes an excellent base. Other foundation tints can be made by mixing shading colors with white greasepaint or clown white. Gray, gray-blue, and gray-violet are useful for shadowing.

Whether or not the makeup should be powdered will naturally depend upon the material of which the statue is supposed to be made. If the finish would naturally be shiny, a grease base without powder should be used. A dull finish requires either a liquid base or a powdered grease one. If the statue is not white, the appropriate color may be used with the same technique. For large areas liquid makeup is always better.

Gold, silver, or bronze statues can be made with metallic body makeup. The effect is excellent, but unless the technique is used with care, it may cause suffocation. (See the discussion in Appendix A under "Metallic makeup" and under "Glycerine.")

Toys. Makeups for toys other than china dolls—as, for example, wooden soldiers and rag dolls—can best be copied from the actual toys. Their unreality should always be stressed in order to counteract the obvious lifelike qualities of the actor.

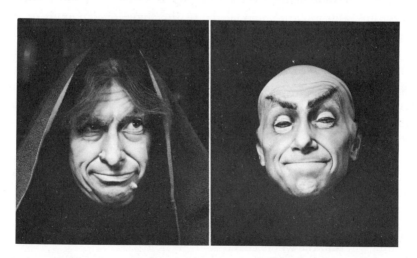

FIGURES 166, 167. Witch and troll. The witch makeup is basically realistic. Nose and warts are of putty and eyebrows of crepe hair. The troll is more stylized in both design and color (green, yellow, purple, and white). Hair is covered with a plastic cap. Cake makeup was used for both. Model in Figure 7.

Trolls. In Scandinavian folklore these are supernatural beings, either very large or very small, living underground or in caves. Trolls are usually thought of as being ugly, though not necessarily repulsive, and not very friendly. The trolls in *Peer Gynt* slit their eyeballs and proposed to do the same to Peer. They could be green, yellow, gray, or almost any color you cared to make them. But they should look grotesque in some way and not kindly. (See Figure 167.)

Witches. In much the same way as gnomes and goblins, witches provide an opportunity for originality in makeup. Sharp, hooked noses; prominent cheekbones; sunken cheeks; thin lips, small sunken eyes; prominent, pointed chins; and numerous wrinkles are common characteristics (see Figures 166, 168). Traditional witches seldom have more than one or two good teeth, straggly hair, and clawlike hands. The complexion may be

FIGURE 168. **Traditional witch.** Gray wig, crepe hair eyebrows, rubber nose, putty warts. Student makeup by Alja Hurnen. Compare with other makeups of Mrs. Hurnen in Figures 57, 63, 159, and 160.

light or dark, but in either case it tends toward the yellow. It may even be green. Prosthetic applications on the nose, chin, and cheekbones are often essential. Hair on the face and warts are common.

But witches can be good or bad, young or old, ugly or beautiful. And each of these could be realistic or stylized. Whereas a wicked old witch might have a face the texture and color of a dried apple, a good young witch might have a face of alabaster with hair of metallic gold. A bad (but sophisticated) young witch, on the other hand, could have a face with a glint of steel, slashed with jet black eyebrows over heavily lashed, slanted eyes. The possibilities seem to be limited only by one's imagination. And then there are those witches who look exactly like everybody else and not like witches at all.

For those with an active imagination, nonrealistic makeup should prove to be more fascinating and more challenging than almost any other. It is the one opportunity for the makeup artist to escape from the confines of realism and demonstrate his creative ability.

PROBLEMS

1. Make clay models of several different types of heads for nonrealistic characters. Create makeups on the basis of these.

2. Make up yourself or someone else as several of the following characters: Pierrot; Oberon, Titania, Puck, Peaseblossom (*A Midsummer Night's Dream*); Manikin, Minikin (*Manikin and Minikin*); Mephistopheles; a Witch (*Macbeth*); The Magistrate (*Liliom*); Ivan Borolsky (*Captain Applejack*, Act II); The Green Thing (*The Gods of the Mountain*); Red Queen, White Queen, King of Hearts, Queen of Hearts (*Alice in Wonderland*); He (*He Who Gets Slapped*); Ariel, Caliban (*The Tempest*); Elvira (*Blithe Spirit*); Pagliacci; Ghost (*Hamlet*); Trolls (*Peer Gynt*); Insects (*The Insect Comedy*); Arturo, Old Hindborough, Roma, Ragg, Givola, Giri (*Arturo Ui*); Orcs (*Lord of the Rings*). Do at least one of the characters in two different styles, one using a realistic technique, the other, a flat, decorative style.

3. Make yourself up as any character you wish, following the style of one of the less realistic portraits in Appendix F or of an artist with whose work you are familiar. It would, of course, be best to choose a character from a play which might logically be given a stylized production.

18

LIGHTING AND
MAKEUP

Perhaps you have observed in moonlight scenes on the stage the unflattering effects of the light on the actors' faces. As the moonlight is turned on, a perfectly healthy young lady is likely to lose very suddenly her pink and ivory complexion and take on instead a deathly pallor, punctuated by large black spots on each cheek and one below the nose where the mouth ought to be. If she is fortunate enough to have brown or black eyes, they may withstand the sudden transformation, but blue ones are likely to disappear. Strong firelight results in similar pallor, minus the black spots.

In order to circumvent such unpleasant results of unfortunate combinations of makeup and lights, the makeup artist in choosing his paints must know what effects the various colors of light used on the stage will have on those paints. An understanding of the principles of color in light as well as in pigment is basic to such knowledge.

COLOR IN LIGHT

We mentioned briefly in Chapter 6 that pigment depends for its color upon the light which illuminates it. In other words, trees are not green at night—unless, of course, they are artificially illuminated. Nothing has color until light is reflected from it. If all the light is absorbed, the object looks black; if all the light is reflected, we say it is white. If certain of the rays are absorbed and certain others reflected, the reflected rays determine the color.

These various colors of rays which make up what we call white light

271

can be observed when they are refracted by globules of moisture in the air, forming a rainbow. The same effect can be obtained with a prism. The colored rays are refracted at different angles because of their different lengths, red being the longest and violet the shortest. All matter has the ability to reflect certain lengths of light waves but not others, resulting in color sensations in the eye.

Just as white light can be broken up into its component hues, those hues can be synthesized to form white light again as well as various other colors. As with pigments, three of the colors can be used as primaries and combined to form any other color of light as well as the neutral white. However, the three primaries are not the same in light as in pigment. In light they are *red* (scarlet), *green*, and *ultramarine* (a deep violet-blue). In mixing lights, red and green give yellow or orange, green and ultramarine give turquoise or blue-green, and ultramarine and red give purple. A mixture of all three primaries produces white light. On the stage these various colored rays are produced by placing a color medium (sheets of transparent gelatine or glass rondels) in front of some source of nearly white light, such as a spot or a flood.

LIGHT ON PIGMENT

If the colored rays fall on pigment which is able to reflect them, then we see the color of the light. But if they fall on a pigment which absorbs some of them, the color is distorted. Suppose, for example, red rays fall on a "red" hat. The rays are reflected, and the hat looks red. But suppose green rays are thrown on the "red" hat. Since the hat is able to reflect only red rays, the green rays are absorbed, nothing is reflected, and the hat looks black.

Imagine a "green" background behind the "red" hat. Add green light and you have a black hat against a green background. Change the light to red, and you have a red hat against a black background. Only white light will give you a red hat against a green background.

The principle of light absorption and reflection can be used to advantage in certain trick effects such as apparently changing a white man into a colored one before the eyes of the audience. But ordinarily your problem will be to avoid such effects. Fortunately, since intense hues of light are seldom used on the stage, usually you need vary your makeup colors only slightly. Moonlight and firelight scenes are the most notable exceptions in realistic plays.

The problem of becoming familiar with the specific effects of the vast number of possible combinations of light and greasepaint is a far from simple one. It is impossible to offer a practical panacea for all of the difficulties one may encounter. A chart could be made, but it would be inaccurate, for not only do exact shades of makeup vary among manufacturers and from tube to tube, but gelatine varies, even within a given brand, from sheet to sheet. And of course light sources vary widely.

Thus the only solution seems to be to generalize and to leave details to the artist himself. A few suggestions follow which may be of some practical value.

In the first place, try to do your makeup under lighting similar to that under which it will be viewed by the audience. Dressing room or makeup room lights should be arranged to take colored gelatine slides which can be matched with those on the stage. Figure 17 shows a possible arrangement. Since dressing rooms are almost never so equipped, some temporary arrangement should be made if possible. A small floodlight or two in a central makeup room is far better than nothing.

Secondly, whenever possible look at the makeup from the house. This can usually be done during a full dress rehearsal. If you are doing your own makeup, have someone whose judgment you trust look at you from the house and offer criticisms. Theoretically, the director should do this, but more often than not he has other problems which he considers of more importance, and he is therefore likely to be less critical than he should be of the makeup. Final approval of the makeup must lie with him, but he cannot always be counted on for constructive suggestions. If a professional makeup artist is in charge of all the makeup, then he will check the makeup under lights and get final approval from the director.

In the third place, you ought to have a reasonably accurate knowledge of the general effects of a certain color of light upon a certain color of makeup. Generally speaking, the following principles will hold:

1. Gelatine colors of low value will have a maximum effect upon makeup; colors of high value, a minimum.

2. A given color of light will cause a similar color of pigment to become higher in intensity, while a complementary color will be lower in both value and intensity.

3. Any shade of pigment will appear gray or black if it does not contain any of the colors composing a given ray of light which falls upon it.

Listed below are some of the common colors of gelatine with their effects upon various colors of greasepaint. You must remember that these effects are only approximations and may upon occasion vary widely from those indicated here.

Dubarry pink and *rose pink* tend to make all colors warmer except greens and blues, which are slightly grayed. The greens and blue-greens become more blue. Most of the base colors tend to become a more intense pink or orange.

Flesh pink does not seriously affect makeup but, like other shades of pink, tends to intensify slightly the majority of base colors and to gray somewhat the cool shading colors.

Fire red will ruin nearly any makeup. All but the very darkest base colors will virtually disappear. Light and medium rouge become a pale orange and fade imperceptibly into the foundation, while the dark reds turn a reddish brown. Yellow becomes orange, and all other shading colors become gray and black.

Bastard amber is one of the most flattering colors to makeup. It may gray the cool shading colors slightly but picks up the warm pinks and flesh tones and adds life to the makeup.

Light amber will cause most base colors and rouge to become slightly higher in value. All will be somewhat more orange. Blues turn gray-violet; blue-greens become grayer and somewhat more green; greens are grayed and tend toward yellow-green. With all shades of amber a darker base and rouge than usual must be used. The base may also need to be somewhat more red.

Dark amber and orange have an effect similar to that of red, though somewhat less severe. All base colors, except the dark browns, become higher in value. Light rouges tend to turn yellow or pale orange. The darker ones may appear somewhat brown or even gray. The blues tend to become more violet, and both blues and greens are grayed. If dark amber illumination cannot be avoided, a very deep foundation color should be used.

Light straw has very little effect upon makeup, except to make the colors slightly warmer. Violet may be grayed a little but not much.

Lemon and *yellow* intensify the yellowish bases and yellow shading paint. The O's become more yellow; the RO's and R's, more orange. The blues will be greener and the violets somewhat gray. The darker the gelatine, of course, the stronger the effect upon the makeup.

Green is a very difficult color to use. It grays all base colors in proportion to its intensity. Rouge may become a deep brownish purple or reddish brown—even gray. Violet is also grayed. Yellow and blue will become more green, and green will become more intense and higher in value.

Light blue-green tends to lower the intensity of the base colors. Light red becomes darker, and dark red becomes brown. Use very little rouge under blue-green light.

Green-blue will cause all colors except the Y and YO groups to become dull grays and browns. The Y colors tend to turn an ugly shade of grayish green-yellow. Reds become a deep grayish purple, the darker ones approaching black. Blues and greens become higher in value.

Daylight blue tends to gray very slightly all colors except green, blue, and violet. The effect can usually be disregarded. One must always be careful, however, not to use too much rouge.

Light and *medium blue* will gray base colors. The Y group will turn slightly green. Red will become a grayish or brownish purple. Blues, greens, and violets are intensified though made higher in value.

Dark blue will gray everything except the greens, blues, and violets. If the blue has a slightly purplish cast, as it often does, the yellows, oranges, and reds will become very low in value but not be as greatly decreased in intensity as for pure blue.

Violet (*light* and *surprise*) will turn the Y bases yellow-orange and orange and the O group, red-orange. The RO's and R's will be lower in value. Rouge will be more intense, and yellow will turn orange. Greens are likely to be a little lower in value and intensity. Be careful not to use too intense a red in either base or rouge.

Dark violet will cause all base colors (except brown) to become shades of pink and brilliant red and red-orange. Reds, Orange-Reds, and Oranges will become very brilliant (except the 4's and 5's, which may tend toward a deep brownish red). Yellow will be red-orange. Greens will be grayed.

Surprise purple will have an effect similar to that of surprise violet, except that the reds and oranges will be intensified to a much greater degree.

Dark and *rose purple* will cause base colors to become orange or pink. Rouge will turn orange. The greens will be strongly grayed, and the blues will turn purple.

One problem remains. Since stage lights are likely to change from time to time during a performance, be aware of any radical changes, especially in color, and have your makeup checked under the various lighting conditions which prevail. If such changes do affect your makeup adversely and there is no opportunity for you to adjust the makeup to the lights, try to modify your basic makeup to minimize the problem under all lighting conditions. If this is not successful, consult the director about the possibilty of some adjustment of the lighting. After all, it is to the advantage of the whole production that every makeup be as effective as possible at all times.

Although you may often consider stage lighting a hindrance to your art, try to make the best of all the advantages it has to offer. Plan your makeups so that the lighting will contribute to rather than detract from their effectiveness.

PROBLEMS

1. What makeup color and what colors of light would you use to make a white man apparently change suddenly into a colored one?

2. What color would each of the following appear to be under the colors of light indicated: A yellow hat under red and green lights? A green hat under red and yellow lights? A red hat under blue and green lights? A red and green hat under yellow lights? A red and yellow hat under green lights? A green and yellow hat under red lights? A red and blue hat under blue lights? A red, yellow, and blue hat under red, green, and ultramarine lights? A purple and white hat under red, green, and ultramarine lights?

3. It has been stated in the chapter that a given color of light raises the intensity of a similar color of pigment. Yet on a stage flooded with red light, all of the clear, bright reds seem to be "washed out." Why is this so?

19

SPECIAL PROBLEMS

Thus far we have been discussing makeup from the point of view of a single actor doing his own makeup or a makeup artist concerned only with the problems of one actor. We have further assumed that the actor would be portraying a dramatic character in a legitimate stage show and would have plenty of time in which to do his makeup.

There are, however, other situations which cause special problems for the makeup artist, such as group makeup and quick changes. These are the problems we shall discuss in this chapter.

GROUP MAKEUP

This is a problem encountered almost exclusively in the nonprofessional theater. Any makeup artist who has attempted to do makeup for very large casts in any kind of theatrical production is well aware of the uniqueness of the problem. To use the same procedures as for individuals or for small casts is sometimes possible but seldom practicable.

Efficient group makeup commonly requires the following:

1. A director of makeup and as many assistants as can work successfully in the space allotted for makeup.

2. A standardized written description of the makeup for each character.

3. Adequate space for taking care of large groups and adequate equipment.

4. A detailed schedule or plan of makeup procedure.

5. A proctor of some sort to maintain order.

The makeup crew. The crew should be headed by a competent makeup artist who will consult with the director and the light man about the makeup, determine the exact procedure to be followed, and assign to other crew members their specific duties. Other people on the crew should also know something about makeup! More often than not, makeup "committees" are composed of girls and women whose experience has been confined to painting their own faces. The more competent the crew, the better the makeup.

Makeup charts. After consultation with the director, the head makeup artist should plan each makeup and fill out a chart indicating all details of the makeup. The forms for these charts should be carefully prepared, then mimeographed or printed. They will be useful for plays with average-sized casts as well as for larger productions.

The form shown in Figure 169 is a practical one which can serve for either simple or complicated makeups and for use by the makeup artist himself as well as by members of his staff if he has one. If a makeup artist has several characters to do, he should always plan the makeups as best he can on the chart before the first makeup rehearsal; then when the makeup is set, he should make necessary changes and complete the chart so that he can duplicate the makeup exactly at the next rehearsal or performance. If the makeups are complicated, the makeup artist should begin to work with the actors long before the first dress rehearsal. If possible, he should set the makeups, then teach the actors to do their own, following the chart.

The colors of makeup used should be listed under "Color," and if there are any special remarks about application, they may be listed under the appropriate heading. Since any prosthetic pieces which are to be used must be applied before the rest of the makeup, there is a place at the top for indicating generally what they are. More detailed information can be put on the back of the sheet.

The full-face and profile heads can be used to make sketches for hair and prosthesis and to indicate such requirements as shadowing, highlighting, eyeshadow, and rouge. The most practical scheme is to use colored pencils—for example, black for hair, eyebrows, and eye accents; brown for shadows; yellow for highlights; red for rouge; green for eyeshadow; and blue for prosthesis, as suggested on the chart.

The separate drawing of the eye is included so as to make possible a more detailed diagram of the makeup to be used. The box in the lower right-hand corner will be used only when there is a staff and the charts are made out by the head makeup artist. The box in the upper left-hand corner may be used for any number of miscellaneous purposes—as, for example, to indicate that this is a quick-change makeup, that it is only one of several makeups on the same actor in the same production, that the actor has a skin condition which requires special handling, or that the makeup will be

MAKEUP WORKSHEET

PLAY..

ctor...Character...Age...........................

PROSTHESIS..

	COLOR	APPLICATION
Base		
Shadows		
Highlights		
Cheek Rouge		
Lip Rouge		
Eyeshadow		
Eye Accents		
Eyelashes		
Eyebrows		
Neck		
Hands		
Powder		
Hair		

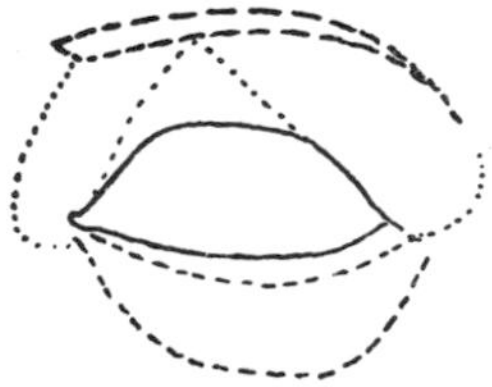

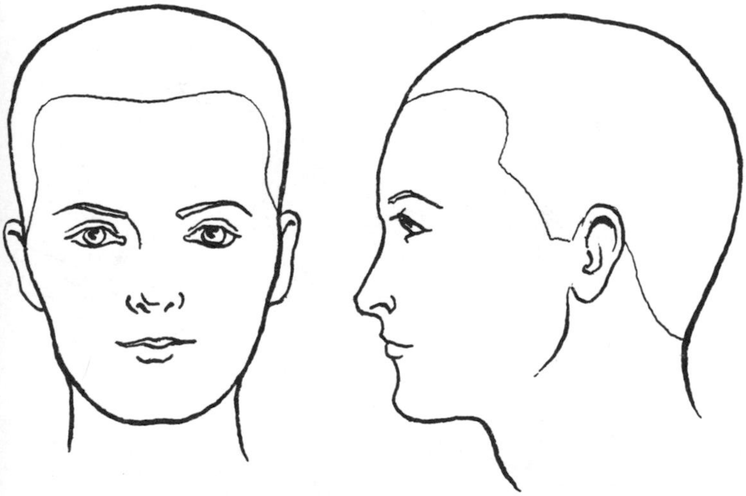

COLOR CODE
RED—Rouge, lipstick
YELLOW—Highlights
BROWN—Shadows
GREEN—Eyeshadow
BLUE—Prosthesis
BLACK—Hair, beard,
eyebrows

Makeup assigned to:

FIGURE 169. Makeup worksheet. Makeup color numbers and remarks on application can be listed in the appropriate columns. Shading, coloring, hair, and prosthesis can be indicated on the diagrams of the head and eye with the colors of pencils indicated in the box. Additional drawings or notes can be made on the back of the sheet.

seen under unusual lighting. Additional drawings or information can be put on the back of the sheet.

Physical equipment. The requirements of a room suitable for making up large groups are the same as those for an ordinary general makeup room. The best arrangement probably is to use a regular makeup room and have an adjoining waiting room. That eliminates the confusion of people milling about and talking. The makeup room should always be kept comfortably cool.

For large groups extra makeup materials will usually be needed. Several tubes each of the most commonly used greasepaints and several each of moist rouge, eyebrow pencils, dry rouges, shadowing and highlighting colors, and boxes of powder are a great help unless, of course, the specialized-labor system, to be described presently, is used.

It may sometimes be necessary to provide temporary or portable makeup facilities for a large number of people, such as students in a makeup class or extras in crowd scenes who are all doing their own makeup. An extraordinarily simple and practical arrangement involves the construction of wooden frames (Figures 170–172) on which inexpensive mirrors can be hung. It is possible to use either individual small mirrors (Figure 171) or long, narrow mirrors (Figure 172) running the length of the frames. Both have their advantages. The long mirrors are less confining to

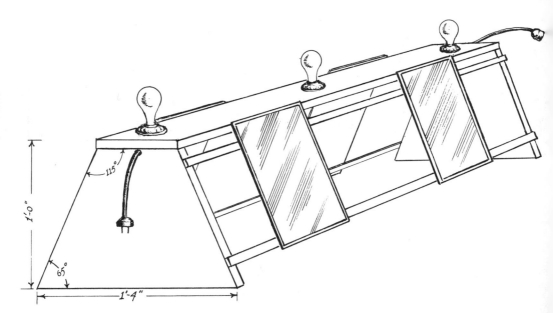

FIGURE 170. **Diagram of frame for portable makeup table.** Designed by Dr. Harold K. Stevens, Eastern Washington State College at Cheney.

FIGURE 171. Makeup class on stage at Eastern Washington State College using tables with portable frames and mirrors.

FIGURE 172. Makeup class at the University of North Carolina using a modification of the frames designed by Dr. Stevens.

the actors, but the small ones afford him access to storage space inside the frame. Both arrangements have proved very satisfactory. In either case, the frames are set on tables, the mirrors hung on nails or hooks, the lights plugged in, and chairs set up along either side.

The lighting for each unit is self-contained—that is, any unit can be plugged directly into the power source, or any number of units can be connected. The most satisfactory arrangement of lights is to have 75-watt bulbs spaced equidistant between the mirrors. This gives each actor a light source from two sides.

A number of units can be set up end to end to make a long makeup table, or they can be divided into smaller sections. In order to take maximum advantage of available space, the frames should be about the same length as the tables on which they are to be used or perhaps an inch or two shorter to allow for plugging the light cords together; however, they will work just as well no matter what the length. The tables should be wide enough to allow work space for the actor on either side of the frame but not so wide that he cannot get close to the mirror.

The units can be set up and taken down very quickly, the frames can be stored or transported in a relatively small space, and any available tables can be used. For classes, the ideal arrangement is to set up as many units as needed on an empty stage. This gives the students adequate space to step back and look at themselves in the mirrors. It enables the instructors to work with much greater freedom than in a crowded dressing room, and it makes it possible to see the makeups under stage lights with maximum convenience. It is extremely useful, when possible, to have spots focussed so that when the student stands back to look at himself, both he and the instructor will be seeing the makeup under stage lights.

Makeup schedule. Before any makeup is started, a detailed plan of procedure should always be made out and then adhered to strictly. There are two general types of procedure possible.

The first is that usually used for plays and the more commendable from an artistic standpoint. Each artist completely makes up certain members of the cast. Then all makeups are approved by the head makeup artist. For large groups, however, such a system requires a more or less complete makeup kit for each artist—certainly one for not more than two artists. Any less equipment will mean loss of time and a great deal of confusion. For very large casts requiring the assistance of a number of makeup people, another system is more practical.

Under this system, a makeup line is formed, and each artist has a specific job assigned to him. For each person who comes to him he does only this one thing. The actor thus starts at the head of the line and passes

successively from person to person—through base, rouge, eye makeup, powder, etc. The head makeup artist is last in the line and checks the completed makeups.

It is best to put only the chorus or simple juvenile character makeups
through the line and have one or two makeup artists to take care of more
complicated character makeups. When using this system of specialization,
each actor should procure his own makeup chart from a proctor at the head
of the line and carry it through himself, showing it to each makeup artist
who works on him. The chart can be checked at the end of the line.

A system such as this one, though artistically deplorable, is usually the
best possible solution to the mass production problem so frequently encountered in the nonprofessional theater. So long as the more important
characters and more difficult makeups receive individual attention, the
system has much to recommend it.

Proctors. In working with large groups one of the makeup artist's most
valuable assets is a proctor or two who can keep order. The proctors should
see that there is always someone ready to be made up, that people are not
milling about waiting to be made up, and that all those who are made up
leave the makeup room immediately.

THE MAKEUP ARTIST IN THE PROFESSIONAL THEATER

Although makeup artists are not widely used in the professional theater, there are productions which require their services. We will be concerned here only with the special problem which arises when a makeup
artist designs all the makeups for a production and works with the entire
cast in the execution of those makeups. Since professional actors, regret-
tably, are seldom prepared to cope with anything more than the most elementary makeups, the "working with" frequently means teaching followed
by strict supervision.

A makeup artist may on rare occasions be employed in the professional
theater to make up a leading actor each night if there are difficult technical
problems involved, but one is almost never expected to do this for an entire cast, as one is in the nonprofessional theater. Once the show has
opened, the actors are on their own, and the makeup artist may or may not
be expected to check up on what they are doing. If his name is listed in the
program, he will probably wish to do so.

If the cast is large or the makeups are difficult, the makeup artist
would be wise to do all his preliminary work before rehearsals start so as to
be ready to work with the actors as soon as they are available. For the
Broadway production of Paddy Chayefsky's *The Passion of Josef D.,* in

which thirty-five actors were required to play more than a hundred historical characters, this preliminary work consisted of discussions with the director (who, in this case, was also the playwright), library research, making
sketches of the leading actors and the characters they were to play (see
Chapter 20), and filling out tentative makeup charts for all of the characters, including notes on the length of time the actor would have for
makeup changes.

Then, throughout the entire rehearsal period, arrangements were made
with the stage manager to send actors to the makeup room as needed.
When a satisfactory makeup had been achieved and approved by Mr.
Chayefsky, the actor was given a duplicate makeup chart and taught to do
his own makeup. He was then free to come to the makeup room and practice it whenever he wished to do so. Makeups were checked nightly during
dress rehearsals and previews and once a week after the opening.

As a result of the advance planning and the weeks of work with individual actors, there was no uncertainty about what was expected or how
it should be done. Problems were solved early, and changes necessitated by
rewriting of the script were made without confusion. Although one seldom
encounters a makeup situation of quite this magnitude, the same procedure
might profitably be followed for smaller casts. (For makeup pictures from
the production see Figures 185–188.)

QUICK-CHANGE MAKEUPS

The secret of quick changes is to plan the makeups carefully, keeping
them as simple as possible, and to do the various operations in each
makeup in a specified order and with no waste motion. Adequate rehearsal
is essential. Cake makeup is preferable to grease because it can be applied
quickly and does not require powdering.

Since no two problems in quick change are alike, perhaps it will be
best to give as examples two monodramas, one requiring a progression in
age, the other several complete changes in character. Makeup and costume
changes combined range from 1 to 5 minutes, the 5-minute changes being
permitted only for old-age makeups.

The use of rubber pieces is indicated in *Journey to Rages* (see below).
However, it would be quite possible to do without them. The time required
is much the same either way, but the effect with the rubber is more convincing. The final makeup in *Should Anyone Call* is done with rubber also,
but for the benefit of those who do not find it convenient to use rubber, the
procedure which would be used with paint only is indicated.

Should Anyone Call

(Beau Brummel in all scenes)

Scene 1 (1812): RO7 cake, Red-Orange 1 moist rouge. Eyes shadowed and accented. Wig.

Scenes 2 and 3 (1812). No change.

Scene 4 (1820): Tone down rouge with more base. Add shadows and highlights with RO9g cake and O3 Cake. Change wig.

Scene 5 (1840): Run over entire makeup quickly with RO5g cake. Deepen shadows with P13g cake, and strengthen highlights with O1 cake. Run white stick liner through eyebrows. Shadow and highlight hands. Change wig.

Journey to Rages

Scene 1, TOBIT: Rubber pieces covering eyebrows and representing flesh sagging over eyes. Rubber eye pouches. Rubber nose. Rubber hands. RO5g cake base. Shadows with R9g cake and highlights with O1 cake. Wrinkle accents with P13g cake.

Scene 2, TOBIAS: Remove all makeup with cream. Wipe off cream. Add moist rouge to cheeks, lips, and below eyebrows (area 2, plane C). No powder.

Scene 3, AZARIAS: Remove rouge on cheeks and under brows. Add Blue-Green 1 eyeshadow.

Scene 4, TOBIAS: Remove eyeshadow. Add rouge to cheeks and under eyebrows.

Scene 5, ASMODEUS: Cover entire face with YO8 cake base. Add green eyeshadow. Pencil in mustache and slanting brows. See Figure 56.

Scene 6, AZARIAS: Remove all makeup with cream. Wipe off cream. Rouge lips slightly. Add Blue-Green 1 eyeshadow.

Scene 7, TOBIT: Repeat Scene 1 makeup.

Scene 8, THE ARCHANGEL RAPHAEL: Remove all makeup. Cover face with O4 cake base. Rouge lips very slightly. Add gold eyeshadow.

For quick-change makeups it is well when possible to rely largely on wigs, accessories, and rubber pieces to effect the basic change. In progressive makeups, when there is no change in character, it is simply a matter of planning the makeups so that shadows and highlights can be added, eyebrows changed, and so on, without disturbing the basic makeup.

20

ACHIEVING A LIKENESS

For most makeups we have considerable latitude in our choice of details—the height of the forehead, the line of the mouth, the shape of the nose. But in recreating real people whose faces are well known we are obligated to achieve as accurate a likeness as possible.

We begin by comparing the face of the character with that of the actor who is to portray him, noting points of difference and of similarity. The analysis should include shape of the face; shape, length, and color of the hair and the beard; color of the skin and the eyes; and precise conformation of individual features. The points of similarity can be emphasized and the differences minimized. If the actor's nose is too small, it can be enlarged and reshaped with putty. If it is too large, it can be shadowed to make it seem less large and attention drawn to other features. Wigs, beards, and spectacles can be enormously helpful.

An excellent way of training yourself to observe details and to reproduce them is to copy portraits. Photographs, with their myriad of details, may prove less useful to the beginner than works of art (paintings, drawings, engravings) with their simplifications and their emphasis on significant features. In using these artists' representations, however, you must keep in mind that your objective, except when you are deliberately working with stylization, is to achieve a realistic, believable makeup. It should be your purpose to recreate in three dimensions the artist's subject, not to reproduce his technique. Whereas the artist is permitted to show brush marks and to use a cross-hatching of lines to represent shadows, the makeup artist is permitted no such license.

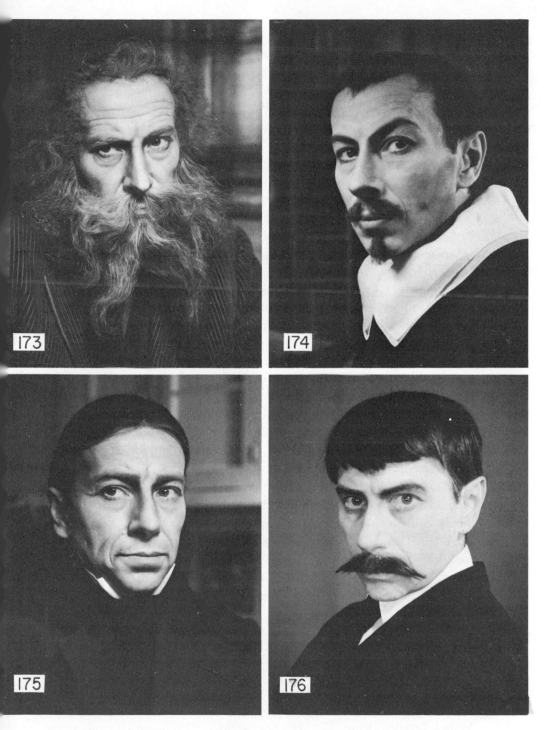

FIGURES 173–176. Four painters. Based on three self-portraits and one photograph: Vincenzo Gemito, 1852–1929 (see Figure 217); Giovanni Mannozzi da San Giovanni, 1592–1636; Jean-Auguste-Dominique Ingres, 1780–1867; Bruce Crane, late nineteenth century. Model in Figure 7.

One final caution—choose a portrait which can conceivably be done on your own face (or that of the model you are using) without a major reconstruction job. If you are concerned about major structural changes, you will not be concentrating on subtlety of detail.

FOUR PAINTERS

Figures 173–176 show four examples of makeups based on portraits. Note that all four faces, though very different in overall effect, were sufficiently similar to the face of the actor in Figure 7 not to require major structural changes. Although some of the changes resulted in striking alterations in the appearance, they were not difficult, requiring only accurate observation and skillful application.

Vincenzo Gemito (Figure 173). Based on a self-portrait. Nose lengthened slightly with putty-wax. Cake makeup base—RO5g; highlights—YO4; shadows—R9g, P13g. Gray wig, beard, and mustache. Beard was in three sections (see Figure 134).

Giovanni Mannozzi da San Giovanni (Figure 174). Based on a self-portrait. Cake makeup base—RO6; highlights—O3; shadows—RO7g, R9g, R14. The darkest shadow was used only around the eyes. Dark brown eyebrow pencil. Upper lip overpainted to thicken. Dark brown wig and crepe hair mustache and goatee. Crepe hair glued on left cheek for hairy mole. Shadows and highlights were used not for aging but for emphasis and changing apparent facial structure.

Jean-Auguste-Dominique Ingres (Figure 175). Based on a self-portrait. Cake makeup base—RO5g; highlights—YO4; shadows—RO7g, R9g, P13g. Small mole on nasolabial fold of nose putty. Cotton in cheeks. Note thin, sharp upper lip and slightly bent nose.

Bruce Crane (Figure 176). Based on a portrait photograph, probably retouched. Cake makeup base—O6; highlights—O3; shadows—RO7g, R9g. Dark brown eyebrow pencil. Dark brown wig and real-hair mustache on lace.

MAKEUP FOR WOODROW WILSON

Let us consider step by step the creation of the makeup for Woodrow Wilson shown in Figure 178. It is apparent at a glance that the actor (Mr. Wilson Brooks, Figure 177) has a bone structure lending itself easily to the makeup. Since President Wilson's face was wider, Mr. Brooks' hair was

FIGURES 177, 178. Actor Wilson Brooks as Woodrow Wilson.
Notice toupee, rubber eyelids, and subtle shadowing and highlighting
used to achieve the likeness.

puffed out a little at the sides to increase the apparent width of the head,
and a small ventilated hairpiece on nylon net was used to match Wilson's
hair style. Observe carefully the following relatively minor but extremely
important changes in individual features:

1. Wilson's eyes have a heavy-lidded effect caused by sagging flesh
which actually conceals the upper lid completely when the eye is open. For
this makeup a rubber piece was used over the eye. The piece was made by
the method described in Chapter 14. Since Wilson's eyebrows are straighter
than Mr. Brooks', the rubber was allowed to cover part of the inner end
of each brow.

The shape of the eyebrows is always important and should be copied
as accurately as possible. In this case the inner ends were raised slightly, the
brows darkened, and the point just beyond the center of each brow was
exaggerated. Shadows under the eye were deepened with cake makeup R9g
and a brush.

2. The nostrils were highlighted, though this does not show in the
photograph, and the nose was narrowed slightly by shadowing with R9g.

3. The shape of both upper and lower lips was altered slightly, and
the lower lip was highlighted with RO3. Shadows at the corners of the
mouth were deepened with R9g. Observe also the highlights and shadows
just below the mouth.

4. A slight cleft in the chin was drawn in with R9g and O1.

5. Forehead wrinkles were deepened with RO6g and R9g and high-lighted with O1. Frown wrinkles between the eyebrows were modeled with the same colors. The superciliary arch was highlighted with O1.

6. Shadows under the cheekbone were deepened with RO9g and the bone highlighted with O1. The nasolabial folds were deepened with RO9g and R14 and highlighted with O1. Although the line of Mr. Brooks' folds is not quite the same as Wilson's, the difference has little effect on the likeness. An actor's own wrinkles, particularly the nasolabial folds, can be deepened or flattened out, shortened or lengthened; but if they are at all pronounced, the natural line must be followed. Otherwise, a smile will reveal that the real fold does not coincide with the painted one, and the credibility of the makeup will be destroyed.

7. The ears were made to stick out slightly with nose putty.

8. The final touch was added with a pair of pince-nez.

It was observed frequently during the makeup that very slight changes in the shape of the lips or the eyebrows, a shadow here, a highlight there, made considerable difference in the likeness. Since it is impossible to have every detail perfect, it is important to make the most of what the actor's face will permit. In most cases there are one or two characteristic features which help more than anything else to identify the character. Cartoonists use these features regularly to depict people in the news.

There are relatively few characters in dramatic literature with faces familiar enough to require extreme accuracy of detail. Wilson is one be-cause, like Lincoln, his picture has been frequently reproduced. Although people have a general idea of what Queen Elizabeth I and Henry VIII looked like, they won't be too critical of details. And for years to come if you want to do Zola or Pasteur, you need only copy Paul Muni's film versions of them and your characterization will be accepted as authentic.

MAKEUP FOR MARK TWAIN

Actor Hal Holbrook (Figure 179), who in his brilliant re-creation of Mark Twain comes startlingly close to achieving the impossible in art—a perfect performance—is as meticulous in his makeup as in his acting. No detail is too small or too unimportant to be given careful attention each time the makeup is applied. And for every performance he devotes more than three hours to perfecting these details. That his makeup takes so long is perhaps less significant than that he is willing to spend that amount of time doing it.

In discussing his problems of re-creating Mark Twain physically, Mr. Holbrook says: "The jaw formation is similar, and so is the cheekbone. My eyes have the *possibility*. His eyes had an eagle sort of look, but you can create that with makeup. And, of course, his nose was very distinctive—long and somewhat like a banana. Mine's too sharp. The nose alone takes an hour. I have a smooth face, and if I don't break it up, the texture is wrong. Also, I have to shrink three and one-half inches. Part of this is done by actual body shrinkage—relaxation all the way down as though I were suspended on a string from the top of the head. Part of it is illusion—the way the suit is made and the height of the furniture on stage. The coat is a little bit longer than it should be. There's a downward slope to the padded shoulders. There's a belly, too—not much of one, but it pulls me down. The lectern, the table, and the chair are built up a little higher."

Materials. The makeup is done with a combination of Pan-Stik, grease stick liners, pencils, and powder. Three shades of Pan-Stik are used—2N (RO3) for the base, 4A (R2) for highlights, and 7A (RO10) for shadows. Three grease sticks are also used—a deep brown, a maroon, and a rose. All three are used for shadows and accents and the red for additional pink color in the cheeks, on the forehead, eyelids, and ears, for example. There are also brown and maroon pencils for accenting.

Application. Except for the base and the first general application of Pan-Stik shadows to the cheeks and eye sockets and sides of the nose, all of the makeup is done with brushes. Most of these are flat sables in various widths. The smaller wrinkles are done with ⅛-inch and ³⁄₁₆-inch brushes and some of the larger areas with a ⅜-inch brush. The makeup is taken directly from the stick. The color is sometimes taken up from the two sticks and mixed on the brush; but more frequently, the various shades are applied separately, one after the other. The importance of using more than one shadow color has been emphasized in this book. Mr. Holbrook uses three—the RO10, the maroon, and the dark brown—and he sometimes adds a bit of rose to give the shadow more life.

All shadows and highlights, as can be observed in Figure 181, are exaggerated since they are to be powdered down. If cake were being used instead of grease, this initial heightening would not be necessary. However, once one has determined what effect the powder will have, one way is as effective as the other. For the detailed brushwork used on this makeup (the whole makeup is approached almost as if it were a painting), the Pan-Stik and grease method is probably easier. As always, choice of materials is a personal matter.

One of the greatest problems in making up youth for age is to elimi-

FIGURES 179, 180. Actor Hal Holbrook, 34, as himself and
as the 70-year-old Mark Twain. The makeup is done entirely

FIGURES 181, 182, 183, 184. Steps in the makeup for Mark Twain. Observe
the wealth of carefully worked out detail, particularly around the neck, jaw line,

with paint, powder, and hair and requires 3 hours.

and eyes. The stippling in 3 colors on the cheeks and temples (Figure 184) is especially effective.

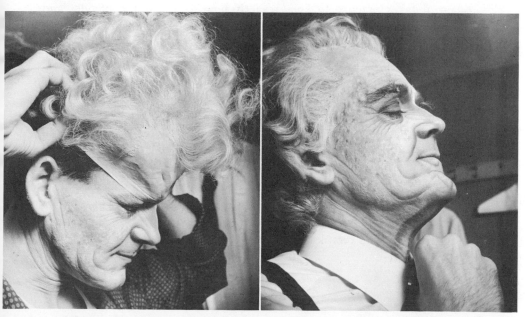

nate expanses of smooth skin. It is at this point that otherwise technically competent makeups often fail. The problem has been solved in this case by covering the smooth expanses with wrinkles, puffiness, hollows, and sagging flesh. You can observe in the accompanying photographs, especially Figure 184, that the entire face and neck (except for the forehead, which is concealed by the wig blender, and the upper lip, which will be concealed by a mustache) is almost completely covered with shadows and highlights. Very little of the original base color shows through.

One additional highly effective technique has been used. After the makeup has reached approximately the stage shown in Figure 183, the cheek area in front of the ears is stippled (using a small brush) with dots of maroon, rose, and the Pan-Stik base. This is then softened somewhat with a clean ⅜-inch brush. When further toned down with powder, the effect, even in the dressing room, is remarkably realistic. (See Figure 184.)

After the stage shown in Figure 182 has been reached and that much of the makeup powdered, the lower part of the forehead across the bottom of the sideburns to the ears is covered with spirit gum, and the wig is put on in the usual way (Figure 183). Ordinarily it is safer to put the wig on first, then apply the spirit gum underneath the blender, though with a very tight wig this may be difficult. Practice makes it possible, however, to apply the spirit gum in the right place and to put the wig on exactly right the first time so as to avoid the difficulties with the gum. The blender in this case extends down to the eyebrows.

The next problem, and a crucial one, is to adjust the blender perfectly so that there are no wrinkles, no air bubbles, nothing to destroy the illusion. This must be done quickly, before the spirit gum becomes too sticky. Again, it takes practice to know exactly how to adjust the blender and what sort of minor imperfections are likely to cause trouble later. Once the blender is perfectly adjusted, it is pressed hard with a towel all along the edge in order to stick it tight to the skin and to make it as smooth as possible. The blender is always cleaned with acetone after the performance to make sure the edge will be as thin as possible.

One of the greatest technical achievements of this makeup is in the treatment of the blender itself and the concealing of the edge. The Pan-Stik 2N base is applied to the blender somewhat irregularly with a ⅜-inch brush. Then the Pan-Stik 7A shadow is applied with a brush to the temples, crossing the edge of the blender. A little light red is worked spottily into either side of the frontal area, keeping away from the hairline. Wrinkles are then drawn on the blender with maroon and 7A and highlighted with 4A. Then the temples are stippled with maroon and rose and 2N.

This is a very important step since it further helps to hide the blender line by breaking up the color in the area. When the blender is powdered, it is impossible to detect even in the dressing room at a distance of six feet. (See Figure 184.)

The eyebrows are made shaggy by sticking bits of gray hair with spirit gum into the natural brows. These are tufts of real hair ventilated into silk gauze. The tuft is cut out leaving only enough gauze to hold the hair together.

The mustache (ventilated on gauze) is attached with spirit gum, the hair is combed, and the makeup is completed. (See Figure 180.)

The preceding paragraphs about Mr. Holbrook's makeup were written in 1959. It is interesting to note that by the time *Mark Twain Tonight* appeared on Broadway in 1966, Mr. Holbrook had made several changes in his makeup—notably, from a blender wig to one with a lace front (putting on the wig was far easier and the effect from the audience was the same) and in the use of sponges for stippling (as described in Chapter 8) instead of brushes. The effect was equally good though not quite the same. Whereas the sponge method took away the youthful smoothness of the skin, which then looked convincingly aged, the brush technique, giving equal age, suggested discolorations of the skin typical of old age. For Mr. Holbrook's television special in 1967 a three-dimensional makeup had to be created for Mark Twain using foamed latex (see Figure 192).

There are several lessons to be learned from Mr. Holbrook's makeup, and they seem to be worth stating specifically:

1. An effective makeup cannot be a hit or miss, last-minute rush job. It must be carefully planned and rehearsed. Except, perhaps, for the professional makeup artist of long experience, any but the simplest sort of makeup requires a certain amount of experimentation, frequently a great deal. Even experienced makeup artists do careful research and planning on any makeup involving historical characters.

2. The makeup should be an integral part of the characterization. Mr. Holbrook over a period of years studied photographs and even an old film of Mark Twain, read everything he could find by or about him, and talked with people who had known or seen him. His makeup developed along with his performance and was not added as decoration before the first dress rehearsal.

3. It is important in making up to adapt the makeup to the actor's face. Mr. Holbrook does not duplicate a portrait of Mark Twain on his own face. As he makes up, he continually twists and turns and grimaces in order to make sure that every shadow or wrinkle he applies follows the

natural conformations of his own face so that there is not the slightest chance that a passing movement or expression will reveal a painted wrinkle different from a real one.

4. One of the secrets of aging the youthful face is to concentrate on eradicating all signs of youth. Blocking out eyebrows, sinking the eyes, modeling marvellously convincing nasolabial folds will all go for nought if the jaw line is firm and the skin is smooth. A firm jaw line may get by if combined with a weatherbeaten skin; or a smooth skin is possible if combined with jowls. But if you can eliminate both, so much the better. The numerous wrinkles in the Mark Twain makeup are less important individually than their effect in breaking up smooth areas of skin with light and shade and color. Unwrinkled areas are broken up with stippling. Mr. Holbrook has taken a definite, positive approach to every area of the face and has made sure that there is no untouched spot remaining to betray his own youthfulness.

Since the remarkable recreation of Twain's likeness is essential to the effectiveness of the performance, Mr. Holbrook feels that he must cut no corners. And, significantly, he takes the attitude that even if the audience were unaware of any imperfections, *he* would know, and in his own mind the performance would suffer. Here is an example of the dedicated artist to whom no amount of effort is too great or too tedious if it will in any way contribute to his performance.

MAKEUPS FOR STALIN AND TROTSKY

In designing the makeup for a historical character, it is helpful to work from photographs of the actor. Perhaps the simplest technique for doing this and making reasonably sure at the same time that the likeness is really feasible, is one used for the major roles in Paddy Chayefsky's *The Passion of Josef D.*

The first step was to place tracing paper over portrait photographs of Peter Falk and Alvin Epstein and to make accurate pencil sketches (Figures 185, 187). This procedure was then repeated with another piece of tracing paper, the features being drawn in lightly but not shaded. This second tracing was then altered to look as much as possible like the historical figure the actor was to play.

In doing such a character drawing, one must be careful to do only that which can actually be done with makeup in the given situation. If, for example, the makeup has to be done quickly (as in the change from the young Stalin to the older one), changes have to be kept simple. But if time is unlimited, one is free to plan more elaborate alterations.

As for the pair of drawings, it would be possible to eliminate the first one and do only the character sketch, which could then be placed over the photograph to show how it corresponded to the actor's face. But if one is able to draw well enough to make the sketch of the actor convincing, it adds considerably to the effectiveness of the presentation in discussing the makeup with the director and the actor and in reassuring them that the transformation is feasible.

Two cautions must be given in connection with this method—be sure the photograph is a reasonably recent one, and use both front view and profile. If all your preliminary work is based on a firm jaw and a smooth skin, an unexpectedly wrinkled face with sagging muscles can be disastrous. Furthermore, a face which appears from the front reasonably easy to make into the likeness of a historical personage can be quite another thing in profile.

Peter Falk as Stalin. The major elements in the change to the young Stalin were the mustache and the eyebrows. The mustache (real hair ventilated on lace) was a simple matter; the eyebrows were not. Whereas Mr. Falk's eyebrows were heavy and slanting down, Stalin's had to be thin and slanting up. Thus, the actor's natural eyebrows had to be completely blocked out. After some experimentation, it was decided to use medical gauze. Although a latex or a plastic piece would have been more effective for close viewing and would have been necessary for screen or television, the use of gauze avoided the necessity for making plaster casts and molds and served well at stage distance.

The natural eyebrows were soaked with spirit gum (Figure 186-A) and pieces of gauze cut to the appropriate shape were laid over them, then brushed with more spirit gum. When this top coat was tacky, Stalin's eyebrows (real hair ventilated on lace) were placed in position on the gauze and the whole area pressed down with a dampened chamois. When the spirit gum was dry, the gauze was covered with Pan-Stik to match the cake base which was to be used. Base (RO5g), shadows (RO7g), and highlights (RO3g) were then applied, the beard area covered with gray cake and stippled with O15 for an unshaven effect, and finally the mustache attached with spirit gum. Mr. Falk's own hair was arranged to suit the character.

For the more mature Stalin, the wig was put on (Figure 186-C) and the lace front attached with spirit gum. Then the lace and the rest of the youthful makeup were covered with light sallow cake base (RO3g). Cake shadows (R9g, P13g) and highlights (O1) were added last.

Alvin Epstein as Trotsky. Alvin Epstein presented an additional problem in that he had not only to look like Trotsky but to achieve the likeness

Peter Falk

Falk as Stalin, Acts I & II

Act III

FIGURE 185. Preliminary pencil sketches of Peter Falk as himself and as Stalin. This is the first step in planning the makeup.

FIGURE 186. Peter Falk to Stalin. (A) Blocking out natural eyebrows. (B) Real-hair eyebrows being glued on. (C) Wig being adjusted, front lace not yet trimmed. (D) Makeup completed, wig being combed.

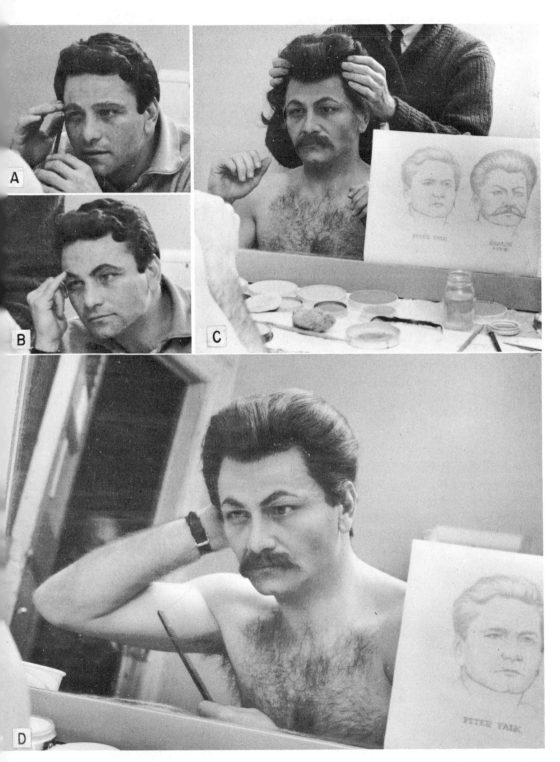

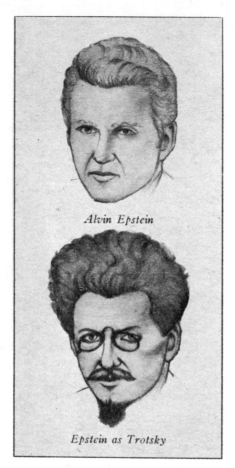

Alvin Epstein

Epstein as Trotsky

FIGURE 187. Preliminary pencil sketches of Alvin Epstein as himself and as Trotsky. Sketch of Mr. Epstein was traced from a photograph.

FIGURE 188. Alvin Epstein to Trotsky. (A) Mustache on hair lace being attached with spirit gum. (B) Pressing goatee into spirit gum. (C) Right eyebrow darkened with black pencil. (D) Makeup completed and wig in place. (Glasses were temporary substitutes for the correct ones.)

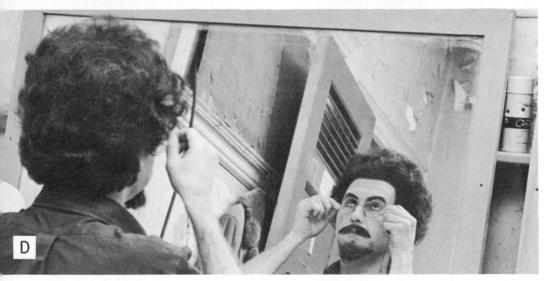

in a quick change. He was playing three characters, each one totally unlike any of the others; but only Trotsky had to be a recognizable historical personage.

The major elements in the Trotsky change were the wig, the goatee, and the mustache (Figures 188-B-D). Mr. Epstein's own blonde eyebrows (Figure 188-B) had to be changed to Trotsky's upward-slanting dark ones, but it was possible to make the change with judicious pencilling (Figure 188-C). The pale, translucent skin which Mr. Epstein wanted for Trotsky was achieved with white cake lightly applied, then partially removed with liquid cleanser, letting the natural skin color below show through and leaving a very slight shine. The bone structure was then lightly accented with cake shadows (R9g) and grease highlights (RO1). The eyes were accented with black and light red pencils. A touch of red pencil was added immediately under the eyebrow.

PROBLEMS

1. Make yourself up as one or more of the following: Sir Thomas More, King Henry VIII (*A Man for All Seasons*); Martin Luther (*Luther*); Abraham Lincoln (*Abe Lincoln in Illinois*); Henry V (*King Henry V*); Stalin, Trotsky, Lenin (*The Passion of Josef D.*); Benjamin Disraeli (*Disraeli*); Franklin D. Roosevelt (*Sunrise at Campobello*); Richard II (*King Richard II*); Richard III (*King Richard III*); Oliver Wendell Holmes (*The Magnificent Yankee*).

Elizabeth I (*Elizabeth the Queen*); Eleanor Roosevelt (*Sunrise at Campobello*); Victoria (*Victoria Regina*).

2. Reproduce as accurately as possible on your own face or someone else's one of the portraits in Appendix F or one from your own collection.

21

FASHIONS IN MAKEUP

One of the determining factors in any realistic makeup is the historical period to which the character belongs. This applies not only to the hair style but, in many cases, to the facial makeup as well. The kohl-lined eyes of the ancient Egyptians, the whitened faces of eighteenth-century ladies, the fashionably pale lips of the early 1960's—all must be taken into consideration in creating makeups for those periods.

The brief notes in this chapter are intended to give an overall view of the subject and to serve as a reference in doing period plays. Although hair styles are mentioned from time to time, along with the makeup, more extensive information can be found in the 21 plates of hair-style drawings in Appendix G.

ANCIENT PEOPLES

Among the Egyptians, both men and women used makeup. The eyelids were frequently colored with green malachite and the eyes heavily lined and the eyebrows darkened (Figure 189) with black kohl (powdered antimony sulfide). Carmine was used on the lips; for coloring the cheeks, red clay was mixed with saffron. Veins, especially on the bosom, were sometimes accented with blue. White lead was occasionally used for whitening the skin.

Both men and women shaved their heads and wore wigs. The hair was usually dark brown or black, though at the height of Egyptian civilization it was sometimes dyed red, blue, or even green. Beards were usually false and tied on with a ribbon or a strap; no attempt was made to make them look natural. Sometimes they were even made of metal.

FIGURE 189. Egyptian king (Tutankhamen) showing eye makeup and the top of the false beard.

Egyptian wigs can be constructed of crepe hair sewn onto a tight-fitting cap. The braids of hair can be used as they are or partially or completely unbraided (see Plate 3). A large number of braids is required to give the wig adequate fullness.

The Assyrians and the Persians also dyed their hair and their beards, the Assyrians preferring black; the Persians, henna color. The eyes were lined with kohl, though not so heavily as those of the Egyptians. The brows, however, were often made very heavy and close together.

Both natural hair and wigs were worn, and the hair was curled with tongs. On special occasions it was sometimes decorated with gold dust and intertwined with gold threads.

Greek women reddened their cheeks and lips with lead oxide, sometimes whitened their faces with white lead, darkened their eyebrows and, upon occasion, dyed their hair or wore wigs. Red hair was popular; and blue, it is reported, was not unknown.

Fashionable Roman men and women whitened their faces, rouged their cheeks and lips, darkened their eyebrows, and sometimes dyed their hair blond or red. During the period of the extremely elaborate and rapidly changing hair styles for women, wigs were frequently worn. Men sometimes wore wigs or painted on hair to cover their baldness. Both sexes sometimes wore beauty patches made of leather.

THE MIDDLE AGES

Medieval women liked a pale complexion and in the late Middle Ages frequently used white lead to achieve it. Cheek and lip rouge were often used. Both black and blond hair were fashionable, but red was not and would not be until Elizabeth I made it so. In the fourteenth and fifteenth centuries women shaved or plucked the hairline so that no hair would show below the headdress. The plucking was even done in public, much as twentieth century women often apply makeup in public. Eyebrows were also plucked to a fine arched line.

THE SIXTEENTH CENTURY

The Renaissance brought a marked increase in the use of cosmetics but not, unfortunately, much improvement in the knowledge of how to make them safe for the skin. Frequently, irritating and poisonous artists' pigments were used to paint the face as if it were a living canvas. The skin was whitened and the cheeks and lips rouged. In *Love's Labours Lost* Biron says:

> Your mistresses dare never come in rain,
> For fear their colours should be washed away.

Spanish wool and Spanish papers (wool or small leaves of paper containing powdered pigment) were popular for rouge (and sometimes for the white as well) and continued to be used for several centuries.

Wigs were sometimes worn (both Elizabeth I and Mary Queen of Scots had large numbers of them), false hair was used, and hair and wigs were dyed. Elizabeth favored red hair and thus made it a popular color. White or tinted powder was sometimes used on the hair. Venetian women in particular sat for days in the sun bleaching their hair and, according to contemporary reports, occasionally suffered severe reactions from over-exposure to the sun. Blonde wigs were sometimes worn instead.

THE SEVENTEENTH CENTURY

There was relatively little change in cosmetics except, perhaps, a tendency toward greater delicacy in their use. Spanish papers in red and white were still used. Samuel Pepys in his diary referred to his cousin,

Mrs. Pierce, as being "still very pretty, but paints red on her face, which makes me hate her." On the other hand, the Earl of Chesterfield wrote to his well-painted Miss Livingston: "Your complexion is none of those faint whites that represents a Venus in the green sickness, but such as Apollo favours and visits most. . . . Smiles from a new-fashioned mouth doe . . . shew such beauties of red and white that all other mouths can never prayse enough."

But painting the face was confined largely to the sophisticated society of the larger cities. Country girls still relied on their natural charms. It is important to remember this in doing Restoration plays. The ladies who would be wearing makeup should be more artificially pink and white than those who would not. Dark complexions were considered common and ugly.

Patches were worn in profusion by fashionable ladies—according to Beaumont and Fletcher, "some cut like stars, some in half moons, some in lozenges." There were other shapes as well. Their placement on the face was not without significance—a patch close to the eye was called *la passionée*, one beside the mouth, *la baiseuse*, on the cheek, *la galante*, and so on. Ladies were seldom content with one patch. According to John Bulwer, writing in 1650 in his *Anthropometamorphosis*, "Our ladies have lately entertained a vaine custom of spotting their faces out of an affectation of a mole, to set off their beauty, such as Venus had; and it is well if one black patch will serve to make their faces remarkable, for some fill their visages full of them, varied into all manner of shapes and figures." Bulwer includes an illustration of a "visage full of them" (Figure 190).

FIGURE 190. A well-patched English lady of about 1650. From John Bulwer's *Anthropometamorphosis*.

Eight years later, in *Wit Restored*, there appeared a few lines on the subject:

> Their faces are besmear'd and pierc'd
> With severall sorts of patches,
> As if some cats their skins had flead
> With scarres, half moons, and notches.

The patches were usually made of black taffeta or Spanish leather (usually red) or sometimes of gummed paper. It was also suggested in *Wit Restored* that patches might be of some practical use in covering blemishes:

> Her patches are of every art
> For pimples and for scars
> Here's all the wandring planett signes
> And some of the fixed starrs
> Already gum'd to make them stick
> They need no other sky.

It is reported, in fact, that the Duchess of Newcastle wore "many black patches because of pimples around her mouth." Plumpers, made of balls of wax, were sometimes carried in the mouth by aging ladies to fill out their sunken cheeks.

The fashion of wigs for men was begun by Louis XIII; black wigs were popularized by Charles II. At the end of the century light powder (mostly gray, beige, and tan, but not white) was used on the hair. Hair styles even developed political significance for a time—whereas the Cavaliers wore their hair long, the Puritans cut theirs short and were called Roundheads. Beards and mustaches were carefully groomed with special combs and brushes and kept in shape with perfumed wax.

THE EIGHTEENTH CENTURY

Face painting became more garish in the second half of the eighteenth century. The ladies "enamelled" their faces with white lead and applied bright rouge heavily and with little subtlety. Horace Walpole, in writing of the coronation of George III, mentions that "lord Bolingbroke put on rouge upon his wife and the duchess of Bedford in the Painted Chamber; the Duchess of Queensberry told me of the latter, that she looked like an orange-peach, half red, half yellow."

In *The Life of Lady Sarah Lennox* we read that a contemporary of Lady Caroline Mackenzie remarked that she wore "such quantities of white that she was terrible" and that the Duchess of Grafton "having left red and white quite off is one of the coarsest brown women I ever saw."

A guest at a party in 1764 was described as wearing on her face "rather too much yellow mixed with the red; she . . . would look very agreeable if she added blanc to the rouge instead of gamboge."

The white paints, according to *The Art of Beauty* (written anonymously and published in 1825),

. . . affect the eyes, which swell and inflame and are rendered painful and watery. They change the texture of the skin, on which they produce pimples and cause rheums; attack the teeth, make them ache, destroy the enamel, and loosen them. . . . To the inconveniences we have just enumerated, we add this, of turning the skin black when it is exposed to the contact of sulphureous or phosphoric exhalations. Accordingly, those females who make use of them ought carefully to avoid going too near substances in a state of putrefaction, the vapours of sulphur . . . and the exhalation of bruised garlic.

The latter problem conjures up interesting possibilities.

The warnings about the white lead paints were hardly exaggerated. Walpole wrote in 1766 that the youthful and attractive Lady Fortrose was "at the point of death, killed like Lady Coventry and others, by white lead, of which nothing could break her." At least they did not lose their lives through ignorance of the dangerous nature of their paints.

Despite the seemingly excessive makeup used by English ladies, they still lagged behind the French. Walpole reported that French princesses wore "their red of a deeper dye than other women, though all use it extravagantly." Lady Sarah Lennox found the Princess de Condé to be the only lady in Parisian society who did not "wear rouge, for all the rest daub themselves so horribly that it's shocking." Most of the cosmetics used by the English came from Paris.

But it was not only the women who used cosmetics. In 1754 a correspondent wrote to *Connoisseur*:

I am ashamed to tell you that we are indebted to Spanish Wool for many of our masculine ruddy complexions. A pretty fellow lacquers his pale face with as many varnishes as a fine lady. . . . I fear it will be found, upon examination, that most of our pretty fellows who lay on carmine are painting a rotten post.

Patches were still worn and in the reign of Queen Anne even took on political significance—Whig sympathizers patching the right side; Tories, the left. Those who had not made up their minds or did not care patched both sides.

Wigs were almost universally worn by men, much less frequently by women. Powdered hair was in fashion until near the end of the century. White powder was introduced in 1703; but tinted powder—gray, pink, blue, lavender, blond, brown—continued to be worn. Facial hair was never fashionable and rarely worn except, in some instances, by soldiers. Military hair styles were strictly regulated.

But the wigs and high headdresses and powdered hair passed and with them the garish makeup. At the end of the century a more-or-less natural makeup was in vogue.

THE NINETEENTH CENTURY

The nineteenth century brought a long respite from the ostentatiously painted faces, though there were still some holdouts against conservatism in makeup. Early in the century the Countess of Granville wrote disapprovingly to her sister of ladies whose makeup she considered ill-bred: "Mrs. Ervington, dressed and rouged like an altar-piece but still beautiful . . . Miss Rodney, a very pretty girl, but with rather too much rouge and naivete . . . Lady Elizabeth Stuart by dint of rouge and an auburn wig looks only not pretty but nothing worse." A Mrs. Bagot she described as being "rouged to the eyes."

The author of *The Habits of Good Society*, published in 1859, looked back disapprovingly on these early years:

Until the first twenty years of this century had passed away, many ladies of *bon ton* thought it necessary, in order to complete their dress, to put a touch of rouge on either cheek. The celebrated Mrs. Fitzherbert was rouged to the very eyes. . . . The old Duchess of R— enamelled, and usually fled from a room when the windows were opened, as the compound, whatever formed of, was apt to dissolve and run down the face. Queen Caroline (of Brunswick) was rouged fearfully; her daughter, noble in form, fair but pale in complexion, disdained the art. . . . I once knew a lady who was bled from time to time to keep the marble-like whiteness of her complexion; others, to my knowledge, rub their faces with breadcrumbs as one should a drawing. But worst of all, the use of pearl powder, or of violet powder, has been for the last half century prevalent.

The Art of Beauty, published in 1825, was more permissive:

Ought people to use paint? Why not? When a person is young and fresh and handsome, to paint would be perfectly ridiculous. . . . But, on the contrary, when an antique and venerable dowager covers her brown and shrivelled skin with a thick layer of white paint, heightened with a tint of vermilion, we are sincerely thankful to her; for then we can look at her at least without disgust. . . . It is not the present fashion to make so much use of red as was done some years ago; at least, it is applied with more art and taste. With very few exceptions, ladies have absolutely renounced that glaring, fiery red with which our antiquated dames formerly masked their faces.

It was then suggested that ladies compound their own rouge in order to avoid the risk of dangerous metallic paints. One of the cosmetics used at the time was called "Portuguese rouge" and was of two types:

One of these is made in Portugal and is rather scarce; the paint contained in the Portuguese dishes being of a fine pale pink hue and very beautiful in its application to the face. The other sort is made in London and is of a dirty, muddy, red colour; it passes very well, however, with those who never saw the genuine Portuguese dishes or who wish to be cheaply beautified.

Spanish wool was still in use, the type made in London being preferred, "that which comes from Spain being of a very dark red colour, whereas the former gives a bright pale red; and, when it is very good, the cakes, which ought to be the size and thickness of a crown-piece, shine and glisten, between a green and a gold colour." Spanish papers were also used.

Then there were Chinese boxes of colors, each containing "two dozen of papers, and in each paper there are three smaller ones, viz. a small black paper for the eyebrows; a paper, of the same size, of a fine green colour, but which when just arrived and fresh, makes a very fine red for the face; and, lastly, a paper containing about half an ounce of white powder (prepared from real pearl), for giving an alabaster colour to some parts of the face and neck."

As to the application of the colors, the reader was informed that the red powders "are best put on by a fine camel-hair pencil. The colours in the dishes, wools, and green papers are commonly laid on by the tip of the little finger, previously wetted. As all these have some gum used in their composition, they are apt to leave a shining appearance on the cheek, which too plainly shews that artificial beauty has been resorted to."

With Victoria came a reaction in England against any form of paint on the face, though creams and lotions and a little powder were acceptable. Makeup was used nonetheless, but so subtly (by "nice" women, that is) that it was often undetectable. A woman who would not dare buy rouge in a public shop was usually not above rubbing her cheeks with a bit of red silk dipped in wine or trying some other home-made artifice.

This was, in fact, the century of do-it-yourself cosmetics. As the century wore on, the pretence that well-bred women did not use makeup faded away, and magazines gave recipes for concocting one's own cosmetics— not only soap and face creams, but perfumes, face powder, rouge, lip salve, and even mascara. Bolder, more sophisticated, or wealthier women bought commercial products and were sometimes taken in by quacks who made impossible claims for their products, which they sold at outrageous prices. By the 1860's a safe rouge was available, though dangerous ones continued to be used. In 1878 Mary Haweis, a London vicar's wife, was advising young women to make the most of their appearance:

It seems to be an inexpressibly absurd and inconsistent "crack" of modern middle-class society, that if an honest girl is known to use a *soupçon* of colour or tinted powder, she is sneered at and laughed at by her virtuous female friends, and so she gives in; but let me remind her that she is also laughed at if she has great feet or scarcely any hair or thick fingers or any other defect. Crows will always persecute their weaker brethren. . . . If a girl has the trial of a complexion so bad that the sight of it gives one a turn, it is simply a duty for her either not to go into society at all or, if she does, to conceal it as she would not scruple to conceal lameness or leanness. You have no right to inflict your misfortunes on everybody—it is an unpardonable offence against good taste.

In 1889 the author of *Beauty and How to Keep It* noted that "the use of rouge and pearl powder seems to have become more fashionable now than it has been for many years."

By the end of the century the shops were well supplied with fascinating and irresistible cosmetics. Not only did women not resist them, but they were known brazenly to repair their makeup in public. In 1895 the editor of the *London Journal of Fashion* wrote:

FIGURE 191. English cosmetic shop, about 1886. This is presumably the one run by "Madame Rachel," who gave her name to a shade of face powder.

Rouge, discreetly put on, of course, forms a part of every toilet as worn by fashionable women, and some among these are beginning to use their toilet-powders somewhat too heavily. Even those who do not use rouge aim at producing a startling effect of contrast by making the lips vividly red and the face very pale, with copiously laid on powder or enamel—which when badly put on is of very bad effect, and, in point of fact, greatly ages a woman. Still, the entirely unaided face is becoming more and more rare, almost everybody uses other makeup effects, if not rouge, and an almost scarlet lip-salve.

It should be particularly noted, in planning your own makeup for a Victorian woman, that well-bred young girls never used makeup, though they did pinch their cheeks occasionally. Married women might resort to a delicate rouge, very subtly applied so as to look like natural color; but they did not rouge their lips. They might, however, employ various methods of bringing the blood to the surface, such as biting; and they might soften the lips with cream. But lipstick was used only by actresses when on stage and by courtesans.

Early in the century, wigs for women were fashionable. Black and blonde were both popular colors. By the 1820's black was favored. *The Art of Beauty* included a recipe for "Grecian Water for Darkening the Hair," which, the reader was warned, was not only dangerous to the skin, but might eventually turn the hair purple. In the second half of the century the preference was for brown or black hair, and dyes were freely used by both men and women—the men for their beards as well as their hair. Richard Wright Procter, in *The Barber's Shop*, cautioned that in dyeing the hair, one must be wary:

Only the other day a perfumer of Marseilles was sued for damages to the amount of four hundred francs because he unfortunately dyed a lady's hair violet instead of red. And not long ago I observed an elderly, unsuspecting gentleman, whose hair was glittering in the bright sunlight—an unmistakable green.

In 1878 Mrs. Haweis wrote that red hair was all the rage; and in 1895 the *Journal of Fashion* announced that "the coming season will be one of complexions out of boxes . . . and the new colour for the hair a yellow so deep as to verge on red. It is not pretty, it is not becoming, and it is somewhat fast-looking because manifestly unreal."

THE TWENTIETH CENTURY

At the turn of the century many women were using henna to turn their hair fashionably auburn. The purpose of makeup was still to enhance the natural beauty rather than to look frankly painted. Some women, including Queen Alexandra, tended to defeat their purpose by applying their makeup quite heavily, though the colors used were delicate. The English and the Americans lagged behind the French in the frank and open application of paint. In the second decade the use of eyeshadow, eyebrow pencil, mascara, and lipstick became widespread.

As the twenties dawned, beauty experts in England and America were still advising natural-looking makeup, but it was a losing battle. Paris won; and by the end of the decade, heavily painted, "bee-stung" lips, plucked eyebrows, and short hair were the mark of the emancipated woman.

It was in the late twenties that sun-tanned faces became popular, and dark powders were made available for those who did not tan well or had no time to lie in the sun. Cosmetics were available in a great variety of colors, natural and unnatural, all of them attractively packaged and safe to use.

In the thirties even schoolgirls used makeup. Their older sisters bleached their hair platinum, and their mothers or even their grandmothers rinsed away their gray. Hollywood set the styles. For the first time in history women made their mouths larger—Joan Crawford style. The bee-stung lips were gone. Fingernails and toenails were painted various shades of red, gold, silver, green, blue, violet, and even, for a time, black. Polish had been used for some years, but it was either colorless or natural pink.

In the forties and fifties extremes of artificial makeup subsided somewhat, though lips were still heavily painted. Rouge became less and less used and eventually was omitted entirely by fashionable women. Makeup bases in both water-soluble cake and cream form were available in a variety of shades, ranging from a pale pink to a deep tan, and were often applied rather too heavily. Eye makeup was still more or less natural. Eyebrows were no longer plucked to a thin line, colored eyeshadow was used mostly for evening wear, and mascara and false eyelashes were usually intended to deceive the viewer.

But in the early half of the sixties the natural look was out. Makeup became as extreme as the hair styles, with a shift of emphasis from the mouth to the eyes. Lips were not only pale (either unpainted or made up with a pale lipstick), they were, for awhile, even painted white. This fashion, like most others, began in Paris. Eye makeup became heavier and heavier with colored eyeshadow generously applied for daytime wear and the eyes heavily lined with black in a modified Egyptian style. False eyelashes became thick and full, and sometimes several pairs were worn at once. It was a time for restless dissatisfaction and experimentation. White and various pale, often metallic, tints of eyeshadow were tried. Eyebrows were even whitened to try to focus attention on the eye itself, and extremely pale makeup bases were worn. The objective seemed to be great dark eyes staring out of a colorless blob. Hair was tinted, rinsed, dyed, teased, ironed, and wound on enormous rollers, which were even, on occasion, worn in public. Sometimes the hair was just left to hang (possibly a beatnik influence), framing a pale face with great black furry-lashed eyes.

22

MAKEUP FOR
OTHER MEDIA

Although the province of this book is specifically makeup for the theater and it is not intended to cover other fields, it is sometimes convenient or necessary to adapt a stage makeup for photographs, for platform appearances, or for television. For those interested primarily in makeup for photography or television, there are good books available. The brief discussions in this chapter are intended only as practical aids for the stage artist who may be working temporarily in other media.

MAKEUP FOR THE PLATFORM

Platform appearances are frequently made on a stage, of course, but the term is used to refer to occasions when the performer is appearing as himself at least part of the time. Monologists, interpretive readers, singers, pianists, magicians, and others are considered platform artists. Since they are usually appearing on a stage, they must, in order to project their features and to counteract the effect of stage lights, usually wear makeup. The makeup must, however, be relatively subtle, especially if the program is in an intimate hall or theater or if the performer appears primarily on the stage apron, close to the audience.

There is an additional problem which occasionally comes up. Sometimes there are no dressing rooms, no adequate lighting off stage (or even on stage for that matter), no opportunity before the performance to apply makeup, and none afterward to take it off (tea with the ladies immediately following the program, for example). It may, therefore, be wise to apply makeup before going to the theater or the club. The problem, then, is to apply it subtly enough that one can meet people without being uncomfortable and still not look washed-out on stage. The difficulty is not too great for women but is rather an imposing one for men. For them the best solution is a natural tan, but if that is impractical, a transparent liquid makeup works quite well (see Appendix A). For women, a cake or Pan-Stik makeup in not too dark a shade is satisfactory.

In general, cake or Pan-Stik are preferable to a grease foundation. In any event, the principles of corrective makeup should be followed, though very subtly. White lights are much more common than in legitimate shows. You must, therefore, be very careful with the reddish hues frequently used on stage. Colors in the O or RO group are safest. The value will depend largely on how dark you want to look. But if you decide you want a good suntan, be sure your hands and your neck are tanned too.

For men, very little else is usually necessary unless the eyes need accenting. For women, eyeshadow should be chosen with both the costume and the eyes in mind, and rouge in relation to costume and complexion.

For platform makeup there is no necessity for carrying a large kit. Platform artists who travel a great deal, as many do, should try to condense their makeup kits as much as possible. For the ultimate in compactness there is a lipstick-sized plastic purse kit which is described in Appendix A.

For character makeup in platform work the two things to be kept in mind are the proximity of the audience (there is not always a significant difference from the usual theater situation, but there may be) and the lighting. A carefully executed, subtle makeup done with the particular lighting situation in mind will usually serve the purpose. You might refer to the discussion of Hal Holbrook's Mark Twain makeup, which is as effective on the lecture platform as in the theater.

MAKEUP FOR PHOTOGRAPHY

The principles of makeup for photography are essentially like those for stage makeup except that in making up you must work specifically for your mirror and not for an imagined audience many feet away. If you have been following the suggestions in this book and doing carefully modeled, realistic makeups which are convincing to the front row, you will have no trouble in toning down the contrasts just a little and exercising special care in blending and with all details of the makeup. Never delude yourself into thinking that what you see in your mirror won't show up in the camera. In fact, the camera will pick up things your eye may gloss over.

If you are working in black and white, you must remember that red photographs dark and therefore should not be used as rouge. There is no objection to using red in shadows if you normally use it, but if used on the cheeks it will photograph as a shadow. If a dark lipstick is being used for the performance, it should be lightened for the photograph. In doing makeup specifically for black and white photography, one ordinarily uses a panchromatic scale of colors, but it is not necessary to change your usual makeup colors for photographs.

Photographs are frequently taken after a performance or a rehearsal. This, of course, is the worst possible time. Aside from the fact that the actors are tired, the makeups will certainly not be at their best, and the pictures will suffer. If photographs are taken after a rehearsal or a perform-ance, be sure to touch up the makeup, remove rouge, and take a fresh look at it with the camera in mind. Portraits should always be taken at a special time with the makeup done specifically for the camera.

MAKEUP FOR TELEVISION

Television makeup is both like and unlike makeup for the stage. The principles of modeling with paint and with prosthetic pieces are basically the same and vary only in the matter of color, in the lack of necessity for projection to a theater audience, and in the extreme care which must be taken with details in order to permit close-ups. Nose putty and crepe hair are used less frequently. Wigs and beards are usually of high quality, ven-tilated on silk or nylon net. Rubber prosthesis is used extensively, and some of the newer plastics are occasionally used, though much less frequently than for movie makeup, which is even more demanding. As for photog-raphy, in television work you make up for the mirror in front of you, not for an imaginary audience many feet away.

Pan-Stik and cake makeup are usually used for the foundation color. Grease is seldom used, though rubber mask grease must be used over latex prosthetic pieces.

For black and white television, women usually use Pan-Stik 5N or 6N, sometimes one shade lighter for cake makeup. Men usually use 7N or 8N. For corrective makeup for men, a "beard stick" is customarily used. This is Pan-Stik 5N or 6N applied over the beard area first to counteract the normal beard shadow. Then the regular makeup base is applied over the entire face, including the beard area.

Some corrective makeup is almost always necessary for television for both men and women. The principles are the same as for stage makeup. However, the overhead lighting in television may tend to accentuate the shadows in deep-set eyes. If the eyes are deep-set, a highlight will offset the natural shadow. Since television lighting is fairly flat, it is frequently desirable to shadow the sides of the nose so that it will not flatten out. As for the stage, facial proportions should be carefully checked and improved, if possible, and other corrections made. (See Chapter 10.)

Highlights are usually three shades lighter than the base, and shadows three shades darker. It is easier to get a subtle blend if you apply the shadows and highlights first to the clean skin, as with the beard stick, then carefully cover the entire face with foundation. If any of the shadows and highlights need to be intensified, they can easily be touched up over the base. If there are pouches or dark circles under the eyes, an even lighter highlight may be necessary.

Although rouge is occasionally used in black and white television, there would seem to be little point to it since it photographs as a shadow. In fact, such a shadow may be quite undesirable. A cherry red lipstick is usually used for women, ordinarily no lip rouge for men unless the lips are extremely pale. Men's eyes are not ordinarily lined since the makeup would probably be visible in closeups. In making up men, be extremely careful that the makeup does not show on the screen.

For color television a special Pan-Stik and Pan-cake CTV series is available. CTV-4W or CTV-5W is usually used for women and CTV-6W or CTV-7W for men. One or two shades lighter or darker are used for shadowing and highlighting. (See note under *Cake makeup* in Appendix A.) A very light rouge with an orange tone (such as Factor's Light Technicolor dry rouge) is used for women and none for men. Lipstick should be fairly light. Beard stick is not usually used for men, and less contrast in corrective makeup is desirable than in black and white television. The makeup colors to be used depend to some extent on the cameras and how they pick up the reds. Experimentation is usually necessary.

For character makeups in black and white, highlights may be much lighter and shadows much deeper. White may be used for strong highlights and dark brown for deep shadows. The base color may be lighter or darker than the shades usually used for corrective makeup. Since texture is more important than it is in stage makeup, a dark stipple (sponge and cake makeup) over the completed makeup may sometimes be helpful in suggesting an aged skin if a darker-than-normal effect is desired.

Special techniques for three-dimensional textured effects (such as

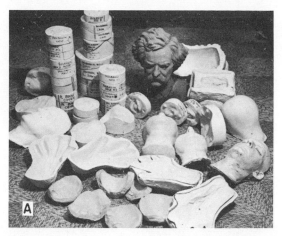

FIGURE 192. Television makeup for Hal Holbrook's Mark Twain. The series of photographs on the following pages shows the step-by-step creation of Dick Smith's makeup for the CBS-TV special of *Mark Twain Tonight*. Although Mr. Holbrook does his own Mark Twain makeup for the stage (see Figures 179–184), the color television cameras required special three-dimensional constructions for complete credibility in closeups. Mr. Smith spent 8–10 weeks preparing for the makeup. This involved making more than 50 casts (A) and a number of experimental tests. Three complete makeups were created before the final one was chosen. With the help of an assistant, Mr. Smith was able to cut the 5-hour application time to 4½ hours and removal time to 1 hour. The method of making casts and foamed-latex pieces like those on the following pages is described in Chapter 13.

The makeup involved both expected and unexpected problems. During the performance Mr. Holbrook puts his hands into the pockets of his white suit. Any actor knows what this can lead to. In order to prevent smearing, Mr. Smith painted the backs of the hands (after the foamed-latex pieces had been attached) with a mixture of latex and acrylic paint. Edges of the pieces on the hands and the neck were blended with George Bau's Scar Plastic Blending Liquid. A light stipple of Pan-Stik was added to the hands and neck and powdered.

At the dress rehearsal it was discovered that the edges of the large latex appliance were working loose around the mouth because of muscular activity. This is a common problem with any prosthetic application in that area. The solution was to use Slomon's Medico Adhesive in troublesome spots. The adhesive is very sticky and more difficult to apply than latex or spirit gum, but it prevented any loosening of edges during the performance.

Although the three-dimensional television makeup shown here was nearly as effective at stage distance as it was on the screen, it would obviously not be practical for regular use in the theater. Some of the techniques used, however, might very profitably be incorporated into makeups for the stage. In fact, Mr. Holbrook now uses the latex nose in combination with his painted makeup for stage performances.

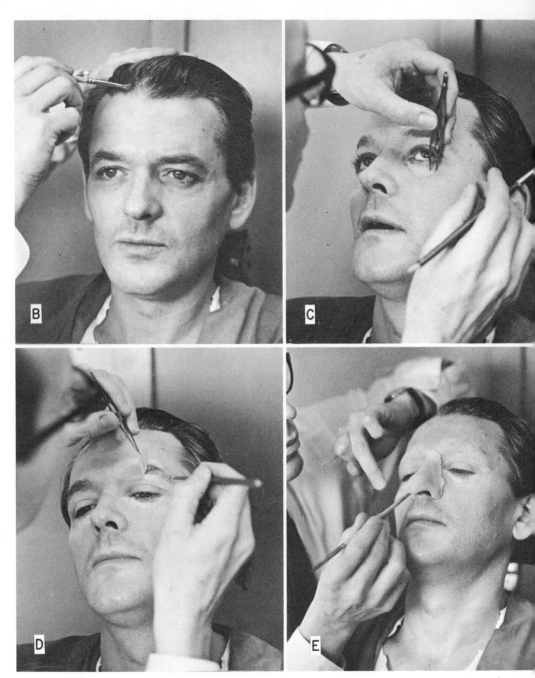

The first step was to flatten Mr. Holbrook's front hair with spirit gum. After the gum was brushed on (B), it was pressed down with a wet towel. Stipple-latex (George Bau's Old Age Stipple) was then applied to the eyelids, dried with a hair drier, and powdered to prevent sticking. Foamed-latex eye pouches were attached with stipple-latex and adjusted with tweezers (C). Eyebrows were flattened with spirit gum (see Chapter 12) and covered with foamed-latex pieces (D). The foamed-latex nose was attached with spirit gum

MAKEUPS BY DICK SMITH, S.M.A.

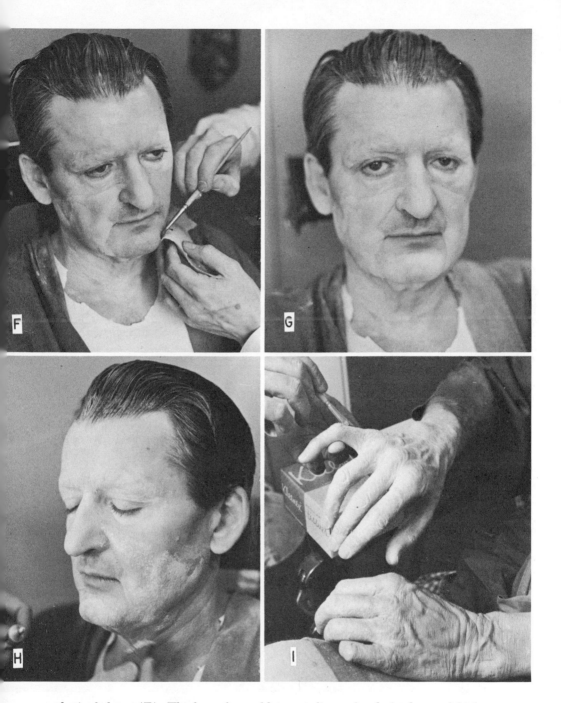

and stipple-latex (E). The large foamed-latex appliance (neck, jowls, nasolabial folds) was set in place and attached with spirit gum on the lower parts and stipple-latex on the top edges (F). Photograph G shows the piece completely attached. Duo adhesive was then applied as a sealer (H). Meanwhile, foamed-latex pieces were being attached to the backs of the hands (I) by assistant Scott Cunningham.

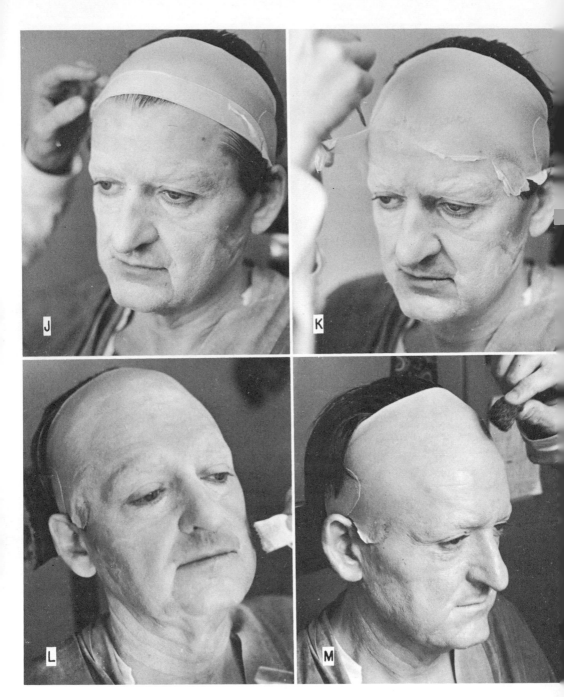

A plastic forehead piece (J) was needed to give an effect of seeing the scalp through the thin and fluffy front hair of the wig. After it was attached with gum, the edge of the plastic piece was dissolved with acetone (K) to blend it imperceptibly into the natural skin. A light rubber-mask greasepaint base was applied over the entire face (L), then stippled with other colors, using a coarse sponge (M) and in some cases a brush. Eyebrows were attached over the latex covers (N). The wig was then put on, the front lace glued down with matte

MAKEUPS BY DICK SMITH, S.M.A.

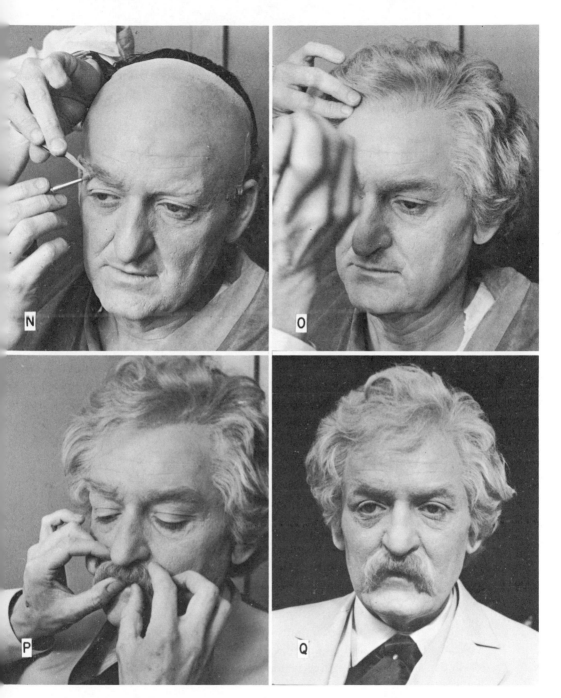

plastic (O), and the hair brushed. After the mustache (ventilated on a net foundation) was attached (P), the entire makeup was touched up wherever necessary. Photograph Q shows the final result. Although the three-dimensional, television makeup shown here was very nearly as effective at stage distance as it was on the screen, it would obviously not be practical for regular use in the theater. Some of the techniques used, however, might very profitably be incorporated into makeups for the stage.

latex or sealer and tissue) are more widely used than they are for stage purposes because of the closer work.

High quality wigs are always used. Crepe hair is sometimes used, but usually not for characters who will have close-ups.

Three-dimensional makeup is used to a much greater extent in television than it is in stage makeup, and there is of necessity much greater emphasis on precision of detail. Rubber prosthesis is extensively used, especially foamed rubber, which makes it possible to construct jowls, double chins, and the like far more successfully than by other methods (see Chapter 14). Special plastics which require double molds, heat, and pressure are sometimes used. Although these give excellent results for close-up work, they are hardly practical for stage use. Not only is the procedure a long and exacting one, but since the edges of the pieces may be destroyed in blending them into the skin, they cannot always be reused. This is not an insurmountable problem for television or movie work, but for stage use it is. Furthermore, the perfection of blending to be achieved with plastic prosthesis is not important on the stage. But for the benefit of those who may wish to do some advanced experimentation and those who are curious about some of the special effects used in television and the films, an abbreviated explanation of the process is included here.

Prosthesis with plastics. The molds used are essentially like those used for foamed latex except that they must usually be larger to withstand the pressure which must be applied, and the surface of the stone casts must be sanded so as to be perfectly smooth.

The plastic material can be made as follows:

1. Mix 9 fluid ounces of dry plastic (such as Vinyl Butyral Resin XYSG, a product of the Union Carbide and Chemical Company) with 64 fluid ounces of isopropyl alcohol, making sure the plastic is thoroughly dissolved before proceeding. This may take several days.

2. Add 13 ounces of plasticizer. This is made by mixing 25% castor oil, 25% dibutyl phthalate, and 50% isopropyl alcohol.

3. Drop plastic material (compounded as above) into cold water and knead it for three or four minutes. Then remove from the water and continue to knead until all of the water is removed. An absorbent, lintless cloth will be required for this. The kneading will take four or five times as long as the first.

4. When the plastic is dry, slap it onto the cleaned and greased positive mold, cover with the negative mold (or the reverse if you prefer), and apply several hundred pounds of pressure for at least ½ hour. Iron stage

weights serve very well for the pressure. Allow the plastic to dry overnight. (Always keep the piece on the cast for storage.)

5. Remove the piece from the cast. Prepare the face by brushing on liquid plastic where the prosthetic piece will be. Let this dry, then set the piece carefully in place. Soften the plastic underneath the edges with isopropyl alcohol and press together. The alcohol will also soften the edge of the plastic piece, and the edges will blend into the skin. The plastic piece and the skin can be made up with Pan-Stik or greasepaint base and powdered.

Plastic caps. We have already discussed the method of making rubber caps to stimulate bald heads, receding hairlines, and the like. This same sort of cap can be made with plastics. The procedure is as follows:

1. The plastic compound can be made up by dissolving 25% by volume of vinyl resin (VYNS) in 70% by volume of methyl ethyl ketone. Then add 15–20 parts of dioctylphthalate (Flexol DOP, Union Carbide). This can be colored by adding a few drops of dye or a small amount of greasepaint.

2. A stone head mold can be made by taking a negative cast of the actor's head with moulage, then making a positive stone cast from this. The cast or mould should be lightly greased, then wiped thoroughly, to make removal of the cap easier.

3. The plastic solution can be flowed on with a brush, keeping the edges thin (only a few coats) and building up the rest of the cap with as many as 25 coats if necessary. Each coat must dry before another is applied. The finished cap should dry overnight before being removed.

4. If a positive mold is used, the cap can be turned inside out to give a less shiny surface on the head. If a negative mold has been used, the matte surface will already be out. After the cap is fitted on the actor's head, the desired blending line can be marked on the cap with a pencil and the cap removed and trimmed. The cap can be attached with spirit gum in the same way as a rubber cap, and Duo adhesive or Flexol can be stippled along the edges to improve the blend. Makeup is applied as usual.

It is possible to ventilate hairs into the cap, but it is easier to build a net foundation into the plastic. This can be done very simply with a positive mold by laying on the net in the proper place and embedding the edges with additional layers of plastic. The hair can be ventilated into the net afterward, or the ventilated piece itself can be embedded. It is, of course, possible to attach a hair piece to the plastic cap with spirit gum in cases in which the cap is to be used for different purposes at different times. If lace is to be embedded, it is wise to make the cap about twice as thick as you normally would.

For a perfect blend it is necessary to dissolve the edges of the cap with acetone (Figure 192-K) in much the same way as is done with other plastic pieces. This, however, destroys the edge, and for stage purposes this is impractical.

This is obviously only a very brief look at the field of television makeup which has of necessity kept pace with other technical developments in the field. The demands of convincing three-dimensional detail work place their problems far beyond those we encounter in the theater.

Many of the television makeup artists are highly imaginative and tireless in their experiments with new ideas and materials, both likely and unlikely. Stage makeups could profit a good deal from a similar interest in developing new techniques. Perhaps when audiences become more demanding, the improvements in makeup will, let us hope, be forced upon us.

23

CONCLUSION

No matter how great your natural talent and no matter how admirable your progress while working with this book, it is safe to say that you have not now learned to do makeup—you have only begun to learn. You will never have finished.

Makeup is by no means a static art. It is far different today from what it was ten years ago. Ten years hence you may expect it to have gone through many more changes. Unless you progress as rapidly as the art itself, you will soon be in the position in which far too many actors and makeup artists now find themselves—they are doing makeups for the theater of fifty years ago and putting them into modern, realistic settings. The result, of course, is ludicrous.

Do not be afraid, then, to discard materials or techniques suggested by books and teachers of today in favor of something better which may appear tomorrow. By all means, don't fail to experiment with every new material or idea, likely or unlikely, which is even so much as rumored. Better yet, try to develop your own. Then, perhaps, you will be able not only to keep up with your art but—what is still better—to keep ahead of it.

And perhaps most important of all, never lose sight of the fact that the art of makeup has only one reason for being—it is a means of assisting an actor to reveal to the audience the character he has in his mind. So long as makeup successfully serves that end, it will be fulfilling its intended function.

A

MAKEUP MATERIALS

On the following pages are listed all of the makeup materials you are likely to use. The list is reasonably complete at the present writing, but since makeup products are continually being improved in form, quality, effectiveness, and packaging, the comments here will not be completely accurate for an indefinite time. A conscientious actor or makeup artist will want to keep abreast of all new developments and to formulate his own opinions upon the basis of actual experimentation with new products.

The four best-known manufacturers of makeup today are Factor, Mehron, Stein, and Leichner. Leichner's makeup is the favorite in Britain and, though not so extensively used in the United States, most of the Leichner products are available. All references in this book are to the English Leichner products, not the German ones, which are not entirely the same.

The brand selected for use depends largely on personal preference and in some cases on local availability. There is, however, no particular advantage in using one brand of makeup exclusively. Since available products and especially colors vary from brand to brand, the most satisfactory kit can be made up from a combination of brands.

Factor has a high-quality makeup, available in cakes (Pan-Cake), tubes (greasepaint), sticks (Pan-Stik), bottles, and tins. Unfortunately, Factor's interest in the legitimate theater and particularly in the nonprofessional theater appears to be considerably less than in other areas. This in no way detracts from the quality of their product, but it does mean that emphasis in materials and colors seems to be slanted toward other mediums. It also means that Factor products are frequently difficult to obtain, orders are not always filled promptly, and many colors are available only on special order. If you want Factor makeup, you would probably be wise not to order it directly from the company. Since Factor discontinues items without notice, their products may or may not be available when you need them.

Stein, on the other hand, caters to the theater and is particularly popular in the nonprofessional theater. They have a wide selection of materials and colors and are continually adding new ones. Colors sometimes vary from batch to batch. Their foundations are available in cakes, bottles, tubes, and sticks, and their rouges and shading colors are packaged in jars, tins, sticks, and transparent plastic containers.

Mehron's makeup is widely used in the New York theater. The quality of all Mehron products is extremely high and entirely dependable, and Mr. Mehron is very co-operative about making up new colors for special projects. Foundation colors are available in cakes, jars (instead of tubes), and bottles. Rouges and shading colors are packaged in jars and plastic containers. New products and colors are continually being added.

Leichner's makeup, available in sticks, tubes, tins, and bottles, is of uniformly high quality and has a good color range. Emphasis seems still to be on sticks, which are used for lip, cheek, and eye makeup as well as for the foundation color. Plastic jars of eye makeup are available, however, and some foundation colors are available in tubes.

Makeup materials can be obtained directly from the manufacturer, from your local drugstore (which usually has a very inadequate supply if they handle theatrical makeup at all), from most costumers, or from a makeup supply house.

If you are ordering by mail and you are using one brand exclusively, you may wish to order directly from the makeup company. If you wish to order more than one brand, however, the best source is probably Paramount Theatrical Supplies in New York (see address in Appendix B). They handle all brands of makeup as well as a few items of their own, and they will try to obtain for you anything which they do not have in stock. In fact, they have agreed specifically to supply any item of makeup mentioned in this book provided it is still available.

Mehron has a sales office in New York City where you can purchase makeup directly. Stein sells only through retail outlets, including Paramount, or by mail. The Makeup Center in New York carries all brands, including their own (On Stage), and specializes in personal service to actors, models, makeup artists, and others who can actually visit their shop, though they will also fill mail orders. In London, Leichner has a conveniently located studio offering personal service. Max Factor has a salon in Hollywood. All addresses are listed in Appendix B.

In the following alphabetical listing the starred (*) items are those with which you should become familiar first.

Absorbent cotton. Used for stuffing in the cheeks to enlarge them and for building up the face, neck, or hands in combination with spirit gum, collodion, latex, or sealer (see Chapter 13).

Acetone. A clear liquid solvent for removing spirit gum and collodion. Since it evaporates very rapidly, it must be kept tightly sealed. Obtainable at drugstores in pound bottles (it is measured by the pound rather than the pint) or much more reasonably at beauty supply houses by the gallon. When purchased at beauty supply houses it may sometimes be labeled "Nail Polish Remover." If you are buying it at a drugstore, try to get the cheapest grade available. If your local store does not have less expensive brands (usually they have only Merck), they may be willing to order it for you. For those who find acetone irritating to the skin, Stein has a Spirit Gum Remover.

Adhesives. There are several adhesives of various types used in makeup—gum, latex, and plastic. Spirit gum is used to attach beards, mustaches, hairpieces, and sometimes rubber prosthetic pieces. Johnson and Johnson's Duo Surgical Adhesive and Mehron's Flexol Adhesive (cream latex types) are used to attach prosthetic pieces and for stippling to conceal edges of prosthetic pieces and wig blenders. Dicor Adhesives 209 (paste) and 210 (liquid) are used largely in prosthesis. Slomon's Medico Adhesive is sometimes used to attach rubber and plastic pieces to the skin but may often prove irritating. Spirit gum is obtainable from any makeup supply house, Duo Adhesive from drugstores, Flexol from Mehron or Paramount, Dicor and Medico from the sources listed in Appendix B.

Adhesive tape. Occasionally used to draw the skin in order to change the shape of the eyes or the mouth or to construct false Oriental eyelids. For drawing the skin, Air Vent (clear), a transparent plastic tape available in drugstores, is recommended.

Alcohol. Common rubbing alcohol can be used to remove spirit gum. However, acetone is preferable. Obtainable at drugstores.

Aquacreme. See *Makeup removers.*

Atomizers. Useful for spraying brilliantine on the hair, diluted spirit gum on crepe hair to help it hold its shape, and alcohol on the face and on rubber pieces to remove spirit gum. Hair lacquer atomizers with rubber stoppers are recommended for the makeup kit since they are not easily clogged and do not spill. Brilliantine, however, will eventually rot the rubber stoppers.

Bandoline. A thick hair-setting liquid.

Beards. Instructions for making in Chapter 15. Ready-made beards can be purchased from Paramount and from some wigmakers.

Black wax. A preparation for blocking out teeth. It must be softened by holding it in the palm of the hand or next to a warm light bulb, then molded into a thin sheet and placed over the teeth that are to be blocked out. The teeth must be dry before the wax is applied. Preparing the wax is sometimes a slow process, and the actor may find the wax uncomfortable. Black tooth enamel serves the same purpose and has neither of these disadvantages but possesses certain others which may occasionally prove even more undesirable (see **Tooth enamel**). Black eyebrow pencil can sometimes be used as a substitute (see Chapter 12). Black wax can be obtained from Mehron, Stein, or Paramount.

    Blending power. See **Face powder.**

    Blood, artificial. Used in any situation calling for visible blood. It is a heavy, viscous liquid with the consistency of real blood. For specific purposes gelatine capsules can be filled with it and at the right moment crushed by the actor in the hand or the mouth to release the blood. Obtainable from Stein, Factor, Leichner, or Paramount. Stein's is called "Stage Blood," Factor's "Panchromatic Blood," and Leichner's "Stage Blood" and "Congealed Blood." Empty gelatine capsules can be obtained from your local pharmacist in various sizes.

    Body makeup. See **Liquid makeup, Metallic makeup,** and **Texas Dirt.**

    Brilliantine. Useful for giving a pleasing sheen to the hair and keeping unruly hair in place. Any good brand is satisfactory for stage purposes. After the brilliantine has been sprayed on, the hair should be combed or brushed. Obtainable at dime stores, drugstores, and elsewhere. Also avail-

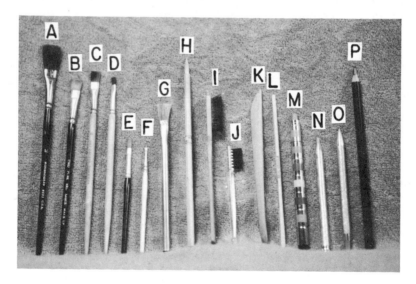

FIGURE 193. Brushes and pencils. (*a*) ½-inch flat camel's hair brush (Mehron), (*b*) ⅜-inch flat sable brush (Stein), (*c*) ⅜-inch oxhair brush (Factor), (*d*) ³⁄₁₆-inch flat oxhair brush (Factor), (*e*) ³⁄₁₆-inch flat sable brush (Mehron), (*f*) sable eyeliner brush (Mehron), (*g*) glue or paste brush for applying spirit gum, latex, or syrup, (*h*) pointed Chinese water-color brush, (*i*) dye brush, (*j*) eyebrow brush (Mehron), (*k, l*) orangewood modeling tools, (*m*) multiple eyeshadow stick (Paramount), (*n, o*) mechanical eyebrow and lining pencils (Paramount), (*p*) wooden eyebrow pencil.

able in solid form. Aerosol sprays and commercial hair dressings are more frequently used.

Brushes, Chinese (or *Japanese*): Water-color brushes with a fine, sharp point, useful in accenting wrinkles. Obtainable at art supply stores. (Figure 193-H.)

Brushes, dye. Shaped like toothbrushes and used for applying acetone to hairlace in removing wigs, toupees, beards, and mustaches. Obtainable from beauty supply shops. (See Figure 193-I.)

Brushes, eyebrow. Stiff-bristled brushes (see Figure 193-J) for brushing the eyebrows. Mehron has very good ones. They are by no means essential, but professional actresses usually like to have them. The small brush which often comes with mascara serves the same purpose.

Brushes, moulage. For applying moulage in casting. Obtainable from Paramount.

Brushes, shading or *tinting.* Several flat sable brushes (or the cheaper camel's hair or oxhair if you can't afford sable) are indispensable in doing character makeups. The bristles should be soft and smooth, yet springy. They must lie flat and not spread. Mehron has an excellent eye-liner brush and a $\frac{3}{16}$-inch shading brush (the most generally useful width). Stein has exceptionally fine sable brushes in five widths, ranging from the tiny eye-liner to the $\frac{3}{8}$-inch width. The $\frac{3}{16}$-inch brush is the most useful one for wrinkles. The $\frac{3}{8}$-inch one is good for blending or for making up larger areas. The narrow brushes can also be used for applying lipstick. Sable brushes can be obtained from art supply stores, but the handles are often inconveniently long. Paramount has a good variety of both sable and oxhair. (Figure 193 shows a number of shading brushes.)

Brushes, stiff-bristled. These are flat brushes, usually about $\frac{3}{8}''$ or wider, useful for applying spirit gum or sometimes latex. Obtainable in art stores, dime stores, and sometimes stationery stores.

Brushes, water color. Used to apply collodion or sealer. Either round or flat camel's hair brushes are satisfactory. They should be cleaned in acetone immediately after use. Obtainable in various sizes at artists' supply stores or dime stores. Moulage brushes can be used instead. Mehron has a good flat Grumbacher brush ($\frac{1}{2}''$) which they call a "character brush" (Figure 193-A). It is useful for applying powder to small areas or for removing the excess.

Burnt cork. Used for minstrel makeup only. It can be procured from Paramount or the makeup companies. Stein has nongreasy Blackface Makeup in tubes. It is now available in Indian, Hawaiian, and Creole as well as black.

Cake makeup. A greaseless, water-soluble foundation paint which is applied with a dampened sponge. Many actors find it preferable to greasepaint. Its chief advantages consist of simplicity of application, comparative cleanliness, and smoothness of the completed makeup. It does not encourage perspiration as a grease foundation does. The only serious disadvantages are the relatively high cost and the impossibility of mixing colors. It is obtainable in plastic cases (Factor, Stein) or jars (Mehron). Although the plastic cases (Figure 194-J) are lighter in weight and take up less space in the kit, the jars (Figure 194-I) contain approximately twice as much makeup for about the same price, and the cakes do not break and crumble as they sometimes do in the thinner plastic cases. The color comes up from the Mehron cake with merely a touch of the sponge, whereas some of the other cakes (especially with certain colors) require considerable rubbing. Stein occasionally has trouble in the manufacture of certain cake colors, resulting in cakes so hard as to be nearly useless. Both Stein and Mehron cakes are available in a wide range of stage colors. Stein also makes small-sized cakes (Figure 194-K) in all colors. These are invaluable for student kits or for shadow and highlight colors in any kit. By the time this book is published, Mehron expects to have a new color television series of cakes which may very well improve upon the Factor colors.

Carbon tetrachloride. Used for cleaning wigs. Obtainable in drugstores.

Castor oil. Used on rubber pieces when they are to be covered with greaseless makeup (see Chapter 14). Obtainable in drugstores.

Chamois. Used in attaching hairlace wigs, beards, and mustaches with spirit gum. Can also be used in applying crepe hair. Obtainable at art supply, paint, or hardware stores.

Cleansing cream. See *Makeup remover.*

*Cleansing tissues. Indispensable for removing makeup. The large boxes are the most economical. Nearly any brand is satisfactory. Pocket-size packs of tissues, cellophane wrapped, are especially handy for the individual makeup kit though more expensive than tissues purchased by the box.

Clown white. A white greasepaint used for such characters as clowns, statuary, and dolls. It can be obtained from Paramount, Mehron, Stein, or Factor. Zinc oxide is sometimes substituted by professional clowns.

Collodion. There are two kinds of collodion used by the makeup artist —flexible and nonflexible. They must not be confused. The flexible type is painted over absorbent cotton to build up the face and neck (see Chapter 13). It should be diluted with acetone. Spirit gum can be substituted if collodion is not available. Nonflexible collodion is used directly on the dry skin for making scars (Chapter 13). Both types of collodion are obtainable at most drugstores or from Paramount. Mehron carries the nonflexible type. Collodion can be peeled off the skin or removed with acetone.

Color Sprā. Trade name of a spray for coloring the natural hair, wigs, beards, and the like. The color does not rub off but can be washed out. Colors can be mixed. Available from Paramount in aerosol spray cans and in bottles to be used with an atomizer. There is a wide variety of colors available, including silver, gold, pink, blue, brown, black, chartreuse, lavender, golden blond, light ash blond, platinum blond, dark red, and copper red.

Combs. A wide-toothed comb is necessary for combing out crepe hair and wigs. The kit should also contain a comb to be used for hair with temporary coloring in it, one to be used with clean hair, and a rat-tail comb.

Cornstarch. Formerly used for graying the hair. White mascara, white cake makeup, special hair whitener, or silver spray should be used instead. For quick-change makeups or when the gray must be removed during the play, it may be necessary to use white blending powder, which is not satisfactory but is preferable to cornstarch.

Cosmetic or **cosmetique.** Used for beading the eyelashes when very heavy ones are required. False eyelashes are more effective, but cosmetic can serve as a cheap substitute. The cosmetic must be heated before use. Available from Paramount, Stein, or Mehron. Mehron's is called "Beadex."

*Cream stick. A velvety, nongreasy stick makeup base applied with the fingers or (for shadows and highlights) with a brush. If you object to the slight natural sheen of the makeup, a little neutral powder can be

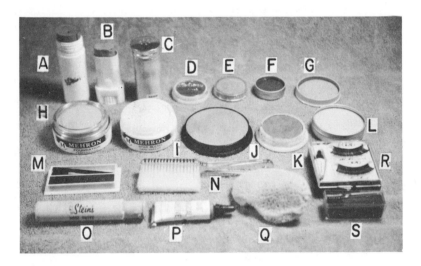

FIGURE 194. Makeup materials. (*a*) Velvet Stick (Stein), (*b*) Pan-Stik (Factor), (*c*) powdered rouge (Mehron), (*d*) eyeshadow (Mehron), (*e*) eyeshadow (Stein), (*f*) soft liner (Stein), (*g*) dry rouge, (*h*) foundation greasepaint (Mehron), (*i*) cake makeup (Mehron), (*j*, *k*) cake makeup (Stein), (*l*) Naturo Plasto (Paramount), (*m*) mascara (Stein), (*n*) nylon powder brush (Mehron), (*o*) nose putty (Stein), (p) J & J Duo Adhesive, (q) natural silk sponge (Paramount), (r) false eyelashes (Mehron), (*s*) mascara (Mehron).

applied over it to give a matte finish. A sort of compromise between cake and greasepaint with some advantages of both, it is sold under the trade names of Pan-Stik (Factor) and Velvet Stick (Stein). Since it is less opaque than greasepaint, shadows can often be applied under the foundation. The possibility of color mixing represents its primary advantage over cake makeup; but the necessity for powdering, even a little, is a slight drawback. Both cream stick and cake makeup are considerably more expensive than greasepaint, though Velvet Stick, figuring by cost per ounce, is less than half the price of Pan-Stik (see Figure 194-A-B). Figure 195-A illustrates a method of combining a number of shades of cream stick (in this case Pan-Stik) in one small container. Cream stick is available from Paramount.

Crepe hair. Indispensable for male character makeups. Crepe wool, as it is sometimes called, comes in tightly woven braids and is purchased by the yard. It can be obtained in a number of colors such as blond, auburn, light brown, medium brown, dark brown, light gray, and medium gray, and in some very useful shades which are a mixture of gray and brown. These gray-browns are available from Paramount and from most of the makeup companies. Crepe hair must usually be dampened and straightened before use.

Derma wax. A soft wax commonly used by undertakers in restoring features disfigured by accident or illness. It can be used as a substitute for nose putty, and though it can be removed much more easily than putty, its adhesive qualities are poor. It can also be mixed with nose putty as explained in Chapter 13. It can be obtained in various sized tins from Paramount, Stein, or Factor. Stein's comes in three shades. Mehron's wax is too soft for building up the nose but can be used for blocking out eyebrows and smoothing out prosthetic applications. Paramount has Naturo Plasto, a high quality wax, in both firm and soft consistencies.

Drawing mats. Used in wigmaking for drawing hair (Figure 146-B). See description and explanation in Chapter 16. Available through Paramount.

Duo adhesive. A Johnson and Johnson cream latex adhesive (Figure 194-P) obtainable in drugstores or from Paramount. Will eventually deteriorate in the tube. See *Adhesives.*

Dye brushes. See *Brushes, dye.*

Dye colors. Liquid food coloring is a safe, useful, and inexpensive dye for tinting liquid latex or for changing the usual tan color of transparent liquid makeup. Obtainable at grocery stores.

Eau de Lys. Leichner's liquid powder for body makeup. Available in a number of greasepaint shades.

Eyebrow pencils. Wooden pencils with soft grease lead used for darkening eyebrows and also for accenting eyes and wrinkles, outlining lips, and similar purposes (Figure 193-P). They are sometimes sold as "lining pencils" or "makeup pencils." Available in a wide variety of colors in addition to the usual brown and black, including auburn, maroon, blue, green, carmine, gray, and white. Every manufacturer does not have all colors, but any brand and any color can be obtained from Paramount. They also have mechanical lining pencils available in single or double points (Figure 193-N-O). The double ones take thick leads in one end and thin in the other. The single-end ones have space for storing extra leads as well as a device in the cap for sharpening the point of the lead. Although these are listed as lip-liners and come only in pink, red, and orange, other colors can be used in them just as well. Grease leads are obtainable for these pencils in a somewhat softer consistency than is found in most of the pencils. The white is especially useful since the average white pencil is too hard to be of much value. Similar pencils can be obtained from dime stores, drugstores, and cosmetic counters but not in a wide variety of colors.

Eyebrow-pencil sharpeners. Ordinary pencil sharpeners are not satisfactory for eyebrow pencils, and razor blades often result in cut fingers. Paramount has a tiny sharpener, and Maybelline has an even better one, obtainable at most dime store cosmetic counters. The Maybelline sharpener catches its own shavings so that you don't have to run to a wastebasket every time you sharpen your pencil.

*Eyelashes, artificial. Widely used by women for routine eye makeup or when the character requires heavy lashes. To some extent they can be used to change the shape of the eyes, though that is not their normal function. They are sold in pairs and must usually be trimmed before using. Ordinarily each lash can be cut in half to make a pair (see Chapter 10), but it is possible to buy ready-trimmed lashes with a "feathered" look. Artificial eyelashes can be obtained at any cosmetic counter or from Paramount. Very high quality ones are made by Mehron (Figure 194-R) and are obtainable in black or brown in three different weights—thin, medium, and heavy. The thin ones are used for street or television, the others for stage. Stein has natural hair lashes as well as self-sticking nylon lashes, which are less expensive than the real hair. Artificial eyelashes are expensive but with proper care should last for a long time. They are applied with special adhesive or with Flexol or Duo adhesive.

Eye-liner brush. A narrow sable brush suitable for lining the eyes. Both Mehron and Stein have excellent sable ones.

*Eyeshadow. Stein has a special eyeshadow (Figure 194-E) in a wide variety of colors, including metallics, and in two sizes. Mehron's Shadoliners serve as eyeshadow as well as for general shading purposes. They also have irridescent colors. For street wear as well as stage, Paramount has three excellent eyeshadows put out by Nu-Masca. One is a cake which comes in a plastic case with a brush and is called "Shadow 'n Brush." The

cake is of a creamy, powdery consistency which comes off easily on the brush with no moistening and gives a smooth, matte finish. There is also a lipstick-size eyeshadow stick in a gold swivel case, available in 7 colors. And for the traveler who wants to keep the makeup kit as compact and light as possible, there is a multiple eyeshadow stick containing 6 miniature sticks of colors in a 5-inch metal tube, color coded on the outside (Figure 193-M). Some of the cosmetic manufacturers specializing in street makeup, package two colors together, one for shading and one for highlighting. Leichner's Form G liners (small, pointed, greasepaint sticks) serve as eyeshadow. Consistency and colors are both excellent.

Face powder. Used over foundation paint to set it. It comes in a wide variety of tints and shades, most of which are unnecessary. A special translucent face powder, which causes very little distortion in the color of the foundation, shadows, and highlights and can thus be used with any base color, is obtainable from any of the makeup companies. Mehron's is called "Colorset," Stein's and Leichner's are called "Neutral," and Factor's is called "Translucent." Alcone Neutral Face Powder, packaged by Paramount, is as good as the others and less expensive. When an ordinary face powder is used, the shade of powder must be slightly lighter than the lightest paint on the face. The very dark shades are sometimes useful for crowd scenes when large numbers of makeups must be done very quickly. The skin can be darkened merely by the application of the dark powder without using any foundation.

Filmed silk. See *Gauze, silk.*

Fishskin. Sometimes used to draw the skin into various shapes. One end may be attached to the skin with spirit gum and the other tied over the head with a string. Fishskin is semitransparent and very strong. Obtainable from music stores, particularly those specializing in repairing, or from Paramount. Not a very useful item in the kit. Transparent plastic adhesive tape can be substituted.

Fluorescent paints. See *Luminous paints.*

Gauze, silk. This is a term used to refer to two different products. Ordinarily for makeup purposes it refers to a thin, tough silk foundation material for wigs and beards (see Chapters 15 and 16). It is available in three qualities—domestic, imported, and Swiss—and in various grades. Obtainable through Paramount. The term is sometimes used to refer to *filmed silk*—a medical product available in drugstores and sometimes used over cotton constructions in building up the face.

Glycerine. May be brushed or sponged on the body to make it shine or used as a base for metallic powders. The powders can be either patted on over the glycerine or mixed with it before it is applied (see **Metallic makeup**). Obtainable at drugstores.

Greaseless makeup. See **Cake makeup** and **Liquid makeup.** Mehron's makeup is technically greaseless since it contains a lanolin rather than a grease base, but its method of use requires that it be listed with greasepaints.

Greasepaint. The traditional foundation paint used to give the basic skin coloring. It is manufactured in a great variety of colors and in both a soft and a hard consistency. Most artists find the soft paint more satisfactory than the hard stick type because it gives a smoother foundation, is more sanitary, and keeps fresh longer. Stein, Factor, and Leichner supply soft greasepaint in tubes. Mehron's foundation paint is not strictly a greasepaint since it contains a pure lanolin base; but since it is used for the same purpose, it will be included under this heading. It is packaged in jars (Figure 194-H). The Mehron foundation paint does not separate as the regular greasepaints frequently do.

The chief advantages of greasepaint over cake makeup are that the colors are easily mixed, skin blemishes and irregularities in prosthetic applications are easily covered, and the paint is inexpensive. The chief disadvantages are that it is messy to use, rubs off easily on clothing, encourages perspiration, and requires powdering, which modifies the character work, often obliterating detail. All grease makeup is subject to the powder risk.

The more nearly pure hues of greasepaint are usually referred to as lining colors or liners. Since that term is very misleading, a preferable though still unsatisfactory term, *shading colors* or *shaders*, is used in this book to refer to the more intense colors of greasepaint. Shading colors are used for shadows and highlights, eye makeup, rouge, and lip rouge and are of firmer consistency than greasepaint foundation. The paint is of a consistency which makes it easily applicable with a brush. Stein and Leichner have stick liners. Leichner's are of a suitable consistency for use with a brush.

Hackle. An instrument combining the qualities of a comb and a brush, constructed of metal spikes in a wooden block, used for combing or untangling skeins of hair. (See Chapter 16.)

Hair coloring. See **Color Sprā.** Various manufacturers of beauty products also have temporary hair coloring products as well as permanent dyes. Mascara (black, white, brown, blond, for example) can also be used but is less effective. Colored powders can be used in an emergency but are not satisfactory. Temporary color sprays are available in drugstores and at cosmetic counters.

Hair, crepe. See **Crepe hair.**

Hair drier. Useful in force-drying molded latex and such materials as plastics, sealer, spirit gum, collodion, and moulage. Obtainable from drugstores, appliance shops, and elsewhere.

Hair, human. Used for fine wigs, toupees, falls, and other hairpieces, and sometimes for beards and mustaches. The hair comes in a loose corkscrew curl, which forms a natural wave in the wig. Unlike crepe hair, real hair should not be straightened before use. It is available in lengths from 10 to 24 inches, in a variety of colors, and is sold by the pound (or the ounce). The price per pound varies with the length and the color. It is also possible to have a sample of hair matched perfectly. This adds to the cost and though necessary for toupees and sometimes wigs, there is little need for it on the stage. For falls there must be a reasonably close match, but it need not always be perfect. All hair goods are obtainable through Paramount.

Hair, synthetic. See discussion in Chapter 15. Nylon-saran has a high sheen and is suitable largely for stylized wigs. Nylon-saran-dynel with human hair (NSD-H) is more nearly like real hair and can be ventilated or made into weft for wigs, beards, and mustaches. Both are available from Paramount in a number of colors. The colors can easily be mixed. Synthetic hair is sold by the ounce, and the cost is about a third that of the cheapest human hair.

Hair, yak. Sometimes used for wigs but more often for beards and mustaches. It has more body than human hair, and it comes straight rather than waved. It is also less expensive.

Hairlace. A netlike foundation used in making high-quality wigs, toupees, beards, and mustaches. See Chapters 15 and 16. Obtainable through Paramount.

Hair spray. Any spray used for keeping the hair in place. See also *Hair coloring* and *Color Sprā.* Colorless aerosol hair sprays in a variety of brands are available in drugstores, at cosmetic counters, and from Paramount.

*Hair whitener. A liquid whitener for graying hair. It is brushed on, then combed into the hair. Removable with soap and water. White cake mascara or white cake makeup can also be used. The mascara is applied with a brush, the cake makeup with a sponge. Hair whitener is obtainable from Paramount or from any of the makeup companies.

Karo syrup. Can be used as a quickly removable adhesive, especially with tissue in creating wrinkled skin effects. See Chapter 13. Obtainable at grocery stores.

Knotting needles. See *Ventilating needles.*

K-Y Lubricating jelly. Can be used for giving makeup a slight natural sheen (see Chapter 14) or as a protective film over a grease makeup, which is, in turn, removed for a quick-change. Since the K-Y is water soluble, it and the makeup covering it can be removed with water, leaving the grease makeup more or less intact, though some detail is likely to be lost. Available in large and small tubes at drugstores.

Lipsticks. Usually available in the same shades as lip rouge. They are usable in the individual makeup kit but for sanitary reasons have no place in group kits. Stein has a variety of colors. Some of the Video shades are particularly interesting.

Liquid latex. A liquid rubber used for building up flexible prosthetic pieces (see Chapter 14), attaching crepe hair (Chapter 15), or making a variety of skin textures (Chapter 13). Obtainable from Paramount, Mehron, or Stein. Latex is normally an off-white but can be easily colored by the addition of small amounts of concentrated dye, food coloring, or even makeup powders to arrive at whatever flesh tone is needed. When dry, however, the latex is normally darker than when wet. The Paramount latex is available in two colors, in addition to the clear latex (which they call Vultex), the flesh color being preferable for most purposes. The Stein latex is a yellowish sallow color and Mehron's is a pink flesh tone. Both can be obtained in small bottles with brush and larger bottles without brush. The larger bottles are, naturally, much more economical. If a bottle with a brush is used, the brush must always be returned to the bottle immediately and not be exposed to the air any longer than absolutely necessary. Once latex dries on the brush, the brush is ruined.

Latex foamed sponge compounds can be obtained from Paramount or from UniRoyal Chemical in four parts to be combined when used. See Chapter 14 for details.

Liquid makeup. This is a greaseless foundation comparable to cake except that it comes in liquid form. It can be obtained from Paramount or from the makeup companies in a wide variety of colors paralleling their greasepaints. Leichner's is called Eau de Lys. Liquid makeup is also applied with a sponge and is removable with soap and water. It can be used for the face but is most useful as a body makeup. For water-soluble body makeup in powder form, see **Texas Dirt,** p. 348. There is also a transparent tan liquid made by Helena Rubinstein called Tan-in-a-Minute. Leichner makes a similar transparent liquid called "Tan Klear" in two shades. Transparent liquid makeup is only for coloring the skin and does not cover blemishes or provide a foundation for other makeup. The clear tan color can be varied by adding red, yellow, or blue food coloring.

Luminous paints. Occasionally it is necessary to have a makeup glow in the dark, as, for instance, Death in *Death Takes a Holiday*. The transition from the makeup of the Count to that of Death can be very simply accomplished by the use of luminous paints or pigments. For the exact technique see Chapter 17. Both fluorescent and phosphorescent paints and pigments can be used. The fluorescent ones must be excited by an ultraviolet light. The phosphorescent ones require no ultraviolet light but are less brilliant. A number of shades are obtainable in both kinds of paints and pigments. The yellow is perhaps the most effective. The paints are expensive, but only a small amount is required for an ordinary makeup. Obtainable from Paramount.

Makeup cape. For protecting clothing. Paramount has an excellent translucent white plastic cape.

Makeup removers. Available in solid or liquid form. Cleansing creams are available from all makeup manufacturers, drugstores, dime stores, and cosmetic counters. McKesson's Solid Albolene is a good-quality, reasonably priced remover. Aquacreme is a special cream remover which is soluble in water. It can be obtained from Paramount but is expensive. Mehron has two excellent removers called "Makeup Remover" and "Liquefying Cream." Stein also has a very good liquefying cream called "Makeup Remover" as well as other types of creams. Some actors prefer to use baby oil or light mineral oil or simply soap and water for cake makeup. Stein has a special spirit gum remover which can be used instead of acetone for those who prefer it. Paramount carries an antibacterial liquid remover called "Lav-a-Derm," which is designed for actors with skin problems. It is relatively expensive. The choice of remover is a matter of personal preference.

Mascara. Used primarily for coloring the eyelashes, sometimes the eyebrows, and occasionally the hair. It is made in brown, black, white, and various colors, such as blue, green, blond, and henna. Available from Paramount, the makeup companies, or any cosmetic counter. Stein's and Mehron's both come in convenient plastic cases with brush (Figure 194-M-S). Stein also makes a liquid mascara in gold and silver. Paramount has a good cream mascara with brush in a metal tube, a tube of cream mascara, which can be used with its accompanying brush or squeezed as a refill into the metal tube mentioned above, and a Nu-Masca cream mascara with Lash-Lengthener. Astonishingly enough, the product actually does seem to lengthen the lashes slightly. The lashes tend to stick together in groups, however, rather than to remain separated. Paramount also carries Nu-Masca Mascara Remover, which effectively removes all eye makeup.

Masslinn towels. Disposable cotton and rayon (nonwoven) towels which can be used with latex for skin-texture effects (Chapter 13). Obtainable in department stores.

Metallic makeup. Greasepaints are available in stick form in gold and silver from Leichner. Metallic shading colors or eyeshadow are available from Mehron, Stein, and Factor. Stein has an effective body makeup in gold and silver. It is easily removable with soap and water.

Gold and silver powders can be used on the hair for graying or adding brilliance. The effect is usually striking, but the powder is harmful to the scalp, exceedingly difficult to remove, and ruinous to any grease makeup upon which it happens to fall. Silver and gold sprays (see *Color Sprā*) are preferable. The powders can be mixed with glycerine and isopropyl alcohol and applied to the body for special effects. The mixture should not remain on longer than an hour and a half or two hours and then only when the actor is in good health. It is usually harmless for very short periods, but if it is left too long on the entire body or a large portion of its area, it can result in suffocation and death, though authorities agree that there is little danger to the healthy actor. However, should the actor wearing the metallic makeup show any sign of faintness, it should be removed immediately. Available in silver (aluminum), gold, copper, red, blue, and green. Larger flakes or sequins are also available. These are useful for certain scintillating, sparkling effects in stylized makeups. Obtainable at paint stores, art supply stores, theatrical costumers, and elsewhere. See also *Texas Dirt* (*gold and silver*).

Metallic sprays. See *Color Sprā.*

Mineral oil. Can be sprayed on the face to simulate perspiration. It can also be used as a makeup remover.

Mirror. A round, double-faced mirror is very useful in the makeup kit, especially the individual one. One side of the double-faced mirror is usually magnifying, but this is not important. Whenever possible, of course, makeup should be done before a large, well-lighted mirror, but the small mirror is essential in getting back and profile views. Obtainable at dime and drugstores.

Modeling clay. Oil-base modeling clay (does not dry out), used in modeling heads when studying facial structure and also in modeling features for prosthesis, is obtainable at art supply stores, usually in 1 lb. or 5 lb. blocks. Various colors are available, but the color is of no importance.

Modeling wax. See *Derma wax.*

Modeling tools. Shaped orangewood sticks used in clay modeling, also in modeling nose putty or derma wax. Available from art supply stores in a variety of styles. (See Figure 193-K.)

Moist rouge. See *Rouge, moist.*

Moulage. An elastic, gelatinous material used in making plaster or stone casts for prosthesis (see Chapter 14). Obtainable from Paramount when available. Paramount also carries braces for reinforcing the molds.

Mousseline de soie. A gauzelike silk or rayon cloth often used in making facial lifts. Obtainable at dry goods counters.

Mustaches. Can be purchased ready-made on gauze in various forms and colors from Paramount. Instructions for making beards and mustaches are given in Chapters 15 and 16.

Needles, knotting or *ventilating.* See *Ventilating needles.*

Netting. Foundation for wigs, toupees, beards, and mustaches. Available in silk, nylon, plastic, and cotton. The English silk vegetable netting is the most expensive and the English cotton vegetable netting the cheapest. The more expensive nettings (or hairlace) should always be used on good wigs or toupees. Cotton netting can be used for practice work. All nettings and laces available from Kalinsky or through Paramount.

*Nose putty. A sticky, pliable material used for building up the nose and other bony parts of the face. Both Stein and Mehron have excellent nose putty. Both now come in stick form (Figure 194-O), though Stein's formerly was packaged in a tin box.

Nylon-saran and *nylon-saran-dynel.* See *Hair, synthetic.*

Orangewood sticks. Sometimes used for modeling nose putty or derma wax. However, the larger clay-modeling tools are more satisfactory. Can be used for applying cosmetic. Obtainable from dime and drugstores. (See Figure 193-L.)

Pan-Cake. Factor's trade name for cake makeup.

Pan-Stik. A Factor stick foundation with a very smooth, creamy consistency. See *Cream stick.*

Phosphorescent paints. See *Luminous paints.*

Plaster of Paris. Used in making both positive and negative casts in rubber prosthesis (see Chapter 14). Obtainable at paint and hardware stores.

Plastic caps. For the screen and often for television, plastic caps are used for bald heads instead of latex. They are very thin and have considerable stretch. For close work the edge across the forehead is adhered with spirit gum, then brushed repeatedly with acetone till it dissolves and blends into the skin. This, of course, destroys the cap. For the stage the edge can be stuck down with latex, which can be peeled off the inside of the cap after it is removed. The outside edge can be stippled with latex or Duo adhesive to help cover the join. Hair on lace can be glued to the cap. The exposed plastic can be covered with greasepaint, cream stick, or rubber mask grease and powdered. The caps, made by George Bau (see Appendix B), are now available from Paramount, along with other very useful Bau products, including Aging Stipple, Invisible Adhesive, and Scar Plastic. (See Paramount catalog.)

Powder brush. A soft brush used to remove excess powder from the finished makeup. Obtainable from Paramount, Mehron, Stein, and Factor and often from dime stores and drugstores. Camel's hair baby brushes are satisfactory substitutes. (See Figure 194-N.)

Powder, face or *blending.* See *Face powder.*

*Powder puff. Used to apply face powder. Any good brand will do. Can usually be obtained more reasonably at drug and dime stores than from makeup companies. The puffs should be washed frequently for sanitary reasons.

Purse kit. A small plastic tube, lipstick-shaped, constructed in sections which can be unscrewed, making available four different sections for makeup. The amounts of makeup are tiny, of course, but the convenience of a kit which fits into the purse or pocket is considerable. It can often be quite adequate for a number of makeups and it is especially valuable for touching up. The tube can be purchased empty or filled, the empty one being much more practical. As a matter of fact, two tubes can be screwed together, giving seven sections for makeup. It is frequently used by models for touching up but can also be very handy for others, including platform

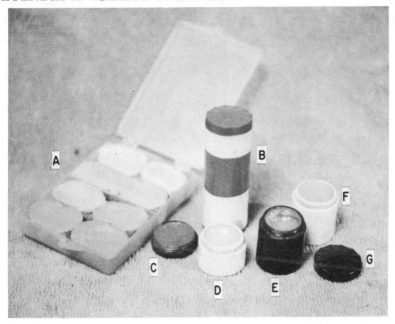

FIGURE 195. Compact makeup containers for traveling. (*a*) Flat plastic box with hinged cover containing 8 shades of Pan-Stik sliced off the top of the original sticks; (*b*) plastic lipstick-size makeup container, shown separated into sections in *c-g*; (*c*) eyeshadow; (*d*) moist rouge; (*e*) cream remover; (*f*) Pan-Stik base; (*g*) cover.

artists and photographers. Obtainable from some cosmetic counters. (See Figure 195.)

Putty. See *Nose putty.*

Rabbit's Paw. Can be used in applying dry rouge or in removing excess powder, but it is no longer a commonplace item in the makeup kit. Obtainable from Paramount, Mehron, or Stein.

*Rouge, dry. A cake rouge which can be applied dry directly from the cake with a puff or a soft brush for touching up completed make-ups or with a damp sponge in the same manner as any cake makeup. The damp-sponge method is usually preferable. A good variety of colors is available from both Stein and Factor. Mehron packages dry rouge in powder form only (Figure 194-C).

Some manufacturers of street makeup have an extremely useful cake rouge which is applied with a brush. This brush-on rouge is highly recommended for both men and women. It is available in natural, subtle colors and can be purchased at cosmetic counters. The Nu-Masca brush-on rouge called "Touch 'n Blush" is available from Paramount in four shades—

Very Pale Pink (RO1c), Rusty Amber (RO5), Fashion Peach (RO5c), and Perky Pink (R6c). The Rusty Amber is especially useful for men, though the Fashion Peach can also be used. The Very Pale Pink is too light for anything but soft highlights. The cake of rouge comes in a plastic case with a brush.

Rouge, moist. For coloring the lips and cheeks. Red shading color can be used instead but is sometimes more difficult to blend, depending on the brand. Under Rouge is more easily blended when the rouge is to be used without a makeup foundation. There is a good selection of rouges in all brands. Stein's #8 Pinktone is an extraordinarily effective rouge for both men and women. Although it is a bright coral (Orange-Red 1), it gives a remarkably natural effect. Mehron's #9 is the same color but with somewhat more concentrated pigment.

Rubber. See *Latex.*

Rubber mask grease. A special castor-oil-base greasepaint for use on rubber. Obtainable from Mehron or from Paramount.

Scalp Masque. Trade name for a liquid color for touching up the scalp to conceal thinning hair. Obtainable from Don-Lee Studios in various colors or from Paramount.

Scissors. Necessary for trimming crepe hair and frequently useful for other purposes, such as trimming latex pieces. Barbers' shears are best for hair work.

Sealer. A liquid plastic skin adhesive containing polyvinyl butyral, castor oil, and isopropyl alcohol, sometimes used medically as an adhesive and as a protective coating. It is especially useful in makeup to provide a protective surface for derma wax constructions, for blocking out eyebrows, and often in place of flexible collodion with cotton. Can be obtained from Mehron or from Paramount.

If you wish to make your own sealer, you can do it very simply by dissolving 1 oz. VYNS (a vinyl chloride-acetate resin) and ½ oz. DOP (dioctylphthalate, a plasticizer) in 10 oz. acetone. Materials obtainable from Bakelite. This will give a fairly stiff film and a fast drying one. For a softer film the amount of plasticizer can be increased 2 or 3 times. The sealer does not deteriorate but must be kept in a tightly closed container to prevent evaporation. It is applied with a soft brush.

Shading colors. See *Greasepaint.*

Silk gauze. See *Gauze, silk.*

Skincote. This is the trade name of a cream used to coat the skin before applying makeup in order to prevent allergic reactions. There is no reason to use it ordinarily, but for the occasional person who does experience an allergic reaction to makeup, Skincote may be helpful. In any case of allergy, it is always well to experiment with various brands of makeup since the allergy may well be caused by a particular ingredient of one brand not present in others. Obtainable from Paramount.

Soap. For blocking out the eyebrows. See Chapter 12. Other methods are usually more satisfactory. Any small bar (sample size most convenient) of toilet soap is satisfactory.

Spirit gum. A liquid gum adhesive used to attach crepe hair, hairlace, or rubber prosthetic pieces. Factor's spirit gum is now called simply "Adhesive." There is some difference in drying time among the various brands of spirit gum, and it is necessary to experiment with the gum you are using to determine about how long it takes to become tacky. The gum should be applied over the powdered makeup when used to attach crepe hair and directly to the skin when used to attach wigs, toupees, beards, or mustaches made on hairlace. Most brushes which come in the bottles are too small. Any suitable brush can be used instead. In applying crepe hair, you should wipe the brush from time to time with an old cloth to remove the hair that sticks to it. And it's not a bad idea to tape the bottle to your makeup table to avoid the possibility of knocking it over. Spirit gum is obtainable from Paramount and the makeup companies.

Sponges. Used primarily for applying cake or liquid makeup. Natural silk sponges (Figure 194-Q) are the most useful. Large ones can be cut in two. These are irregular in shape but roughly round or oval. Artificial sponges, flat and rectangular in shape, are sometimes useful in shadowing or highlighting when more precision is needed than can be achieved with the natural sponge. Red rubber sponges are especially good for creating the illusion of irregular skin texture. The natural silk sponges can also be used in the cheeks for making them fatter or for creating jowl effects. Sponges can be obtained from Paramount, from the various makeup companies, in drugstores, and in dime stores. The flat rubber sponges often sold for street makeup are not recommended for applying foundation.

Stone, dental. This comes in powder form to be mixed with water and is used for making casts in the same way as plaster. The resultant cast is considerably harder than plaster and must be used when the cast is to be subjected to considerable pressure. Dental stone can be obtained from dental supply houses, or as "Duroc stone" from Ransom and Randolph, Toledo, Ohio, or from a retail outlet in your area which they can recommend.

Spray-on bandage. Packaged in aerosol cans under the trade name Safeguard. Sprays on a thin plastic film which is useful in setting beards or mustaches or as an adhesive. Obtainable at drugstores.

Student makeup kits. The best available student kit is put out by Mehron, handsomely packaged in transparent plastic containers in a 5 x 7-inch black and transparent plastic box. It contains 5 foundation colors, 6 shading colors, neutral powder, powder puff, makeup remover, 1 piece of brown crepe hair, spirit gum, black and brown eyebrow pencils, and a ⅛-inch brush. Foundation colors in the men's kit are #4 (OY2), 6 (RO7), 11 (R6g), H(O7), and M (YO9c). Two lighter colors are substituted in the women's kit. Shading colors are #2 (Blue 3), 7 (Gray 4), 8½ (RO14c), 9 (Red-Orange 1), Cherry (Red 3), and White. The color selection is a very practical one. Although the brush is too narrow for most shading and should be supplemented with a 3/16-inch one, the kit is otherwise most useful and is highly recommended for students who prefer to work with greasepaint. It is to be hoped that Mehron will eventually have available a student kit with cake makeup.

A slightly less expensive kit, made up largely of Stein's makeup, is packaged in a flat cardboard box by Paramount. It contains 5 small tubes of greasepaint (much larger than the old Factor ones, however), 4 soft liners, 2 moist rouges, 2 eyebrow pencils, 3 stumps, 2 colors of crepe hair (but no spirit gum), nose putty, neutral face powder, powder puff, and a tube of cold cream. If you plan to use this kit, be sure to buy at least one 3/16-inch flat shading brush and use the stumps only for drawing with charcoal and chalk. If you try to do much mixing of colors, you will find you also need some black shading color, though you might use your black eyebrow pencil in a pinch. The blue will be too light for most mixing, though it will serve as it is for eyeshadow. If you plan to use the crepe hair, you will need spirit gum, which is also useful to have for blocking out eyebrows. The makeup chart in the cover is best ignored.

Stumps. Paper stumps are small, pointed, pencil-like rolls of paper sometimes used for shadowing and highlighting. Brushes should be used instead. But stumps are useful for drawing with charcoal and chalk. They can be obtained from Paramount, the makeup companies, or any artists' supply store. Chamois stumps are somewhat more expensive but last much longer.

Tan Klear. Leichner's transparent liquid makeup in two shades, Suntan Light and Suntan Dark. See *Liquid Makeup.*

Tape, adhesive. See *Adhesive tape.*

Temple Silver. A German Leichner stick for streaking the hair with silver. Obtainable from Paramount.

Texas Dirt. An effective body makeup which comes in powder form and is applied quickly and easily with a damp sponge. It is easily removable with soap and water. Obtainable from Paramount and Mehron. Mehron's Plain is an RO12 in color and dries with a dull finish. Their Gold is about the same color but has a gold sheen. Mehron's Texas Dirt, Silver and Paramount's Texas Dirt are similar in color. Paramount's is an R9g with a very subtle silvery sheen. Mehron's has a slightly more definite silver sheen. Since the effects of the various versions of Texas Dirt are quite dissimilar, you should decide whether or not you want the slightly metallic sheen and if so, whether you want the strong suntan color with gold or the silvery bronze.

Thread. Common cotton or silk thread is useful in removing nose putty. When the thread is passed between the skin and the putty, most of the putty will come off easily.

Toupees. Can be made to order by any wigmaker. However, those made by John E. Jevnikar (see Appendix B) are recommended above all others. They are made on plastic lace by a special patented process resulting in a front edge which is not cut and therefore does not ravel. This makes it possible to extend the hairline to the edge of the lace, eliminating the usual extra half inch of lace, which is always difficult to conceal. It also means that the hairpiece will last perhaps twice as long as conventional ones. With regular wearing and good care it should last more than a year, as compared to six months for the average lace-front hairpiece. The initial cost of others may be lower in some cases, higher in many others. But ultimately Jevnikar's are probably the most economical as well as the most effective. In buying a hairpiece, it is well to remember that the best ones are not always made by those who take the biggest ads and charge the highest prices. It is preferable to have measurements taken in person, but if that is not convenient, any wigmaker will send you instructions for making your own pattern. Jevnikar usually requires four to six weeks to fill orders. If you wish to wear a hairpiece regularly, it is important to have two available so that one can be sent out for cleaning, blocking, and any necessary repairs.

Toupee tape. A cloth tape with adhesive on both sides for securing wigs or toupees to the head. Sometimes also used for quick change mustaches or beards. Obtainable from Paramount, Mehron, or less expensively in large rolls from Robert Spector (see Appendix B). Also known as "toupee plaster" or (from Spector) as "double-faced adhesive." Mehron's tape, which has somewhat better adhesive properties than Spector's, comes in small sheets rather than in rolls. Paramount has a good imported tape in rolls.

T-pins. T-shaped pins for tacking wigs to wig blocks (can be seen in Figures 131 and 132). They come in various sizes and can be obtained from Paramount or from wig supply companies.

Tweezers. Often handy for removing stray hairs in dressing crepe hair applications. Any good tweezers will do.

Velvet Stick. Stein's equivalent of Factor's Pan-Stik. Not only is it slightly cheaper than Pan-Stik, but the stick is more than twice the size of the Factor product (see Figure 194-A). At present it is made only in a grayed series (O1g-O12g) designed for color TV. But these colors are useful for certain stage makeups, including base color, shadows, and highlights.

Ventilating needles. For knotting hair into net or gauze for wigs or beards. See Chapters 15 and 16. Obtainable from Paramount. Should be ordered by number, the number indicating the number of hairs the needle will extract from the hank at one time. The needle holder is ordered separately. One holder is sufficient, but you should have several sizes of needles.

Vultex. See **Liquid latex.**

Wax, black. See **Black wax.**

Wax, derma. See **Derma wax.**

Weaving frames. For weaving hair. See Chapter 16. Available through Paramount.

Wig blocks. Available in balsa wood, styrene, canvas covered, and leatherette covered. Obtainable through Paramount.

Wigs. Instructions for wigmaking can be found in Chapter 16. Wigs can be rented or bought from most theatrical costumers and from wigmakers, such as Bernner, Lerch, and Zauder. No particular wigmaker is recommended for renting wigs since complaints from nonprofessional groups tend to indicate that in general the wigs sent out are not entirely satisfactory. Their work with professional actors and makeup artists appears to be considerably more commendable. This may not be entirely the fault of the wigmakers since amateurs tend to mistreat rented wigs and do not usually know how to adjust the fit or change the styling if the wig is not entirely suitable as it comes to them. Wigmakers cannot be expected to send out their best wigs to groups which often handle them carelessly. Buying wigs is always more satisfactory than renting. Paramount has a variety of stock wigs of varying types and qualities at reasonable prices. In addition, they will make up wigs to order. Time must be allowed for this, of course. In order to make the designation of style as simple as possible, they have agreed to make up real hair wigs to match any style illustrated in Appendix G. It is necessary only to give the plate number and letter of the style in Appendix G, specifying "4th edition," and the usual wig measurements (see Chapter 16). Prices vary according to style. In addition to real hair wigs, Paramount has a number of styles available in nylon-saran-dynel and a blend of nylon-saran-dynel with real hair. They also have mohair wigs.

For professional made-to-order wigs, Bob Kelly is highly recommended (see Appendix B). But he does not rent wigs or handle ready-made wigs. His prices, though reasonable by professional standards, are far beyond the budgets of most nonprofessional groups.

Wig springs. Used only if you make your own wig foundations. They hold the wig snugly to the head. Obtainable through Paramount.

Wig stands and **holders.** Necessary for holding wig blocks in place when wigs are being dressed. They can be in the form of floor stands, table clamps, or a small rubber stand with a suction cup (called Wigways) which can be attached to any smooth surface. Floor stands are cumbersome to have around unless you have plenty of space, but they do make it possible to work on your wig anywhere in the room. The table clamps usually allow tilting the wig block to any convenient angle, but they require a suitable table or bench to which they can be attached. Wigways is a handy portable gadget useful for attaching to makeup or dressing table tops and for carrying about. It is very light in weight and easily stored. Wig stands and clamps are available from Paramount.

APPENDIX

B

SOURCES OF
MAKEUP MATERIALS

BAKELITE Co. (Division of Union Carbide Corp.), 270 Park Ave., New York City.

Materials for prosthesis with plastics, including XYSG, VYNS, and Flexol DOP. Ask for pamphlets and price lists on vinyl resins.

BAU, GEORGE T., 3271 Laurel Canyon Blvd., Studio City, Calif.

Plastic caps, plastic scar material, Aging Stipple, Invisible Adhesive. Does not sell items in small quantities and prefers to deal only with professionals. Most items available through Paramount.

OSCAR BERNNER, 152 West 44th St., New York City.

Wigs.

DON-LEE STUDIOS, 130 West 57th St., New York City.

Scalp Masque.

MAX FACTOR MAKEUP STUDIOS, 1655 North McCadden Place, Hollywood 28, Calif.

Complete line of stage makeup. Write for price list.

FIBRE PRODUCTS MFG. Co., 601 West 26th St., New York City.

Large variety of sample cases suitable for makeup kits. Write for catalog, specifying particular interest in makeup or mention *Stage Makeup*.

JOHN E. JEVNIKAR, 1030 Euclid Ave., Cleveland 15, Ohio.

Toupees and wigs for street wear only. Write for quotations. Mr. Jevnikar makes regular visits to New York for those in that area who wish to see him. No theatrical wigs of any kind.

SAM KALINSKY AND SON, 110 West 17th St., New York City 11.

Hair goods and wigmakers' supplies. Send for price lists. Their supplies are also available through Paramount.

KELLY, BOB, WIG CREATIONS, 151 West 46th St., New York City.

Highly recommended for high quality, made-to-order wigs for the professional theater, television, movies, and street wear. Mr. Kelly does not rent wigs or supply ready-made ones. Prices are not within the range of average nonprofessional budgets.

LERCH WIGS, 21 West 46th St., New York City.
Wigs.

MEHRON, INC., 150 West 46th St., New York City.
Complete line of stage makeup. Write for price list. If you are in New York, you can buy Mehron's products at the address above.

MAKEUP CENTER LTD., 150 West 55th St., New York City.
The best general source of makeup of all brands for New York customers or visitors to the city. The owners are very friendly and helpful and even allow professional customers to try various shades of makeup in their makeup room. A makeup service (especially valuable for models) is also available. Mail orders are accepted.

PARAMOUNT THEATRICAL SUPPLIES (Alcone), 32 West 20th St., New York City.
Best mail-order source of makeup and hair supplies of all brands. Write for catalog. Mr. Cohen will do his best to obtain for you any makeup or hair item listed in this book.

PLASTODENT, INC., 1310 Jerome Ave., New York City 10052.
Dental supplies.

SLOMON'S LABORATORIES, 43–28 Van Dam St., Long Island City 1, N.Y.
Medico adhesive.

SPECTOR, ROBERT, 12 Warren St., New York City.
Adhesive tapes.

M. STEIN COSMETIC Co., 430 Broome St., New York City 10013.
Complete line of stage makeup. Write for catalog. Mail orders only.

UNIROYAL CHEMICAL, Elm Street, Naugatuck, Connecticut 06770.
Latices, including their compound for foaming, LOTOL L-7176. (See Chapter 14 for formula and instructions for use.) Sold in minimum quantity of 1 gallon. Also available from Paramount.

VERNON-BENSHOFF Co., 929 Ridge Ave., Pittsburgh, Pa.
Dicor Adhesives #209 and #210.

S. S. WHITE DENTAL MFG. Co., 220 West 42nd St., New York City.
Dental supplies. Manufacturers of Texton and Duz-all.

WIGWAYS, INC., 55 West 39th St., New York City 10018.
Portable rubber wig stands with suction cup for attaching to table tops. Write for brochure.

ZAUDER BROTHERS, 75 West 45th St., New York City.
Wigs, hair goods, makeup.

SOURCES IN GREAT BRITAIN

AMALGAMATED DENTAL Co. LTD., 26 Broadwick St., London, W. 1.
Dental plaster.

ASH, CLAUDIUS, SONS & Co., LTD., 26 Broadwick St., London, W. 1.
Inlay wax, tooth plastics.

BAKELITE LTD., 12 Grosvenor Gardens, London, S.W. 1.
Sealers, VYNS.

BATEMANS, Young Corner, British Grove, London, W. 4.
Latex adhesives.

CAFFERATA & Co. LTD., Newark-on-Trent, Nottingham.
Casting plaster.

DENTAL FILLINGS LTD., 49b Grayling Road, London, N. 16.
Tooth plastics.

DENTAL MANUFACTURING Co. LTD., Automotive House, Great Portland St.,
London, W. 1.
Dental plaster.

DUNLOP RUBBER Co. LTD., St. James's House, 25 St. James's St., London,
S.W. 1.
Latex.

EDE & RAVENSCROFT LTD., 93 Chancery Lane, London, W.C. 2.
Legal wigs.

EYLURE LTD., 60 Bridge Road East, Welwyn Garden City, Herts.
Eyelashes, brushes, pencils, sponges, false nails, brush-on eyeshadow.

GEMEC CHEMICALS Co., 120 Moorgate, London, E.C. 2.
Plasticizer (DOP).

GOTHAM Co. LTD., Bentinck Buildings, Wheeler Gate, Nottingham.
Casting plaster.

HOECHST CHEMICALS LTD., Portland House, Stag Place, London, S.W. 1.
Polyvinyl butyrals.

LEICHNER'S CREATIVE STUDIOS, 44a Cranbourn St., London, W.C. 2.
Complete line of makeup materials, studio for consultation, and ad-
visory service. Inquiries from outside Great Britain are welcomed. Open
9:30 A.M. to 5:30 P.M. weekdays. Phone REGent 7166 for appoint-
ments.

MACADAM & Co., 5 Lloyd's Ave., London, E.C. 3.
Latex.

MAX FACTOR, 16 Old Bond St., London, W. 1.
Complete line of makeup materials.

MONSANTO CHEMICALS LTD., Monsanto House, Victoria St., London,
S.W. 1.
Sealing compounds, plasticizers.

NAGELE'S, 8 Broadwick St., London, W. 1.
Hairdressing supplies.

NATHAN, L. & H., LTD., 141 Drury Lane, London, W.C. 2.
Wigs.

OSBORNE, GARRETT & Co., LTD., 51 Frith St., London, W. 1.
Hairdressing supplies.

PYTRAM LTD., Pytram Works, Dunbar Road, New Maldon, Surrey.
Negocoll.

REVERTEX LTD., 51 Strand, London, W.C. 2.
Latex.

RUBBER LATEX LTD., Mosley Road, Trafford Park, Manchester, 17.
Latex adhesives, Easifoam #457.

RUBBER TECHNICAL DEVELOPMENTS LTD., 78 Bridge Road East, Welwyn
Garden City, Herts.
Latex.

SERVENTI, HENRY, LTD., 61 Beak St., London, W. 1.
Human hair.

STATHAMS, Uttoxeter, Staffs.
Casting plaster.

VINYL PRODUCTS LTD., Butler Hall, Carshalton, Surrey.
Sealing compounds.

WHITE, S. S., CO. OF GREAT BRITAIN, LTD., 126 Great Portland St., London, W. 1.
Tooth plastics.

WIG CREATIONS LTD., 22 Portman Close, Baker St., London, W. 1.
Wigs and hairpieces.

WIG SPECIALTIES, 173 Seymour Place, London, W. 1.
Wigs.

WITCO CHEMICAL CO. LTD., Bush House, Aldwych, London, W.C. 2.
Latex.

C

MAKEUP KITS

The following are suggested makeup kits for various purposes. They should be revised and supplemented to suit the individual need. All makeup color numbers refer to those used in this book. For equivalents in commercial brands see the color chart in Appendix F.

No single brand of makeup is superior in every way to all other brands, though certain specific materials or colors made by one company may be of higher quality, more practical, more conveniently packaged, more economical, or more dependable. There is no particular advantage in using one brand of makeup exclusively. It is usually wiser to choose items individually, selecting the best each manufacturer has to offer. For sources of makeup materials see Appendix A.

Good professional makeup boxes can be obtained from a variety of sources. They are discussed in Chapter 5.

STUDENT MAKEUP KIT: Male

Grease	*Cake*
Foundation: O6 or O7	Cakes: O1, O5, RO5g, RO7(8),
Shading colors and rouge: Red 3,	R9g (or RO9g), P13g, (or R14),
Yellow 3, Blue 3, Black, White,	White
RO13 (or RO14c), Red-Orange 1	Dry rouge: Red-Orange 1
	1 natural silk sponge

2 flat shading brushes (³⁄₁₆-inch)
1 flat shading brush (³⁄₈-inch)
Eyebrow pencils: dark brown and black
Nose putty

Crepe hair: light gray, gray brown, color to match own hair
Spirit gum
Acetone
Scissors
Comb
Face powder: neutral
Powder puff
Makeup remover
Tissues
Eyebrow-pencil sharpener
(Liquid latex)

STUDENT MAKEUP KIT: Female

Grease	*Cake*
Foundation: RO4(5)(c) or O5c Shading colors and rouge: Red 3, Orange-Red 3, Yellow 3, Blue 3, Green-Blue 2 or 3, Black, White, RO13 (or RO14c), Red-Orange 1	Cakes: O1, O3, RO5(4), RO5g R9g (or RO9g), P13g (or R14), White Natural silk sponge Dry rouge: Red 1 or 2, Orange-Red 1 or 2 Shading colors and rouge: Red 3, Orange-Red 3, Blue 3 (or assorted rouges and eyeshadows of whatever type preferred)

2 flat shading brushes ($\frac{3}{16}$-inch)
1 flat shading brush ($\frac{3}{8}$-inch)
Eyebrow pencils: black and brown
Face powder: neutral
Nose putty
Comb
Spirit gum
Powder puff
Mascara: black
Makeup remover
Tissues
Eyebrow pencil sharpener
(False eyelashes)

PROFESSIONAL MAKEUP KIT: Male

Grease

Foundation: O7(6), RO3(4), R7, R9g, R10, O10, YO8, YO13(14)
Shading colors and rouge: Orange-Red 3 (or Red 3), Red-Orange 1, Yellow 3, Green 3, Blue 3, Violet-Purple 4, Black, White, Gray 3, RO13, (or RO14c)

Cake

Cakes: O1, O7(8), O12, YO7, RO5g, RO7g (or O7g or O9g), R9g (or RO9g), R14, P13g, White
Greasepaint or cream stick: O7, O7g, or RO7g

Dry rouge: Red-Orange 1
Face powder: neutral
2 flat shading brushes (³⁄₁₆-inch)
2 flat shading brushes (³⁄₈-inch)
2 flat shading brushes (⅛-inch)
1 or 2 pointed Chinese brushes (medium)
Eyebrow pencils: black, brown, maroon, (red)
Nose putty
Derma wax (firm)
Sealer or flexible collodion
Modeling tool
Crepe hair: assorted shades
Spirit gum
Acetone
Liquid latex
Duo adhesive
Natural silk sponge
Red rubber sponge
Toupee tape
Scissors
Combs
Hair whitener
Powder puff
Hairpins
Dye brush
Eyebrow-pencil sharpener
Hair cream or brilliantine
Hair spray
Makeup remover
Tissues
Lintless towel or chamois
Plastic makeup apron

PROFESSIONAL MAKEUP KIT: Female

Grease

Foundation: P4c (or P5), R2(3, 3c), R9g, RO4(5), Y4(5)

Shading colors and rouge: Red 3, Red-Orange 1 and 3, Yellow 3, Green 3, Green-Blue 3, Blue 3, Violet-Purple 4, Gray 3, Black, White, RO13 (or RO14c)

Dry rouge: Red 1 (2), Red-Orange 1

Cake

Cakes: O1, O5(6), O12, RO6(5), RO5g, RO7g (or O7g), R9g (or RO9g), R14, P13g, White

Greasepaint or cream stick: O5(6), O5g, or RO5g

Shading colors and rouge: Red 3, Red-Orange 1 and 3, Green 3, Green-Blue 3, Violet-Blue 3(4), Violet-Purple 4, or personal choice of assorted rouges and eyeshadows

Face powder: neutral
Powder puff
2 flat shading brushes (¾₁₆-inch)
2 flat shading brushes (⅜-inch)
2 flat shading brushes (⅛-inch)
1 or 2 pointed Chinese brushes (medium)
Nose putty
Derma wax (firm)
Sealer or flexible collodion
Natural silk sponge
Red rubber sponge
Hairpins
Combs
Hair whitener
Hair spray
Eyebrow pencils: black, brown, maroon, (red)
Artificial eyelashes
Mascara
Duo adhesive
Spirit gum
Acetone
Crepe hair: small amount for eyebrows
Modeling tool
Dye brush
Eyebrow-pencil sharpener
Makeup remover
Tissues
Scissors
Plastic makeup apron
Lintless towel or chamois

GROUP MAKEUP KIT

Foundation: O7(6), O10, Y4(5), YO8, YO13(14), RO1(2), RO7, RO10,
   P4(5), RO9g, Lavender
Cakes: White, Black, Gray 3, Y1, Y7, OY9g, O1, O3, O6, O9, O12, RO3,
   RO6, RO8, RO10, RO5g, RO7g (or O7g), RO9g, R2, R9g, R14, P13g
Dry rouge: Red 1 or 2, Red-Orange 1 or 2, Orange-Red 1 or 2
Shading colors and rouge: Purple-Red 4(3), Red 3, Orange-Red 1 and 3,
   Red-Orange 1 and 3, Yellow 3, Green 3, Green-Blue 3, Blue 3(4), Vio-
   let-Blue 3(4), Violet-Purple 4, Gray 3, Black, White, RO13 (or RO14c),
   YO13(14)
Eyeshadow: Gold
Face powder: neutral (colored powders if desired)
Liquid body makeup: to match greasepaint shades, as needed
Texas Dirt
Natural silk sponges
Red rubber sponges
Flat shading brushes ($\frac{3}{16}$-inch, $\frac{3}{8}$-inch, $\frac{1}{8}$-inch)
Pointed Chinese brushes (medium)
Dye brushes
Spirit gum
Acetone
Liquid latex
Duo adhesive
Nose putty
Derma wax (firm)
Sealer or flexible collodion
Scissors
Crepe hair: assorted shades
Curling iron, hair curlers, and rollers
Hair whitener or white hair spray
Silver hair spray (also such additional colors as brown, black, blond, and
   auburn if desired or as needed)
Hair spray (lacquer)
Hair cream or brilliantine
Toupee tape
Powder puffs
Makeup remover
Tissues
Eyebrow-pencil sharpener
Hairpins

Eyebrow pencils: assorted colors
Absorbent cotton
Clown white
Mascara: black, brown
Black tooth wax
Lintless towels or chamois
Plastic makeup capes

APPENDIX

D

OUTLINE FOR A SHORT COURSE IN MAKEUP

The following outline for an extremely condensed workshop course is included as a practical guide for teachers and students when time does not permit covering the entire book in detail. A hard-working student should be able to complete the material outlined in 30 hours of laboratory work, preferably divided into ten 3-hour sessions or a one-semester course meeting once a week for 2 hours.

There need be no lectures or class demonstrations; the entire time should be spent in actually working on the assignments. Students should be helped individually, and problems of general interest should be brought to the attention of the class. The student should try continually to criticize his own work rather than waiting for a verdict from the instructor. This can usually be done simply by asking and answering two questions: Is the makeup believable? Have I accomplished what I set out to do? Until he has met his own standards, a student's work can hardly be considered satisfactory. Experience shows that most students, when put to the test, have high standards for their own work and will be disappointed if the instructor is willing to accept less than their best efforts.

Many important aspects of the work, though not included in the assignments, can be discussed briefly by the instructor when questions arise. Emphasis in this condensed course is on mastering fundamentals, one detail at a time. It is assumed that the student, having done that, will be able to use what he has learned in order to go ahead on his own after the course is completed.

Since most students seem to work more effectively with cake than with grease, cake makeup is recommended for the student kit. The following kit, though it does not give a wide variety of colors, has proved adequate for the techniques to be learned:

362

CAKE MAKEUP—White, O1 (or RO1), O6, RO4c, RO3g, RO5g, RO7g, R9g (or RO9g), P13g (or R14)

MAKEUP PENCILS—Black, dark brown, (maroon)

DRY ROUGE—Orange-Red 1 or 2 (or one of the brush-on cake rouges in a natural shade suitable for the individual student)

MOIST ROUGE—Red-Orange 1 (and any other shades of their own that women students may wish to use)

GLAMOR EYE MAKEUP (for women)—False eyelashes and personal choice of eyeshadow

BRUSHES—Two ³⁄₁₆-inch flat shading brushes, one ⅜-inch flat shading brush, (one ⅛-inch flat shading brush), (one Chinese water-color brush or one eye-liner brush)

MISCELLANEOUS—Natural silk sponge, makeup remover, tissues. In addition, the student will need a half sheet of gray charcoal paper, 1 stick of hard charcoal, and 1 piece of white chalk. Usually these can be furnished to the student, along with spirit gum, crepe hair, acetone, and nose putty should he progress rapidly enough to need them.

It is suggested that the following assignment sheet be given to the student or that he be instructed to refer to the one here:

MAKEUP WORKSHOP ASSIGNMENT SHEET

Since this is an extremely condensed course, it is absolutely essential that you study the text in advance of each class, *including the first one.* There will be no lectures and no demonstrations covering text material, but you will have an opportunity to ask questions. Since this is a workshop course, you will spend your time actually making up. By following the assignments below, you will be able to progress at your own speed. When one assignment has been approved, you will be free to proceed to the next. It is more important to master fundamentals, however, than to cover a lot of ground.

1. PREPARATION. Study Chapters 1–12 before the first class.
2. LIGHT AND SHADE. Chapter 11, problems 1 and 2 (1 cylinder, 1 cube, and 1 sphere will be sufficient).
3. OPTICAL ILLUSIONS. Chapter 10, problems 2, 3, 6.
4. CORRECTIVE MAKEUP. Chapter 10, problem 10.
5. MODELING WITH PAINT. Chapter 12, problems 3, 4, 6, 8, 9, 11, 12.
6. COMPLETE MAKEUP. After finishing the problems above, do a complete makeup of a specific middle-aged or elderly character from a play—one that you feel you know fairly well. The character should require a realistic not a stylized makeup and should not require nose putty or crepe hair.

7. THREE-DIMENSIONAL MAKEUP, BEARDS, MUSTACHES. Read Chapters 13 and 15. Probably only students who work very rapidly or work extra time will get this far. If you do, it is suggested that you model a nose with putty and/or construct any sort of beard or mustache you wish. If you have time to complete a makeup with the nose or beard, do so.

APPENDIX

E

RACIAL CHARACTERISTICS

The accompanying reference table should be used only as a general guide in solving racial problems in makeup and not as a final authority on ethnology. Peoples are classed by both race and geography, whichever seems more convenient. Chinese, for example, are classed under "Chinese" because no other group has like characteristics. But Swedish is classed under "Nordic," which includes other groups as well as the Swedes. The French are classed under both Alpine and Mediterranean since both types are common in France. India contains many racial strains, but the people can be classed roughly into two groups, Dravidian and Aryan, which are indicated in the table. The Mongolian element is small. Minor racial groups who rarely if ever appear in plays are omitted.

A wide latitude is given in skin coloring since there is wide variation within any given group. In general, women have lighter skins than men. Aside from that, the important thing is to notice whether the colors suggested are generally light, medium, or dark and the general tendency in the hue. All races other than the Caucasian have brown skins, but the brown may be yellowish or copper-toned or so very grayed and dark that it approaches black. For realistic makeups never use red for Indians, yellow for Orientals, or black for Negroes. And though in general you will probably use browns slanted toward those colors, bear in mind that Orientals (particularly the women) are not invariably yellowish, Indians are frequently not reddish at all, and Negroes range from light to very dark in a variety of browns.

In your analysis settle upon the racial characteristics which are most significant to the character and to the play and consider those characteristics as only a part of the total picture of the individual character.

In the chart on p. 367 the numbers listed under "Skin Color" indicate normal variations in hue, value, and intensity of foundation color. The method of indicating intensity may need some explanation. O5-11g, for example, includes all colors between O5g and O11g whereas O5-11(g)

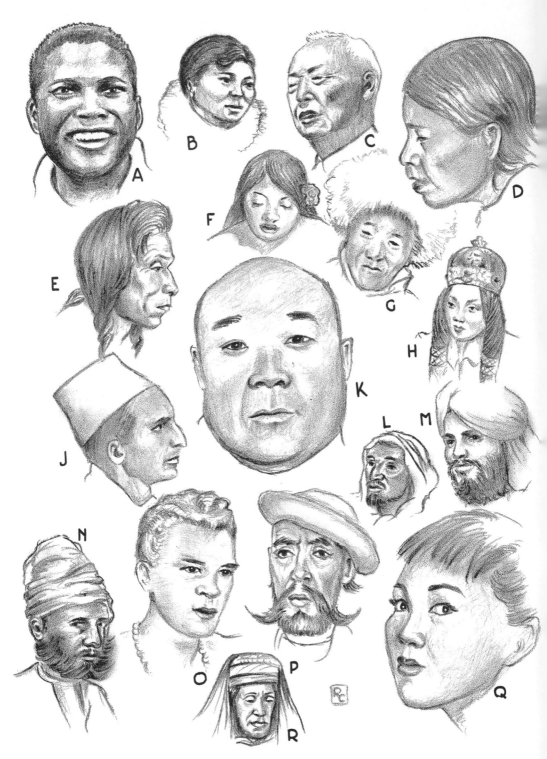

FIGURE 196. Contrasting racial types: A—Negro, B—Eskimo, C—Korean, D—Mexican, E—American Indian, F—Tahitian, G—Mongolian, H—Chinese, J—Turk, K—Chinese, L—Arab, M, N—East Indian, O—Samoan, P—East Indian (Aryan), Q—Japanese, R—Persian.

GENERAL PHYSICAL CHARACTERISTICS OF RACIAL GROUPS

	SKIN COLOR	FACE	EYES	NOSE Profile	NOSE Front	HAIR Form	HAIR Color
ALPINE: N. French, Swiss, Czech, Russian, Balkan	O4-9, EO4-9	Broad Short	Brown	Straight	Med. or narrow	Wavy	Brown
ARMENOID: Turkish, Syrian, Persian, Russian, Greek	OY9g, YO4-12, O4-10g	Narrow Long	Brown	Convex Long	Medium	Wavy	Dark
ARYAN: East Indian	YO6-11(g), O6-11(g)	Narrow	Dark	Convex	Narrow	Wavy	Dark
CELTIC: Scotch, Irish, English, Welch	O4-8, 3O4-8, R4-8	Long	Dk. Blue or hazel	Straight	Narrow	Wavy	Red or brown
CHINESE	OY9(g), YO6-11(g), O5-11g	Broad	Oblique	Concave	Broad	Straight	Black
DRAVIDIAN: East Indian	YO15g, O9-13g	Medium	Dark	Convex	Broad	Curly	Black
EAST BALTIC: Russian, Finnish, German, Balkan	O4-8, RO4-8, R4-8	Broad	Blue or gray	Concave	Medium	Wavy	Ash blond
ESKIMO	OY9g, YO5-12(g), O4-9g	Broad	Almond	Concave	Medium	Straight	Black
INDIAN (American)	YO8-14, O8-14(g), RO7-9g	Broad	Dark	Convex	Medium	Straight	Black
INDONESIAN-MALAY: Siamese, Tibetan, Chinese, Indian	OY9(g), YO4-11(g), O5-11g	Broad Short	Almond Dark Brown	Concave	Medium	Straight	Black
JAPANESE	OY5-9(g), YO4-11(g), O5-11g	Long or broad	Dark Almond	Concave Convex	Narrow or broad	Straight, wavy	Black
MEDITERRANEAN: S. Ital. and French, Spanish, Portuguese, Egyptian, Arab	YO5-12(g), O5-12(g), RO5-9g	Narrow	Brown	Straight or convex	Med. or narrow	Wavy	Black or brown
MEXICAN (Indian)	YC5-14(g), O5-14g	Broad Long	Dark	Concave Convex	Medium	Wavy, straight	Black
NEGRO	OY9g, YO12-15(g), O12-15(g)	Broad	Dark	Concave	Broad	Wooly	Black
NORDIC: Scand., N. German, Dutch, English, Scotch	O4-8, RO4-8, R4-8	Long Narrow	Blue or gray	Straight or convex	Narrow	Wavy	Gold or ash blond
NORDIC-ALPINE (Beaker): German, French, British	O5-9, RO5-9, R5-9	Broad Long	Blue or brown	Straight or convex	Med. or broad	Wavy	Brown or blond
POLYNESIAN: Hawaiian, Tahitian, Samoan	YO4-12, O5-12(g), RO5-9g	Narrow Long	Dark brown	Straight or convex	Broad or medium	Wavy or straight	Black or brown

includes from O5 to O11 as well as from O5g to O11g. In other words, a parenthetical (g) means that both "normal" and "grayed" colors are suitable.

COLOR FOR RACIAL GROUPS

The foregoing suggestions are directed to actors of one race who wish to make themselves up as members of another. But there is the additional problem, not considered in the body of the text, of actors of races other than Caucasian who wish to make themselves up as characters of their own race.

Except for the suggestions offered for the use of specific colors, most of the material in the book is as applicable to one race as to another. But all makeup colors must obviously relate to the natural skin color. Since one of the purposes of stage makeup is to counteract the paleness of the Caucasian skin under stage lights, it follows that for darker-skinned races a foundation color will not always be necessary, though the actor may wish to use it to provide a base for other makeup to cover blemishes. In that case, he will probably choose a color similar to his natural skin color.

If, on the other hand, he is doing a character for which a lighter or darker base would be appropriate, then he will choose a suitable shade within his own general color group—Y's, OY's for Orientals and Y's, OY's, YO's, and O's for Negroes. If, for example, a Negro family is being represented, and an actor playing one of the brothers is very dark and all the others very light, the dark-skinned actor will presumably need to lighten his own skin color to match that of the other actors—unless there is some clear indication in the script to the contrary. Age, environment, and health will also need to be taken into account.

The use of rouge for cheeks and lips will depend on the natural skin pigmentation and on whether natural or artificial coloring is being represented. If the color is to look natural, the actor must adhere to what is natural for his face; but if the color is to represent makeup, then any color which the actor and the director believe the character would wear becomes appropriate.

As with any makeup, highlights and shadows must be co-ordinated with the base color or, if a base is not being used, with the natural skin tone. For example, the OY and YO shadows, which can rarely be used for Caucasians, are excellent for Orientals and often for Negroes. Black is extremely useful as an accent or even a shadow color for dark Negroes but not for lighter or for redder-skinned races.

With Negroes particularly, the wide variation in skin color gives a similarly wide latitude in value for shadows and highlights. The basic skin tone, whether coffee-colored, warm brown, cool brown, or burnt umber, will be the determining factor in selecting colors. For corrective makeup, shadows and highlights about three shades darker and lighter than the base, but of approximately the same hue, should be chosen. For age a much wider variation in value is needed, and some variation in hue is possible. For accents one can go even further afield in choice of hue in order to give greater depth to the shadows. Violet, maroon, red-brown, yellow-brown, gray-brown, and black are all useful when they relate to the base color. For stylized makeups the actor need not be inhibited by his natural skin color, whether black, white, yellow, brown, or red, but can free his imagination and his palette.

APPENDIX

F

PORTRAIT COLLECTION

Reproductions of a number of paintings, prints, and drawings, as well as photographic collages of facial features, are included on the following pages for easy reference when one's personal picture morgue is not available or for the use of students who have only begun their own morgue. It should prove useful in two ways—for reference to individual features, such as noses, eyes, mouths, wrinkles, beards, and so forth, and as portraits for the student to copy. The careful copying of portraits, in addition to preparing one for recreating familiar historical personages (see Chapter 20), provides excellent training in observing and reproducing precise details and evaluating their effect on the overall makeup.

It would be a useful exercise, with the pages showing only parts of faces, to try to reconstruct mentally the entire face and the personality traits suggested by a single feature. Is a particular mouth, for example, likely to be found on a face with small deep-set eyes and shaggy brows, or one with prominent eyes and heavy pouches, or with troubled eyes and knit brows? Does it suggest warmth and friendliness; strength and determination; a devious and calculating mentality? Search your mind for a character for whom it would be especially suitable.

In using the full portraits as source material, always observe the single feature in relation to the whole face and avoid reproducing the feature on a face on which it will seem totally out of place. In the case of beards and hair styles, note the period and ask yourself if the same style could conceivably be worn in the period of the play on which you are working or if it would have to be modified. It might be interesting (and possibly even productive) to imagine what sort of beard or wig, if any, the subject of the portrait might have chosen to wear had he lived in another period of history.

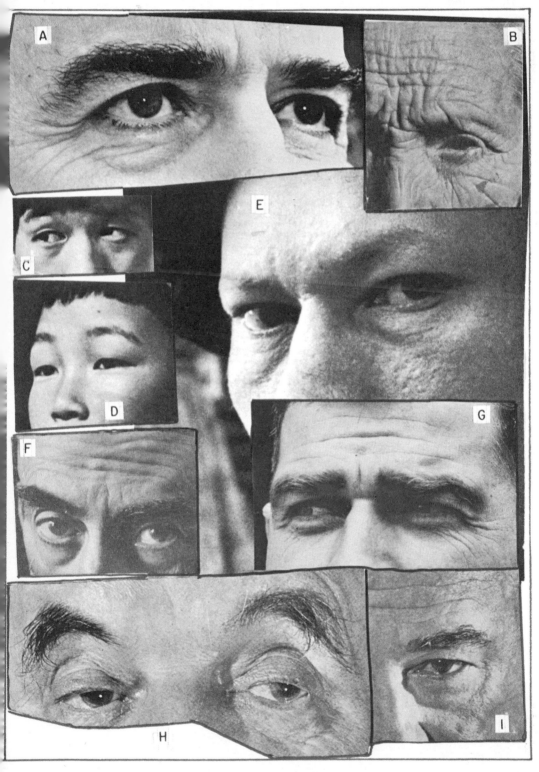

FIGURE 197. Eyes.

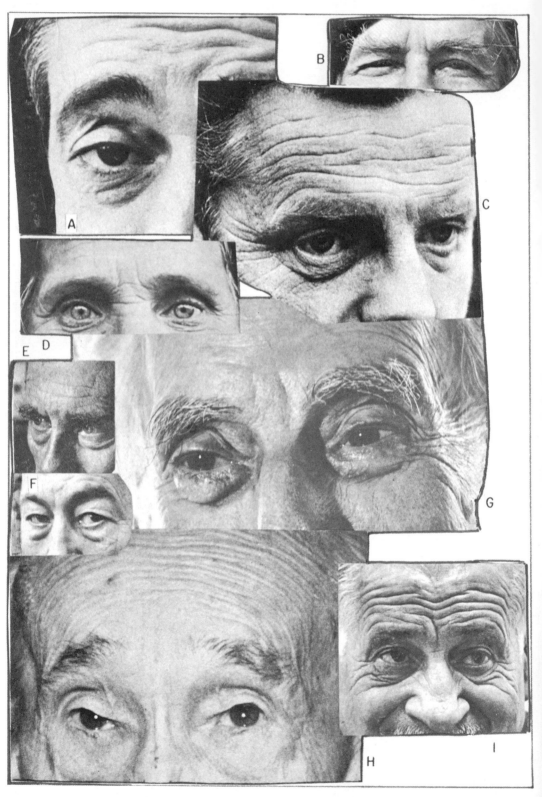

FIGURE 198. Eyes.

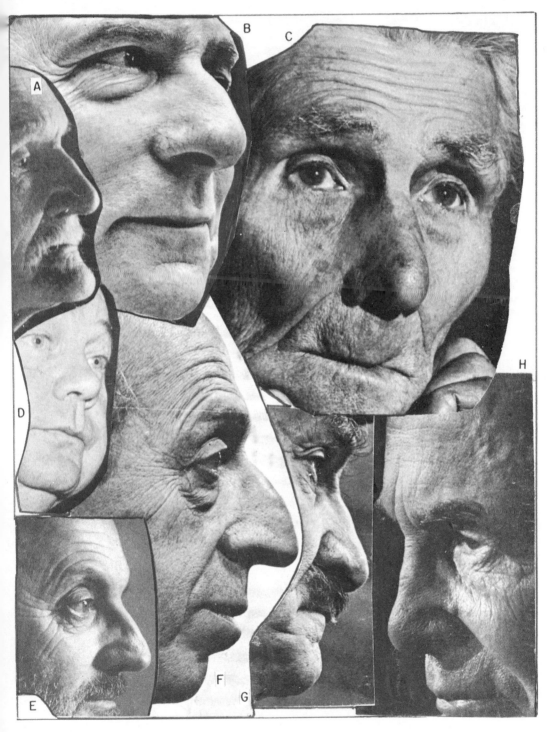

FIGURE 199. Noses.

FIGURE 200. Noses.

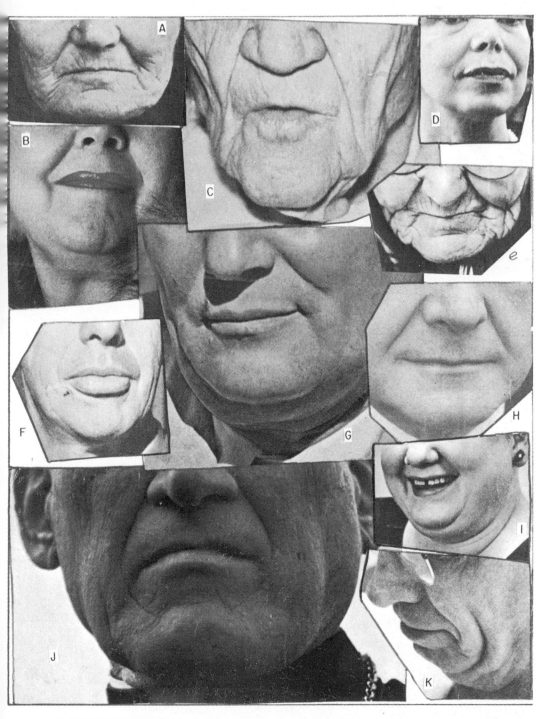

FIGURE 201. Mouths and chins.

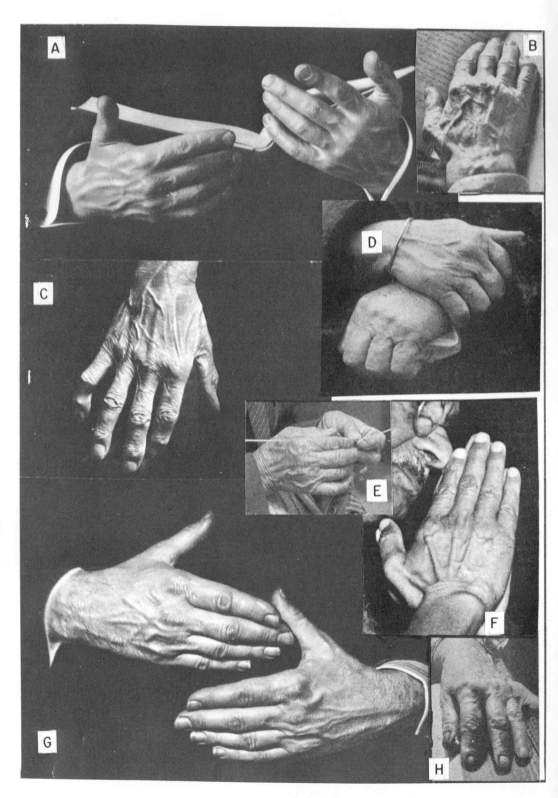

FIGURE 202. Hands.

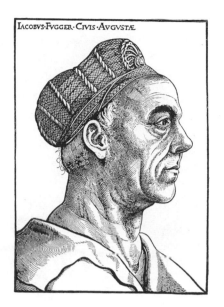

FIGURE 203. Jacob Fugger. Early sixteenth century, Augsburg, Germany.

FIGURE 204. Albrecht Dürer's portrait of his mother, 1514.

FIGURE 205. Philip Melanchthon. Engraving by Dürer, 1526.

FIGURE 206. Luther's mother. Painting by Cranach, 1531.

377

FIGURE 207. Prominent fifteenth-century Florentines. Engraving.

FIGURE 208. Head of Saturn.
Crayon drawing by Baldung,
1516.

FIGURE 209. Old Man of 93.
Brush drawing by Dürer, 1521.

FIGURE 210. Pieter Bruegel the Elder. Self-portrait, mid-sixteenth century.

FIGURE 211. Heironymus Holzschuher. Painting by Dürer, 1520.

FIGURE 212. Henri IV of France.
Late sixteenth century.

FIGURE 213. Sassoferrato. Self-
portrait, mid-sixteenth century.

FIGURE 214. Louis XII of
France, 1462–1515. Engraving.

FIGURE 215. Samuel Pepys,
1633–1703.

FIGURE 216. Raffaello Sernesi, 1838–1866. Self-portrait.

FIGURE 217. Henri Monnier. Caricature by Carjat, 1862.

FIGURE 218. Käte Kollwitz, 1867–1945. Self-portrait.

FIGURE 219. Karl Schmidt-Rotluff. Self-portrait, twentieth century.

FIGURE 220. The Duchess from *Alice in Wonderland*. With Alice, Cook, Baby, and Chesire Cat.

FIGURE 221. Illustration from Lewis Carroll's *The Three Voices*. By A. B. Frost.

FIGURE 222. The Mad Hatter from *Alice in Wonderland*. Illustration by Sir John Tenniel.

FIGURES 223–228. Stylized masks for *The Caucasian Chalk Circle*. Designed by James Hart Stearns for the Lincoln Center Repertory Theater production. The masks were made of fiberglass and painted. The actor's mouth and chin were painted to match the mask. In these photographs the masks are being modeled without makeup or costumes.

G

PERIOD HAIR STYLES

The twenty-one plates of hair styles which follow are intended as a general guide for period plays. The captions opposite each plate date each style as specifically as possible, often identifying the wearer. This does not mean that the style was confined to that year or that decade, but only that it is known to have been worn then. How fashionable it was can usually be determined by observing other styles of the period or from the social status of the person identified as the subject. A style worn by Marie Antoinette may be assumed to be in the latest fashion, whereas a style worn by a French peasant would not be. In general, young women are more likely to wear extremes in fashion than older ones, though social status and personality must always be considered.

In preparing to do any period play, you will need to study fashions in both makeup and hair styles. Chapter 21, though it is devoted primarily to period makeup, contains occasional supplementary notes on hair styles.

Keep in mind always that the closer you come to the present, the more precise you must be in dating a hair style. Whereas a few hundred or even a thousand years' discrepancy in ancient Egyptian styles may not be noticed, a year or two is the most you should allow in the mid-twentieth century. You may deliberately choose a hair style which is ten or fifteen years out of date for a character who might wear it, but you must never select a style which is even so much as a year ahead of its time. Such carelessness reflects on the quality of the whole production.

The drawings on the following plates are extracted from *Fashions in Hair—The First Five Thousand Years,* published (1965) in London by Peter Owen Limited and in New York by Hastings House. In the 700 pages of text, reproductions of works of art, and plates of drawings you will find detailed information on all periods of history.

PLATE 1: ANCIENT PEOPLES, MEN

a. c.2800 B.C., Sumerian. The bundle of hair at the back is typical of the Sumerian hairdo.

b. c.2700 B.C., Egyptian. The hair is braided and the braids stitched to a woven foundation to keep them firmly in place. The ends of the braids are fringed.

c. c.2500 B.C., Egyptian. Senodem, a magistrate. This style was quite common. Rows of small, tight, spiral curls were stitched onto a well-ventilated cap or woven foundation.

d. c.2500 B.C., Egyptian.

e. c.2500 B.C., Sumerian. Wig and false beard. The beard style strongly resembles both the Assyrian and the Greek, but the hair seems more closely related to the Phoenician and the Semitic Akkadian.

f. c.1875 B.C., Egyptian. Sehetep-Ib-Rē'-'Ankh, steward of the king. The body of the hair is slightly waved and is curled only at the ends. The beard is presumably real.

g. c.1500 B.C., Hittite warrior from Carchemish.

h. c.1450 B.C., Egyptian. Kha'-Em-Wēset. Black wig in typical tile-like arrangement of hundreds of tiny curls.

i. c.1420 B.C., Egyptian. Roy, Scribe and Steward of the Queen. The fullness of the wig results from many layers of curls.

j. c.1400 B.C., Egyptian. The hair is stitched down from forehead to crown to form a center parting.

k. c.1250 B.C., Egyptian. The curls in the top layer radiate from a central point. The lower side sections are formed of tile-like layers of tiny curls.

l. c.860 B.C., Phoenecian. The binding up of the hair in back is typical and distinguishes the hair style from that of the Assyrians, which it otherwise resembles.

m. c.740 B.C., Assyrian king. Hair and beards were always carefully curled.

n. c.740 B.C., Assyrian. Bearer of the king's bow.

o. c.700 B.C., Assyrian.

p. Late seventh century B.C., Etruscan.

q. c.600 B.C., Etruscan.

r. c.525 B.C., Etruscan. The shaved upper lip was not uncommon among bearded men.

s. Late sixth century B.C., Etruscan youth.

t. c.500 B.C., Persian.

PLATE 2: ANCIENT PEOPLES, MEN

a. Late sixth century B.C., Greek. Young men were beginning to wear shorter hair, though older ones often let theirs grow. A braid sometimes replaced the fillet and was arranged in various ways. Here the ends of the braid are concealed under the front hair.

b. Sixth century B.C., Greek.

c. 440–400 B.C., Greek. Back hair looped over fillet.

d. 470–450 B.C., Greek. The fillet here is in the form of a braided cord.

e. Fifth century B.C., Greek. The style of turning the hair over the fillet was followed by both men and women. The long, hanging ends come from both the front and the back hair.

f. Dionysius the Elder, 430(?)–376 B.C. Tyrant of Syracuse. The hair radiates from the crown, and the ends are curled.

g. Fourth century B.C., Greek.

h. Fourth century B.C., Greek.

i. Caius Julius Caesar, 102(?)–44 B.C.

j. Marcus Junius Brutus, 85–42 B.C.

k. Julius Caesar, 102(?)–44 B.C. Later than *i* above.

l. Pompey, 106–48 B.C.

m. c. A.D. 10, Roman boy.

n. Claudius, 10 B.C.–A.D. 54. Emperor, A.D. 41–54.

o. Vespasian, A.D. 9–79. Emperor, A.D. 69–79.

p. End of the first century A.D., Roman.

q. c. A.D. 134, Roman. L. Julius Ursus Servianus, Hadrian's brother-in-law.

r. Lucius Verus. Died A.D. 169.

s. Second century A.D., Egyptian. Natural hair, resulting from Roman influence.

t. Third century A.D., Roman.

u. Constantine I (the Great), A.D. 280(?)–337.

v. Early fifth century A.D., Roman.

w. Fifth century A.D.

x. c. A.D. 400, Roman.

PLATE 3: ANCIENT PEOPLES, WOMEN

a. c.2900 B.C., Egyptian. The braids are stitched firmly onto a foundation. Braids were usually smaller than this.

b. c.2800 B.C., Sumerian.

c. c.2500 B.C., Semitic Akkadian. Wig.

d. c.2200 B.C., Egyptian servant. Notice the lack of a center part in the wig.

e. c.1500 B.C., Egyptian. Wig.

f. c.1450 B.C., Egyptian. Metal headband. Hair of the wig is crimped for fullness and the ends tightly curled.

g. c.1450 B.C., Egyptian. Metal headband, decorated with blossoms, belonging to a lady of the court. The body of the hair is frizzed and puffed out and the curled ends tightly bound and waxed.

h. c.1350 B.C., Egyptian. Queen Mutnezemt.

i. c.1250 B.C., Egyptian. Wig of a queen or a princess. Long, elaborately dressed wigs were worn only by persons of high rank.

j. c. 1025 B.C., Egyptian. Princess Na-ny, daughter of King Pinedjem. The wig, now in the Metropolitan Museum of Art, consists of a long, narrow braid of human hair over linen thread from which numerous plaits set with beeswax hang. The braid is sewn together loosely with a faggoting stitch to form a skull cap or caul. The size was adjusted by linen drawstrings fastened at each temple, which also held the plaits at the forehead in place.

k. Late sixth century B.C., Etruscan girl.

l. Second half of the sixth century B.C., Greek. Sections of the hair running the length of the head are separated and curled, then arranged in parallel rows. The style was still worn in the fourth century and was later popular in Rome.

m. Probably late fifth century B.C., Greek.

n. About fifth century B.C., Greek.

o. Early fifth century B.C., Greek.

p. Probably late fifth century B.C., Greek.

q. Greek. Persephone. Since high foreheads were considered ugly, the hair was usually dressed low.

r. Fourth century B.C., Greek.

s. Fourth century B.C., Etruscan.

PLATE 4: ANCIENT PEOPLES, WOMEN

a. Late fifth or fourth century B.C., Greek.

b. Between 206 and 30 B.C., Egyptian. Wig of one of the Cleopatras.

c. Between 300 B.C. and A.D. 100, Greek. The higher forehead and the knot were popular after Alexander.

d. Mid-first century B.C., Roman. Fulvia, wife of Marc Antony. Died 40 B.C. The puff at the forehead and the coil at the neck are typical of the fashion of the period. Sometimes the hair behind the front puff was braided and the braid carried over the top of the head and down to the coil on the neck. Braids were also worn around the head and over the head.

e. Late first century B.C. or early first A.D., Roman. The fringe at the forehead is probably a development of the puff of the Fulvia style. The hair is beginning to get a little fuller.

f. Early first century A.D., Roman. Livia, 55(?) B.C.–A.D. 29. Typifies early Empire style.

g. Early first century A.D., Roman.

h. Livia. Front view of *f* above.

i. Late first century A.D., Roman.

j. Late first or early second century A.D., Roman. A modification of the *orbis*.

k. Late first century A.D., Roman. Style of Julia, daughter of Titus. *Orbis.* The curls are arranged on crescent-shaped wire frames. The back hair is divided into sections, braided, then curled. Sometimes the hair was coiled without braiding.

l. End of the first century A.D., Roman. Modifications of the *orbis*.

m. Early second century A.D., Roman. The large crown of braids is typical of the Hadrian period.

n. Second quarter of the second century A.D., Roman. Hadrian period.

o. A.D. 195, Roman.

p. Early third century A.D., Roman. Julia Domna, wife of Septimus Severus. Typical of the padded hair style of the period, with massive braids or coils at the back of the head. Wigs were common.

q. Third century A.D., second quarter, Roman. Orbiana, wife of Alexander Severus. The hair is less massive, and the coil at the back has shrunk. Hair is lower in back. Later it rose again.

r. Third century A.D., Roman.

s. Fourth century A.D., Roman.

t. Fourth century A.D., Roman.

PLATE 5: MEDIEVAL MEN

a. Sixth century, Gaul.

b. Byzantine.

c. c.547, Byzantine. A dignitary in the court of Justinian. Some of the members of the court were bearded, some not. Although Justinian's hair style was much like this one, he was clean-shaven. An earlier mosaic shows him bearded.

d. c.750.

e. c.879. Long hair, full mustaches, and shaven chins seem to be typical of many of the barbaric tribes.

f. Late tenth century.

g. 1130–1135. Although beards were commonly worn by older men, young men were usually beardless. The front hair was ordinarily combed forward and cut relatively short; but the back was sometimes left long, as it is here, or cut shorter.

h. c.1150, Italian. Note that the hair radiates from a point on the natural hair-line rather than at the crown. This was not an unusual style among the Italians.

i. French.

j. c.1150, French. The hair was occasionally plaited in the eleventh century as well.

k. c.1160, French.

l. c.1235, French.

m. c.1245.

n. Mid-thirteenth century.

o. Thirteenth century, last quarter. The ends of the hair were curled with irons.

p. Early fourteenth century, Italian. Monk wearing tonsure of St. Peter.

q. Fourteenth century, second quarter.

r. Fourteenth century, English. Richard II, ruled 1377–1399.

s. Fourteenth century, last quarter, French.

t. c.1376, French. Fashionable young man.

u. c.1390.

v. 1390, French. Fashionable young man.

w. c.1400, English.

a

b

c

d

e

f

g

h

i

j

k

l

m

n

o

p

q

r

s

t

u

v

w

PLATE 6: MEDIEVAL WOMEN

a. c.400, Byzantine. Athenais Endocia, wife of Emperor Theodosius.

b. Sixth century, Byzantine. The hair was built up over rolls and pads. Often it was studded with jewels.

c. Sixth century, Byzantine.

d. 1083, French. Queen Mathilde.

e. 1180, French queen. The braids were worn very long and extended with artificial hair if necessary.

f. c. twelfth century, German.

g. Thirteenth century, Italian.

h. Late thirteenth century, Italian.

i. Thirteenth century.

j. Late twelfth or early thirteenth century.

k. c.1340, French.

l. French.

m. Fourteenth century, first quarter, French. Woman wearing a *gorgière*.

n. c.1310, French.

o. Mid-fourteenth century, German.

p. After 1320. It was in the fourteenth century that women began plucking or shaving the hairline to give a higher forehead, as shown here.

q. 1364, English.

r. Fourteenth century, French.

s. c.1360.

a

b

c

d

e

f

g

h

i

j

k

l

m

n

o

p

q

r

s

PLATE 7: FIFTEENTH CENTURY MEN

a. Louis II, Duc d'Anjou, Comte de Provence, 1377–1417.

b. 1412. This style remained fashionable until about 1460 and was still worn somewhat later.

c. Henry V, 1387–1422. King of England, 1413–1422. This was the fashionable and popular hair style during the first half of the century. Frequently the ends were curled under, as in *b* above.

d. 1416. The pointed or forked beard without side-whiskers was worn at the beginning of the century but in 1416 was disappearing.

e. Charles VII, 1403–1461. In 1429 Joan of Arc had him crowned king at Rheims.

f. German.

g. c.1440, French.

h. 1448. Alfonso V (the Magnanimous), 1396–1458. King of Aragon and Sicily, 1416–1458, and of Naples, 1443–1458.

i. 1445.

j. Mid-century, French king. Beards were not fashionable, but long ones were sometimes worn by dignitaries as a symbol of their importance.

k. Johann Fust, c.1400–1466, German printer, partner of Gutenberg. Issued first dated book in 1457.

l. 1480, French.

m. 1476, Italian.

n. 1491, Italian. Lorenzo de' Medici, 1449–1492.

o. 1488.

p. Italian. Piero de' Medici, 1471–1503.

q. Last quarter, Italian. Fashionable young man.

r. 1486, Italian. Fashionable young man.

s. Giovanni Pico della Mirandola, 1463–1494. Brilliant Italian humanist. Fashionable hair style.

t. c.1490. Long bangs were fashionable in the last decade.

u. Italian. Probably a wig.

v. c.1495, German. Fashionable style.

w. Last quarter, Italian. Young gentleman.

a   b   c   d   e   f   g   h   i   j   k   l   m   n   o   p   q   r   s   t   u   v   w

PLATE 8: FIFTEENTH CENTURY WOMEN

a. c.1400, probably Italian.
b. First half, Italian.
c. Mid-century or third quarter, French.
d. First half, Italian.
e. c.1440, French. Jeanne de Saveuse, wife of Charles d'Artois.
f. 1447, Italian. Cicilia Gonzaga.
g. c.1470, German.
h. Last quarter.
i. 1488, Italian. Fashionable lady.
j. Last quarter (before 1491), German.
k. Last quarter, German.
l. Last quarter, German.
m. Last quarter, Italian. Fashionable style.
n. Last quarter.
o. Last quarter, Italian.
p. 1495, Italian. Elisabetta Gonzaga, wife of Guidobaldo da Montefeltro, son of the Duke of Urbino.
q. Noble Italian lady. Back hair is probably false.
r. 1492, Italian. Worn only by fashionable upper-class ladies.
s. Italian.
t. c.1500, Italian. Isabella d'Este, 1474–1539, wife of Francesco Gonzaga.

a   b   c   d   e   f   g   h   i   j   k   l   m   n   o   p   q   r   s   t

PLATE 9: SIXTEENTH CENTURY MEN

a. French. Louis XII, 1462–1515. Succeeded Charles VIII in 1498
b. 1510, German. Unusually large *round* or *bush* beard.
c. Francis I, 1494–1547. King of France, 1515–1547. For later hair style see *k* below.
d. 1520, German. Hieronymus Holzschuher.
e. 1520, German. Martin Luther, 1483–1546. For later hair style see *l* below.
f. German.
g. 1529, German. Philip Künstler, age 7.
h. 1530, German.
i. 1530, German. Martin Luther's father.
j. 1535, German. Count Ulrich von Württemberg.
k. Francis I. For earlier style see *c* above.
l. Martin Luther. For earlier style see *e* above.
m. Gustavus I, 1496–1560. King of Sweden, 1523–1560.
n. German. Martin Bucer, 1491–1551. Reformer.
o. Flemish. Gerardus Mercator (Gerhard Kremer), 1512–1594. Geographer.
p. English. Cornelius Vandun, 1483–1577. Soldier with King Henry, Yeoman of the Guard and usher to King Henry, King Edward, Queen Mary, and Queen Elizabeth.
q. Italian. *Marquisette* beard.
r. c.1575, Scotch.
s. French. Henri de Lorraine, duc de Guise, 1550–1588. *Pique devant* beard with inverted mustache.
t. Henri II, 1519–1559. King of France, 1547–1559.
u. c.1594, Italian. Small *bush* beard.
v. 1596, English. *Swallow-tail* beard.
w. 1599, English. Sir Henry Neville.

PLATE 10: SIXTEENTH CENTURY WOMEN

a. c.1512, Italian.

b. Italian. Lucrezia Borgia, 1480–1519.

c. c.1515, Italian.

d. Before 1520, Italian.

e. 1520, Italian.

f. First quarter, Italian.

g. Mid-century.

h. c.1550, French.

i. c.1550, Italian.

j. Mid-century, Italian.

k. c.1560, probably English.

l. 1560.

m. German peasant.

n. c.1575, French. Hair dressed over pads.

o. Last quarter, French. Probably a wig.

p. English. Hair dressed over pads.

q. Marguerite de Valois, 1553–1615. Queen of France and Navarre, wife of Henri IV. Wig.

r. Probably French.

s. Elizabeth I, 1533–1603. Queen of England, 1558–1603. Wig.

t. c.1595, French. Wig.

u. 1597, Italian. The same treatment of the front hair was also used without the cone-shaped arrangement at the back. This was a short-lived style worn in Italy. Hair dressed over wire frames.

a

b

c

d

e

f

g

h

i

j

k

l

m

n

o

p

q

r

s

t

u

PLATE 11: SEVENTEENTH CENTURY MEN

a. William Shakespeare, 1564–1616. (The drawing is based on the Chandos portrait.)

b. 1614, Italian. Francesco de' Medici, brother of the Grand Duke.

c. 1614, German. *Pique devant* beard.

d. 1628, Spanish peasant.

e. Christian IV, King of Denmark and Norway, 1577–1648. Notice the small braid in front of the ear. The fashion of wearing a single pearl earring was started by Henri de Lorraine, duc d'Harcourt, who subsequently became known as *le Cadet à la perle.*

f. Bavarian. Gottfried Heinrich, 1594–1632. Imperialist general in the Thirty Years War. *Stiletto* beard.

g. Captain John Smith, 1579–1631. English adventurer. *Round* beard.

h. English. William Slater, D.D.

i. c.1630, Dutch. Crispin Van de Passe the Younger. *Square cut* beard.

j. English. John Endicott, 1589–1665. Governor of Massachusetts colony. *Needle* beard.

k. Anthony Van Dyck, 1599–1641. *Stiletto* beard, later called a *Van Dyck* or *Vandyke.*

l. English. Thomas Howard, Earl of Arundel, 1586–1646.

m. 1632, Spanish. Charles of Austria, son of Philip III.

n. 1633, French. Fashionable gentleman with *lovelock.*

o. c.1635.

p. 1645, English. Fop with two *lovelocks.*

q. 1645, English. Oliver Cromwell, 1599–1658.

r. 1649, English. Cavalier with *lovelock.*

s. c.1650, French. Molière, 1622–1673.

t. c.1650, French.

u. Charles II, 1630–1685. King of England, 1660–1685.

v. Louis XIV, 1638–1715. King of France, 1643–1715. Wig.

PLATE 12: SEVENTEENTH CENTURY WOMEN

a. c.1610, French. Probably a wig.

b. 1610, French. Wig.

c. 1615, probably Spanish.

d. c.1630, French.

e. c.1630, Dutch. Hélène Fourment, wife of Peter Paul Rubens.

f. c.1635, French.

g. 1640, French.

h. c.1640, Dutch.

i. German.

j. 1643, French.

k. c.1650, Spanish.

l. French. Anne of Austria, 1601–1666. Queen of France, mother of Louis XIV.

m. c.1650, Dutch.

n. c.1650, Spanish.

o. 1660, Dutch. Catherina Horft.

p. 1665, French. Side curls are wired to stand out.

q. 1680, English. *Hurluberlu.* The style was created by Martin in 1671 in Paris.

r. English. Nell Gwynn, 1650–1687. Actress and mistress of Charles II after 1669.

s. 1680's, French. Early *fontange.*

t. 1690's, French. *Fontange* with *tour,* decorated with jeweled pins.

a

b

c

d

e

f

g

h

i

j

k

l

m

n

o

p

q

r

s

t

409

PLATE 13: EIGHTEENTH CENTURY MEN

a. Baron Gottfried Wilhelm von Leibnitz, 1646–1716. German philosopher and mathematician. *Full-bottom* wig.

b. c.1718. *Full-bottom* wig.

c. King George II, reigned 1727–1760. *Full-bottom* wig. This was no longer a fashionable style, and the enormous full-bottoms had disappeared completely.

d. c.1735, English clergyman. *Long* bob—sometimes called a *minister's* or *clergyman's* bob.

e. *Campaign* wig or *knotted* wig. This bushy version was also known as a *physical tie.*

f. 1735, English. Composer. Powdered *knotted* wig.

g. 1736, English.

h. 1750, English. *Scratch* wig or natural hair.

i. 1747, English. Alderman's clerk. *Bob* wig.

j. 1735, English.

k. Henry Fielding, 1707–1754. *Physical* bob.

l. 1761, English. *Physical* bob, worn by bishops. The foretop was not always so high.

m. *Full-bottom* or *square* wig, worn mostly by gentlemen of the Law.

n. Voltaire, 1694–1778. *Long* bob.

o. c.1750, English. *Physical* bob, very popular with the medical profession.

p. c.1760, English. *Short* or *minor* bob. Ends of the hair are frizzed into a bush and the wig powdered. (See other versions of long and short bobs.)

q. c.1763, English. Gentleman wearing *cauliflower* or *cut* wig.

r. 1758, English. *Short* bob.

s. 1762, English. Natural hair.

t. 1770's, French soldier. Wig with *horseshoe* toupee and *twisted* queue, raised and secured with comb.

u. 1773. *Bob* wig.

v. 1773, English. *Major* wig, sometimes a *brigadier.*

411

PLATE 14: EIGHTEENTH CENTURY MEN

a. 1772, English. Variation of *cadogan* or *club* wig.

b. 1771, German. *Bag* wig. The high toupee was very fashionable at this time.

c. 1772, German. *Bag* wig. The bag tended to be quite large in the 1770's.

d. 1776, French. Gentleman at home. The back hair is pulled up and secured with a comb. It would be worn this way only at home.

e. 1770's, French. Wig *à l'enfant* or *à la naissance* or *naissante,* popular primarily in France in the last quarter of the century. Style *d* above might be worn this way in public.

f. c.1775. Double *pigtail* wig with *grecque*. The double queue was largely French. The *grecque* is the horseshoe-shaped toupee.

g. Jean d'Alembert, 1717–1783. French mathematician and philosopher. *Bag* wig. Note the large and elegant bow.

h. Benjamin Franklin, 1706–1790. Natural hair.

i. John Howard, 1726(?)–1790. Powdered *cadogan* or *club* wig, popular after the late 1760's.

j. Wolfgang Amadeus Mozart, 1756–1791. Powdered *tie* wig.

k. Marquis de Lafayette, 1747–1834.

l. Jacques Necker, 1732–1804. French banker and financial expert, minister of state under Louis XVI. *Bag* wig.

m. 1782, English.

n. Late 1780's. *Pigtail*. Probably natural hair.

o. 1789, French. *Tie* wig.

p. 1786, Italian. *Club* wig.

q. 1786, Italian. *Pigtail* wig.

r. c.1790, French. *Cadogan*.

s. 1790's, French.

t. 1794. William Bligh, British admiral, captain of the *Bounty*. Natural hair.

u. John Adams, 1735–1826. Became president of the United States in 1796. Natural hair with queue.

413

PLATE 15: EIGHTEENTH CENTURY WOMEN

a. c.1700, French. *Fontange* style with pearls, jeweled pins, and *favorites* (curls at temple).

b. c.1702, English. Queen Anne.

c. 1732, English.

d. c.1730, French. Known as the "Dutch coiffure." Usually powdered. Popular into the 1750's.

e. c.1735, French.

f. c.1750.

g. 1750's. Style worn by Marie Joseph of Austria.

h. 1760's, French.

i. 1764. Style of Madame de Pompadour.

j. c.1770, French. Madame du Barry.

k. c.1770, French.

l. 1774, French.

m. 1773, German. Hair in this period was dressed back and low with a fairly high toupee and a number of small puffs or curls down the sides. Most coiffures were powdered.

n. 1774, French. À *la Venus*.

o. c.1776, French. Coiffures at this time were high and narrow.

p. Marie Antoinette.

q. 1776, French. Coiffure *à la Syrienne*, originated in 1775.

r. 1778, French. Coiffure *en rouleaux*. The high coiffures were built up on elastic cushions or sometimes stuffed with horsehair or wool, teased (although that term was not used), thoroughly greased with pomatum, and heavily powdered.

PLATE 16: EIGHTEENTH CENTURY WOMEN

a. 1778, French. *Chien couchant*. Coiffures were decorated with ropes of pearls, jewels, ribbons, plumes, flowers, fruit, vegetables, chiffon kerchiefs, ornaments of blown glass, reproductions of gardens, parks, carriages, ships, planets, tombstones, and almost anything else one can imagine.

b. 1780, French. Marie Antoinette.

c. 1780, French. Frizzed toupee and side hair.

d. 1780, French. *Le bandeau d'amour*. Frizzed toupee and sides. The hanging curls were always smooth. Later in the 1780's the side curls were not always worn.

e. c.1782, French.

f. 1781, English. *Hérisson* or *hedgehog*. Originated in Paris, it was an extremely popular style and lasted for some years in both France and England, in many versions. The essential was the bouffant frizzle, which gives the style its name.

g. 1788, French. *Hérisson*.

h. 1798, English.

i. 1794, English.

j. 1796, French. *Titus* cut. This style signalled the end of long hair.

k. Late 1790's, French.

l. c.1788, French.

m. 1797, French. Wig *à la grecque*.

n. 1798, French. "Garland of flowers and moss."

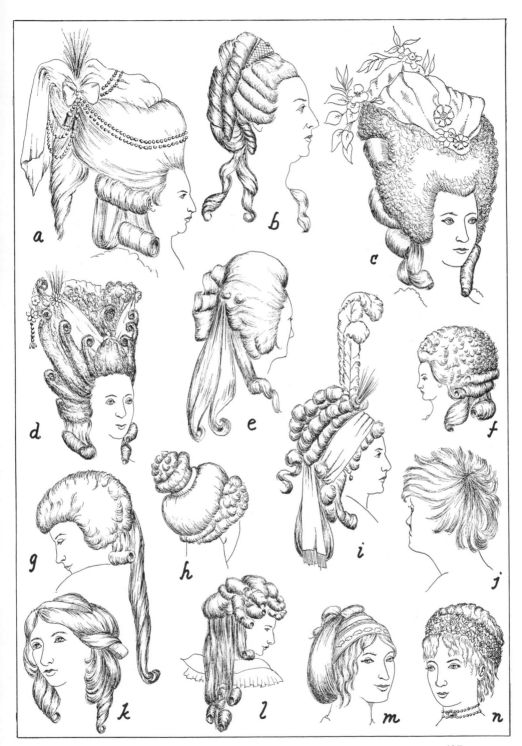

a   *b*   *c*   *d*   *e*   *f*   *g*   *h*   *i*   *j*   *k*   *l*   *m*   *n*

PLATE 17: NINETEENTH CENTURY MEN

a. Early years, English.
b. Joseph McKeen, 1757–1832. First president of Bowdoin College, 1802–1807. Long hair was still worn by conservative men but was not fashionable.
c. George IV, 1762–1830. King of England, 1820–1830.
d. 1820, English.
e. English. Benjamin Disraeli, 1804–1881.
f. Frédéric Chopin, 1810–1849.
g. American. Matthew Brady, 1823–1896. Pioneer photographer.
h. Napoleon III, 1808–1873.
i. German. Robert Schumann, 1810–1856.
j. Benjamin Franklin Kelley, 1807–1891. *Uncle Sam* beard.
k. Johann Peter Eckermann, 1792–1854. German writer.
l. c.1860. E. A. Sothern as Lord Dundreary in *Our American Cousin*.
m. American. Benson John Lossing, 1813–1891. Historian and journalist.
n. Algernon Charles Swinburne, 1837–1909.
o. Russian. Alexander II, 1818–1881.
p. Andrew Adgate Lipscomb, 1816–1890. Author and educator. *Billy* whiskers or *billies*.
q. English. Benjamin Disraeli, 1804–1881. In America this small beard was called a *breakwater*.
r. American. Ralph Waldo Emerson, 1803–1882.
s. 1880's. Watson Robertson Sperry, born 1842. American journalist.
t. 1880's. John Meredith Read, 1837–1896. U.S. Minister to Greece.
u. 1880's. Washington C. DePauw, 1822–1887. Founder of DePauw University.
v. 1880's, American. Richard Grant White. *Dundrearies*.
w. 1880's, American. General George Crook, 1828–1890.
x. 1880's. Irving Ramsay Wiles, born 1861. American artist.

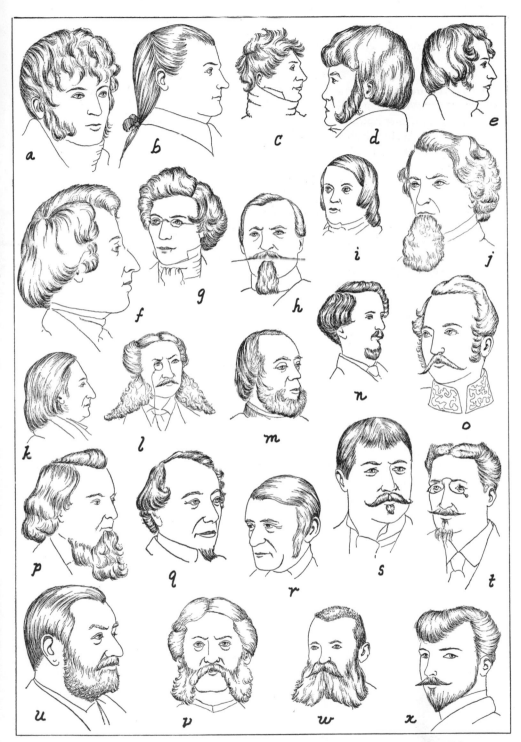

a

b

c

d

e

f

g

h

i

j

k

l

m

n

o

p

q

r

s

t

u

v

w

x

419

PLATE 18: NINETEENTH CENTURY MEN

a. 1890's, Norwegian. Fridtjof Nansen, 1861–1930. Explorer, scientist, states-man, humanitarian, and first Norwegian minister to Great Britain.
b. 1890's, American. Edward Mitchell. Lawyer.
c. 1890's, American.
d. 1890's, Scotch. Robert Louis Stevenson, 1850–1894.
e. 1892, American. William Collins Whitney, Secretary of the Navy, 1885–1889.
f. 1890's. Armand Capdervielle. American editor and publisher.
g. 1890's, American merchant, soldier.
h. 1890's, American. John Mason Loomis.
i. 1890's, American. H. M. Alexander. Attorney.
j. 1890's, American. James Roosevelt. Steamship official.
k. 1890's, American. Rev. Charles K. Parkhurst.
l. 1890's. Charles Carroll Walcutt, 1838–1898. American soldier.
m. 1890's, American. John Philip Sousa, 1854–1932. Composer.
n. 1890's, American merchant, philanthropist. *Imperial* beard.
o. 1890's, American journalist.
p. 1890's. Edward Gay. Irish-American artist.
q. English. Sir Arthur Sullivan, 1842–1900.
r. 1890's, American. Business executive. *Burnsides.*
s. 1890's, American. John F. Shera. Stockbroker.
t. 1890's, American banker.
u. 1890's, American. Paul L. Thebaud. Shipping merchant. *Swallow-tail* beard.
v. 1890's, American broker. *Dundrearies.*
w. 1890's, American. Thomas S. Hastings. President of the Union Theological Seminary.
x. 1890's. Daniel Smith Lamb, 1843–1929. American pathologist and anato-mist. A variation of the *imperial.*
y. Hermann Sudermann, 1857–1938. German dramatist and novelist.

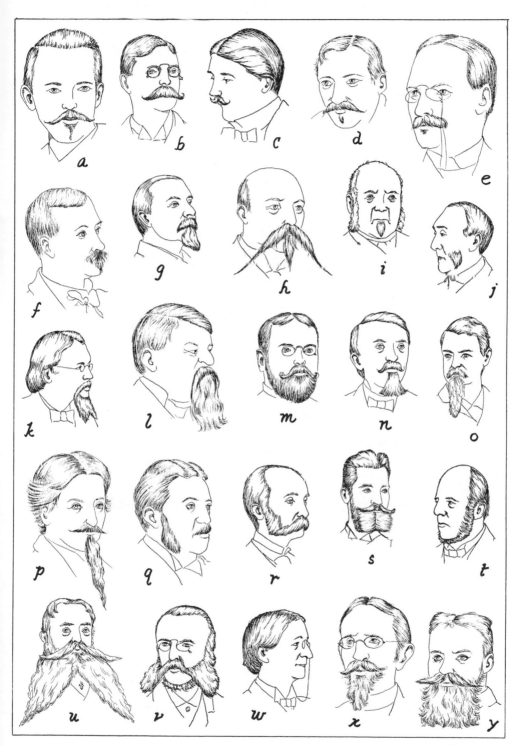

a   b   c   d   e

f   g   h   i   j

k   l   m   n   o

p   q   r   s   t

u   v   w   x   y

PLATE 19: NINETEENTH CENTURY WOMEN

a. 1803, French.
b. 1808, French.
c. 1813, French.
d. c.1820, American. Maria Monroe Gouverneur, daughter of James Monroe.
e. 1827. Coiffure for a ball.
f. 1831. The high, lacquered bows were wired in place and the coiffure decorated with feathers, flowers, leaves, ribbons, beads, or jewels.
g. 1841, English. Queen Victoria, 1837–1901. Hair was worn flat to the head and parted in the center. Ears were exposed, and braids and spiral curls were popular.
h. 1848. Hair was still straight, front and back sections of the hair were usually separated, and braids were more popular than ever.
i. 1855. Slight waves were beginning to appear. Braids were less popular.
j. 1860. Hair was much fuller. Curls and braids were popular. Feathers were worn in the evening.
k. 1862. Low chignons, often false, were in fashion.
l. 1865, French.
m. 1869, French. Curls probably false. Sometimes an entire coiffure was made up of false hair pieces.
n. 1869, French. Coiffures were becoming higher.
o. 1874, French. Most of the hair is probably false.
p. 1877, French. Hair at the temples is natural, but the rest may be a combination of various pieces of false hair.
q. 1879, French. Top hair was lower and nearly always waved or curled.
r. 1880. Combs were very fashionable.
s. 1885, French. Back hair entirely false. Wispy bangs softened the line of the forehead.
t. 1888. The hair was heading upward again.
u. 1894, French. Tight marcels were no longer fashionable, and the hair was beginning to puff out.
v. 1894, French. Topknots vied with puffs.
w. 1894, French.
x. 1899, French.

PLATE 20: TWENTIETH CENTURY MEN

a. 1905, American engineer.

b. John Philip Sousa, 1854–1932. American bandmaster and composer. Beards were not fashionable but were still being worn by older men.

c. Georg Morris Cohen Brandes, 1842–1927. Danish writer.

d. Piotr Kropotkin, 1842–1921. Russian anarchist.

e. Rupert Brooke, 1887–1915. English poet.

f. Woodrow Wilson, 1846–1924. 28th U.S. President.

g. c.1922, American senator.

h. 1926, American actor. Most fashionable men were clean-shaven. Mustaches, when worn, were small.

i. 1929. John Barrymore.

j. 1930's, English. Military hair style. The American military cut was much the same.

k. 1937, American actor.

l. 1940, American.

m. 1953, American. *Crew* cut.

n. 1956, American. Elvis style. Long hair, rising in a high wave in front, often worn with sideburns. Worn by Elvis Presley, American entertainer.

o. c.1958, British. *English* cut. Hair long on top and sides, full over the ears and in back, and combed back from the forehead.

p. 1959, American actor.

q. 1961, American college student.

r. 1961, French. *Caesar* cut. Hair combed down over forehead. Very popular with young men.

s. 1961, French. *Caesar* cut. Small beards were being seen increasingly on young men, even in the United States.

t. 1962, American. *Caesar* cut.

u. 1962, English.

v. 1963, English.

w. 1965, English. Beatle style.

x. 1966, American college student. Not typical but indicative of the trend toward longer hair.

y. 1966, American. The majority of teen-agers and young men were combing the hair forward and letting it grow fuller.

425

PLATE 21: TWENTIETH CENTURY WOMEN

a. 1904, American. Fashionable. Gibson girl style.

b. 1910, American.

c. 1914, French. Fashionable.

d. 1917, American. Ornate tortoise-shell combs were fashionable.

e. 1919, American. Hair turned under to look like a bob. A style designed for women who hesitated to take the plunge and have their hair cut off.

f. 1919. The latest bob from Paris.

g. 1924. *Egyptian* bob.

h. 1923, American.

i. 1925. *Marcelled* bob.

j. 1925. The latest *shingled* bob. The *boyish* bob, a bit shorter at the crown, was equally fashionable.

k. 1934, American. Soft waves were back, hair was longer, and the full face was exposed.

l. 1940, American. Front hair up and back hair down was the fashionable style.

m. 1940, American.

n. 1941, American. Side part, hair long and slightly waved, partially concealing one eye. Style popularized by Veronica Lake.

o. 1945, American.

p. 1948. A popular and durable style.

q. 1954, French. Zizi Jeanmaire. Singer and dancer. The vogue for very short hair did not last long.

r. 1959, American.

s. 1961, American. *Beehive* style. Hair was teased to give it volume.

t. 1961, American. Jacqueline Kennedy style.

u. 1964, English. Fashionable and popular style.

v. 1964, English. False topknots had been worn for several years. Hair partially concealed the forehead.

w. 1965, English and American. A Vidal Sassoon style. Sassoon's chunky, boyish cuts, reflecting the men's style popularized by the Beatles, had considerable influence on young sophisticates.

x. 1966, American. Hair was worn both up and down, short and long. When up, a good deal of it was false.

a
b
c
d
e
f
g
h
i
j
k
l
m
n
o
p
q
r
s
t
u
v
w
x

427

H

MAKEUP COLOR CHART

On the following pages makeup colors from Factor, Leichner, Mehron, and Stein are indicated in both list and chart form by actual color, by the commercial number under which they are sold, and by the standardized numbers by which they are referred to in this book.

The color chart can be used in three ways: (1) It is possible to find in the chart the actual color of makeup you need. Along with the color block, you will find not only the standardized number but also a listing of all makeup from greasepaint to eyebrow pencils available in that color. (2) In studying this text, you may wish to know either the exact color of a particular number referred to or the equivalent makeup paint. The chart will give you both. (3) You may wish to find the number of the paint in one brand which is equivalent to a certain number in another brand. Then you refer first to the listing by manufacturer (pp. 429–435) to find the standardized number, which enables you to refer to the correct color block in the chart. There you will find all equivalent paints listed.

In using the chart, bear in mind that although the color blocks and the makeup paints were equated as precisely as possible, makeup colors sometimes change from batch to batch, occasionally in hue and more frequently in value. Therefore, the particular paint you are using may not be exactly the same as the one used in the analysis for the chart.

The colors shown represent the color of the makeup on the skin, not in the tube or cake or jar. The difference is sometimes quite marked. In addition to appearing lighter or occasionally darker on the skin, a color may sometimes change in hue, often becoming considerably redder.

There are a few colors shown for which there is at present no equivalent in makeup. However, should such makeup colors become available in the future, they can easily be inserted into the appropriate places.

MAKEUP COLOR CHART

An Organization of Colors Used in Theatrical Makeup and Their Equivalents in Commercial Brands

Code of Abbreviations

F—Factor
L—Leichner
M—Mehron
S—Stein

f—foundation paint
c—cake makeup
s—shading colors
ps—Pan-Stik
vs—Velvet Stick
es—eyeshadow

mr—moist rouge
dr—dry rouge
lr—lip rouge
l—lipstick
ur—under rouge
p—makeup pencils

Standardized Number	Color	Commercial Numbers
Y1		S: f 1
Y2		F: f 4
Y3		L: f Colorfilm 1
Y4		M: f 4½ S: f 5
Y5		F: f 5
Y7		F: f 12; c Chinese S: f 12; c 40½
Y10		L: f 8B
Y10g		L: f 6½
Y15g		F: s 2; p Light Brown S: f 11
OY2		L: f 5 M: f 4; c 4B
OY3		S: f 22
OY9		S: c 40
OY9g		L: f Colorfilm 6
YO5c		M: f 16; c 16B S: c 39½

Standardized Number	Color	Commercial Numbers
YO6c		
YO8c		F: f 8, 30 L: f Tan Klear Light M: f L
YO9c		F: f 31 L: f Tan Klear Dark M: f M
YO10c		L: s 28A
YO4		L: f 5½ M: c 25
YO5		M: c 26
YO6		M: c 27 S: f 23
YO7		M: c 28
YO8		M: f K; c 30
YO9		
YO10		
YO11		
YO12		F: s 21; ps 665-K S: s 6
YO13		F: f 16; ps 665-P M: f 14; s 8

Standardized Number	Color	Commercial Numbers
YO14		F: *c* Negro 2; *s* 3; *ps* 665-Q M: *f* 15; *p* Lt. Brown S: *f* 16
YO15		F: *f* 11; *c* Negro 1 L: *s* 28
YO10g		
YO15g		F: *p* Brown L: *f* 11 S: *p* Brown
O4c		F: *c* 24 S: *c* 24
O5c		F: *c* 25 L: *f* Lit K S: *f* 3½, 5½, 25F; *c* 25
O6c		F: *f* 7, 26; *c* 26 M: *f* G; *c* TV9 S: *f* 26F; *c* 26
O7c		F: *f* 27; *c* 27 M: *f* F; *c* TV 10 S: *f* 6, 27F; *c* 27
O8c		F: *f* 28; *c* 28 S: *f* 28F; *c* 28
O9c		F: *f* 29; *c* 29 L: *f* 13 S: *f* 14, 29F; *c* 29, 30
O10c		F: *c* 30; *mr* 5 S: *f* 10, 24, 30F; *c* 31, 42
O11c		F: *c* 31 S: *f* 31F; *c* 35
O12c		M: *p* Auburn S: *f* 19; *c* 36
O13c		F: *f* 8A S: *f* 20; *s* 1

Standardized Number	Color	Commercial Numbers
O14c		L: *p* Light Brown
O15c		
O1		F: *f* 4A; *c* Natural 1 M: *c* 21 S: *c* Cream A
O2		M: *c* TV4 S: *c* TV1
O3		F: *c* Cream Rose L: *f* Colorfilm 2 M: *c* TV5, TV6
O4		F: *c* 5N; *ps* 5N M: *c* TV7 S: *c* C 4
O5		F: *c* 6N; *ps* 6N M: *c* TV8 S: *c* C-5
O6		F: *f* 6A; *c* 7N; *ps* 7N L: *f* Colorfilm 3 S: *c* C-6
O7		F: *f* 5½; *c* 8N; *ps* 8N L: *f* Colorfilm 4 M: *f* H; *c* 31 S: *c* TV7, C-7, Tan Bl. 3
O8		F: *c* 9N; *ps* 9N M: *c* 29 S: *f* 7; *c* TV8, C-8; *vs* C-8
O9		F: *c* 10N; *ps* 10N S: *c* TV9, C-9; *vs* C-9
O10		F: *f* 9 M: *f* 8; *c* 8B S: *c* TV10, C-10; *vs* C-10
O11		M: *c* 34 S: *c* TV11, C-11; *vs* C-11
O12		S: *c* C-12; *vs* C-12

Standardized Number	Color	Commercial Numbers
O13		S: c 37
O14		
O15		M: f 17 S: c 32, TV12; s 7
O5g		L: f 6
O6g		L: f Colorfilm 5
O7g		F: c Lt. Egyptian; ps Golden Tan
O8g		
O9g		F: c Indian
O10g		
O11g		F: c Dark Egyptian
O12g		
O13g		
O14g		F: c Eddie Leonard
O15g		F: f 17 L: f 16; p Dark Brown M: c 17B; p Dark Brown

Standardized Number	Color	Commercial Numbers
RO1c		M: f A L: f Peach S: f 1½; c TV3, C-1
RO2c		F: f 21; c 21 M: f C; c 23 S: c 21, TV2, C-2
RO3c		F: f 22; c 22 M: f D S: f 2; c 22, 44, C-3
RO4c		F: f 23; c 23 L: f Peach Dark M: f E S: f 2½; c 23
RO5c		L: f Peach Special S: c 2, 45
RO6c		S: f 3
RO7c		
RO8c		L: f 4 S: f 8
RO9c		S: f 7F
RO10c		L: f 9 M: f 12; c 12B S: f 9
RO11c		L: f 8
RO12c		S: c 41
RO13c		F: mr 7, s 22
RO14c		M: s 8½ S: s 2; es 1

Standardized Number	Color	Commercial Numbers
RO1		F: c 4A M: f B; c 22 S: f 4; c Nat. A; vs C-1
RO2		F: f 4½; c 1N; ps 1N M: c 24A S: vs C-2
RO3		F: f 5A; c 2N; ps 2N M: c 25A S: f 21; c TV4, Tan Blush
RO4		F: f 2A, 24; c 3N, 4N; ps 3N, 4N M: f 3; c 3B, 26A
RO5		F: f 25 M: f 2A; c 27A S: c TV5, Tan Blush 2
RO6		F: c 2A; ps 2A L: f 3½ M: f 6½; c 6½B, 28A S: c TV6
RO7		M: f 6; c 29A
RO8		L: f 4½ M: c 30A S: c 7
RO9		F: f 7A; c 7A M: c 31A
RO10		F: ps 7A
RO11		
RO12		
RO13		S: s 22
RO14		F: p Maroon L: f 7

Standardized Number	Color	Commercial Numbers
RO3g		F: ps Olive S: c Tan A; vs C-3
RO4g		S: vs C-4
RO5g		F: c Tan 2; ps Deep Olive S: c Tan B; vs C-5
RO6g		F: ps Natural Tan S: f 13; c 38; vs C-6
RO7g		S: c 39; vs C-7
RO8g		
RO9g		S: c 50
R1c		F: f 1 L: f 1
R2c		L: f 2 M: f 1; c 1B
R3c		
R4c		F: f 2
R5c		L: f 2½
R6c		L: f 3
R7c		

Standardized Number	Color	Commercial Numbers
R8c		
R9c		F: f 3½
R10c		F: f 10 M: f 10; c 10B S: l 9
R11c		
R1		
R2		F: ps 4A
R3		F: f 2½ M: f 5
R4		F: f 1A M: c 5B
R5		
R6		
R7		F: f 3 M: f 7
R8		M: f 9; c 9B S: l Video Pink 1
R9		
R10		

Standardized Number	Color	Commercial Numbers
R11		
R12		M: c Red Brown
R13		
R14		M: c 37
R15		
R6g		F: f 6 M: f 11
R9g		M: c 11B
R12g		
P1c		
P2c		M: f 2; c 2B
P3c		F: f 1½
P10		F: dr Natural S: dr 20
P10g		
P13g		M: c 38

Color	Commercial Numbers	Color	Commercial Numbers
	PURPLE-RED 1 F: *ur* 1 S: *ur* 1		RED-ORANGE 1 F: *dr* Light Technicolor M: *mr* 9 S: *mr* 8; *dr* 5; *l* Video Bl. 1
	PURPLE-RED 2 F: *dr* 18; *ur* 2 S: *dr* 18		RED-ORANGE 2 M: *dr* Geranium
	PURPLE-RED 3 F: *ur* 3 S: *mr* 4; *l* 7		RED-ORANGE 3 M: *lr* Light L: *s* 320 S: *dr* 22; *c* 48; *f* 18; *s* 18
	PURPLE-RED 4 F: *mr* Studio Special M: *lr* Crimson L: *s* 25 S: *s* 13		RED-ORANGE 4 F: *mr* 6 S: *mr* 9
	RED 1 F: *dr* Rose 2 M: *mr* 11		RED-ORANGE 5 M: *lr* Special 5
	RED 2 F: *dr* Carmine S: *dr* 14, 16; *ur* 2		ORANGE 1
	RED 3 F: *mr* 2; *ur* 4; *dr* Rasp. M: *lr* Cherry, Dark L: *s* 322 S: *mr* 3, 5, 6, 7; *l* Video Med.		ORANGE 2 S: *dr* 12
	RED 4 F: *mr* 3 L: *s* 323 S: *s* 12		ORANGE 3 F: *mr* Light Cinecolor M: *dr* Coral L: *s* 324 S: *l* Video Blush 2
	RED 5		ORANGE 4 F: *dr*, *mr* Dark Technicolor
	ORANGE-RED 1 F: *dr* Day Orange L: *s* 328 M: *dr* Natural; *mr* 10 S: *l* Video Pink 3		ORANGE 5 F: *mr* 8 L: *s* 30
	ORANGE-RED 2 F: *dr* Flame, Blondeen S: *l* Video Pink 2; *p* Red		YELLOW-ORANGE 3 M: *mr* 15; *f* Orange
	ORANGE-RED 3 F: *mr* 1 L: *s* 321 M: *lr* Med.; *f* Red S: *mr* 2; *ur* 4		YELLOW-ORANGE 4 F: *mr* Dark Cinecolor
	ORANGE-RED 4 F: *mr* 4		ORANGE-YELLOW 3 L: *s* 327; *f* Chrome
	ORANGE-RED 5 F: *mr* 9 S: *p* Maroon		YELLOW 3 F: *s* 11 L: *f* 8A M: *f* Yellow S: *s* 16

Color	Commercial Numbers		Color	Commercial Numbers
	YELLOW-GREEN 3 S: *es* 16			**VIOLET-BLUE 3** F: *s* 16 L: *s* 326M; *f* Med. Blue S: *s* 9; *es* 2
	YELLOW-GREEN 4 S: *s* 19; *es* 17			**VIOLET-BLUE 4** F: *s* 4 M: *s* 1 L: *s* 326D S: *es* 20
	GREEN 3 F: *s* 10 M: *s* 4			**BLUE-VIOLET 2** M: *s* 6
	GREEN 4 M: *s* 5; *p* Green S: *c* 46			**BLUE-VIOLET 5** S: *s* 10
	BLUE-GREEN 1 L: *s* 334 S: *es* 6			**VIOLET 1** F: *f* 14 L: *s* 337L M: *f* 20
	BLUE-GREEN 3 L: *s* 335; *f* Green II M: *f* Green			**VIOLET 2** L: *s* 337M S: *es* 4; *c* 49
	BLUE-GREEN 4 L: *s* 336			**VIOLET 3** L: *s* 337D; *f* Dark Mauve S: *s* 23
	GREEN-BLUE 2 M: *s* 2½			**VIOLET 4**
	GREEN-BLUE 3 S: *s* 20; *es* 3			**VIOLET-PURPLE 2** F: *s* 8
	GREEN-BLUE 4 L: *s* 39			**VIOLET-PURPLE 4** S: *es* 5; *s* 21
	BLUE 3 M: *s* 2 S: *s* 11			**GRAY 2** L: *s* 31 M: *f* 18 S: *s* 3
	BLUE 4 M: *p* Blue S: *p* Blue			**GRAY 3** F: *s* 15 S: *s* 4; *c* 34
	VIOLET-BLUE 1 L: *s* 325, 326L			**GRAY 4** M: *s* 7 S: *s* 5
	VIOLET-BLUE 2 F: *s* 5, 17 M: *s* 3; *f* Blue S: *s* 8; *es* 19; *c* 47			**GRAY 5** F: *s* 6 L: *s* 32; *p* Gray M: *p* Gray

Commercial Makeup Color Numbers and Their Equivalent Standardized Numbers

FACTOR GREASEPAINT:

1—R1c	5½—O7	16—YO13
1A—R4	6—R6g	17—O15g
1½—P3c	6A—O6	21—RO2c
2—R4c	7—O6c	22—RO3c
2A—RO4	7A—RO9	23—RO4c
2½—R3	8—YO8c	24—RO4
3—R7	8A—O13c	25—RO5
3½—R9c	9—O10	26—O6c
4—Y2	10—R10c	27—O7c
4A—O1	11—YO15	28—O8c
4½—RO2	12—Y7	29—O9c
5—Y5	14—Violet 1	30—YO8c
5A—RO3	15—White	31—YO9c

FACTOR PAN-CAKE:

1N—RO2	22—RO3c	7A—RO9
2N—RO3	23—RO4c	Tan 2—RO5g
3N—RO4	24—O4c	Natural 1—O1
4N—RO4	25—O5c	Cream Rose—O3
5N—O4	26—O6c	Chinese—Y7
6N—O5	27—O7c	Light Egyptian—O7g
7N—O6	28—O8c	Dark Egyptian—O11g
8N—O7	29—O9c	Indian—O9g
9N—O8	30—O10c	Negro 1—YO15
10N—O9	31—O11c	Negro 2—YO14
21—RO2c	2A—RO6	Eddie Leonard—O14g
	4A—RO1	

FACTOR PAN-STIK:

1N—RO2	8N—O7	Olive—RO3g
2N—RO3	9N—O8	Deep Olive—RO5g
3N—RO4	10N—O9	Natural Tan—RO6g
4N—RO4	2A—RO6	Golden Tan—O7g
5N—O4	4A—R2	665-K—YO12
6N—O5	7A—RO10	665-P—YO13
7N—O6		665-Q—YO14

FACTOR SHADING (LINING) COLORS:

1—Black	11—Yellow 3
2—Y15g	12—White
3—YO14	15—Gray 3
4—Violet-Blue 4	16—Violet-Blue 3
5—Violet-Blue 2	17—Violet-Blue 2
6—Gray 5	21—YO12
8—Violet-Purple 2	22—RO13c
10—Green 3	

FACTOR MOIST ROUGE:

1—Orange-Red 3	8—Orange 5
2—Red 3	9—Orange-Red 5
3—Red 4	Studio Special—Purple-Red 4
4—Orange-Red 4	Light Technicolor—Orange 3
5—O10c	Dark Technicolor—Orange 4
6—Red-Orange 4	Light Cinecolor—Orange 3
7—RO13c	Dark Cinecolor—Yellow-Orange 4

FACTOR UNDER ROUGE:

1—Purple-Red 1	3—Purple-Red 3
2—Purple-Red 2	4—Red 3

FACTOR DRY ROUGE:

Raspberry—Red 3	Light Technicolor—Red-Orange 1
Blondeen—Orange-Red 2	Dark Technicolor—Orange 4
Day Orange—Orange-Red 1	Carmine—Red 2
Natural—P10	Rose 2—Red 1
18 Theatrical—Purple-Red 2	Rose 3—Purple-Red 2

Flame—Orange-Red 2

FACTOR EYEBROW PENCILS:

Light Brown—Y15g   Brown—YO15g   Maroon—RO14

LEICHNER GREASEPAINT:

1—R1c	6—O5g	16—O15g
2—R2c	6½—Y10g	20—White
2½—R5c	7—RO14	Lit. K—O5c
3—R6c	8—RO11c	Peach—RO1c
3½—RO6	8A—Yellow 3	Peach Dark—RO4c
4—RO8c	8B—Y10	Peach Special—RO5c
4½—RO8	9—RO10c	Med. Blue—Violet-Blue 3
5—OY2	11—YO15g	Green II—Blue-Green 3
5½—YO4	12—Black	Dark Mauve—Violet 3
	13—O9c	Chrome—Orange-Yellow 3

LEICHNER SHADING COLORS (LINERS):

22—White	324—Orange 3
25—Purple-Red 4	325—Violet-Blue 1
28—YO15	326-L—Violet-Blue 1
28A—YO10c	326-M—Violet-Blue 3
30—Orange 5	326-D—Violet-Blue 4
31—Gray 2	327—Orange-Yellow 3
32—Gray 5	328—Orange-Red 1
39—Green-Blue 4	334—Blue-Green 1
42—Black	335—Blue-Green 3
320—Red-Orange 3	336—Blue-Green 4
321—Orange-Red 3	337-L—Violet 1
322—Red 3	337-M—Violet 2
323—Red 4	337-D—Violet 3

LEICHNER EYEBROW PENCILS:

Light Brown—O14c   Dark Brown—O15g

Gray—Gray 5

LEICHNER TRANSPARENT LIQUID MAKEUP (TAN KLEAR):

Suntan Light—YO8c   Suntan Dark—YO9c

LEICHNER SPECIAL GREASEPAINT (COLORFILM):

1—Y3	3—O6	5—O6g
2—O3	4—O7	6—OY9g

MEHRON DRY (POWDERED) ROUGE:

Natural—Orange-Red 1   Geranium—Red-Orange 2

Coral—Orange 3

MEHRON SHADING COLORS (SHADO-LINERS):

1—Violet-Blue 4	5—Green 4
2—Blue 3	6—Blue-Violet 2
2½—Green-Blue 2	7—Gray 4
3—Violet-Blue 2	8—YO13
4—Green 3	8½—RO14c

Also irridescent colors

MEHRON CAKE MAKEUP:

24A—RO2	21—O1	1B—R2c
25A—RO3	22—RO1	2B—P2c
26A—RO4	23—RO2c	3B—RO4
27A—RO5	24—O3c	4B—OY2
28A—RO6	25—YO4	5B—R4
29A—RO7	26—YO5	6½B—RO6
30A—RO8	27—YO6	8B—O10
31A—RO9	28—YO7	9B—R8
TV4—O2	29—O8	10B—R10c
TV5—O3	30—YO8	11B—R9g
TV6—O3	31—O7	12B—RO10c
TV7—O4	34—O11	16B—YO5c
TV8—O5	37—R14	17B—O15g
TV9—O6c	38—P13g	Other shades in B
TV10—O7c	Red Brown—R12	series being added

MEHRON MOIST ROUGE (CHEEK ROUGE):

9—Red-Orange 1	11—Red 1
10—Orange-Red 1	15—Yellow-Orange 3

MEHRON FOUNDATION:

1—R2c	11—R6g	E—RO4c
2—P2c	12—RO10c	F—O7c
2A—RO5	14—YO13	G—O6c
3—RO4	15—YO14	H—O7
4—OY2	16—YO5c	K—YO8
4½—Y4	17—O15	L—YO8c
5—R3	18—Gray 2	M—YO9c
6—RO7	19—Pale Blue	Red—Orange-Red 3
6½—RO8	20—Violet 1	Yellow—Yellow 3
7—R7	A—RO1c	Blue—Violet-Blue 2
8—O10	B—RO1	Green—Blue-Green 3
9—R8	C—RO2c	Orange—Yellow-Orange 3
10—R10c	D—RO3c	

MEHRON LIP ROUGE:

Light—Red-Orange 3	Cherry—Red 3
Medium—Orange-Red 3	Crimson—Purple-Red 4
Dark—Red 3	Special 5—Red-Orange 5

MEHRON PENCIL LINERS:

Light Brown—YO14	Green—Green 4
Dark Brown—O15g	Gray—Gray 5
Auburn—O12c	Blue—Blue 4

STEIN SOFT GREASEPAINT:

1—Y1	8—RO8c	20—O13c
1½—RO1c	9—RO10c	21—RO3
2—RO3c	10—O10c	22—OY3
2½—RO4c	11—Y15g	23—YO6
3—RO6c	12—Y7	24—O10c
3½—O5c	13—RO6g	25F—O5c
4—RO1	14—O9c	26F—O6c
5—Y4	15—White	27F—O7c
5½—O5c	16—YO14	28F—O8c
6—O7c	17—Black	29F—O9c
7—O8	18—Red-Orange 3	30F—O10c
7F—RO9c	19—O12c	31F—O11c

STEIN SOFT SHADING (LINING) COLORS:

1—O13c	12—Red 4
2—RO14c	13—Purple-Red 4
3—Gray 2	14—Red 3
4—Gray 3	15—White
5—Gray 4	16—Yellow 3
6—YO12	17—Black
7—O15	18—Red-Orange 3
8—Violet-Blue 2	19—Yellow-Green 4
9—Violet-Blue 3	20—Green-Blue 3
10—Blue-Violet 5	21—Violet-Purple 4
11—Blue 3	22—RO13

23—Violet 3

STEIN CAKE MAKEUP:

2—RO5c	39½—YO5c	TV3—RO1c
7—RO8	40—OY9	TV4—RO3
21—RO2c	40½—Y7	TV5—RO5
22—RO3c	41—RO12c	TV6—RO6
23—RO4c	42—O10c	TV7—O7
24—O4c	43—White	TV8—O8
25—O5c	44—RO3c	TV9—O9
26—O6c	45—RO5c	TV10—O10
27—O7c	46—Green 4	TV11—O11
28—O8c	47—Violet-Blue 2	TV12—O15
29—O9c	48—Red-Orange 3	C-1—RO1c
30—O9c	49—Violet 2	C-2—RO2c
31—O10c	50—RO9g	C-3—RO3c
32—O15	Tan A—RO3g	C-4—O4
33—Black	Tan B—RO5g	C-5—O5
34—Gray 3	Natural A—RO1	C-6—O6
35—O11c	Tan Blush—RO3	C-7—O7
36—O12c	Tan Blush 2—RO5	C-8—O8
37—O13	Tan Blush 3—O7	C-9—O9
38—RO6g	Cream A—O1	C-10—O10
39—RO7g	TV1—O2	C-11—O11
	TV2—RO2c	C-12—O12

STEIN MOIST ROUGE:

1—Red-Orange 3	5—Red 3
2—Orange-Red 3	6—Red 3
3—Red 3	7—Red 3
4—Purple-Red 3	8—Red-Orange 1
9—Red-Orange 4	

STEIN VIDEO LIPSTICK:

Video Pink 1—R8	Video Blush 2—Orange 3
Video Pink 2—Orange-Red 2	Video Light—Red-Orange 3
Video Pink 3—Orange-Red 1	Video Medium—Red 3
Video Blush 1—Red-Orange 1	Video Dark—Red 3

STEIN UNDER ROUGE:

1—Purple-Red 1	3—Red 3
2—Red 2	4—Orange-Red 3

STEIN DRY ROUGE:

5—Red-Orange 1	16—Red 2
12—Orange 2	18—Purple-Red 2
14—Red 2	20—P10
22—Red-Orange 3	

STEIN EYESHADOW:

1—RO14c	6—Blue-Green 1
2—Violet-Blue 3	16—Yellow-Green 3
3—Green-Blue 3	17—Yellow-Green 4
4—Violet 2	19—Violet-Blue 2
5—Violet-Purple 4	20—Violet-Blue 4
(7–15 are metallic shades)	

STEIN EYE SHADING PENCILS:

Brown—YO15g	Red—Orange-Red 2
Maroon—Orange-Red 5	Blue—Blue 4

STEIN VELVET STICK:

C-1—RO1	C-5—RO5g	C-9—O9
C-2—RO2	C-6—RO6g	C-10—O10
C-3—RO3g	C-7—RO7g	C-11—O11
C-4—RO4g	C-8—O8	C-12—O12

FIGURE ACKNOWLEDGMENTS

p. 103, Figs. 52, 53, photograph by Bert Roth, ABC-TV
p. 182, Fig. 101, photograph by Jock Lauterer
p. 206, Fig. 118, photograph by Bert Roth, ABC-TV
p. 236, Fig. 141, from Garsault's *Art du Perruquier*, 1767
p. 237, Fig. 142, from Garsault's *Art du Perruquier*, 1767
p. 239, Fig. 146, wigs from Bob Kelly Wig Creations, New York
p. 242, Fig. 148, from Garsault's *Art du Perruquier*, 1767
p. 243, Fig. 149, from Garsault's *Art du Perruquier*, 1767
p. 248, Fig. 150, wigs from Bob Kelly Wig Creations, New York
p. 266, Fig. 165, photograph by Bert Roth, ABC-TV
p. 281, Fig. 172, photograph from U.N.C. Photo Lab
pp. 292, 293, Figs. 179, 180, *Chicago Tribune* photographs by John Austad
p. 298, Fig. 186, photographs by Werner J. Kuhn
p. 300, Fig. 188, photographs by Werner J. Kuhn
p. 304, Fig. 189, Musée Egyptian, Cairo
p. 306, Fig. 190, from John Bulwer's *Anthropometamorphosis*
pp. 319–323, Fig. 192, photographs by Dick Smith, S.M.A.
p. 377, Fig. 204, Kupferstichkabinett der Staatl. Museen, Berlin-Dahlem
p. 380, Fig. 211, Staatliche Museen Berlin, Gemäldegalerie Dahlem
p. 381, Fig. 213, Galleria degli Uffizi, Firenze
p. 382, Fig. 216, Galleria degli Uffizi, Firenze
p. 382, Fig. 219, Reproduced by permission of the artist

INDEX

(Italic numerals refer to page numbers of illustrations)